Making It Happen

Making It Happen

Interaction in the Second Language Classroom

From Theory to Practice

Patricia A. Richard-Amato

Longman

New York & London

Making It Happen

Longman , 95 Church Street, White Plains, N.Y. 10601

Associated companies:
Longman Group Ltd., London
Longman Cheshire Pty., Melbourne
Longman Paul Pty., Auckland
Copp Clark Pitman, Toronto
Pitman Publishing Inc., New York

Executive editor: Joanne Dresner
Production editors: Helen Greer/Robert Goodman
Text design: Joseph DePinho
Cover design: Joseph DePinho
Cover illustration: Joseph DePinho
Text art: Joseph DePinho
Production supervisor: Eduardo Castillo

Library of Congress Cataloging-in-Publication Data

Richard-Amato, Patricia A.
    Making it happen.

    Bibliography: p.
    Includes index.
    1. Language and languages—Study and teaching.
2. Second language acquisition.   3. English language—
Study and teaching—Foreign speakers.   I. Title.
P53.R49 1988   418'.007   87-32472
ISBN 0-8013-0027-4

8 9 10-AL-95949392

For my father
Wallace Marvin Abbott

Contents

Preface

The question of how best to teach a nonprimary language has troubled language teachers over the years. Some have flirted with various cognitive approaches. Many have tried the newer communicative methods. Others have chosen to remain with audiolingualism or even grammar–translation because these seem familiar and nonthreatening.

Unfortunately, many language teachers have come to believe that they are derelict in their responsibilities if they don't teach by the book, in a sequential fashion. They feel guilty if they allow the students' mistakes to slip by without immediate, direct correction. They are likely to think that time is being wasted when students communicate about things that interest them.

Stevick (1980) tells of a teacher who was at first very casual in approach, not knowing much about ESL methodology. The students were simply presented with relevant topics about which they could express their ideas, without the fear of making mistakes. In later years, the same teacher became more "conscientious," relying on textbooks, probably in an effort to cover the structures systematically. The teacher's style became authoritative rather than facilitative, as it had once been. Eventually it became obvious that the students were not progressing as quickly as they had during that first teaching experience. In retrospect, the teacher remarked, "I can look back on these four years and see a gradual decline in the performance of my students . . . I never see successes like those first six ladies" (1980, p. 6).

While I do not favor a *laissez-faire* classroom, I am advocating a low-anxiety, interactional one in which communication is emphasized rather than syntactic form. That is not to say that a study of form should be avoided. On the contrary, there are many situations in which such a study may be highly appropriate and may help to facilitate the acquisition process, especially for older learners. The point being made here, however, is that the target language should be the medium of communication in the classroom and a tool for learning rather than the main subject for study. Moreover, the student should be encouraged to be an initiator and a creator of output as well as a receiver of input.

This book offers a theoretical orientation in order to lay a solid foundation for the methods and activities that follow. I first came to know the theories and ideas explored here in an intuitive sense as a practicing language teacher. Later, when I was formally introduced to them, they made sense to me and I was able to relate them to what had happened in my own classrooms over the years.

All of the activities included here have been carefully screened and tested in the classroom. Most have evolved out of my own experience and/or that of other practicing teachers. I have tried to determine the original sources of adapted activities in order to give proper credit. However, if I have overlooked any source, I hope the reader will feel free to call the oversight to my attention so that it may be set right in any future editions of the materials.

This book is an attempt, however limited, to bridge the gap between theory and practice. The theories, methods, and activities presented are not intended to be the final word on language teaching, nor will each one be applicable in every program. It is hoped that many of them will be of use to teachers developing programs tailored to the needs and interests of their students.

Patricia Abbott Richard-Amato
California State University, Los Angeles

Acknowledgments

First I am indebted to my former ESL students at Alameda High School and Alameda Junior High in Lakewood, Colorado. Many of the activities presented in this book could not have been developed had it not been for them.

My graduate students at the University of New Mexico and at California State University, Los Angeles, have been especially instrumental in helping me work out several of the ideas and see them in practice. Many a fleeting notion has become fleshed out through lengthy class discussions. A few, to whom I owe a special thanks, even shared parts of their libraries with me: Pamela Branch, Linda Sasser, and Ramon Diaz.

Appreciation goes to Ruth Cathcart-Strong, whose clear perspective and expert advice were invaluable. Also to Mary McGroarty and Carolyn Madden, whose careful reading and comments helped a great deal. And to John Oller, Jr., my collaborator on *Methods That Work*. He was the one who suggested that I write this book in the first place, and later read the manuscript, offering many encouraging and insightful comments. Support and guidance, particularly during the book's initial stages, came also from other professors at the University of New Mexico, whom I wish to thank: Robert White, Rod Young, Steve Strauss, and Bess Altwerger.

In addition I would like to express my gratitude to the following people in the field, who read the manuscript and made many very practical suggestions: Leslie Jo Adams, Marty Furch, Sue Gould, and Wendy Hansen. Thanks also to Jennifer Claire Johnson, who helped conceptualize some of the illustrations; to Rey Baca, who commented on the section dealing with placement tests; to James Wiebe, who gave me suggestions on computer programs; to

Alan Crawford, who commented on the development of literacy materials; and to Dick Evans, who took care of the business aspects of this project.

Appreciation goes, too, to the following: Marilyn Greenberg, who strongly encouraged me to apply for affirmative action funds, making it possible for me to complete the book; and Joanne Dresner and the many others at Longman who were wonderfully supportive and helpful in preparing the final manuscript.

I am grateful also to the following publishing companies and individuals for permission to reprint or adapt materials for which they own copyrights:

Bonne, Rose. Excerpt from "There Was an Old Woman Who Swallowed a Fly," illustrated by Pam Adams. Copyright Michael Twinn, Child's Play Ltd. Reprinted by permission of Michael Twinn, Child's Play (International) Ltd. An excerpt only— taken from last page in book.

Breen, Michael and Candlin, Christopher. "The Essentials of Communicative Curriculum in Language Teaching" from *Applied Linguistics,* volume I (2): 1979, pp. 99–104. Reprinted by permission of Oxford University Press.

Brown, H. D. *Principles of Language Learning and Teaching,* second edition, pp. 99–110, 114–119, Copyright © 1987. Reprinted by permission of Prentice-Hall, Inc., Englewood Cliffs, New Jersey.

Christison, Mary Ann. Illustration by Kathleen Peterson, *English Through Poetry,* p. 29, 1982. Reprinted by permission of Alemany Press/Janus Book Publishers, Inc., Haywood, California.

Cummins, James. "Language Proficiency, Bilingualism, and Academic Achievement" from *Bilingualism and Special Education: Issues in Assessment and Pedagogy,* pp. 136–151. San Diego, California: College-Hill. Copyright © 1984 by James Cummins. Reprinted by permission of College-Hill, San Diego, California.

Ellis, Rod. "Theories of Second Language Acquisition" from *Understanding Second Language Acquisition,* pp. 248–276. Copyright 1986. Reprinted by permission of Oxford University Press.

Evans, Joy and Moore, Jo Ellen. Adaptation of illustration, p. 57, from *Art Moves the Basics Along: Units About Children;* 1982. Reprinted by permission of Evan-Moor, Carmel, California.

Evans, Joy and Moore, Jo Ellen. Adaptation of illustration, p. 80, from *Art Moves the Basics Along: Animal Units,* Copyright © 1979. Reprinted by permission of Evan-Moor, Carmel, California.

Gliedman, John. "Interview (with Noam Chomsky)," *Omni,* edited by Patrice Aderet, 6 (2): November, 1983. Copyright 1983 by John Gliedman and reprinted with permission of Omni Publications International, Ltd.

Harper & Row/Newbury House. *Methods That Work,* edited by J. Oller, Jr. and P. Richard-Amato. Adaptation of Chapter 32, pp. 393–413. Copyright 1983, Harper & Row/Newbury House.

Krashen, Stephen. "Providing Input for Acquisition," from *Principles and Practice in Second Language Acquisition*, pp. 57–73, Copyright © 1982 Stephen Krashen. Reprinted with permission of Oxford: Pergamon.

Krashen, Stephen. Figure 2, "The relationship between affective factors and language acquisition," p. 110 in *Second Language Acquisition and Second Language Learning;* Copyright © 1981 by Stephen Krashen. Reprinted by permission of Oxford: Pergamon.

Krashen, Stephen. Figure from "Immersion: why it works and what it taught us," in *Language and Society* 12 (Winter 1984), p. 63. Reprinted by permission of the Office of Official Languages, Ontario, Canada.

Krashen, Stephen. Figure 2.1 from *Principles and Practice in Second Language Acquisition;* Copyright 1982 by Stephen Krashen. Reprinted by permission of Oxford: Pergamon.

Krashen, Stephen and Terrell, T. From *The Natural Approach*, pp. 67–70. Copyright 1983. Reprinted by permission of Alemany Press/Janus Book Publishers, Inc. Haywood, California.

Palmer, Hap. "Put Your Hands Up in the Air," from *Songbook: Learning Basic Skills Through Music I.* Copyright 1971. Reprinted by permission of Educational Activities, Inc., Baldwin, New York.

Prelutsky, Jack. "The Creature in the Classroom," from *The Random House Book of Poetry for Children*, selected and introduced by Jack Prelutsky. Copyright © 1983 by Random House, Inc. Reprinted by permission of the Publisher.

Silverstein, Shel. "Gooloo" from *A Light in the Attic.* Copyright © 1981 by Snake Eye Music, Inc. Reprinted by permission of Harper & Row Publishers, Inc. and Jonathan Cape Ltd. London.

Vygotsky, L. S. *Mind in Society: Development of Higher Psychological Processes.* Edited by M. Cole, V. John-Steiner, S. Scribner, and E. Souberman. Cambridge, Massachusetts: Harvard University Press. Copyright © 1978 by the President and Fellows of Harvard College.

Whitecloud, Thomas. Adaptation of "Blue Winds Dancing" from *Scribner's Magazine*, February, 1938. Copyright 1938 Charles Scribner's Sons; copyright renewed. Reprinted by permission of Charles Scribner's Sons.

Widdowson, H. G. © Oxford University Press, 1979. Reprinted from Explorations in *Applied Linguistics* by H. G. Widdowson (1979) by permission of Oxford University Press.

I am grateful also to the following individuals for allowing me to summarize their programs: Pamela Branch (ABC Unified School District, Cerritos, California), Sandra Brown (North Hollywood Adult Learning Center, North Hollywood, California), Ken Cressman (Lakehead Board of Education, Thunder Bay, Ontario, Canada), Carolyn Madden and John Swales (University of Michigan, Ann Arbor, Michigan), Beverly McNeilly (Los Angeles Unified

School District, Los Angeles, California), Christina Rivera (ABC Unified School District, Cerritos, California), and Lorenzo Trujillo (Jefferson County Public Schools, Lakewood, Colorado).

And last to my husband, Jay, whose love, encouragement, and advice kept me going through the very last page. Many weekends were lost to ''the book.'' He, more than anyone, was glad to see it finished.

Making It Happen

Introduction

A frequent lament heard among former second language students across many cultures is that they never really learned the languages they studied even though they spent several years in classrooms. This common complaint has led to a reassessment of the theories and methods popular during the last twenty to thirty years. Several theoretical concepts are currently under consideration by those attempting to determine what direction we should take to be effective second language teachers. This book explores some of these concepts as well as the methods and activities to which they gave birth.

The second language student, like a first language acquirer, must *grow* (in the Chomskyan sense) within the language environment. As Wilkins points out, a grammatical focus will probably not facilitate the process for most people, but then on closer inspection neither will a notional–functional focus (see Chapter 1). Perhaps Vygotsky's Zone of Proximal Development and Krashen's $i + 1$ concepts (see Chapter 3) bring us closer to what "growing" means. Both view optimal input as being essential through interaction and guidance. Oller expands this notion of optimal input to include a kind of heightened awareness provided by the episodic organization of materials. Quality input is not an all or nothing proposition. Rather, various kinds of input fall along a continuum beginning with nonsense at one end and fully motivated, logical discourse at the other. The former is almost totally divorced from experience; the latter is fully in tune with it (see Figure 0.1).

Although some language programs include strings of nonsense (e.g., contrastive sounds, tongue twisters for phonetic practice) and others include strings of real but unrelated words (e.g., vocabulary lists, minimal pairs), a serious problem can arise in language teaching when whole programs center on strings of unrelated sentences and on temporally structured but unmotivated discourse ("unmotivated" in the sense that there appears to be little contextual justification—see Chapter 4). In such programs meaningful interaction between student and teacher, student and student, and student and text is very limited at best.

This book concentrates on ways of providing opportunities for meaningful interaction in second language classroom settings. Part I presents a theo-

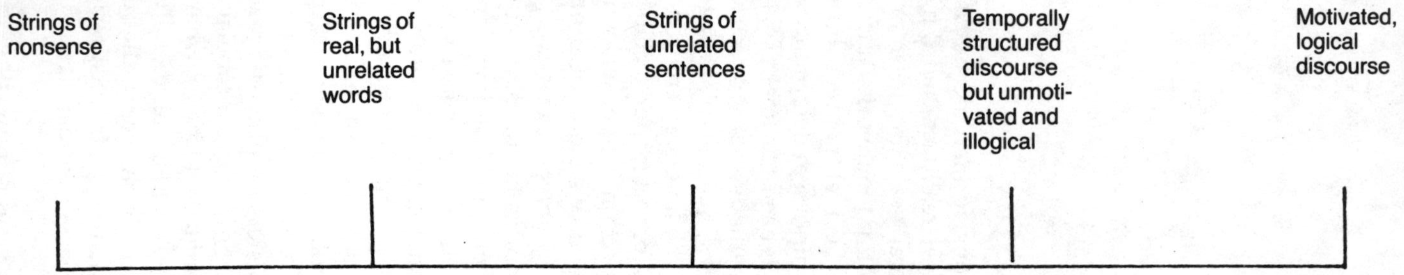

Figure 0.1. Quality Input Continuum

Strings of nonsense

Strings of real, but unrelated words

Strings of unrelated sentences

Temporally structured discourse but unmotivated and illogical

Motivated, logical discourse

2

retical orientation to the remaining chapters. It begins with a brief overview of the grammar-focused methods of the past and goes on to highlight some of the seminal ideas of Chomsky, Wilkins, Widdowson, Breen and Candlin, and others (Chapter 1). Then it presents evidence supporting the notion that acquisition can and does take place in the classroom under certain conditions (Chapter 2). Next it attempts to develop an interactional approach drawing from the insights of Vygotsky, Krashen, Bruner, John-Steiner, Seliger, Schumann, Carroll, and many others (Chapter 3). It then looks at Oller's episode hypothesis in relation to materials selection (Chapter 4). Finally, it examines the important role played by the affective domain in second language acquisition in the classroom (Chapter 5).

Part II explores several methods and activities that are for the most part compatible with an interactional approach: the total physical response and the audio-motor unit (Chapter 6); the natural approach and its extensions (Chapter 7); jazz chants, music, and poetry (Chapter 8); storytelling, role play, and drama (Chapter 9); games (Chapter 10); and affective activities (Chapter 11).

Counseling learning and suggestopedia are not included in Part II, although they have in many cases had an indirect influence on several methods and activities described. *Counseling learning* (discussed in Related Reading 7) is a method requiring that students gradually establish their independence from the counselor-translator. It appears to have potential in foreign language teaching, where all the students generally have a language in common. However, in second language teaching,[1] where only a few groups of students have a common language, it loses some of its appeal. *Suggestopedia*, an approach whereby students (under the control of an "expert" teacher) are brought to greater heights of awareness through relaxation, has had its triumphs, particularly in Bulgaria under Lozanov, who originated the method. Although it is not included in Part II, a version of it is described in Chapter 15.

Part III discusses several considerations to be taken into account when one is developing and implementing programs: classroom management (Chapter 12); the selection of tools of the trade, including textbooks, placement tests, and computer programs (Chapter 13); and teaching through the content areas (Chapter 14).

Part IV presents programs in action. Chapter 15 (ESL Programs) discusses an ESL intensive learning center at Alameda High School in Lakewood, Colorado; a sheltered English model at Artesia High School in Artesia, California;

---

[1]*Second* language teaching usually refers to a target language that is being taught in the country where *it is the dominant language;* foreign language teaching, on the other hand, usually refers to a target language that is being taught in a country where it is not the dominant language. Sometimes the terms are used interchangeably, however, particularly when contrasting the terms "first language acquisition" and "second language acquisition." In this case "second" usually refers to any language that is not the first one learned.

a kindergarten ESL program within a Spanish bilingual school at Loma Vista Elementary in Maywood, California; a life-skilis adult basic education program at the North Hollywood Adult Learning Center in North Hollywood, California; and a university English language institute at the University of Michigan in Ann Arbor. Chapter 16 (Foreign Language Programs) describes Jefferson County's approach to foreign language teaching in Lakewood, Colorado; a high school Spanish program at Artesia High School in Artesia, California; and a French immersion model for elementary students in Thunder Bay, Ontario, Canada. All these programs were selected because of the quality of some of their more salient features. However, they are not meant to be representative of all the programs available.

The Conclusion reiterates many of the main points of the book and provides a retrospective look at its major themes.

The Related Readings section provides edited readings from a few of the people who have contributed, either directly or indirectly, to the development of second language pedagogy: Chomsky, Widdowson, Breen and Candlin,

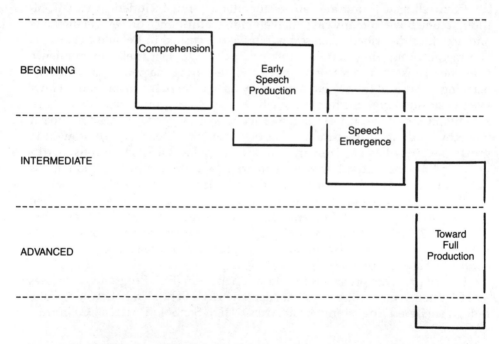

Figure 0.2. Classification of Proficiency Levels

The terms *beginning, intermediate,* and *advanced* refer to the levels to which students are often assigned for work in the second language. *Comprehension, Early Speech Production, Speech Emergence,* and *Toward Full Production* refer to stages within the levels. The first three stages come from the natural approach (see Chapter 7). The last stage is sometimes called "Intermediate Fluency" by natural approach advocates.

Ellis, Krashen, Vygotsky, H. D. Brown, Oller, and Cummins. While the section is intended for anyone desiring supplemental materials, it will probably be most useful to the teaching of theory and/or methods courses, since it offers additional areas for thought and classroom discussion.

In order to facilitate an understanding of the proficiency levels and stages referred to throughout the book, an explanation of the nomenclature used to identify them is in order. Classifications such as *beginning, intermediate,* and *advanced* refer to the various levels to which the students are assigned for work in the second language. Classifications such as *comprehension, early speech production, speech emergence,* and *toward full production* refer to stages of development within the levels (see Figure 0.2). The first three (comprehension, early speech production, and speech emergence) come from the natural approach (see Chapter 7). At the comprehension stage, students develop the ability to understand spoken language and to react to simple commands. During this time students experience their "silent period" when they are not expected to speak, although they may respond with a word or two. At the early speech production stage, students are able to produce a few words and can often recognize their written versions. At the speech emergence stage, they begin to use simple sentences and can read and write simple text in the target language. As students become capable of fuller production (sometimes referred to by natural approach advocates as the period of "intermediate fluency"), they can express themselves in a variety of ways and can understand much of what is said. (See pages 212–213 for a more comprehensive list of typical language behaviors found at each level.)

It should be noted that there is much overlap between one level and the next and one stage and the next. Students may be beginners at some tasks but advanced learners at others. In addition, an intermediate or advanced student might be thrown back temporarily into the comprehension stage typical of beginners whenever new concepts are introduced. It has been my observation that students need several "silent periods" as they move from one group of concepts to another.

PART I

A Theoretical Perspective

Presented here are selected theories and hypotheses intended to serve as an undergirding for the methods, activities, and ideas presented in the remainder of the book. No attempt has been made to include all of the people involved in furthering the development of an interactional approach. It is hoped that those included will, in some sense, represent many whose contributions may have been just as important.

Because second language acquisition is so complex, no two learners will get there by exactly the same route. However, in spite of the variations, it is possible to describe some of the processes that seem to be common to large numbers of people struggling with a new language and, in many cases, a new culture. Most people agree that simple exposure to the new language and/or culture is not enough. By understanding more about those processes that language learners seem to share, we can be in a better position to plan classroom experiences that are conducive to second language acquisition. Thus we can continue to develop means by which both language and culture are made more accessible to second language students.

1

From Grammatical to Communicative Approaches

> *Not to let a word get in the way*
> *of its sentence*
> *Nor to let a sentence get in the way*
> *of its intention,*
> *But to send your mind out to meet the*
> *intention*
> *as a guest;*
> *That is understanding.*
>
> *Chinese proverb,*
> *Fourth Century* B.C.
> *(in Wells, 1981)*

As Wilkins (1979a) has noted, changes that have taken place over the last three decades in both second and foreign language teaching have for the most part been limited to *methods* of language teaching as opposed to *content*. In other words, we have concerned ourselves with the how rather than with the input itself. Input has rather consistently focused on grammar until recently.

GRAMMAR-BASED APPROACHES

Many language teachers have felt that language teaching is facilitated by focusing on grammar as content and/or by exposing the student to input in the target language that concentrates on one aspect of the grammar system at a time—present tense before past, comparative before superlative, first person singular before third person singular, and so forth. The approaches used have included grammar–translation, audiolingualism, cognitive approaches, and the direct method. The most characteristic features of these approaches are presented below. Many variations exist, however, that are not noted in this brief analysis.

Grammar–Translation

Grammar–translation, also known as the "Prussian Method," was the most popular method of foreign language teaching in Europe and America from about the mid-nineteenth to the mid-twentieth century. Versions of it still exist today in many countries around the world. Its goal was to produce students who could read and write in the target language by teaching them rules and applications.

A typical grammar–translation lesson began with a reading (to be translated into the first language) followed by the rule it illustrated. Often several strings of unrelated sentences were given to demonstrate how the rule worked. New words were presented in a list along with definitions in the first language. These new words were also included in the reading, which, more often than not, was syntactically and semantically far above the students' levels of proficiency. The topics may have involved a trip to the library, a brief historical sketch of an area, a shopping expedition, a trip by train, or the like. Lessons were grammatically sequenced and students were expected to produce errorless translations from the beginning. Little attempt was made to communicate orally in the target language. Directions and explanations were always given in the first language.

Audiolingualism

Audiolingualism (ALM) was the new "scientific" oral method that was developed to replace or enhance grammar–translation. It was introduced as a component of the "Army Method" used during World War II (a version of it had been developed earlier by Bloomfield for linguists to use when studying languages). It was recognized as the "audiolingual method" when it began to gain favor in teaching English as a foreign language and English as a second language in the 1950s. In America it was closely related to structural linguistics and contrastive analysis[1] (see Fries, 1945; Lado, 1977).

Through the use of this method, structures of the target language were carefully ordered and dialogues were repeated in an attempt to develop cor-

---

[1]*Structural linguistics* is a grammatical system whereby the elements and rules of a language are listed and described. Phonemes, morphemes and/or words, phrases, and sentences are ordered linearly and are learned orally as a set of habits. *Contrastive analysis*, emphasizing the differences between the student's first language and the target language, was relied upon in an effort to create exercises contrasting the two. The first language was thought of chiefly as an interference, hindering the successful mastery of the second.

rect habits of speaking. Sentences in the substitution, mim-mem (mimic and memorize), and other drills were often related only syntactically ("I go to the store," "You go to the store," "He goes to the store"), and they usually had nothing to do with anything actually happening. Sometimes, however, they did resemble real communication in that the situational scenarios to be memorized included greetings and idiomatic expressions. Rules were presented but often not formally explained, and activities such as minimal pairs (seat—sit, yellow—jello, etc.) were commonly used in an effort to overcome the negative transfer (interference) of L1 (first language) sounds. Listening and speaking skills took precedence over reading and writing skills. However, in most of the applications, there was very little use of creative language,[2] and a great deal of attention was paid to correct pronunciation. Often practice sessions took place in fully equipped language laboratories.

Cognitive Approaches

Cognitive approaches, most evident since the 1960s, are often referred to rather vaguely in the literature as "cognitive-code" methodology. According to Richards and Rodgers, the latter term is ". . . sometimes invoked to refer to any conscious attempt to organize materials around a grammatical syllabus while allowing for meaningful practice and use of language" (1986, p. 60).

Persons claiming to advocate a cognitive approach believed, for the most part, that subskills in listening, speaking, reading, and writing such as sound discrimination, pronunciation of specific elements, distinguishing between letters that are similar in appearance, forming capital and small letters, and so on needed to be mastered before the student could participate in real communication activities. Generally speaking, it was felt that phonemes needed to be learned before words, words before phrases and sentences, simple sentences before more complicated ones, and so forth.

Lessons were usually highly structured through a deductive process, and the "rule of the day" was practiced. Although creative language was used at higher levels during the practice, students generally had to produce correctly right from the first. A great deal of time was devoted to temporally related but often unmotivated (contextually unjustified) discourse (see Chapter 4).

The Direct Method

Also known today as "Berlitz," this approach was derived from an earlier version called the "Natural Method," which was developed by Sauveur in

---

[2]One exception was Fries's own language program at the University of Michigan. According to Morley, Robinett, Selinker, and Woods (1984), Fries utilized a two-part approach: one part focused on the structural points being drilled and the second part on automatic use through meaning. The "personalized" elements which were considered vital to the program somehow became lost in most of its adaptations.

the mid-nineteenth century and later applied by de Sauzé. It was *natural* in the sense that it made an effort to "immerse" students in the target language. Teacher monologues, formal questions and answers, and direct repetitions in the input were frequent. Although the discourse was often structured temporally and motivated logically, the method fell short of being optimal in that the topic for discussion was often the grammar itself. The students tried inductively to discover the rules of the language. Those interested in grammar as a topic of conversation may have found such lessons stimulating; however, most students needed something more relevant to keep their interest.

Although these methods varied from one another, they all generally adhered to the same principle: grammar is the foundation upon which language should be taught.

Even as early as 1904, Otto Jespersen saw the artificiality inherent in this principle. He criticized the French texts of his era by saying,

> The reader often gets the impression that Frenchmen must be strictly systematical beings who one day speak merely in futures, another day in *passé définis* and who say the most disconnected things only for the sake of being able to use all the persons in the tense which for the time being happens to be the subject for conversation while they carefully postpone the use of the subjunctive until next year (1904, p. 17; also in Oller and Obrecht, 1969: 119).

Those advocating cognitive approaches are of particular interest with respect to their interpretation of Chomsky, who developed what is commonly known to linguists as transformational grammar. For example, Philip Smith, an advocate of cognitive approaches, claimed to use a transformational model[3] by teaching language from "deep to surface structure." He felt that "teachers can teach a finite set of phrase structure rules and expand them via the application of transformations" (1981, p. 33). By this means, a student can then produce more language. He further said that this was different from the behaviorist approach[4] because it gave a "new slant" to grammatical explanations and drills. It encouraged sentence recombining and other kinds of exercises centering on form. He offered "deep structure questioning" as a way to reduce native-speech utterances to simple units within the student's linguistic repertoire. For example, "The dingbat was fizzled by the glompus in the gloaming" could be understood if one broke it into smaller parts: "Who got fizzled? When? What happened to the dingbat? Who fizzled the

---

[3]A transformational model is based on Chomsky's generative approach to grammatical analysis. Sentences are "transformed" into other sentences economically by application of phrase structure rules to what is called the *deep structure* (sometimes referred to as *kernel* sentences). For example, the rule of extraposition can be applied to the sentence "That summer follows spring is a known fact," transforming it to "It is a known fact that summer follows spring." The latter is known as its *surface form*.

[4]A behaviorist approach adheres to the theory that language is acquired principally through the process of habit formation and the stimulus/response association. Its chief proponent is B. F. Skinner. Audiolinguistic drills constitute its most direct application to language teaching methodology.

dingbat?'' etc. (1981, p. 65). Thus the "deep structure," according to Smith, was used to pedagogical advantage.

Others advocating cognitive approaches recommended that early instruction in language be limited to kernel sentences, particularly when translation was involved in second language teaching. They thought that kernel sentences of different languages would be very similar and that positive transfer would then occur. At later stages transformations could be applied.

Second language teachers who agreed with cognitive approaches believed that comprehensible input involved teaching sentences that were neither temporally sequenced nor logically motivated. Rather their main reason for existence seemed to be to demonstrate the use of some grammatical structure or other in an effort to aid the development of linguistic competence. These teachers were disappointed to find that Chomsky himself did not advocate such a method, nor any specific method, for that matter. In his address to the 1965 Northeast Conference on the Teaching of Foreign Languages, Chomsky stated that neither the linguist nor the psychologist had enough knowledge about the process of language acquisition to serve as a basis for methodology.

> I am, frankly, rather skeptical about the significance, for the teaching of languages, of such insights and understanding as have been attained in linguistics and psychology. . . . I should like to make it clear from the outset that I am participating in this conference not as an expert on any aspect of the teaching of languages, but rather as someone whose primary concern is with the structure of language and, more generally, the nature of cognitive processes (in Allen & VanBuren, 1971, p. 152).

He cautioned teachers against passively accepting theory on grounds of authority, real or presumed.

Is it true that there are no implications of Chomskyan thought for second language teaching, and more specifically for optimal input for second language acquisition? In the same speech at the Northeast Conference on the Teaching of Foreign Languages, Chomsky admitted that "there are certain tendencies and developments within linguistics and psychology that may have some potential impact on the teaching of language" (in Allen & VanBuren 1971, pp. 155–156). He named these main areas of possible impact: the creative aspect of language use, the abstractness of linguistic representation, the universality of underlying linguistic structure, and the role of intrinsic organization in cognitive processes. However, he stressed that the implications of these ideas are not yet clear, nor is their substance.

Inferences drawn from Chomsky's rationalist theory[5] are perhaps more

---

[5]Rationalist theory in general is a belief in reason as opposed to the empiricism associated with a behaviorist philosophy. Chomsky's rationalist theory embraces the idea that language development is too complicated a phenomenon to be explained on the basis of behaviorism alone. That children seem to have a mastery over their first language by the age of five or earlier points to the idea that there must be a great deal about language that is innate.

important to second language teaching than any of the applications of transformational grammar, which appear for the most part to be misguided. Transformational grammar was not meant to be used as a model of performance, as the reader will see later.

CHOMSKY'S CONTRIBUTIONS

Chomsky proposes the notion of a "language organ" which he calls the *Language Acquisition Device* (LAD).[6] We do not yet know enough about it to determine its full implications in second language teaching. Bruner feels that it is a "powerful idea, one that we will want to revisit after other aspects of language become clearer" (1978a, p. 43). However, Bruner does remind us that simply writing a grammar for a language does not explain how it is acquired. To understand that, we need to investigate perception, motor skills, concept formation, and social as well as linguistic aspects. Chomsky himself agrees:

> . . . we must investigate specific domains of human knowledge or systems of belief, determine their character, and study their relation to the brief and personal experience on which they are erected. A system of knowledge and belief results from the interplay of innate mechanisms, genetically determined maturational processes, and interaction with the social and physical environment. The problem is to account for the system constructed by the mind in the course of this interaction (1971, p. 21).

But Chomsky's (1959) challenge of Skinnerian theory and, indirectly, of most of the applications of behaviorism to second language teaching is perhaps his most important contribution to date. Bruner gives Chomsky credit for "freeing us from the paralyzing dogma of the association-imitation-reinforcement paradigm" (1978b, p. 245). Chomsky opposed the idea that the mind is simply a *tabula rasa*. He refused to believe that grammar is simply an "output" on the basis of a record of data. However, he did not deny that the mind is capable of the abilities attributed to it by behaviorism. He reminded us that language is not "made" by us but rather develops as a result of the way we are constituted, when we are placed in the "appropriate external environment" (1980, p. 11). He felt that it remains to be seen just how much of language is actually shaped by experience and how much is intrinsically determined.

Support for the idea that at least some aspects of language are innate comes from psycholinguistic research. Roger Brown (1973) has discovered much about universal trends in language acquisition by recording the speech of several children in natural situations over a period of years. Slobin (1971)

---

[6]There is much speculation as to the possible functions and structure(s) of the LAD. Some even question that it exists at all.

and others have added to this body of research. They have found that children across languages use similar linguistic structures in their language development and that they make the same kinds of errors. In addition, they have found that the linguistic structures are learned in the same order.

These findings have led researchers to believe that the brain is more than simply a blank slate upon which humans store impressions. It contains highly complex structures which seem to come into operation through an interactional process.

What does all this mean for the provision of optimal input in the second language classroom? Although the implications are, to a large extent, indirect, they nevertheless are important. If we are convinced that there is at least some validity in rationalist thought, we would not be inclined to rely so heavily on behaviorism and the classroom activities that fall under its umbrella. Patterned drill, with its endless, often mindless repetition (see Lamendella, 1979, Krashen, 1981b), and memorization of dialogue that more often than not is far removed from anything real, might be replaced by a more natural kind of activity. The target language should be allowed to *grow* and develop within the person when he or she is placed in an appropriate environment (see Related Reading 1).

WILKINS AND BEYOND

Chomsky has been criticized rather severely (and perhaps deservedly) by those who point out that his basic linguistic model[7] is too restrictive in failing to include the societal aspects of language (Hymes, 1970; Halliday, 1979; and many others). Most (other than Halliday) agree with the competence/performance distinction but feel that competence should include not only grammatical sectors but psycholinguistic, sociocultural, and de facto sectors as well, to use Hymes's terms. Halliday rejects the distinction between competence and performance altogether by calling it misleading or irrelevant. Halliday feels that the more we are able to relate the grammar system to meaning in social contexts and behavioral settings, the more insight we will have into the language system. It is this basic idea that Wilkins uses in constructing his notional–functional syllabus as a structure for input in the classroom.

Wilkins is concerned with helping the student meet specific communication needs through the input. Such input for the student would be organized into a set of notional categories for the purpose of a syllabus design: semantico-grammatical categories (time, quantity, space, matter, case, deixis), and

---

[7]Chomsky's basic linguistic model distinguishes two aspects of language: competence (the underlying knowledge of the grammatical system) and performance (the use of that knowledge to communicate).

categories of communicative function (modality, moral evaluation and discipline, suasion, argument, rational inquiry and exposition, personal emotions,
emotional relations, interpersonal relations). Syllabi based on a notional approach often include such topics as accepting/rejecting invitations, requesting
information, and expressing needs or emotions of various kinds.

Although Wilkins feels that a notional syllabus (which includes categories
of function) is superior to a grammatical one, he is not yet ready actually to
replace grammatically focused systems for teaching with functionally focused
ones. He does, however, see a notional approach as providing another dimension to existing systems. It "can provide a way of developing communi-
catively what is already known, while at the same time enabling the teacher
to fill the gaps in the learners' knowledge of the language" (1979b, p. 92).
Widdowson (see Related Reading 2) warns us, however, that although some
linguists might boast of ensuring communicative competence through the use
of a notional syllabus, such an approach does not necessarily mean such competence will be the result. For one thing, a notional syllabus isolates for study
the components of communication. He states:

> There is one rather crucial fact that such an inventory [typically included in
> a notional syllabus] does not, and cannot of its nature, take into account,
> which is that communication does not take place through the linguistic expo-
> nence of concepts and functions as self-contained units of meaning. It takes
> place as discourse, whereby meanings are negotiated through interaction
> (1979a, p. 253).

Perhaps it is because a notional approach utilizes an artificial breakdown
of communication into discrete functions, that most of its applications lose
their potential as providers of effective input. As the reader will see, activities
based on a notional approach do not always involve real communication situations any more than repetitive dialogues or "structures for the day" did.

Consider the following excerpt from a currently available textbook utilizing a notional approach (Jones & von Baeyer, 1983):

> Here are some useful ways of requesting. They are marked with stars [in this
> case asterisks] according to how polite they are.
>
>   * Hey, I need some change.
>   I'm all out of change.
>   ** You don't have a quarter, do you?
>   Have you got a quarter, by any chance?
>   Could I borrow a quarter?
>   *** You couldn't lend me a dollar, could you?
>   Do you think you could lend me a dollar?
>   I wonder if you could lend me a dollar.
>   **** Would you mind lending me five dollars?
>   If you could lend me five dollars, I'd be very grateful.
> ***** Could you possibly lend me your typewriter?
>   Do you think you could possibly lend me your typewriter?
>   I wonder if you could possibly lend me your typewriter.

****** I hope you don't mind my asking, but I wonder if it might be at all
possible for you to lend me your car.

Decide with your teacher when you would use these request forms. Can you
add any more forms to the list?

Not only would such an analysis be superficial but the subtleties involved
would be very difficult for an ESL student even at an advanced level. Native
speakers also might have trouble in determining many of the differences. For
example, is "Would you mind lending me five dollars?" more or less polite
than "Do you think you could lend me a dollar?" In addition to the activity's
syntactic problems, semantic and situational differences are not at all clear.
Asking someone for a car is certainly different from asking someone for a
quarter. Important variables are missing, such as the positions, ages, and
other characteristics of the interlocutors and their relationships to one
another. Thus the activity lacks not only meaning but comprehensibility.

What kinds of activities then would be meaningful and comprehensible?
Although some organizing principles might lend themselves to effective communicative approaches more than others, it is not so much the organizational
principle that makes the difference. Nor is it the content itself. For example,
even grammar may be considered a stimulating topic for communication by
some students and their teachers.

Breen and Candlin (see Related Reading 3) characterize an effective communicative approach as being one in which a shared knowledge is explored
and modified as a result. It implies a negotiation of "potential meanings in a
new language" and it implies a socialization process. Breen and Candlin reject systems in which the learner is separated from that which is to be learned
as though the target language could be objectively broken down into isolated
components. They argue further that

> In a communicative methodology, content ceases to become some external
> control over learning-teaching procedures. Choosing directions becomes a
> part of the curriculum itself, and involves negotiation between learners and
> learners, learners and teachers, and learners and text (Related Reading 3,
> page 300).

Thus they feel that a negotiation for meaning is crucial to a successfully
applied communicative methodology. This idea seems to suggest the need
for greater interdependence and a greater flexibility on the parts of teachers
and students to allow the syllabus and its content to develop in ways that
make acquisition of the target language most likely.

SUMMARY

Although methods, like models of cars, have varied over the years, the content of language teaching has remained basically the same until recently. An
analysis of language has been in the driver's seat while meaningful interac-

tion about content of interest has had to find room where it can if it is to be included at all.

Chomsky's transformational grammar has been mistakenly used to justify and perpetuate a focus on structure in language teaching while his real contributions to the field in general have remained largely ignored. His exposure of the cognitive paralysis brought about by behaviorism, while having an impact on theory, is just beginning to be felt in the classroom. Although we are not sure where it will lead us, his concept of a possible language acquisition device may have profound consequences for classroom practice once we have more understanding of its content, structure(s), and networking.

Hymes, Halliday, Wilkins, Widdowson, Breen and Candlin, and many others have added to our knowledge of the sociocultural aspects in defining a language system. In addition, their ideas have been influential in the development of approaches that involve students in meaningful experiences in the new language.

READINGS, REFLECTION, AND DISCUSSION

Suggested Readings and Reference Materials

Austin, J. (1962). *How to do things with words.* Oxford: Clarendon. A seminal work consisting of several lectures given in 1955 at Harvard. Through them we gain insight into the author's ideas concerning speech act theory, which places an emphasis on function as opposed to form.

Brumfit, C. J., & Johnson, K. (Eds.). (1979). *The communicative approach to language teaching.* Oxford: Oxford University. An in-depth analysis of the fundamental arguments underlying communicative approaches. Included are key writings of Hymes, Halliday, Wilkins, Widdowson, and many others who have led the way to a new look at language teaching processes.

Chomsky, N. (1975). *Reflections on language.* New York: Pantheon. In this book, Chomsky attempts to clarify his stand on many issues. For example, he stresses the fact that he did not intend for his term ''deep structure'' in language to represent in any way that which is really deep. He continues his fierce battle with empiricism and all of its ramifications, but here he fights with more literary finesse than before.

Chomsky, N. (1980). *Rules and representations.* New York: Columbia University. Here Chomsky further develops his theme that genetically based structure is an *a priori* basis for higher mental functions which come into being when humans come into contact with external environmental factors. In this book he addresses performance models which, he asserts, must include theories of both grammatical and pragmatic competence. Performance and competence models are mutually supportive, he feels.

Diller, K. (1978). *The language teaching controversy.* Rowley, MA: Newbury House. This book presents a comprehensive overview of several linguistic theories and their contributions over the years to language teaching.

Slobin, D. (1971). *Psycholinguistics.* Glenview, IL: Scott Foresman. Slobin's insights into the development of language in children and the relationship of language to cognitive processes are the focus of this book.

Widdowson, H. G. (1978). *Teaching language as communication.* Oxford: Oxford University. Here Widdowson develops his ideas on what a communicative approach should involve. He emphasizes language "use" (communication) as opposed to "usage" (analysis of language) throughout.

Questions for Reflection and Discussion

1. In the mid-1960s, Chomsky claimed that neither the linguist nor the psychologist knew enough about the language acquisition process to make recommendations concerning methodology. On the basis of your own reading, do you think this assessment was valid at that time? How about today?

2. Many have speculated about what the language acquisition device might contain. Chomsky himself, in an interview (see Related Reading 1), theorizes about the neurological structures that may network to form such a device. He compares these structures to a computer containing what might be called a "universal grammar." According to his view, this universal grammar consists of a series of preprogrammed subsystems responsible for meaning, syntax, relationships between various types of words, and their functions. Within each subsystem, the individual through experience makes choices from a linguistic "menu." Depending on the language environment in which it finds itself, the brain will select items appropriate to the specific language to which it is exposed. Grammars for the different languages might even be defined by specifying the choices from the menu of humanly possible options. Discuss the feasibility of such a hypothesis. What implications might this hypothesis have for future research?

3. Widdowson (1978) argues that "we do not progress very far in our pedagogy by simply replacing abstract isolates of a linguistic kind by those of a cognitive or behavioral kind." Explain what you think he means. Can you think of abstract isolates, other than those mentioned in this chapter, on which programs might attempt to focus?

4. Take a close look at several language textbooks with which you are already familiar or to which you have access. Which activities appear to focus on an analysis of language? Which on communication?

2

The Classroom as an
Environment for
Language Acquisition

*This would not necessarily mean changing or disguising
the classroom in the hope that it will momentarily serve
as some kind of "communicative situation" resembling
situations in the outside world. The classroom itself has
a unique social environment with its own human activities and its own conventions governing these activities.*

M. Breen and C. Candlin, 1979

The positions taken in the remainder of this book are based on the following
two assumptions: (1) *Although important differences must be taken into account,
there are a sufficient number of similarities between first and second language acquisition to support a common theory;* (2) *the classroom can indeed be an appropriate
environment for language acquisition.*

A COMPARISON BETWEEN FIRST AND
SECOND LANGUAGE ACQUISITION

The first assumption is supported by Ervin-Tripp (1974), B. Taylor (1980),
Krashen (1982), and Ellis (1986) as well as by several others.

Ervin-Tripp directly challenges the widely held idea that it is not logical
to attempt to develop a common theory for first and second language acquisition. She points out that one reason for this idea's apparent popularity is the
fact that research traditions have been so different for each of the two areas.
First language (L1) studies have been longitudinal for the most part, have
focused on learner strategies, and have been limited mainly to natural set-

tings in which language is a by-product of communication needs. Second language (L2) studies, with some exceptions, have been cross-sectional. They have focused on a manipulation of structure and methods, and, until recently, they have been limited mostly to classroom settings in which syntactic form rather than communication needs have been emphasized.

According to Ervin-Tripp, the idea that L1 and L2 acquisition have little in common theoretically has been based on two common misconceptions: (1) The foundation for L2 is built largely from a transfer of the rules of L1, and (2) only L2 is constructed from prior conceptual knowledge within the learner.

Concerning the first misconception, Newmark (1979) states that students who have a need to perform before they are ready will revert to L1 syntactic rules. According to Newmark this is more a result of ignorance than interference. The dependence on L1 seems to occur predominantly at beginning stages, when there is an intense desire to communicate. Sometimes the student at this stage will use not only L1 structures with L2 words but L1 words as well. While the L1 is heavily depended upon during initial stages of second language acquisition, the need for it dies out as the student gains proficiency in the L2. It is true that the L1 may be responsible for some errors, especially in cases in which specific linguistic items are similar. In addition, the L1 may account for the avoidance of certain L2 elements in the output. However, most errors appear to be developmental in the second language acquisition process, just as they are in the first.

Regarding the second misconception, it must be noted that L1, like L2, is constructed from prior conceptual knowledge. Bruner, referring to L1, observed that ''language emerges as a procedural acquisition to deal with events that the child already understands conceptually and to achieve communicative objectives that the child, at least partially, can realize by other means'' (1978b, p. 247).

Ervin-Tripp feels that if the human brain is equipped to handle language, then certainly this ability is not meant only for L1. To show that the brain uses similar strategies for L2 acquisition, she points to her study of American children learning French in Geneva. The children utilized three sources for acquiring French: peers (interaction in and out of the classroom), school (content-area subject matter was taught in French), and home (exposure to parents who often spoke French, to servants, and to the mass media). Generally speaking, ''the conclusion is tenable that first and second language learning is similar in natural situations . . . the first hypothesis we might have is that in all second language learning we will find the same processes: overgeneralizations, production simplification, loss of sentence medial items, and so on'' (1974, p. 205).[1]

She did note an important difference in L1 and L2 acquisition in addition

---

[1]See Slobin (1973) for the ''Operating Principles'' associated with the acquisition of L1.

to L1 transfer, particularly at beginning stages. She found that although L2 learners go through essentially the same process as L1 learners, they do it much faster because they are usually more advanced cognitively. In addition, it should be pointed out that older second language learners are able to handle more complex ideas, are able to have more control over the input they receive, and are able to learn and apply rules which may aid in facilitating the acquisition process. Although the differences related to cognition must be taken into account, especially when one is choosing the content of the input, the similarities cannot be ignored or deemphasized, particularly when speaking of the acquisition process itself.

B. Taylor, like Ervin-Tripp, found evidence giving credibility to the notion that second language learners use similar strategies to those learning their first language. He looked at the use of overgeneralization and transfer made by elementary and intermediate students of ESL. By doing an error analysis he found that "reliance on overgeneralization is directly proportional to proficiency in the target language, and reliance on transfer is inversely proportional" (1980, p. 146). In other words, during initial stages of acquisition the learner will depend quite heavily on first language knowledge to communicate in the target language, but once the student is able to form hypotheses about the new language, he or she will begin to work within the framework of that language. The student then will make errors mainly due to overgeneralization of the newly acquired structures. Taylor points out that overgeneralization (and transfer too, for that matter) is the result of a necessity to reduce language to the simplest possible system. He points to Jain's (1969) observation that this phenomenon represents an effort to lessen the cognitive burden involved in trying to master something as complex as language. The second language learner, like the first, attempts to "regularize, analogize, and simplify" in an effort to communicate.

In reference to the natural order hypothesis, Krashen (1982) points to some rather striking similarities between L1 and L2 acquisition orders which, if valid, may add credence to the argument that there are many parallels in cognitive strategies. He bases his conclusions on the following morpheme studies: (1) Dulay and Burt (1974), who found in their research done on Spanish and Chinese children learning English what may be a universal order in L2 morpheme acquisition; (2) Bailey, Madden, and Krashen (1974), who found that adults and children followed a similar order in learning a second language; and (3) R. Brown (1973) and DeVilliers and DeVilliers (1973), who reached similar conclusions in their well-known findings on L1 morpheme acquisition order. Krashen states, "in general, the bound morphemes have the same relative order for first and second language acquisition (*ing, plural, ir past, reg past, third person singular,* and *possessive*) while the auxiliary and copula tend to be acquired relatively later in first language acquisition than in second language acquisition" (1982, p. 13). It is interesting to note that Larsen-Freeman (1978) found in her study that morpheme orders seem to reflect the frequency of certain morphemes in the input. She stresses the importance of carefully examining the input when investigating such orders.

Caution must be used, however, before the morpheme studies are taken at face value (Ellis, 1986; Gregg, 1984; Wode, 1978). First, the evidence may not be sufficient to support a natural order hypothesis. Second, there appear to be some contradictions in the orders. For example, the findings in the studies by R. Brown and by DeVilliers and DeVilliers are not consistent with those of Porter (1977), who used the Bilingual Syntax Measure in obtaining the data for a study of the L1 order. The Bilingual Syntax Measure itself may have affected the order in the L2 studies in which it was used as well as in Porter's study. In addition, equating accuracy order with acquisition order (as in the cross-sectional studies) is a questionable procedure at best. Thus, the significance of these studies remains in doubt.

More convincing evidence supporting a common theory comes from Cazden (1972) and others who based their conclusions on longitudinal studies. To illustrate, Ellis (1986) points out that the L1 orders Cazden noted in the acquisition of the transitional forms of negatives and imperatives are very similar to those of L2 acquisition. For example, rising intonation used to mark questions comes before the incorporation of *wh*-structures, and word order inversion does not occur until later. However, Ellis did note a few minor differences. For example, L2 learners do not seem to go through a one-word stage for questions as do L1 learners. He attributes this difference and others to the more advanced cognitive levels of development in the L2 speakers. He feels that some differences may be due to L1 transfer as well.

Similarity between speech addressed to children in their first language (motherese) and speech addressed to foreigners (foreigner talk) is evidence that others at least perceive the strategies of L1 and L2 acquisition to be similar in many ways. Shorter sentences, high-frequency vocabulary, ''here and now'' items, indirect correction, frequent gesture, and lack of overt attention to form are among the many similarities observed in situations in which the interlocutors are involved in real communication (Henzl, 1973; Freed, 1978; Hatch, Shapira, & Gough, 1978; Arthur, Weiner, Culver, Young, & Thomas, 1980; Long, 1981; Wesche & Ready, 1985; Richard-Amato, 1987.)

Additional support for a common theory comes from Asher, who states ''a reasonable hypothesis is that the brain and nervous system are biologically programmed to acquire language, either the first or second, in a particular sequence and in a particular mode.'' He stresses that both require a *silent period*, i.e., time to simply comprehend language without having to orally produce it. He states, ''if you want to learn a second language gracefully and with a minimum of stress, then invent a learning strategy that is in harmony with the biological system'' (1972, p. 134).

We already know that children learning their first language require a fairly extensive silent period before they begin to produce utterances that are meaningful. It is interesting to note that Postovsky (1977) showed the benefits of a silent period for second language learners in a study of adult American students of Russian at the Defense Language Institute in Monterey, California. The students in the experimental group were asked to *write* their responses to input rather than *speak*; in contrast, the control group had to produce orally right from the beginning. The first group did better than the second not only in syntactic control of the language but in accuracy of pronunciation.

Gary's (1975) research also gives strength to arguments for a silent period. The study involved fifty American children learning Spanish. Half the students were allowed a silent period during which they could respond with nods, pointing, and other gestures. The other half had to respond orally using an audiolingual format. The experimental group outperformed the control group in both listening comprehension and speaking performance.

Thus many studies carried out since the 1970s point to the conclusion that the process of learning a second language is very much like that of learning the first language. Yet classrooms continue to operate as though these discoveries had never been made.

LANGUAGE ACQUISITION IN THE CLASSROOM

The second assumption mentioned at the beginning of this chapter is that the classroom can be an appropriate environment for language acquisition. The view has been expressed that discussions of psycholinguistic research concerning the acquisition process are not relevant, for the most part, to the second language classroom (see Strevens, 1978). Before an attempt is made to refute this view, we need to look at acquisition theory itself.

Several (mostly compatible) second language acquisition models and hypotheses have been described by Ellis (see Related Reading 4). Although many of them are referred to in this and other chapters, the two that seem most appropriate to the present discussion are the Monitor Model proposed by Krashen and the Variable Competence Model proposed by Ellis. The Monitor Model is probably the most well-known of the models and, at the same time, the most controversial.

As part of the rationalization for this model, Krashen distinguishes between two different linguistic systems: acquisition and learning (Krashen, 1981b, 1982). It is his view that acquisition is subconscious and learning is conscious. Below are adaptations of the acquisition and performance models that he has used to help clarify the entire process.

The items that are *acquired* (Figure 2.1) are those that were able to pass through the affective filter, which consists of inhibitions, motivation, personality factors, and so on, and move into the subconscious to become intake. On the other hand, the items that are *learned* (i.e., the formal rules of the target language) become part of the monitor (see Figure 2.2) and are used in

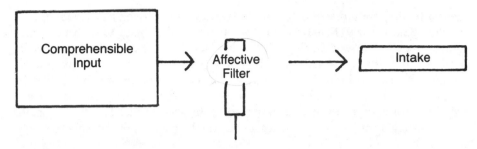

Figure 2.1. The Acquisition Process (Krashen, 1981b)

production only if they are relatively simple, if the speaker is focused on form, and if there is time to apply them. Ordinarily, in the flow of normal discourse, the speaker does not have the opportunity to monitor the output to any great extent unless he or she is what some linguists refer to as a "super monitor user," in other words, one who is adept at applying rules and communicating simultaneously (some language teachers fit into this category). Now and then a language learner appears not to monitor at all; see, for example, Schmidt's (1984) subject W (Chapter 5). He would be referred to in Krashen's terminology as an "underuser." However, Krashen (1981b) also identifies the "optimal user," one who applies the monitor appropriately. There are situations in which the monitor can be maximally effective: when the language learner is taking grammar tests, writing papers, or preparing planned speeches. Although items in the learning store as such do not directly become part of the acquisition store, according to Krashen, the rules of the target language do become acquired, but only by exposure to the language.

He cites supportive evidence from the descriptive studies of Stafford and Covitt (1978) and Krashen and Pon (1975). Stafford and Covitt's subject V demonstrated a high level of proficiency with spoken English, but in an inter-

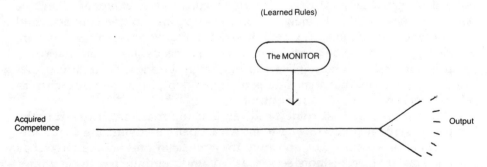

Figure 2.2. Performance Model (Krashen, 1982)

view with him, they discovered that he showed no conscious knowledge of the rules. Conversely, Krashen and Pon's subject P proved to be an optimal monitor user when writing English but did not apply the well-learned, well-practiced rules to her speech production. Instead she made many errors. However, McLaughlin, Rossman, and McLeod (1984) point out that the brain often has difficulty in handling two competitive cognitive demands at once—carrying on a conversation and being accurate grammatically. It is possible that once the cognitive burden is lessened, the learner might be able to apply some of the rules.

Another complication is what Stevick (1980) refers to as the *Eureka* phenomenon, which can occur when the student is made consciously aware of the acquired rule through teaching. This awareness might lead the student into thinking that the learned rule, because it has been learned, goes directly into the acquisition store, when it may actually have been acquired through exposure to the language itself. However, it is highly probable that the subconscious/conscious dichotomy has been too simplistically drawn in the first place. Who is to say that things learned cannot go into the acquisition store? Many have questioned the dichotomy by arguing that it is possible for rules that have been consciously applied over and over in a variety of situations to become automatic and thus internalized (Bialystok & Fröhlich, 1977; McLaughlin, 1978; Stevick, 1980; Sharwood-Smith, 1981; Gregg, 1984; Ellis, 1986).

In addition, we seem continually to "monitor" subconsciously and we become aware of doing so only when there has been a mismatch between our acquired hypotheses and what we hear and/or produce (see also Morrison & Low, 1983). Thus the issues involved here appear to go much deeper and are obviously much more complicated than we have been led to believe.

McLaughlin, Rossman, and McLeod (1984) are also critical of the distinction Krashen has drawn between learning and acquisition. They prefer to speak of controlled and automatic information processing. Either one can be the focus of attention (usually true of controlled processes) or on the periphery of attention (usually true of automatic processes). What differentiates these concepts from Krashen's is that controlled and automatic processes do not fall unequivocally into a conscious/subconscious dichotomy. They see both processes as falling somewhere on a continuum between conscious and subconscious functioning. They emphasize that individual learning styles are an additional factor to be considered. They do concede, however, that when input is comprehensible, implicit learning might be most successful. However, they point out that some adults prefer working from the rules whereas others prefer working from the output.

While it appears that some headway is being made in discovering the nature of language processing systems, we are particularly unsure about how the various processes occur and how they relate to one another. We may hypothesize that acquisition serves as an undergirding for those things learned, producing the Eureka effect. However, we cannot ignore indications that in some circumstances the opposite occurs. Consider, for example, students who have spent years in audiolingual or cognitive-code programs, then go to a country where the target language is spoken and become fluent in a very short time. In those cases, the learning system appears to have predisposed the learner to a more rapid acquisition of the language. However, one might wonder how soon the students would have become fluent had they been exposed to meaningful, comprehensible communication in the target language right from the beginning.

Although the Monitor Model may be flawed as a theory, Krashen has highlighted an extremely important issue. He has brought the point home to many language teachers that the classroom does not have to confine itself to formal instruction in the target language. It can instead provide the kind of input that he feels will best facilitate the second language acquisition process, that is, input that is comprehensible, interesting, and/or relevant, that is not grammatically sequenced, and that is present in sufficient quantity (see Related Reading 5).

While Krashen emphasizes the importance of providing comprehensible input, Ellis (1984a, 1986) in his Variable Competence Model focuses on interaction. He believes it is not enough to be concerned with input. A key factor in the second language acquisition process is "the opportunity afforded the learner to *negotiate* meaning with an interlocutor, preferably one who has more linguistic resources than the learner and who is adept at 'foreigner/ teacher talk'" (1984a, p. 184). (See Chapter 3 for the development of a similar idea.) In his model of second language acquisition, Ellis recognizes a single knowledge store in which variable transitional rules are contained. Some rules tend to be more automatic, others more analyzed. The second language learner demonstrates variation in the production of interlanguage forms. Sometimes the learner will appear to have mastered a particular structure and other times he or she will regress to earlier forms. The variation, according to Ellis, is often the result of whether the process is a primary one (using automatic rules) in unplanned discourse or a secondary one (using analyzed rules) in planned discourse. (See Figure 3 and its description in Related Reading 4.) Primary processes are those that utilize and facilitate the automatic system, and secondary processes utilize and facilitate the analytic system. Both systems represent a continuum rather than a dichotomy. The rate of acquisition depends upon the quantity and quality of the interaction in which the learner is involved. Ellis claims that "Rapid development along the 'natural' route occurs when the learner has the chance to negotiate meaning in unplanned discourse" (1984a, p. 186). However, he reminds us that this process is influenced by such affective factors as motivation and personality (see Chapter 5).

Although relatively little research has been done on the language acquisition process in second language classrooms, progress has been made in accessing the product. Many of the studies, for example, indicate that the

French immersion programs in Canada[2] have been among the most successful (Lambert & Tucker, 1972; Tucker & d'Anglejan, 1972; Selinker, Swain, &
Dumas, 1975; Swain 1975; Swain, Lapkin, & Barik, 1976) as has the Spanish
immersion program in Culver City, California (Cathcart, 1972; Cohen, 1974;
Plann, 1977). What these programs have in common is that the emphasis is
placed on the content to be learned rather than on language itself. At later
levels, formal instruction is also included in varying degrees. All immersion
students are at similar levels in the target language to begin with (unlike
submersion programs, in which they are the minority among native speakers)
and all the content-area subjects are taught in the target language until English is gradually added at later levels (see Chapter 14).

It is interesting to note, however, that Selinker, Swain, and Dumas found
that although the students in French immersion gained proficiency, their
speech contained pidginized forms which may have been due to their lack of
sufficient interaction with peers and others who were native speakers of
French. Plann discovered the same tendency toward the development of pidginized forms in the Spanish immersion program. In fact, he found that the
students appeared to have developed their own classroom dialect. It is likely
that in both situations the students did not have sufficient opportunities for
interaction with native or near-native speaking linguistic models (see discussion of fossilization as related to cooperative learning on pages 193–194; see
also Swain's explanation on pages 41–42).

Other studies also indicate that our knowledge of the second language
acquisition process *is* relevant to the classroom and that acquisition, in fact,
does occur there. This is especially true when the methods themselves are
consonant with our cognitive systems to the extent that they provide input
that can be understood in communicative situations (Asher, 1972; Asher, Kusudo, & de la Torre, 1974; Swaffer & Woodruff, 1978; Voge, 1981). Asher as
well as Asher, Kusudo, and de la Torre compared the total physical response
with traditional methods (see Chapter 6); Swaffer and Woodruff looked at a
college-level reading program in which total physical response, yoga breathing, and gymnastics were used in combination to acquire language through
meaningful reading; and Voge compared the natural approach to the direct
method.

In addition, Wagner-Gough and Hatch (1975) argue that, on the basis of
their observations, the classroom is more than just one more environment
in which acquisition occurs. It can be a place that is especially conducive to
acquisition. They feel that for beginners up to the intermediate level, the
classroom can potentially be more effective than the outside world for acquiring a second language. They remind us that it is often difficult for students

---

[2]The Thunder Bay Program described on pages 274–279 is an example of immersion.

to get comprehensible input from a world that is not aware of their need for it.

SUMMARY

Two assumptions concerning second language acquisition are supported: (1) although important differences must be taken into account, there are a sufficient number of similarities between first and second language acquisition to support a common theory, and (2) the classroom can be an appropriate environment for acquisition.

Related to the two assumptions are Krashen's Monitor Model and Ellis's Variable Competence Model. The first, although it may be flawed as a theory, emphasizes the importance of comprehensible input; the second emphasizes interaction and negotiated meaning in a variety of situations.

Although the natural environment might, in fact, be ideal for some, others might find it difficult to receive comprehensible input and to find the opportunity to participate in quality interaction. For them the classroom may be the best environment available.

READINGS, REFLECTION, AND DISCUSSION

Suggested Readings and Reference Materials

Ellis, R. (1986). *Understanding second language acquisition*. Oxford: Oxford University. In this book, Ellis gives perspective to much of the current research on second language acquisition and its relationship to the theories that have been developed.

Hatch, E. (1978). *Second language acquisition: A book of readings*. Rowley, MA: Newbury House. Representative selections in second language acquisition are presented including papers by Wagner-Gough; Ervin-Tripp; Ravem; Schumann; Dulay and Burt; Bailey, Madden, Krashen; Larsen-Freeman; and many others. An additional section contains abstracts on acquisition research.

Krashen, S. (1982) *Principles and practice in second language acquisition*. Oxford: Pergamon. This book examines the relationship between theory and practice, the processes involved in second language acquisition, the roles of comprehensible input and grammar, and the various teaching approaches currently being used.

Long, M. (1984). Process and product in ESL program evaluation. *TESOL Quarterly*, 18(3), 409–426. Long stresses the importance of process evaluation, which has often been ignored in classroom studies of the past. A particularly valuable reading for anyone planning to do classroom research.

Richards, J. (1978). *Understanding second and foreign language learning: Issues and approaches*. Rowley, MA: Newbury House. A collection of readings on strategies for learning and teaching L2. Among the selections are contributions from Hatch, Corder, Schumann, Strevens, Tucker, d'Anglejan, and Swain.

Questions for Reflection and Discussion

1. Classroom acquisition research has recently come under fire because of what some see as a failure on the part of many researchers to consider carefully both *product* and *process*. Long states, "Product evaluations cannot distinguish among the many possible explanations for the results they obtain because they focus on the product of a program while ignoring the process by which that product came about" (1984, p. 413). What kinds of factors might be overlooked if one focuses on the product alone? What implications does this have for our interpretations of the studies themselves and the conclusions based upon them?

2. In spite of the many similarities between first and second language learning, the important differences must be considered in curriculum development. What implications might they have, particularly for planning the content of language programs?

3. A few people (for example, see Strevens, mentioned earlier) feel that the acquisition process is not relevant to the classroom. On what do you think they base this conclusion? In your opinion, is there any justification for this point of view?

4. Speculate about what role you feel a learner's first language has in the acquisition of the second. Take into account your own experience in language learning. Has its role been given too much or too little importance in the formulation of second language theory? Discuss.

5. What is your reaction to the characteristics of optimal input as described by Krashen (see Related Reading 5)? Do you agree with most of his assertions? Would you modify any of them? If so, how?

3

Toward an Interactional Approach

How can we help the child learn a language?

Believe that your child can understand more than he or she can say, and seek, above all, to communicate. To understand and to be understood. To keep your minds fixed on the same target. In doing that, you will, without thinking about it, make one hundred or one thousand alterations in your speech and action. Do not try to practice them as such. There is no set of rules of how to talk to a child that can even approach what you unconsciously know. If you concentrate on communicating, everything else will follow.

R. Brown, 1977

The Zone of Proximal Development (Vygotsky, 1962, 1978) and the $i + 1$ (Krashen, 1981b, 1982) are both hypotheses that seek to explain, at least in part, the cognitive operations involved in language acquisition. Underlying the surface complexity of these concepts are fundamentals that have remained largely ignored by language teachers until recently.

Although neither one can account for the whole process of language acquisition, they can teach us much about the role of input in the interaction, particularly in full two-way communication.[1] Of course, second language ac-

---

[1]Burt and Dulay (1983) identify three communication phases: one-way (the learner receives input but gives no overt response); partial two-way (the learner responds orally in L1 or by simple gestures); and full two-way (the learner gives messages and responds in the target language to messages of others).

quisition can take place without full two-way communication. Gass and Varonis (1985) found, for example, that in one-way communication, when there is sufficient shared knowledge on the part of participants, there may be less need for interaction. However, current research seems to indicate that interaction involving two-way communication is the best way to negotiated meaning and ultimately to acquisition of the target language (Long, 1983b, 1983c; Pica & Doughty, 1985; Swain, 1985).

Even though the role of input will be the focus of this chapter, the role of output cannot be underestimated in an informed theory of language acquisition. It will be considered later as an independent variable.

THE ZONE OF PROXIMAL DEVELOPMENT AND THE IMPORTANCE OF SOCIAL INTERACTION

Although Vygotsky (1978), like Chomsky, did not speak directly to second language pedagogy, he did formulate ideas concerning learning and development in children that have important implications for second language teaching and the providing of optimal input (see Related Reading 6). Before we proceed, it may be advantageous to compare Vygotsky's view of the relationship of learning and development to Piaget's in order more fully to understand the former.

To Piaget (1979) the processes of learning and mental development are independent of each other. Learning utilizes development but does not shape its course. He believed that maturation precedes learning. Educators who adhere to this idea emphasize the "readiness" principle. A student must be exposed primarily to input that can be handled without difficulty. In other words, the input must be at the student's actual level of development.

Vygotsky differed in that he saw the individual as having two developmental levels which have interacted with learning since the time of birth. In his theory learning precedes maturation. The individual through interaction progresses from what he called an *actual developmental level* to a *potential developmental level*. Between the two levels is the "Zone of Proximal Development," which he defined as "the distance between the actual developmental level as determined by independent problem solving and the level of potential development as determined through problem solving under adult guidance of and in a collaboration with more capable peers" (page 348 in Related Reading 6). The potential developmental level becomes the next actual developmental level through learning which "presupposes a specific social nature and a process by which children grow into the intellectual life of those around them." Learning then should always be one step ahead of development.

Whereas Piaget stressed *biology* as the determiner in universal stages of development, Vygotsky stressed *society* as the determiner of development, although the resulting stages are similar. However, Vygotsky felt that these stages are not universal in nature because each person's history is different; each person's opportunity of interaction is different. He emphasized a dialectical unity or an "interlacement" (a John-Steiner & Souberman term, 1978) between biological foundations and dynamic social conditions. He was convinced that higher psychological functions entail new psychological systems; they are not simply superimposed over the more elementary processes as Piaget believed.

In addition, Vygotsky placed a great deal of stress on play, which he saw as being rule governed. Children don't usually jump around aimlessly. If they do, it is usually for a very brief time. In order for this kind of activity to be fun, they have to have rules. Even being a "mother" requires rules. Play, like school, should create a Zone of Proximal Development. Through it the "child always behaves beyond his average age, above his daily behavior; in play it is as though he were a head taller than himself" (1978, p. 102).

Although learning and development are directly related, they do not increase in equal amounts or in parallel ways. "Development in children never follows school learning the way a shadow follows the object that casts it" (page 353 in Related Reading 6). The relationship between the two is extremely complex and uneven and cannot be reduced to a simple formula. Vygotsky was convinced that *learning itself is a dynamic social process through which the teacher in a dialogue with a student can focus on emerging skills and abilities.*

Freire (1970) enlarges on this concept in *Pedagogy of the Oppressed* in which he distinguishes between two kinds of education: banking and libertarian. Banking education involves the act of depositing. The student is an empty depository and the teacher is the depositor. The students "receive, memorize, and repeat." There is no real communication. The role of the student is a passive one, a sort of "disengaged brain." On the other hand, in libertarian education the teacher and students are partners. Meaning is inherent in the communication. Through it students are involved in acts of cognition and are not simply empty heads waiting to be filled with information. The process is a dialectical one. Sometimes the teacher is a student and the students are teachers in a dialogue through which all individuals can benefit.

This cooperative relationship is particularly important to second language teaching, for it leads to meaningful interaction about some content of interest. Through such interaction the teacher is naturally attuned to the students' emerging skills and abilities. Otherwise, meaningful communication could not take place. If we consider the "development" to include the students' actual levels with the target language and the students' potential levels, then Vygotsky's theory makes sense for students learning a second language at any age, whether cognitive structures are already highly developed or not.

Meaningful interaction seems to be the key.

One example of the importance of interaction comes from John-Steiner (1985), who refers to the study done with Finnish immigrant children entering

Swedish schools. She reports that they experienced "severe difficulties in their academic and linguistic development" because they were at first placed in very structured classrooms where there was little chance for meaningful interaction. The teacher did most of the talking and the activities were written.

John-Steiner, in the same paper, cites Wong-Fillmore's (1976) study of five new arrivals to the United States from Mexico. These children were paired with Anglo peers and their communication was taped over the period of a school year. The children stretched their knowledge of the target language remarkably. Sometimes these extensions were inadequate in getting across intentions but the peers were able to fill in the gaps.

Additional evidence of the importance of meaningful interaction in second language teaching is found in a study by Seliger (1977). He first became interested in social interaction as a phenomenon when he observed his own two-year-old child. She would

> . . . often push her father's newspaper aside to get his attention and then direct a stream of gibberish at him mixed with a few hardly understood words. He, in turn, could discuss the weather, the stock market, her siblings, or American foreign policy with her. It didn't seem to matter what was said as long as some interaction was taking place. As long as the child was answered, she would continue the same for quite some time.

The question Seliger poses is why a child would participate in and prolong an activity without having much understanding of what was being said to her. He concluded that this phenomenon is actually rather typical behavior and that the strategy being used may be important to the acquisition process itself.

In his study, he proposes that a similar strategy is used by adults who are successfully learning a second language. Although his study is not without critics (see Day, 1984),[2] it is an important one. It attempts to measure not only a public willingness to interact in the classroom but a willingness to participate in private classroom interaction as well. His subjects had studied English as a foreign language and were currently enrolled in an upper intermediate level class in the English Language Institute at Queens College, C.U.N.Y. Each student fell into one of two groups: the "high input generator" group at one end of an interaction continuum, or "the low input generator" group at the other end. The members of the high input generator group interacted intensively, not only with the teacher but with each other. In addition, they initiated much of the interaction. The low input generator group,

---

[2]One of Day's findings in his study of ESL students in Honolulu was that there appeared to be no significant relationship between a measure of public exchanges (involving both responses to general solicits by the teacher and student self-initiated turns) and scores given on an oral interview and on a cloze test.

on the other hand, either avoided interaction altogether or remained fairly passive in situations in which they could have interacted. They seemed more dependent upon formal instruction.

Even though (as Day reminds us) Seliger's subjects are few in number (only three in each category), the study, nevertheless, has interesting implications. It was concluded from the scores on pretests and post-tests that by receiving more focused input through interaction, the high input generators were able to "test more hypotheses about the shape and use of L2 thus accounting for increased success." Low input generators, on the other hand, were particularly dependent upon the classroom environment to force interaction because they did not tend to initiate or allow themselves to become involved in it on their own.[3]

More evidence comes from the Heidelberg Project (cited in Schumann, 1978b) to support the notion that social interaction is important to second language acquisition. In this study of Italian and Spanish guest workers acquiring German in Germany, the correlations were extremely high between German proficiency and leisure social contact (.64), and between German proficiency and social contact at work (.53).

Carroll (1967) comes to a similar conclusion based on his study of university students majoring in French, German, Italian, Russian, and Spanish. Even a brief time spent abroad, where they had social interaction, had a substantial effect on proficiency.[4]

Bruner, who believes strongly in the social nature of language acquisition, chastises those who are committed philosophically to the idea that language learning is reducible to a concatenation of simple forms, which thereby become complex forms. Of course, here he is referring to methods advocated by the behaviorists and later by the cognitive-code theorists. Bruner emphasizes the fact that these people "failed to take into account the inherently social nature of what is learned when one learns language and, by the same token, to consider the essentially social way in which the acquisition of knowledge of language must occur" (1978b, p. 244).

---

[3]At the end of the semester Seliger gave a discrete point test of English structure (Lado-Fries) and an integrative test of aural comprehension (The Queens College English Language Institute Test of Aural Comprehension) in addition to a cloze test. It was found that the scores on the pretests were not good predictors of scores on the post-tests. However, measures of social interaction were. The amount of interaction accounted for 85 percent of the variance in the post-test scores on the discrete point test and for 69 percent of the variance in the post-test scores on the Aural Comprehension test.

[4]MLA Foreign Language Proficiency Tests for Teachers and Advanced Students were administered in 1965 to 2,782 seniors majoring in foreign languages at 203 institutions. The correlations between time spent abroad and test scores were .47,[a] .60,[a] .24,[b] and .27[b] for French, German, Russian, and Spanish respectively. (Italian was probably not included because there was not a sufficient number of cases.)

Note: [a]significance at the .01 level or better.
 [b]significance at the .05 level or better.

THE $i + 1$ AND THE NATURE
OF SOCIAL INTERACTION

Krashen concentrates on input and the role it plays in the language acquisition process in his formulation of the $i + 1$ concept. Like the Zone of Proximal Development, it refers to the distance between actual language development (represented by i) and potential language development (represented by $i + 1$).

This distance is perhaps realized most fully in motherese, that special language used by caretakers who wish to communicate with their children. "Children," according to Macnamara "learn their mother tongue by first determining, independent of language, the meaning which a speaker intends to convey to them and then working out the relationship between the meaning and the expression they heard" (1983, p. 250).

Brown (1973) also stresses this concern with content rather than form in motherese. The child forms his or her own hypotheses about the rules and the relationship between meaning and form. Brown states that meaningful communication on one level always serves as the "launching platform" for attempts at a higher level. It is not so much a mechanism to teach language as it is a way to continue or extend the rapport within a conversation for as long as possible.

Motherese involves the simplification of speech in an intense desire on the part of the caretaker to be understood by the child. According to Corder (1978) this simplification is done chiefly in terms of choosing the kinds of topics and range of speech functions, the utterance length, the rate of speech as well as the amount of repetition, rephrasing, and redundancy in the message. In addition it is specifically related to situational context.

It is interesting to note that in motherese there is seldom a direct correction of ungrammatical forms in the output. Krashen (1982) supports Brown's conclusion that the caretaker seems to be more interested in the truth value of the utterance. As an example of this, he points to Brown, Cazden and Bellugi (1973), who report that "Her curl my hair" was not corrected in their study because the statement was true, whereas "Walt Disney comes on Tuesday" was corrected because in reality Walt Disney comes (on television) on Wednesday. Thus content, not form, is the emphasis.

It is interesting also that parents are usually thrilled by any effort at all that the child makes in forming utterances. For example, when the child says "Daddy home" for the first time, no one labels this a mistake or calls it substandard or even considers it an error at all. Instead it is thought of as being ingenious and cute and the child is hugged or rewarded verbally. The utterance is considered evidence that the child is indeed acquiring the language.

What if in the classroom the language teacher treated "errors" as being evidence that the language was being acquired and that generalizations (often overgeneralizations) were being formed by the student? How would that facilitate the acquisition of the language? It is probable that in such an environment, the learner would be more willing to take the risk of being wrong and would be freer and more uninhibited in developing an interlanguage.[5] The forms would thus become acquired, as they are in L1, mainly through extensive use of modified language in meaningful situations (Wagner-Gough & Hatch, 1975; Chaudron, 1985; Ellis, 1985).

What happens in the classroom in which the teacher is concerned both with the accuracy and fluency of the output, as most of us are? Sutherland feels that both of these goals "cannot realistically be achieved in the early stages of learning. Fortunately, and perhaps more importantly, they do not need to be achieved simultaneously in order to ultimately produce effective speakers" (1979, p. 25). He further says that learners in classrooms in which accuracy is first tend to develop very little proficiency in the target language. In such classrooms the teachers often look upon themselves as "Guardians of the Linguistic Norm" and feel that their main reason for being there is to ensure correctness. They often think that if students are allowed to make mistakes at beginning levels, they are doomed to a lifetime of linguistic errors (it's a matter of habit formation, they say). However, Sutherland points out that "Since errors persist in learners anyway—no matter what method is employed—we certainly cannot look to methods to explain this phenomenon" (1979, p. 27).

It appears that most errors found in the interlanguage of learners are developmental (at least after the very beginning stages during which transfer from L1 seems to be a viable strategy). If this is true, what can a teacher do to help the student become more accurate? Yorio (1980) suggests that we keep careful note of the errors our students make to determine whether the errors are systematic (appear with regularity) or random (caused by memory lapse, inattention, not having acquired the rule, or overgeneralization). It is the systematic errors with which we should be concerned. Are the errors increasing? (The student is regressing.) Are the errors decreasing? (The student is learning.) Are they stationary? (The student is fossilizing—the errors have become obligatory in the student's output.)[6] Of course, if the student appears to be regressing, something must be done before the forms have had a chance to

---

[5]The term *interlanguage* (Selinker, 1972) refers to the developmental stages involved in moving from L1 to L2. Various kinds of errors and strategies have been identified with stages along the way. For example, learners at some levels in the early part of their development have difficulty with sentence inversion when asking questions (Why you are here?) and with negative formation (You no like it). It should be noted that learners tend to vary their interlanguage to match the situation. Forms used in informal discourse are often different from those used in more formal discourse. The situation will generally influence the amount of conscious monitoring that occurs. However, the overall natural sequence associated with informal discourse appears to be universal (see Ellis, 1986).

[6]Most second language learners fossilize at some point in their interlanguage development (see Selinker, 1972). Causes of fossilization may include low motivation to become more nativelike, lack of native or nativelike models, or a failure of the hypothesis-testing mechanisms of the brain which may be related to age (see Selinker and Lamendella, 1978a). The danger occurs when learners fossilize early in their interlanguage development and their ability to communicate becomes impaired. (See also Chapter 5.)

fossilize. However, Yorio warns that it is important not to inundate the students' papers with red ink, but to discuss errors in a meaningful way. Perhaps sessions can be held with several students at once who seem to be making the same kinds of errors. He suggests also that students be given a chance to find their own errors and correct them. With oral errors, he recommends we focus on meaning as opposed to form, especially with children. Modeling or repeating what the learner has said, but in correct form, is one way to correct indirectly. However, he notes that adults often want to know the nature of the errors they are making. They may ask for explanations.

There is one rule of thumb that might work well here. It is somewhat analogous to the advice parents are often given on how to answer questions their children ask about sex. Tell them *only* what they have asked for and no more. The same thing can apply to questions about grammar. Thus when students ask about the rule governing the difference between "walk" and "walked," discuss the rule involving the distinction between present and past of regular verbs, but refrain from giving them the complete verb system, including irregular forms, or from explaining the various ways in which "ed" can be pronounced ([t], [d], or as a separate syllable such as in "ragged"). Their asking the question in the first place indicates that they are motivated to learn that particular rule and that they may be ready to incorporate it into their linguistic systems. Because older children, teenagers, and adults are more advanced cognitively and are better able to apply learned rules, introducing them to some rules fairly early in their language development (e.g., regular past tense, plural formation) could aid in the acquisition process. However, if the goal of the student is to understand and to be understood in social and/or academic situations, then methods must focus primarily on real communication in those kinds of situations.

The student, like the child learning a first language, acquires language best through meaningful input addressed directly to him or her, similar to the input of motherese. "It makes rules become more salient and helps (the student) to perceive more easily the relationship between meaning and form" (d'Anglejan, 1978, p. 225). The phrases or rules learned from a book or syllabus may be totally obscured when the student is involved in real conversation, and they will probably not even be recognized.

What kind of input, then, is most conducive to forming generalizations about the language, thereby making acquisition possible? Krashen (see Related Reading 5) suggests that in addition to being relevant and/or interesting (see Chapter 2), the input must approximate the student's $i + 1$. It must be comprehensible in that it is near the student's actual level of development (i), but then it must stretch beyond that to include concepts and structures that the student has not yet acquired ($i + 1$). Free conversation with native speakers does not generally produce input that can be comprehended unless the native speakers are talking directly to the student and are aware of the student's approximate $i + 1$. Neither does TV or radio ordinarily produce such input. The student ideally must be in a situation in which all the interlocutors desire to understand and be understood. It is often through gestures, the context itself, and linguistic modifications that the new concepts become internalized. In other words, the student needs to receive foreigner talk.

The term "foreigner talk" was coined by Ferguson (1975), who defined it as a simplified register or style of speech used when addressing people who are non-native speakers.[7] Foreigner talk in the classroom is generally well formed and includes, but often to a greater degree, many of the same strategies used in regular teacher talk: exaggeration of pronunciation and facial expression; decreasing speech rate and increasing volume; frequent use of pause, gestures, graphic illustrations, questions, and dramatization; sentence expansion, rephrasing, and simplification; prompting; and completing utterances made by the student (Henzl, 1973; Gaies, 1977; Kleifgen, 1985; Wesche & Ready, 1985; Richard-Amato, 1987). The input is automatically adjusted in the attempt to ensure understanding. See the example below:

Two teachers are talking to a group of foreign students in the Intensive English Center at the University of New Mexico.

	Strategy Used
TEACHER 1: Who's the man with the hood on his face? (points to the word "executioner" on the chalkboard)	question gesture graphic aid
TEACHER 2: Yeh. You've seen the pictures . . . they have black hoods (She pantomimes as she crouches and ominously pulls a pretend hood over her head.) . . . with the eyes. (She uses her fingers to encircle her eyes to appear as though she is looking through a mask. Teacher 1 does the same, and they both scan the group as if to frighten them.) . . . You know . . . really creepy looking . . . scary . . . oh . . . what is it called?	decreased rate increased volume pausing expansion dramatization simplification expansion question

(Richard & Lucero, 1980, p. 6)

It is important to point out that comprehensible input is a relative concept determined by the total interaction and cannot be defined simply by a list of features (Tarone, 1981; Ellis, 1985). As Ellis concludes on the basis of his 9-month study of an ESL teacher's interactions with two pupils,

---

[7]An important question here is how does foreigner talk differ from regular teacher talk in the classroom? Studies have been done in an attempt to at least partially answer this question (see Kleifgen, 1985; Wesche & Ready, 1985; Richard-Amato, 1987).

Different features may aid development at different times. For instance, in
this study of T-P [teacher-pupil] interactions, teacher self-repetitions were
more frequent at an early stage of development, and teacher expansions at a
later stage. Also the context of activity in which interaction takes place is
characterized by a dynamic, utterance-by-utterance adjustment by both partners in the conversation. Both the learner and the native speaker adjust their
behavior in the light of the continuous feedback about the success of the
discourse with which they provide each other (1985, p. 82).

The following illustrates the negotiation of meaning in a one-to-one communication situation. In this kind of collaboration between student and
teacher or student and a more advanced peer, the "stretching" to higher
levels of development becomes more obvious.

STUDENT: I throw it—box. (He points to a box on the floor.)
TEACHER: You threw the box.
STUDENT: No, I threw *in* the box.
TEACHER: What did you throw in the box?
STUDENT: My . . . I paint . . .
TEACHER: Your painting?
STUDENT: Painting?
TEACHER: You know . . . painting. (The teacher makes painting movements
          on an imaginary paper.)
STUDENT: Yes, painting.
TEACHER: You threw your painting in the box.
STUDENT: Yes, I threw my painting in box.

The teacher is speaking near the student's $i + 1$. The conversation is
about the immediate environment. The vocabulary is simple. Repetitions are
frequent. Acting out is used. All in response to the feedback. The focus is on
the meaning as opposed to the form. Correct forms are being acquired not
by the process of direct correction, but through the content and the process
of indirect correction or modeling. Notice that *throw* in the student's speech
becomes *threw, in* is incorporated into the prepositional phrase, and the article
the is picked up before *box* but then lost again. It will probably take a lot
more comprehensible input containing these forms before they become firmly
established in the student's acquisition store.

Thus the grammar is being acquired through the natural process of communication. A conscious use of grammatical sequencing does not appear to
be necessary. Similar conclusions are borne out by many others (Long, Adams, McLean, & Castanos, 1976; d'Angeljan, 1978; Krashen, 1982; Hatch,
1983; B. Taylor, 1983).

THE ROLE OF OUTPUT

Krashen (1985; see also Related Reading 5) minimizes the role of output in the acquisition process. He reminds us that language can be acquired simply by comprehending input. He argues particularly against those who believe that output is used for hypothesis testing, a process by which the learner tries out new structures in discourse and acquires a specific rule, provided enough positive responses are received. He feels that second language learners test hypotheses, not through the use of output, but by subconsciously matching forms in the input to their own notions about the language. Of course, he does admit that full two-way communication, because it necessitates more negotiation of meaning, results in more comprehensible input.

Swain (1985) prefers to take a stronger stand for the importance of the role of output in the acquisition process. In fact, she argues that among other functions, output *is* a significant way to test out hypotheses about the target language (also see Seliger, discussed earlier in this chapter). She concludes, on the basis of her study of English-speaking children in a French immersion program,

> Comprehensible output . . . is a necessary mechanism of acquisition independent of the role of comprehensible input. Its role is, at minimum, to provide opportunities for contextualized, meaningful use, to test out hypotheses about the target language, and to move the learner from a purely semantic analysis of language to a syntactic analysis of it (1985, p. 252).

She found that although immersion students comprehended what their teachers said and focused on meaning, they were still not fully acquiring the syntactic system of French. She agrees with those who suggest that "it is not input per se that is important to second language acquisition but input that occurs in interaction where meaning is negotiated" (1985, p. 246). Simply knowing that one will eventually be expected to produce may be the "trigger that forces the learner to pay attention to the means of expressions needed in order to successfully convey his or her own intended meaning" (1985, p. 249). Obviously, there is less chance to give output in subject-matter classes in which the teachers do most of the talking and the students do the listening. She feels that the grammatical development of immersion students will suffer because of their relatively limited opportunity to interact. Output has a much greater role than simply to provide more comprehensible input. She is convinced that when the second language student receives negative input in the form of confirmation checks and other repairs, he or she is given impetus to seek alternative ways to get the meaning across.

Once the meaning has been negotiated, it becomes possible for the student during similar future exchanges to "move from semantic processing to syntactic processing" (1985, p. 249). In other words, once the meaning is understood, the learner is free to focus on form within the interactional situation. Swain laments the fact that in addition to their opportunities for output being limited, immersion students appear to be satisfied with their strategies for getting meaning across, since they are readily understood by those around them. In her words, "There appears to be little social or cognitive pressure to produce language that reflects more appropriately or precisely their intended meaning; there is no push to be more comprehensible than they already are" (1985, p 249).

If Swain is right, then output is more than just a means for receiving more comprehensible input. It is important to the acquisition process itself.

SUMMARY

Vygotsky's Zone of Proximal Development and Krashen's $i + 1$ are similar concepts, both offering insights into the cognitive processes involved in language acquisition. Contrary to Piaget, who proposed one level of cognitive development, Vygotsky and Krashen implied two levels: an actual level and a potential level. While Vygotsky stressed the *importance* of social interaction, Krashen stressed the *nature* of the input.

The pivotal role of social interaction in second language acquisition is supported by the following: John-Steiner's conclusions based on a study involving Finnish immigrant children in Sweden and on a study done by Lilly Wong-Fillmore of Mexican immigrant children in the United States; Seliger's research on the role of interaction in an intermediate English class at Queens College, C.U.N.Y.; Schumann's conclusions based on the Heidelberg Project; and Carroll's study of foreign language students at several universities.

The nature of input is described not only by Krashen but by Brown, Cazden, and Bellugi, in addition to the many others who have looked at motherese and found that it emphasizes meaning rather than form. Applying this knowledge to second language acquisition in the classroom, Sutherland and Yorio address the accuracy-vs.-fluency controversy and its relative significance in instruction. Sutherland feels that the two should not be dealt with simultaneously at beginning levels, at which fluency should be the chief concern. Yorio addresses accuracy and offers some suggestions for dealing with systematic (not random) errors in the student's output.

Although the chapter focuses on the role of input in the interaction, that of output must not be ignored. Output can play a substantial part in the acquistion process. It not only aids in receiving comprehensible input, it offers opportunities for practice and appears to be an important means for testing hypotheses.

READINGS, REFLECTION, AND DISCUSSION

Suggested Readings and Reference Materials

Brown, R. (1973). *A first language: The early stages.* Cambridge, MA: Harvard University. A classic in the study of first language acquisition. The proponents of interactional approaches in second language learning often refer to its insights, particularly to the role the caretaker plays in facilitating the interaction.

Gass, S. & Madden, C. (1985). *Input in second language acquisition.* Rowley, MA: Newbury House. A collection of research papers focusing on the input to which second language students are exposed and on the interactions in which they are involved.

Krashen, S. (1985). *The input hypothesis: Issues and implications.* New York: Longman. In this book Krashen discusses the input hypothesis and its ramifications including supporting evidence, the challenges it has faced, and its implications for teaching second languages.

Mehan, H. (1979). *Learning lessons.* Cambridge, MA: Harvard University. A fascinating, in-depth study of the structure of classroom interaction and the interdependence of its participants. The classroom is viewed as a "community" in which the members perform their roles to carry out its functions.

Richards, J. (1975). The context for error analysis. In M. Burt and H. Dulay (Eds.), *New directions in second language learning, teaching and bilingual education* (pp. 70–79). Washington, DC: Teachers of English to Speakers of Other Languages. An attempt to understand the nature of second language acquisition by examining the output of individuals going through the process. Four issues are addressed: the nature of language, the nature of language systems in contact, the learning of linguistic systems, and their use in communication.

Vygotsky, L. (1978). *Mind in society.* Cambridge, MA: Harvard University. Editors M. Cole, V. John-Steiner, S. Scribner, and E. Souberman spent several years compiling this volume of manuscripts and letters that might have been lost to us had it not been for their efforts. The collection highlights and clarifies Vygotsky's theories of the mind and its higher psychological functions.

Wells, G. (1981). *Learning through interaction: The study of language development.* Cambridge: Cambridge University. A valuable collection of papers on language acquisition and its inextricable relationship to interaction. Contains many examples of actual discourse between children and their caretakers. Identifies key communication strategies.

Questions for Reflection and Discussion

1. After visits to several beginning to early intermediate second or foreign language classrooms, answer the following questions:
   a. In which classrooms were the lessons focused on grammar?
   b. In which classrooms was meaningful interaction the focus?

    c. Did you notice any differences in student attitude between those involved in one type of lesson and those in another?

2. According to Freire, the relationship between teacher and student should be dialectical. What kind of classroom environment might foster this relationship? What sorts of activities might take place in such a classroom?

3. How, in your opinion, should student errors be handled in the classroom? Consider the following:
    a. Level of student proficiency
    b. The age of the student
    c. Systematic versus random errors
    d. Correction of oral versus written output

4. React to Macnamara's (1983) condemnation of language teachers in the quote:

> Language is a particular embarrassment to the teacher because outside school children seem to learn a language without any difficulty whereas in school with the aid of teachers their progress is halting and unsatisfactory.

Assume that all the children to whom he is referring are learning a second language and are of the same approximate age. If his statement has credibility in your opinion, give some possible explanations.

5. In your opinion, is there a place for the explicit teaching of grammar rules in the second language classroom? If so, address the following questions and relate your discussion to the particular language you teach. Which rules would you teach? To whom? When? Under what conditions? How?

4

The Episode Hypothesis
and Materials Selection

. . . The input is never into a quiescent or static system, but always into a system which is already actively excited and organized. In the intact organism, behavior is the result of the interaction of this background of excitation with input from any designated stimulus. Only when we can state the general characteristics of this background of excitation, can we understand the effects of a given input.

K. Lashley, 1961

PREDICTABILITY

The mind, in its attempt to assimilate the ideas with which it comes into contact, organizes and builds sequences of hierarchies (see de Saussuré, 1959; Minsky, 1975; Schank & Abelson, 1977). When the individual comes into contact with a new situation, he or she selects, usually subconsciously, an appropriate structure with which to associate it. Generally some sort of accommodation mechanism is available to help the individual handle information for which there seems to be no perfect fit.

Schema theory (see Becker, 1973; Adams & Collins, 1979; Rumelhart, 1980; Carrell, 1983; and many others) develops a similar idea mainly in relation to the comprehension and retention of texts. The schema (sets of hierarchies) act as frames which aid the reader in predicting the organization and content of what he or she reads.

Natural speech itself is arranged sequentially in highly predictable ways. According to Oller, this high degree of predictability enables us to understand what is being said. "The more predictable a sequence of linguistic elements becomes, the more readily it is processed" (1979, p. 447). In his work with Obrecht in 1969, Oller found that "informational sequences," groups of sentences that present interrelated information in a logical fashion, were easier to remember than sentences forming no such logical order. Two sets of Spanish sentences of equal complexity were taught to a group of high school students enrolled in first year Spanish. *Set A* incorporated informational sequences (e.g., 1. ¿Cómo está? 2. Estoy bien. 3. ¿Y usted? 4. Muy bien); *Set B* did not (e.g., 1. ¿Qué es esto? 2. Voy después. 3. ¿Quién es? 4. Pues voy). Each subject received both sets. The results indicated that informational sequencing is a significant positive factor in one's being able to remember and reproduce phonemes, intelligible words, and sentences in the foreign language.

Oller (1974) uses the term "expectancy grammar" to describe the relationship between language and experience and to explain the mental processes involved in utilizing a temporal integration to comprehend and remember input.

He distinguishes between linguistic and nonlinguistic contexts in what he calls a "pragmatic mapping" of language into experience. The linguistic context involved in natural speech falls into two basic divisions (see Howes & Osgood, 1961): *homogeneous linguistic context*, which is context provided by the person's own previous language behavior, and *heterogeneous linguistic context*, which is context provided by the utterances of other persons in the environment. Linguistic context includes both verbal and gestural behavior.

Nonlinguistic context or extralinguistic context (the latter term is the one Oller uses) refers to the more subjective aspects of language: our perceptions of ideas, people, events (past and present), and relationships (1979, p. 19).

Adams (1982) describes her investigation into the effects of both linguistic and nonlinguistic background knowledge upon determining the meanings of unknown vocabulary words in a reading comprehension task. She used "script activators" (statements given to predispose students to certain interpretations of a text) to find out what the effects would be on the ability to define the unfamiliar words. One of her hypotheses was that subjects receiving the script activators before reading a particular passage would score higher than those receiving none. She then presented her subjects, American college students, with passages in which target words had been replaced with nonsense words. The scores depended on the number of times a word's meaning was correctly recognized. Students who had received script activators did indeed achieve considerably higher vocabulary scores than students who received no script activators.

In another study, this one done by Schallert (1976), the script activator was a title or an introduction that predicted what the passage was about. The subjects were given ambiguous passages to read that could be interpreted in two different ways semantically. For example,

In the last days of August, we were all suffering from the unbearable heat. . . . "All we need now," said the manager in one of his discouraged moods, "is a strike." I listened to him silently but I could not help him. I hit a fly. "I suppose things could get even worse," he continued. "Our most valuable pitchers might crack in this heat. If only we had more fans, we would all feel better, I'm sure . . . ."

The above passage has two concrete interpretations although not equally probable. The "manager" could be a manager of a baseball team or the manager of a glassware factory. The first possibility would be the strong meaning and the second the weak one. When script activators were given, they had a rather powerful influence on the comprehension and memory of the reader. Otherwise, the strong meaning was generally chosen if it was favored by the background experience of the students.

The challenge, as it appears to Oller, is how this knowledge about expectancies can best be utilized in the teaching of a second language. He states:

> If the native speaker's knowledge of his language is characterized as a grammar of expectancy that incorporates pragmatic knowledge of the world, the problem of teaching a second language can be defined as providing the student with a corpus of language in meaningful communicative settings (Abstract, 1974, p. 443).

What should be the nature of such a corpus of language, or, in other words, what should be the nature of the input in order for it to have the best possible chance of becoming acquired?

THE EPISODE HYPOTHESIS

As an answer to that question Oller offers the Episode Hypothesis, which states that *"text (i.e., discourse in any form) will be easier to reproduce, understand, and recall, to the extent that it is motivated and structured episodically"* (1983b, p. 12). Episodic organization requires both motivation created by conflict and the logical sequencing that is necessary to good storytelling and consistent with experience. Thus a text may be structured temporally but not necessarily episodically.

Schank and Abelson (1977) relate episodic structure to memory itself. It is their view that "not only is information stored by humans in episodic form; it is also acquired that way."

Oller agrees and goes one step further by applying this theory to the classroom:

> Language programs that employ fully contextualized and maximally meaningful language necessarily optimize the learner's ability to use previously acquired expectancies to help discover the pragmatic mappings of utterances

in the new language into extralinguistic contexts. Hence they would seem to be superior to programs that expect learners to acquire the ability to use a language on the basis of disconnected lists of sentences (1979, pp. 31–32).

Yet many ESL and foreign language texts written today contain disconnected lists of sentences or, at best, sentences that may be related but are not part of any motivated or logical interaction.

Consider the following example from a typical ESL text. It consists of a group of items related only in that each illustrates the same grammatical form.

Example 1

1. We're *having* a grammar test today.
2. Bob *is having* a party tomorrow.
3. The Smiths *are having* a good time in Paris.
4. My sister *is having* a baby in June.
   (*Pollock, 1982, p. 7*)

Or read the next typical passage, which is temporally structured but lacks sufficient motivation or conflict as well as logical sequencing.

Example 2

Tomás is visiting Ralph and Lucy.

RALPH: How long can you stay, Tomás?
TOMÁS: I'm going to leave tomorrow afternoon. I'm taking the bus.
LUCY: I like taking the bus, but Ralph doesn't.
RALPH: What do you want to do tomorrow, Tomás? Do you want to sleep late?
TOMÁS: No, I like to get up early. Let's go to the park. Do you like playing tennis?
RALPH: I don't like to play, but Lucy likes tennis. She plays every day.
LUCY: Ralph likes jogging. Let's go to the park early tomorrow morning. Tomás and I can play tennis, and you can go jogging. Ralph . . .
(*Sutherland, 1981, p. 11*)

Compare the first two examples with the following:

Example 3

DARLENE: I think I'll call Bettina's mother. It's almost five and Chrissy isn't home yet.
MEG: I thought Bettina had the chicken pox.
DARLENE: Oh, that's right. I forgot. Chrissy didn't go to Bettina's today. Where is she?

> MEG: She's probably with Gary. He has Little League practice until five.
> DARLENE: I hear the front door. Maybe that's Gary and Chrissy.
> GARY: Hi.
> DARLENE: Where's Chrissy? Isn't she with you?
> GARY: With me? Why with me? I saw her at two after school, but then I went to Little League practice. I think she left with her friend.
> DARLENE: Which one?
> GARY: The one next door . . . the one she walks to school with every day.
> DARLENE: Oh, you mean Timmy. She's probably with him.
> GARY: Yeah, she probably is.
> DARLENE: I'm going next door to check.
> (Brinton & Neuman, 1982, p. 33)

Which of these three examples of input would have the best chance for becoming internalized? Of course, the answer would have to be Example 3. It captivates our interest through its episodic organization.

Below are posed a few questions concerning the three examples to reinforce the importance of episodically meaningful text.

Questions for Example 1:

1. Who is having a good time in Paris?
2. Who is having a party tomorrow?

These questions are impossible to answer without referring back to the text. Why? In looking back at the words themselves, we realize that the *Smiths* are having a good time in Paris and that *Bob* is having a party tomorrow. But these people are not important to us in that they do not connect meaningfully to our experience, nor do they connect in any meaningful way to each other. They are not part of any conflict and thus they remain unmotivated. They have made little impression and are not easily remembered.

Questions for Example 2:

1. Who is visiting?
2. What does the visitor plan to do?
3. Who likes to ride on buses?
4. What does Lucy like to do?
5. Who likes jogging?

The above questions, even though the sentences to which they refer are temporally related and perhaps slightly motivated, are just as difficult to answer as those for Example 1. Why? They are not logical according to our experience. Their only reason for existence seems to be to expose the students to the present progressive tense and to gerunds and to teach the comparative structure "I like taking the bus, but Ralph doesn't" or "I don't like to play, but Lucy likes tennis." People in normal conversation do not speak in this fashion; there is no reason for doing so considering that in natural discourse we are not concerned with exposing others to specific grammatical forms.

In addition to there being no justification for the discourse other than a grammatical one, there is little logic in the flow of the conversation. When Tomás says, "I'm going to leave tomorrow afternoon. I'm taking the bus," one would expect either Lucy or Ralph to say something like "Oh, you're leaving so soon" or at least comment on the leaving. Instead, Lucy says, "I like taking the bus, but Ralph doesn't." Thus our sense of expectancy is violated. Grice (1975) relates this sense of expectancy to the maxim of relation which is essential in normal discourse.

Questions for Example 3:

1. Who has disappeared?
2. When was she last seen?
3. Where are they going to look for her?
4. How do the characters feel about her disappearance?

Here we are more apt to remember the details. Why? The structuring is consistent with our own experience, and the dialogue is motivated and logical. Because these requirements are met, we automatically become involved with the language at a subconscious as well as conscious level. We experience a heightened awareness. We become concerned with the little girl's disappearance just as the people in the story are concerned.

APPLICATION TO THE CLASSROOM

Oller states:

> The problem, it would seem, from an educational point of view is how to take advantage of the expectancies that a learner has already acquired in trying to teach new material. The question is, what does the learner already know, and how can that knowledge be optimally utilized in the presentation of new material (1979, p. 31).

He makes six suggestions to the language teacher:

1. Unmotivated texts should be avoided.
2. The story line (in the text chosen) should be carried primarily by stage-

able action. Through this means, the materials would be easier to dramatize and understand.

3. The story line must respect the logic of experience.
4. The basic facts of the story should be understood first before the student is expected to comprehend the subtleties.
5. The story can be broken down into manageable "chunks" for a better grasp of the facts.
6. Each episode can be worked through in multiple cycles, progressing from simple to more complex. On each "pass" through the story the student would go from the basic facts (who, what, and where) and progress to a more in-depth understanding (when, why, and how) and finally to presupposition, associations, and implications (Oller, 1983b, pp. 17–18).

The presentation of episodically organized materials can indeed be an effective language teaching approach. Through materials that do not violate the logic of normal discourse, the student can receive optimal input which can enhance the ability to reproduce, understand, and recall the target language.

SUMMARY

The brain in its effort to store and process information utilizes hierarchical knowledge systems that have been determined by prior experience. Thus sequences that are highly predictable are formed out of what would otherwise be isolated clusters of bits and pieces. We know that appropriate connections within complex structures must be made if we are to make sense out of input and remember it.

The Episode Hypothesis argues that text that is motivated and structured episodically will be more easily incorporated into our linguistic repertoires than other kinds of text.

Many second language textbooks, however, are written mainly to teach specific grammar points or structures without much thought given to what constitutes meaningful prose. This is not to say that "grammar" books as such should not be written, particularly if they are supplemental in nature. There is a place for such books too. However, it seems reasonable that if textbooks are to capitalize maximally on our ability to acquire language, then they must engage our emotions as well as our intellects.

READINGS, REFLECTION, AND DISCUSSION

Suggested Readings and Reference Materials

Hook, J. N. (1963). *Writing creatively*. Boston: Heath. Although this classic on writing may not appear to be an appropriate inclusion, I suggest it particularly for those who may be interested in materials development. The book offers a wide array of ideas for producing compelling fiction that will keep the reader focused on content.

Minsky, M. (1975). A framework for representing knowledge. In P. Winston (Ed.), *The psychology of computer vision.* New York: McGraw-Hill. Minsky reacts to what he feels to be an overemphasis on the ''minute, local, and unstructured'' accounts of knowledge representation. He instead argues for a more encompassing, structured explanation of how the mind organizes and remembers that with which it comes into contact. He is critical of attempts by the behaviorists to represent knowledge as simply a collection of separate elements.

Oller, J., Jr. (1983c). Story writing principles and ESL teaching. *TESOL Quarterly, 17*(1), 39–53. This paper considers four hypotheses: the input hypothesis, the textuality hypothesis, the expectancy hypothesis, and the episode hypothesis. Their relationships are explored and practical applications are offered.

Schank, R., & Abelson, R. (1977). *Scripts, plans, goals, and understanding.* Hillsdale, NJ: Lawrence Erlbaum. A highly theoretical inquiry into human cognitive structures as they relate to artificial intelligence. The authors examine such areas as memory, causal chains, and motivation.

Questions for Reflection and Discussion

1. What is your reaction to the Episode Hypothesis? Would you change it in any way?

2. Consider some language text personally known to you which you believe is effective, and another which you believe ineffective. Does this chapter throw any light upon the reasons for your favorable or unfavorable opinion?

3. Set up some criteria for rating examples from textbooks in terms of their episodic organization. Include additional aspects that you feel might heighten the awareness of the reader or listener. You might consider aspects of character development, dialogue, or literary devices of various kinds.
    Example:

	Yes or No *(check one)*	
Are the characters believable?	_____	_____
Is the dialogue logical?	_____	_____
Is foreshadowing present?	_____	_____

You might want to refine the ratings by giving numerical value to such categories as ''usually,'' ''sometimes,'' ''never,'' and so on.

4. Using the language texts and other supplemental reading materials that are available to you, choose passages that can be looked at in terms of

episodic structure. By rating them according to the criteria you've set up, determine which ones fare best.

5. How might a knowledge of the Episode Hypothesis help you other than in choosing texts and other reading materials? Consider the applicability of such knowledge to other situations used to create an acquisition-rich environment for your students.

5

The Affective Domain

If we were to devise theories of second language acquisition or teaching methods which were based only on cognitive considerations, we would be omitting the most fundamental side of human behavior.

H. D. Brown, 1980

The affective domain includes several variables that can either enhance second language acquisition or hinder it, depending upon whether they are positive or negative, the degree to which they are present, and the combinations in which we find them.

Because these variables are difficult to isolate and are often so subtle they can scarcely be detected, it seems impossible to study them objectively with our current methods, although many have tried. How does one effectively measure inhibition, for example? Or empathy? Or attitudes, for that matter? All of these intangible concepts interact to form changing patterns usually operating out of the subconscious. We do know that factors or combinations of factors having to do with *attitudes, motivation,* and *level of anxiety* are central to the affective domain. These are strongly influenced by the process of *acculturation* and by certain *personality* variables.

ATTITUDES

Attitudes develop as a result of experience, both direct and vicarious. They are greatly influenced by people in the immediate environment: parents, teachers, and peers. Attitudes toward self, the target language and the people who speak it (peers in particular), the teacher, and the classroom environment all seem to have an influence on acquisition.

Attitude Toward Self

Adelaide Heyde (1979) looked at the effects of three levels of self-esteem (global, specific [situational], and task) on the oral performance of American college students studying French as a foreign language. She found that students with high self-esteem at all levels performed better in French (see Related Reading 7). Other studies have resulted in similar conclusions (Heyde, 1977; Oller, Hudson, & Liu, 1977).

In general, self-esteem leads to self-confidence. The degree of self-esteem and/or self-confidence may vary from situation to situation or from task to task. Both may increase as one performs well in a variety of situations. Oller (1981) argues that the relationship between affect and learning is probably bidirectional. We may perform well because our attitude toward self is positive; we may have a positive attitude toward self because we perform well (see also Gardner, Lalonde, & Moorcroft, 1985).

Stevick emphasizes the importance of *self-security*, an important facet of the attitude toward self. "Am I what I would like to be as an intellectual being and also as a social being? Do I have an adequate mind, and am I the kind of person that other people are willing to spend time with?" (1976b, p. 229). If the answer to all these questions is affirmative, then the individual is better able to engage in the often humbling process of acquiring a second language.

Attitude Toward the Target Language and the People Who Speak It

The attitudes that an individual has toward the target language and the target group (especially peers) seem to have a very significant effect on motivation in particular. According to Gardner and Lambert,

> The learner's ethnocentric tendencies and his attitudes toward the members of the other group are believed to determine how successful he will be, relatively, in learning the new language (1972, p. 3).

Here stereotyping often plays a large role. Saville-Troike (1976) reports that the *in-group* often values characteristics that the *out-group* supposedly lacks, such as cleanliness, human traits (as opposed to animal), independence, self-reliance, appropriate behaviors concerning time, and the like. A major effect of stereotyping is to create or perpetuate social distance and social boundaries. Saville-Troike argues that stereotypes build "a social barrier which inhibits communication and learning and they affect the self-image of those who are typed."

When negative stereotypes are attributed to second language students, they may become *internalized* and could undermine attempts at language acquisition. Not only do negative stereotypes affect the self-esteem of the group's members, but they often bring about negative reactions and encourage negative attitudes toward the target language and culture. Students who are considered linguistically deficient or disadvantaged because they have a different first language are particularly at risk. The second language student's self-esteem is in jeopardy if the teacher and peers fail to show respect for the first language and the culture of which it is a part.

Attitudes Toward the Teacher and the Classroom Environment

In classrooms in which mutual respect is lacking, differing values can meet head on. Conflicts are likely to develop between student and teacher and between student and peer. Students who cooperate on a project may be thought to be "cheating" or students who fail to guess on the true or false section of a test are thought to be "not caring." In the first case the students may not value competition as the teacher thinks they should; rather they value group cooperation in completing a task. In the second case, the students may not feel comfortable guessing when not knowing the answer; their motive may be not to get the highest possible score but simply to render a more accurate indication of what they actually know.

We have all probably seen classrooms in which values clashed, student against peer. In one situation, for example, the students had been given a group task to identify problems that might be encountered on a "date," American style. Two fairly recent arrivals insisted that the couple must be chaperoned in order to prevent inappropriate behavior. A much larger number thought that the idea of a chaperone would be silly; they insisted that in a modern world one would never consider such a practice. The discussion resulted in a very angry exchange among the students. This incident might have been prevented had the majority of the students been given a chance to voice differences early on, discuss them, and through the discussion gain an appreciation of others and their differing world views.

To ease tensions which might result in unpleasant situations such as the one described above, some teachers might feel comfortable using affective activities or humanistic techniques (see Chapter 11). Those advocated particularly by Brown and Dubin (1975), Moskowitz (1978), and Simon, Howe, and Kirschenbaum (1972) seek to create good feelings on the part of the students toward the teacher, each other, and the resulting classroom environment.

Moskowitz sets out to gather evidence that the use of such techniques in language classrooms (both foreign and ESL) does indeed "enhance attitudes toward a foreign language, rapport with classmates, and the self-image of foreign language students" (1981, p. 149). She conducted two studies using the language students of eleven teachers enrolled at Temple University in courses on humanistic techniques of teaching a foreign language. The subjects were high school students studying a variety of languages: French, Spanish, German, Italian, Hebrew, and ESL. Each teacher chose one class (from beginners through advanced) in which to do the study. Often they chose classes that had been apathetic or difficult in some way. They gave three questionnaires prior to the humanistic activities and readministered the questionnaires two months later. Had the students' attitudes changed? In both studies there appeared to be significant positive increases in attitude toward themselves, toward the language, and toward each other.[1] The following four hypotheses were accepted (1981, pp. 145–150):

> Using humanistic techniques to teach a foreign language:
> 1. enhances the attitudes of foreign language students toward learning the target language
> 2. enhances the self-perceptions of foreign language students
> 3. enhances the perceptions of foreign language students toward
>   a. the members of their language class
>   b. how their classmates perceive them
> 4. increases the acceptance of foreign language students for members of the same sex and the opposite sex in their class, thus increasing their cohesiveness.

These studies indicate that humanistic activities may increase the development of positive student attitudes overall.

MOTIVATION

In much of the current literature, integrative motivation and instrumental motivation are differentiated. Gardner and Lambert (1972) describe *integrative motivation* roughly as a desire to integrate and identify with the target language group. They describe *instrumental motivation* as a desire to use the language to obtain practical goals such as studying in a technical field or getting a job.

The studies of French classes in Canada done by Gardner and Lambert (1959), and Gardner, Smythe, Clement, and Gliksman (1976) all conclude that integrative motivation is generally stronger than instrumental motivation in predicting French proficiency. In addition, Bernard Spolsky (1969) found that integrative motivation, as determined by a questionnaire that indirectly as-

---

[1]In the 1977 study the students' identities were not revealed and so the pre-post data were treated as though they came from two independent groups; in the 1978 study the identity of the students was retained in code so that pre-post data could be matched. Two questionnaires were administered: the Foreign Language Attitude Questionnaire and *My Class and Me* (see Moskowitz, 1981, p. 150). Sociometric data were collected from each student to see to what extent attitudes changed toward specific peers.

sessed attitudes toward the target language group, is among the strong predictors of proficiency in ESL students.

However, the evidence in this area frequently appears contradictory.
There are cases in which integration appears *not* to be a strong motive but in
which a certain urgency exists to become proficient in the target language for
instrumental reasons. In such cases instrumental motivation becomes the
main predictor (Lukmani, 1972; Oller, Baca, & Vigil, 1977). In addition, the
study of Chinese-speaking graduate students in the United States (Oller,
Hudson, & Liu, 1977) indicated that although the students' main reason for
wanting to be proficient in English was instrumental, the subjects who characterized Americans positively performed better on a cloze test. Thus the
studies are very inconclusive.

What appear to be contradictory findings may simply be evidence indicating that the various motivations studied are difficult if not impossible to isolate and are certainly not mutually exclusive.

Many questions need to be addressed. How do we distinguish the various motivations to begin with? For example, does "integration" mean to
become part of the target language group or just to socialize on a casual basis
with its members?[2] If the latter is true, then might not instrumental motivation be present as well? Imagine, for example, a person who desires to socialize with the target group in order to integrate but does so in a desire to curry
political favor. How would one categorize such motives? Even if they could
be isolated, how could they be measured? In addition, the person may not
want to reveal his or her real feelings or may not even be aware of them.

Oller (1981) probes these and other thorny questions, particularly those
involving the self-report questionnaire as the method of determination. How
reliable can our data be if the information requested is potentially damaging
to the student? For example, a student may indicate by certain choices a dis-
loyalty to his or her first language group. How reliable can the questionnaire
be if the answers reflect the respondent's perception of what it is looking for?
How reliable can it be if self-flattery (Oller & Perkins, 1978) is a tendency on
the part of the examinee? By using the questionnaire, is it possible that we
are, in fact, not even determining motivation at all? Obviously, the issues
involved here are far from settled and probably will not be settled in the fore-
seeable future.

LEVEL OF ANXIETY

H. D. Brown (see Related Reading 7) distinguishes between two kinds of
anxiety: *trait* anxiety (a predisposition toward feeling anxious) and *state* anx-

---

[2]Graham (1984, see Related Reading 7) attempts to clarify by adding yet another category: *assimilative motivation.* Assimilative motivation is present when one desires to "melt" into the target
group to the extent that one becomes indistinguishable from the others.

iety (anxiety produced in reaction to a specific situation). He also distinguishes between anxiety which is debilitative and which is facilitative. Whether the anxiety is an aid or hindrance often depends upon the degree to which it is found in the individual. For example, no anxiety at all might cause the person to be lethargic whereas a small amount might bring the individual to an optimal state of alertness.

⁎ However, in general, it appears that a lowered anxiety level is related to proficiency in the target language (Carroll, 1963; Chastain, 1975; Gardner, Smythe, Clement, & Gliksman, 1976). In the case of ESL, the teacher and peers can promote a lowered level of anxiety by providing a sort of surrogate "family" to serve as a buffer until independence is reached. Sheltered classrooms in the content areas (see Chapters 14 and 15) also provide temporary refuges in which students can receive comprehensible input in low-anxiety environments. Larsen and Smalley (1972), although they don't specifically mention the classroom as serving in this capacity, nevertheless do advocate such a haven. However, students who are sheltered for too long may fossilize early as a result of isolation from target group peers. A wise teacher involves students with native or nativelike speakers as early as possible and pushes the students into independence as soon as they become ready.

Additional potential causes of increased anxiety in both ESL and foreign language classes include not providing a silent period, giving direct corrections, and so forth (see Chapters 2 and 3).

RELATED FACTORS

Acculturation

Acculturation may be an important predictor of target language acquisition (Stauble, 1980; Schumann, 1978a). Stauble argues that second language learners will succeed "to the degree that they acculturate to the target language group" if no formal instruction is attempted. Although the procedures of her research may be open to dispute,[3] the following assumption appears reasonable:

---

[3]In Stauble's study of the process of decreolization, she made a distinction between social distance (domination versus subordination, assimilation versus adaption versus preservation, enclosure, size, congruence, and attitudes) and psychological distance (resolution of language shock, culture shock, and culture stress, motivation, and ego permeability). She measured the negation development of three native Spanish speakers who had been living in the United States for over ten years. They were classified along the Schumann (1979) continuum from Basilang (minimal skills in the target language) to Mesolang (intermediate skills) to Acrolang (nativelike performance).

In an attempt to account for their varying levels, she administered a questionnaire to determine their social and psychological proximity to English. She found that her subject Xavier (in the lower Mid-Mesolang phase) had the least amount of social distance (12.5%) and greatest

The assumption here is that the more social and psychological distance there is between the second language learner and the target language group, the lower the learner's degree of acculturation will be toward that group (1980, pp. 43–50).

Schumann (1978a) compared the linguistic development demonstrated by six second language learners of English—two children, two adolescents, and two adults. The subject who acquired the least was Alberto, a 33-year-old Costa Rican. Of all the subjects, he was the one most socially and psychologically distant from the target language group. He interacted predominantly with Spanish-speaking friends and made no attempt to socialize with English-speaking people. He showed little desire for owning a television set and played mostly Spanish music on his stereo. Although English classes were available, he showed no interest in them. However, as Schumann points out, a Piagetian test of adaptive intelligence revealed no gross cognitive defects which might prevent him from learning a second language. The main reason for his low proficiency, according to Schumann, was his lack of desire to acculturate.[4]

To explain the effect of acculturation on the second language acquisition process, Schumann developed the Acculturation Model (see Related Reading 4). According to his way of thinking, L2 acquisition is dependent upon the amount of social and psychological distance that exists between the learner and the L2 culture. When the distances are great, the learner tends to fossilize during early stages of interlanguage development. The learner may not have received the necessary input because of social isolation or may not have given the target language the attention necessary for acquisition because of psychological distance.

Andersen's Nativization Model (see Related Reading 4) also seeks to explain why some learners fossilize early. He considers the effects of what he calls "nativization" and "denativization" upon the learner. Through nativization, the learner tends to assimilate the target language into an already determined schemata of how the L2 should be. Judgments are made based on a knowledge of the first language and culture. Denativization, on the other

---

amount of psychological distance (62.5%); her subjects Maria and Paz had the same amount of psychological distance (21%) but differed somewhat on social distance, 56% and 67%, respectively. From this she suggested that psychological distance may be more important than social distance. However, one might question this conclusion. Intuitively it would seem that the two factors would be highly correlated with one another and would be difficult to separate so distinctly. She mentions in passing that Paz demonstrated a higher degree of motivation than the other two. Perhaps this should have been pursued as a causative factor. Stauble herself admits that the validity and reliability had not yet been determined on her measurement and that the results should be considered speculative.

[4]It is interesting to note that, according to Schmidt (1984), the poorest learners in the studies referred to by Schumann and Stauble were also the oldest. Age may have been, either directly or indirectly, a contributing factor.

hand, is an accommodation process in which the learner changes the schemata to fit the new language. The learner who tends to denativize is the most likely to become proficient and nativelike.

Giles in his Accommodation Theory (see Related Reading 4) claims that motivation is the key and that it is closely related to ingroup (the L1 group) and outgroup (the L2 group) identification. He places importance on how the individual *perceives* social distance rather than on actual social distance as described by Schumann. Giles argues that feelings of identity are dynamic and are dependent upon continuing negotiations between and among individuals and groups. Schumann sees these feelings as being more constant and slower to change. Fossilization, according to Giles's model, occurs during what he calls "downward divergence," which takes place when the individual is not strongly motivated in the direction of the outgroup.

Schmidt's (1984) study of W seems to contradict a strong version of both the Acculturation Model and Accommodation Theory. His subject W was a 35-year-old native speaker of Japanese who had been living for five years in Hawaii. W was judged by the researcher to be intelligent, sophisticated, and uninhibited. In addition he appeared to be extroverted, socially adept, and self-confident but, at the same time, stubborn and domineering. He conversed readily in English and was not afraid of making errors. He was a successful businessman and had a great deal of professional and social contact with native speakers of English. Although he possessed a high level of integrative motivation to communicate in English, he had no interest in studying English or in analyzing the language and appeared to pay little attention to form during conversation. He made many errors in his speech but seemed not to be aware of them. Schmidt concludes that adults may actually require formal instruction in order to acquire the rules. Interaction may not be enough. However, it is more to the point to say that interaction without any attention to form (either conscious or subconscious) may not be enough. Even children acquiring a first language "pay attention" to form but at a subconscious level. W's ability to acquire normally may have been impaired for two reasons: (1) his inflexibility may have made a denativization process impossible and (2) his apparent success at being socially accepted without having to become more nativelike prevented him from undergoing the acculturation process in a normal fashion.

In his analysis of the literature, H. D. Brown (1980) describes the four stages which have been identified in the normal acculturation process. In the first stage the newcomer feels a type of *euphoria* mixed with the excitement of being in a new (sometimes exotic) place. As the reality of survival sets in, the newcomer moves into the second stage—*culture shock*. It is in this stage that frustration rises to its peak, the individual begins to feel alienated from the target culture, and self-image and security are threatened. The third stage signifies the beginning of recovery. The stress is still felt but the person is beginning to gain control over the problems which seemed insurmountable before. Brown refers to this state as *anomie* (see Srole, 1956), a state in which the individual begins to adapt to the target culture and lose some of the native culture. A feeling of homelessness might develop until the person fully adjusts to the new culture. This stage is considered a "critical period" in that the student is now able to gain a mastery over the new language. The fourth stage brings *full recovery*. The person has become reconciled to his or her role in the new culture. It is the critical period that Schmidt's subject W failed to experience and this failure may, in part, have accounted for his not acquiring the grammatical system of English.

Under normal conditions, persons becoming acculturated pass through all the stages at varying rates. Furthermore, they do not progress smoothly from one stage to the next; instead regression to previous stages is common, depending upon circumstances and the state of mind.

Personality

According to H. D. Brown (see Related Reading 7), certain personality characteristics such as willingness to take risks (Rubin, 1975; Beebe, 1983) and relative lack of inhibition (Guiora, Acton, Erard, & Strickland, 1980; Guiora, Beit-Hallami, Brannon, Dull, & Scovel, 1972) can, in most cases, lead to proficiency in the target language. Extroversion and assertiveness, although not necessarily beneficial traits (Naiman, Fröhlich, & Stern, 1978; Busch, 1982), can be helpful to the degree that they encourage more output and hence more input. In addition, empathy, under normal conditions, can lead to greater proficiency. Being able to identify with members of the target language group is important to communication. Guiora, Brannon, and Dull (1972) feel empathy is essential in order that our ego boundaries be permeable. In other words, we need to be open to the new language and the new people. Schmann (1980) related empathy and ego permeability to a lowering of inhibitions.

> I would submit that empathic capacity or ego flexibility, particularly as operationalized under the concept of "lowering of inhibitions," is best regarded as an essential factor to the ability to acquire a second language. (1980, p. 238).

It should be noted, however, that a person who is extroverted and assertive to the extreme will not tend to be empathic. The three characteristics need to be in balance in order to have a positive effect on language acquisition.

CREATING AN OPTIMAL SCHOOL AND COMMUNITY ENVIRONMENT

Although a teacher may successfully establish an environment conducive to language acquisition in the classroom, what the students face outside of the classroom may have a greater impact on affect in general. Unfortunately, ESL students are often subject to ridicule, prejudice, and sometimes outright hostility. This attitude can come not only from native-speaking peers but from teachers, administrators, and other school staff members, as well as from the community. The form that it takes among teachers and other school personnel, although perhaps subtle, can be especially devastating. Persons of influence can affect the attitudes found in the whole school setting, which often extend to the community itself. I remember an incident that occurred when I was an ESL teacher in a large public high school. One day in the teachers' lounge a fellow teacher asked me, "How's old 'Ho Hum' [a nickname he had given the Asian student we shared] doing today?" I pretended not to know to whom he was referring, although the student's identity was obvious since we had only one Asian student in common. He continued, "You know, what's his name" and then he gave the student's real name. "Oh, *he's* doing just fine," I replied. As it turned out, old "Ho Hum" went on to maintain close to a 4.0 grade-point average throughout school, won the top "Junior of the Year Award," and became a star member of the soccer team. Of course, not all ESL students achieve so much and many are subject to the same learning and/or psychological problems that the rest of us are.

Although we cannot hope to eliminate the prejudices of all insensitive persons with whom our students come into contact, we can perhaps through cultural awareness training make the overt expression of these prejudices unpopular. Through the inservicing of teachers and staff, and the sensitizing of entire student populations and groups within the community, we can achieve a school climate that will be supportive for all of our students, not only those in ESL.

The teacher inservice I would like to present here seemed to be particularly efficacious in exposing cultural biases. It began with the following scenario.[5]

> A man and woman dressed in clothes that represent a very "primitive" hypothetical culture walk slowly through the audience. The woman, who is carrying a basket filled with bread, walks a few paces behind the man (her husband). Once they reach the front of the room, they turn to face the audience and kneel down, side by side. The man places his hand on the woman's head while she bows her head down, touching it to the floor three times. She then rises, walks into the audience, and begins to lead people up to the front of the room as though she is preparing for a ceremony (in this case a wedding ceremony—her husband will take a second bride). First, she quietly leads two men (one at a time) from the audience to the front of the room. The only sounds she utters are pleasing "umms" from time to time. She motions for them to sit in the chairs she has set up previously. She repeats the same procedure except this time she takes two women from the audience. She motions for them to kneel on the floor. Lastly, she leads the

---

[5]Although I have not been able to locate the original source of this idea, I saw a version of it presented at the 1980 NAFSA Conference in El Paso.

new bride to a kneeling position beside the husband. She then passes out the bread from her basket. She gives it to the men first, waits a few moments, and then to the women.

The moderator asks the audience to describe this society. Usually the audience guesses that it is a patriarchal society supported by these facts: the man walked ahead of the woman upon entering, the women had to sit on the floor while the men got chairs, the men were fed first, and the husband pushed the woman's head to the floor three times. This reaction on the part of the audience was expected in that they had little choice but to react from their own world view or *weltanschauung*. Actually the hypothetical society being portrayed was set up as a matriarchal one. The men walked ahead of the women in case of danger lurking around the corner. The women were generally the only persons who could directly receive the spirits who were in the ground. Thus only the women could sit on the ground and bow their heads to it while the men could only receive the spirits indirectly through a hand gently placed on a woman's head. One exception to this rule occurred when a man married. Only at that time could he receive the spirits directly. The bread was served to the men first in case it had poison in it. That way safety for the women could be ensured.

A lively discussion usually follows about perspectives and how they color views of reality. Through activities such as this, people may begin to look at events from the viewpoint of others and may perhaps gain a more global perspective.

Another activity that promotes cultural understanding is to take teachers, students, and community groups through the stages of ethnicity (Banks, 1981) by means of role playing in hypothetical situations. Banks's typology applies to situations in which dominant and nondominant groups coexist in a variety of ways. His definitions of the stages are summarized as follows:

Stage 1: *Ethnic Psychological Captivity*
The member of a nondominant group feels rejection and low self-esteem and may avoid contact as much as possible with the dominant group. This individual has internalized the "image" that the dominant society has ascribed to him or her and may even feel shame.

Stage 2: *Ethnic Encapsulation*
The member of a nondominant group has reacted to Stage 1 by feeling bitterness and, in some cases, a desire for revenge. As a result the person may turn inward to the ethnic group and reject all other groups, particularly the dominant one. In extreme manifestations of this stage, other groups are regarded as "the enemy" and are often seen as racists with genocidal tendencies. Members of this group who try to assimilate into the dominant group are considered traitors.

Stage 3: *Ethnic Identity Clarification*
The member at this stage is able to clarify self in relation to the ethnic group of which he or she is a part. Self-acceptance and understanding are reached. The person is able to see both positive and negative aspects of the primary ethnic group and other groups. Usually, in order to attain this stage, the person must have gained a certain degree of economic and emotional security and must have had productive, positive experiences with members of other groups, particularly those in the dominant group.

Stage 4: *Biethnicity*
The individual is able to function successfully in two cultural groups, the primary group and a nonprimary group. Most individuals belonging to a nondominant group are forced to reach this stage if they wish to become mobile socially and economically in the society in general. Interestingly, members of the dominant group do not have to do this and can (and usually do) remain monocultural and monolingual all their lives.

Stage 5: *Multiethnicity and Reflective Nationalism*
The individual has learned to function successfully in several ethnic groups. The person still feels loyalty to the primary ethnic group but has developed a commitment to the nation state and its idealized values as well.

Stage 6: *Globalism and Global Competency*
The individual has developed global identifications and has the skills necessary to relate to all groups. This person has achieved an ideal but delicate balance of primary group, nation state, and global commitments, identifications, and loyalties.

Individuals do not necessarily move from one stage to the next in linear fashion. Rather they tend to zigzag back and forth, and some may skip stages altogether. Fortunately, Stage 2 is often bypassed, although some feelings from it might exist temporarily, as the person moves from Stage 1 toward Stage 3. By role-playing in hypothetical situations, teachers, students, and community members can "experience" at least Stages 1–3. First the participants decide which groups they want represented, such as Mexican-American, Korean-American, Vietnamese-American, American Indian, Japanese-American, and so on. Then they decide which group they want to join. Once in the group of their choice, they go through a set of planned activities to help them experience the various stages.

For example, in Stage 1 they might bring in pieces of literature, songs, pictures, or anecdotes depicting their people experiencing oppression at the hands of the dominant group. They may want to list negative feelings about the self and the ethnic group created by this experience and discuss how each feeling came about. There is a more general activity that will help the participants to feel the effects of being labeled. Give each participant a paper hat (a simple headband will do).[6] On each hat write a label such as "dumb,"

---

[6]This activity was adapted from one shared with me by Leah Boehne.

"smart," "good-looking," "unbathed," and so on. Place the hats on the participants in such a way that no individual will see the label he or she is wearing. Give the group an interesting topic for discussion and have them during the course of the discussion treat each other according to their labels. Most will be amazed at the intensity of the anger or joy they feel depending on the treatment to which they are subjected.

At Stage 2 the participants may want to discuss the negative feelings to keep them from festering to the point at which bitterness develops. Once these feelings are fully aired, the person is better able to begin to build a positive attitude toward his or her own ethnic group and the groups of others. This time the group may want to share literature and other cultural items that cause them to feel intense pride in their "own cultures."

Stage 3 involves a sort of sitting back just a little to look at the positive attributes and achievements of other groups (share their literatures, etc.) and to achieve a realistic view of their own ethnic group in relation to others.

Still other culture awareness activities can include celebrations, group discussions, films, and other events that bring school and community together. The rewards of such activities can be immeasurable in terms of increased human understanding.

SUMMARY

Because the concepts related to the affective domain are so intangible, they are difficult to define, describe, and measure. Yet despite their ephemeral quality, we cannot give up our attempts to understand what their role might be in second language development. Central to the affective domain are attitudes, motivation, and level of anxiety. They are strongly influenced by acculturation and personality factors.

Attitudes which are largely determined by what our students have experienced and by the people with whom they identify—peers, parents, teachers—influence the way students see the world and their place in it. Motivation also, whether it be integrative or instrumental, is a strong force in determining how proficient the students will become. In addition, level of anxiety has its effect. Have the students been given a chance to try out the language in a nonthreatening environment where stress is kept at a minimum? If so, they will be more able to go through the stages of acculturation without its becoming a debilitating process.

The student's emotional well-being will be enhanced by a positive, accepting school environment. In spite of the fact that prejudices cannot be eliminated completely, much can be done to make the environment a better one not only for language learners but for all students. Cultural awareness activities can involve school personnel, students, and community members. They can sensitize people to the needs and feelings of others.

READINGS, REFLECTION, AND DISCUSSION

Suggested Readings and Reference Materials

Banks, J. (1981). *Multiethnic education: Theory and practice.* Boston: Allyn & Bacon. A sensitive exploration of the nature of ethnicity and multiethnic education in the United States. Offers guidelines for promoting a more global, open society through education. A very readable and important book for all teachers.

Ford, C., & Silverman, A. (1981). *American cultural encounters.* San Francisco: Alemany. This collection of cultural assimilators provides students with many hypothetical encounters such as making dates, deciding who pays in various situations, determining when to arrive at a particular social event, etc. Students make choices from among several possible alternative solutions. Discussions follow.

Gardner, R., & Lambert, W. (1972). *Attitudes and motivation in second language acquisition.* Rowley, MA: Newbury House. Research findings and the measures used in obtaining them are discussed in detail in this book. Several studies on attitudes as they relate to second language acquisition are presented.

Heyde, A. (1977). The relationship between self-esteem and the oral production of a second language. In H. D. Brown, C. Yorio, & R. Crymes (Eds.), *On TESOL '77* (pp. 226–240). Washington, DC: Teaching English to Speakers of Other Languages. A research report of her study on the relationship between three levels of self-esteem (global, specific, and task) and their effects on performance. Offers a review of the literature and makes suggestions for further research.

Moskowitz, G. (1978). *Caring and sharing in the foreign language class.* Rowley, MA: Newbury House. A sourcebook on humanistic methods. Presents a wide array of ideas on relating to others, discovering the self, expressing feelings, sharing, and values. This book is included as suggested reading for Chapter 11 as well.

Zanger, V. (1985). *Face to face: The cross-cultural workbook.* Rowley, MA: Newbury House. By using the activities suggested in this book, the teacher can prepare ESL students to interview native English speakers about American culture. The structure of such interviews is, for the most part, controlled and the questions are relevant but nonthreatening.

Questions for Reflection and Discussion

1. Several language students have mentioned that learning a second language makes them feel "helpless and ineffectual." What demands are typically made on the individual in the following second language situations that might contribute to this feeling?
   a. a child going to kindergarten in the new culture
   b. a tenth-grader in beginning Spanish as a Foreign Language

c. an adult going to work in the new country for the first time

d. a university ESL student attending a class oriented to native speakers

What affective factors will help or hinder the individual's ability to cope in each situation?

2. Savignon (1983) describes an incident involving her son Daniel, a new student in a Paris school. On the first day he met with more than a hundred students at his grade level in the school's courtyard. The school director called out the names of the students. They were to stand and tell what class they were in. When his name was called, he followed the procedure but was immediately chastised for having his hands in his pockets. When he went home that day, he vowed that he would never go back. He had had it with that school.

Explain the incident in terms of what you know about the stages of acculturation, attitudes, values, etc. If you were Daniel's parent, what would you say to him to help him put this incident in perspective?

3. In what ways, other than those mentioned in the chapter, can you aid your own students in developing positive attitudes, strong motivation, and reduced anxiety? Consider kinds of activities, room arrangements, and the general ambiance in the school and classroom environment.

4. Plan a culture awareness inservice for the school personnel (including the secretaries, custodians, cafeteria help, etc.) in your school. Be very specific about the pre-inservice preparation, the inservice itself, and the follow-up.

PART II

Exploring Methods and Activities

In the literature about what to do in classrooms, terms such as "approach," "method," and "technique" are often confusing, at best. Anthony's (1963) definitions, while general, seem adequate for the purposes of this book. He sees the relationship among these concepts as being hierarchical in nature (see Richards and Rodgers, 1986, for refinement and development of the various levels). An *approach* (at the top level) consists of an axiomatic group of related assumptions about language teaching and learning. A *method* is an orderly plan giving direction to the presentation of materials. It must be consistent with the approach under whose umbrella it falls. A *technique* is the lowest level on the hierarchy. It is used to implement a method and accomplish immediate objectives.

Applying this terminology to the book, one could say that Part I describes the fundamental approach with which the recommended methods are compatible. Part II presents the methods and activities themselves. I have added the term "activity," which describes content and a set of procedures falling somewhere between the method and technique levels. Some activities, now in their embryonic states, are capable of becoming methods (e.g., "Story Experience" on pages 130–132); others will never develop into methods but will remain closer to the level of technique. The important thing to keep in mind is that all of the content and strategies suggested (regardless of their labels) are consistent with an interactional approach to second language teaching. In varying degrees, they call for high-quality input, negotiation for meaning, and creative language production in non-threatening environments.

Generally, the activities are intended for elementary, secondary, and/or university second or foreign language programs (see Chapter 14 for descriptions of program types and Part IV for "Programs in

Action"). However, many of the activities, when given modified content, could be used in language programs for special purposes such as preparing students for various technical occupations.

It should be noted that although a majority of the activities are recommended for specific age and proficiency levels, they can, for the most part, be adapted to other levels (see pages 188–189 for sample adaptations).

The particular methods or activities chosen for a specific program will depend upon several factors: the student, the situation, and teacher preference. Not all the methods and activities are for everyone and every situation. They must be chosen carefully to form a workable program. The activities, for the most part, can be successfully integrated with grammar lessons when such lessons are appropriate, particularly for older learners. However, it is important in most programs to keep the main focus on meaningful communication.

6

The Total Physical Response and the Audio-Motor Unit

If the training starts with explicit learning such as audio-lingual that emphasizes error-free production, correct form, and conscious rule learning, the risk is that most children and adults will give up before even reaching the intermediate level.[1]

J. Asher, 1972

THE TOTAL PHYSICAL RESPONSE

It was in the 1960s when James Asher first offered the total physical response (TPR) as one alternative to the audiolingual approach. His method, based on techniques advocated much earlier by Harold and Dorothy Palmer (1925), involves the giving of commands to which the students react. For example, the teacher might say, "Point to the door," and all the students will point to the door. The imperatives are designed to bring the target language alive by making it comprehensible and, at the same time, fun. The students are asked to act with their bodies as well as with their brains—in other words, with their total beings. Thus, the cognitive process of language acquisition is synchronized with and partially facilitated by the movements of the body.

Asher offers theoretical justification for his basic approach by looking at the process by which children master the first language. Mother or caretaker directs the child to look at an object, to pick it up, or to put it in a specific place. Production is naturally delayed until the child's listening comprehen-

---

[1]Asher (1972) bases his opinion on the conclusions of Carroll (1960) and Lawson (1971).

sion has been developed and the child is ready to speak. Thus the child grad-ually becomes aware of language and what it means in terms of the environ-ment and the situation.

It is recommended that the students, too, remain silent until they are ready to speak, usually after about ten hours of instruction. At first they jump, run, sing, or do whatever is necessary to show that the request has been comprehended. Advancing gently, at their own rates, they eventually achieve a productive command of the target language. Through this process, they evolve from silent comprehenders of language to full participants in its nuances. After a few weeks of instruction, a typical class might consist of approximately 70 percent listening comprehension, 20 percent speaking, and 10 percent reading and writing (Asher, Kusudo, & de la Torre, 1974).

The commands are given to the class as a whole, to small groups, and to individuals. Once the student has acquired some basic commands, he or she might be asked to perform a double action such as, ''Walk to the window and open it.'' The teacher or another student generally demonstrates the ap-propriate behavior first, making the actions very clear. Then the student is expected to carry out the request. If he or she does not respond at first, the teacher should repeat both the words and the demonstration rather than demand that the student comply with a repetition of the words alone. Grad-ually, the requests gain complexity as the student becomes more proficient. For example, the teacher might say, ''When Lamm opens the window, Maria will run to the door and close it.''

The students, when ready, move into the production phase by volunteer-ing to give the commands while the teacher and other students carry them out. The students are allowed to make mistakes when they first begin to speak; thus anxiety is lowered. It is expected that their speech will gradually take on the shape of the teacher's as they gain confidence with their new language.

Although Asher recommends a grammatical sequencing of the materials, the lessons themselves are not focused on grammar; instead they are focused on meaning, especially at beginning stages. The grammar is internalized in-ductively. It is expected that certain forms will be more suited than others to the method and will therefore be repeated over and over in the natural course of events.

Concerning the method itself, Asher admits that a few teachers may be skeptical of his basic approach for one reason or another. Although some have accepted TPR for the teaching of simple action verbs, they have ques-tioned its use for teaching some of the nonphysical elements of language—past and future tenses, abstract words, and function words. To defuse this kind of skepticism, Asher (1972) and Asher, Kusudo, and de la Torre (1974) offer a number of studies such as the two field tests described below.

The first field test involved adults who had taken about 32 hours of Ger-man with an instructor using the total physical response. It was found that most of the linguistic forms of German could indeed be incorporated into the commands. Tenses were combined by using clauses in sentences such as "While John is closing the door, Annette will turn out the light." Function words were not a major problem because they were ubiquitous and were acquired naturally through repetition in a variety of situations. Abstract words such as "honor" and "justice" were manipulated as though they were objects. The words were written on cards. The instructor gave commands in German such as "Andy, pick up 'justice' and give it to Sue."

Although the experimental group had had only 32 hours of training, it did significantly better in listening comprehension than a group of college students who had received 75 to 150 hours of audiolingual/grammar–translation instruction in German. It is interesting to note that the experimental group, even though it had no systematic instruction in reading, did as well in that area as the control group which had received such training.

Asher (1972) surmised that if students can internalize listening comprehension of a second language, they can make the transition to oral production, reading, and writing with a fair amount of ease.

The second field test reported by Asher, Kusudo and de la Torre (1974) involved undergraduate college students in beginning Spanish. After about ten hours of concentration in listening comprehension, the students were invited but not coerced into switching roles with the teacher. As each student became ready to do so, he or she assumed the teacher role and gave the commands for brief periods of time. Reading and writing were also accomplished at the student's individual pace. The teacher wrote on the chalkboard any phrases or words that students wished to see in writing. Skits were created and presented, and problem solving was attempted, all in the target language.

After 45 hours of instruction, the experimental group was compared with the control groups whose hours of instruction ranged from 75 to 200. The group exposed to the total physical response exceeded all other groups in listening skill for stories.

After 90 hours of instruction, the group was given a form of the Pimsleur Spanish Proficiency Test that was intended for students who had completed about 150 hours of college instruction, audiolingual style. Even with almost no direct instruction in reading and writing, the students were beyond the 75th percentile for level I and beyond the 65th percentile for level II.

According to Asher, the studies clearly indicated that TPR training produces generally better results than the audiolingual method. He attributes the success to the fact that TPR utilizes implicit learning, whereas the audiolingual approach relies on explicit learning. These two concepts roughly parallel Krashen's acquisition/learning distinction (see Chapter 2). However, Asher suggests that an alternative model of teaching might begin the instruction in the implicit mode and end it in the explicit mode. At later levels a student's skills may be advanced to the point at which teaching rules and correcting errors may be beneficial.

Even though Asher (1982) sees his method as being the focus of classroom activity rather than a supplement, he does recommend that it be used in combination with other techniques such as skits, other kinds of role play, and problem solving.

The commands themselves may be arranged around several topics of interest. For example, lessons may be organized around parts of the body, numbers, spatial relationships, colors, shapes, emotions, clothes, giving directions, and so forth. Asher recommends that only a certain number of new concepts be given at one time depending upon the students' levels of understanding and other factors.

Below is a list of a few typical commands to use with beginners.[2] These may be modified, expanded, or combined in a variety of ways. Some possibilities for modification are suggested in parentheses.

Stand up.
Sit down.
Touch the floor (desk).
Raise your arm (leg).
Put down your arm (leg).
Pat your cheek (back, arm, stomach, chest).
Wipe your forehead (face, chin, elbow).
Scratch your nose (knee, ankle, heel).
Massage your arm (neck).
Turn your head to the right (left).
Drum your fingers.
Wet your lips.
Pucker your lips.
Blow a kiss.
Cough.
Sneeze.
Shout your name ("help").
Spell your name.
Laugh.
Stretch.
Yawn.
Sing.

Giggle.
Make a face.
Flex your muscles.
Shrug your shoulders.
Wave to me (to _____).
                    (name of student)
Tickle your side.
Clap your hands.
Point to the ceiling (door).
Cry.
Mumble.
Talk.
Whisper.
Hum.
Stand up.
Hop on one foot (on the other foot, on both feet).
Step forward (backward, to the side).
Lean backward (toward me, away from me).
Make a fist.
Shake your fist (head, hand, foot, hips).
_____, walk to the door, (window).
(name of student)
_____, turn on (off) the lights (radio).
(name of student)

---

[2]These commands were adapted from a mimeographed sheet (author unknown) distributed by the Jefferson County Schools, Lakewood, Colorado.

It is important to note that Asher intended a lighthearted, relaxed approach to his method, one in which students are encouraged to take on some of the playfulness of childhood, a time when learning language could easily be made a game and "losing oneself" in it was a natural consequence. Therefore, a "barking" of commands, army sergeant style, would not be appropriate. Instead, the commands should be given in an easy, nondemanding manner.

Using some of the commands from the above list, a sample lesson for rank beginners might look like this:

The teacher has one or two volunteer students, peer teachers, or lay assistants (see Chapter 12) come to the front of the room. They are offered chairs through gesture. They sit in them. The teacher also sits in a chair. He or she gives the following commands:

1. Stand up. (The teacher demonstrates by standing.)
2. Sit down. (The teacher demonstrates by sitting.)
   (two repetitions of 1 and 2)
3. Stand up. (The teacher motions to the two volunteer students or teacher assistants to stand up. They stand.)
4. Sit down. (The teacher motions to them to sit down. They sit down.)
   (two repetitions of 3 and 4)

The teacher turns to the class.

5. Stand up (motions to everyone to stand up and they all stand).
6. Sit down (motions to everyone to sit down and they all sit).
   (two repetitions of 5 and 6)

The teacher compliments with a simple "good" at various points and with a lot of smiles. Then he or she continues by giving the commands minus the gestural clues to see if the students are indeed comprehending the words. Gradually other commands are added following similar procedures. For example, the next commands might be "step forward" followed by "step backward." And on it goes until the students have a rather large repertoire of commands that they can comprehend. Often the order of the commands is varied to ensure that students are not simply memorizing a sequence of actions.

I personally like to give commands to volunteers or to the whole class (as in the example above) rather than single out individuals. I feel that anxiety is lowered if students are allowed some anonymity, especially at very beginning stages.[3] In addition, I prefer to use the method in small doses, perhaps for

---

[3] It is interesting to note that even those students who only observe seem to internalize the commands.

fifteen minutes or so three or four times a week at beginning levels. Otherwise, the technique becomes too tiring for the students and for me. Also, if I use it extensively, there is danger that the students will get the impression that the main function of the target language is to give commands. For these reasons, it makes sense to combine it with other kinds of activities that *reinforce* what is being taught. Activities such as cutting and pasting, drawing, painting, jazz chants, story experience, songs, and others (see later chapters) can all be effective ways to increase possibilities for acquisition. Another means of reinforcement is to incorporate key concepts during a common classroom ritual such as grouping students for other activities. For instance, the teacher might want to reinforce colors: "All students with the color red on come to table 1; all students with blue on go to table 2." Or, using the same method, the teacher might reinforce months of the year: "All students born in May or June come to table 1." The teacher can continue reshuffling students by giving similar commands until each group has the necessary number of students in it.

Below are some TPR-based activities which can readily be adapted to almost any age level (provided the students are cognitively ready) or to the teaching of any language.[4] Possible alternative words are given in parentheses.

The Pointing Game

With a small group of students, use a collection of pictures such as those one might find in a mail order catalog to reinforce concepts that have been taught. Ask students to point to various specific body parts (a head, an arm), to colors (something green), or to items of clothing (a dress, a sweater).

Identifying Emotions

After the class has acquired simple commands such as "cry" or "laugh," pictures can be placed across the front of the room of people clearly demonstrating such emotional reactions. Students can be asked to take the picture of a person displaying a specific reaction (someone crying, someone laughing). Later this same procedure can be extended to other kinds of descriptions of emotions, perhaps more subtle ones (someone who is sad, someone who is angry).

Dress the Paper Doll

A large paper doll man, woman, or child with a set of clothes can be made and mounted on a bulletin board. Velcro can be used to make the paper clothes stick to the figure.

---

[4]I would like to thank Sylvia Cervantes, Carol Gorenberg, and Cyndee Gustke for the basic notions involved in "Dress the Paper Doll," "Working with Shapes," and "Following Recipes."

Students are then asked to place various items of clothing on it. Concepts such as checked, polka dotted, and striped can be taught in the same manner along with a variety of fabrics and textures (wool, cotton, velvet, or rough, smooth, soft). For teaching the fabrics and textures, different kinds of materials can be cut in the shape of the paper clothes and glued to them.

Manipulating Rods

Rods of various colors such as those used in Gattegno's Silent Way can provide realia for teaching numbers, spatial relationships, colors, and the like (take the *blue* rod, take *three* red rods, put the blue rod *beside* the red rod). Rods can be used also in advancing students to more complex structures (take a red rod and give it to the teacher).

Bouncing the Ball

Concepts such as numbers, days of the week, and months of the year can be acquired or reinforced simply by having the students bounce a ball (Richard-Amato, 1983, p. 397). For instance, each one of twelve students in a circle could represent a month of the year. The "March" student would be directed to bounce the ball and call out "March, June." The student who is "June" would have to catch the ball before it bounces a second time. Conscious attention is centered on the act of catching the ball while the language itself is being internalized at a more or less peripheral level of consciousness.

Working with Shapes

Another idea is to cut squares, rectangles, triangles, and circles out of various colors of construction paper and distribute them to the students. Shapes (hold up the triangle), colors (hold up the green triangle), and numbers (hold up three triangles) can be taught or reinforced. Ordinal numbers can also be introduced by placing several shapes in various positions along the chalkboard. A student can be asked to place the green triangle in the third position or the eighth position, for example. Each student in the class can then be given a small box of crayons or colored pencils and a handout with rows of squares, rectangles, triangles, and circles drawn on it. Commands such as "Find the first row of circles. Go to the fifth circle. Color it red" can be given to reinforce not only the shape, but the ordinal number and the color.

As a follow-up, students can cut out of old magazines pictures of objects that have shapes similar to those mentioned above. Another follow-up might be to have students cut the various shapes from colored poster board, newsprint, or wallpaper. Have them arrange the shapes into a collage.

Following Recipes

At much later stages, making holiday rice cakes, baking valentine cookies, or preparing enchiladas can provide a TPR experience and can also involve students in the cultures of other countries and those within the United States. First display all the ingredients for any given recipe and introduce each item, one by one. Then present each student with a written recipe. An extra large version to which you and the students can refer can be placed at the front of the room. While you or a student reads the recipe, other students can measure, mix the ingredients, and so on. As a follow-up, students can bring in favorite recipes to share. These can be put together to form a class recipe book to which others can be added.

Information Gaps

Information gaps (Allwright, 1979; Johnson, 1979) can be created in which one student has information that another does not have but needs. One student may give a set of directions or commands to another student, who will carry them out to meet some stated goal. For example, Student A goes to the chalkboard and Student B goes to the back of the room and faces the back wall, with a drawing in hand (simple geometric shapes usually work best at first—see page 102). Student B then gives step-by-step directions to Student A so that A can reproduce the drawing. This activity can be followed by a debriefing if the directions have not produced a configuration fairly close to the original. If the directions have been written down by a teacher assistant as they are given, the specific steps can be analyzed to see how they might be clarified (Richard-Amato, 1983, p. 399).

An alternative might be to have Students A and B seated across from one another at a table with a divider between them, high enough so Student B cannot see what Student A is doing. Next give Student A some blocks of various sizes, shapes, and colors. Student B gets a duplicate set of blocks. Student A then is asked to build an original configuration or structure with the blocks. While student A is accomplishing the task, he or she gives directions to Student B so that B can build a similar configuration or structure. Again a debriefing can take place if there has been a breakdown in the communication.

Although the advantages are obvious, there appear to be a few potential drawbacks in using Asher's method. The first concerns the teaching of words representing abstract concepts. Although words such as "honor" and "justice" might be briefly remembered through use of Asher's technique, it is difficult to see how their meanings would become clear unless they are used repeatedly in some sort of meaningful context based on experience. It should be noted, however, that Asher has attempted to remedy the problem by placing translations of the words into the students' first languages on the back of the cards.

Another possible difficulty is the lack of intrinsic sequencing. Although some of the applications suggested in this chapter do involve a logical sequencing, the method itself does not call for it. It is probable that students, particularly those who are operating at the high beginning levels and up, will lose interest in the activities unless some sort of logical sequencing of events is present in the commands. No matter how much fun or how fast paced they may be, something is lost if they remain isolated from one another and from what we know about human experience. For example, suppose a student is asked to "turn off the light and shout 'help'" (as suggested in the list of commands earlier in this chapter). What motivation does the student have for performing these actions other than to demonstrate that he or she is comprehending? If at some point a context could be provided for such behavior, then perhaps the action would become more meaningful and thus more memorable to the progressing learner. Consider the following situation. A blind person (such as in the now classic Audrey Hepburn movie *Wait Until Dark*) has discovered an intruder in her apartment. Cleverly, she turns off the light so that she and the intruder will be equally handicapped. In spite of this maneuver, she soon realizes she is definitely in a "no-win" situation. She might shout "help" in order to attract her neighbors. Now the commands have taken on another dimension for a student who might be asked to play the part of the blind person. Strings of seemingly unrelated sentences have now taken on meaning and become part of motivated, logical discourse (see Chapter 4).

Often TPR-type activities can begin with a simple story, read and acted out by the teacher and one or more teacher assistants. Later the teacher can act as a director and the students can perform the parts. Directions might include commands such as "Sit down in the chair" or "Shake hands with Mr. Kim (a character in the story)" or "Tell Hong (another character) to take the book from the shelf." The key words and phrases eventually can be written on the chalkboard or placed on cue cards. When the students are ready, they can take turns being the director while the teacher and other students act out the parts. The students can move from predetermined scripts to ones that they create themselves. Perhaps they can even perform their own creations for other groups. (For more ideas involving role play and drama, see Chapter 9.)

THE AUDIO-MOTOR UNIT

Kalivoda, Morain, and Elkins (1971) also recognize the lack of meaningful sequencing as a weakness in the TPR method at later stages and suggest alternative ways of combining commands. Although their ideas may not be as dramatic as the one offered above, they nevertheless add a contextual dimension to the utterances. They call a particular sequence of commands an *audio-motor unit*. A 10-minute tape is played on which a native speaker issues a series of commands for twenty actions, all centering on a single topic. The teacher demonstrates the appropriate responses to the commands, using whatever realia are available to make the actions comprehensible. An audio-motor unit might include such pantomimed or real sequences as "go to the cupboard," "open the cupboard door," "find the largest bowl," "take it out," "set it on the table," and so on. The students are then invited to comply with the commands. Actions may be pantomimed when it is not possible or advisable to use props. For example, climbing a real ladder could prove a difficult and even dangerous task, but a pretend ladder could be almost as effective if one uses a little imagination.

Kalivoda, Morain, and Elkins like to consider the audio-motor unit as supplemental to a larger program (which, unfortunately, they do not describe) rather than as the focus. Although one unit generally lasts only about 10 minutes, it can be made longer or shorter depending on student needs and on the amount of time available from day to day.

They also like to include cultural learning in the lessons. Various customs involving eating, preparing food, telephone conversations, and introductions can be taught through a series of commands given in the context of real or pretend situations.

To examine the effectiveness of the audio-motor unit, they looked at the results of a pilot program in the Southeastern Language Center at the University of Georgia (Kalivoda, Morain, & Elkins, 1971.) The students were given intensive six-week courses in Spanish, French, or German. Beginning classes received one 10-minute lesson each day; advanced classes were given only one or two 10-minute lessons a week. The eight participating teachers had received only enough special instruction to make the presentations similar in execution. After the courses were over, the students filled out questionnaires so that their attitudes toward the audio-motor strategy could be studied. Of the 180 students who took part, 90 percent revealed positive attitudes. They thought that the method improved their listening comprehension and increased their vocabularies. Furthermore, they seemed to like the change of pace that it gave to the daily lessons, and they found it stimulating and entertaining. However, a few of the remaining 10 percent found it not difficult enough, boring, or silly. Some students and teachers felt that the written form of the commands should have been given and a few students thought that they should have been able to participate orally in the lesson.

Six of the eight teachers reacted positively. The benefits they reported are paraphrased below:

1. The vocabulary, structures, and syntax of the language used in their lessons were reinforced by exposure to the audio-motor strategy.
2. Students became strongly interested in the lessons through the physical acting out of cultural aspects.
3. The lessons, even though designed for the development of listening skills, had a real impact on oral production. The teachers noticed increased spontaneity and better pronunciation although they admitted the latter was difficult to verify.
4. The nonnative teachers of the various languages felt that they improved their own skills with the languages they were teaching.

In spite of its qualities, the audio-motor unit may suffer somewhat from its dependence on a tape to give the commands. The activities could become less personalized and less flexible than those in Asher's approach, in which teachers use students' names and react to their changing needs from moment to moment. This is not to say that it is not a good idea to expose students occasionally to taped voices for which there may be no visual clues to meaning.

It must be pointed out that in both methods the teacher is the controlling force. The interaction must be almost completely teacher structured and controlled until the students gain enough proficiency to have more influence. At that time, activities such as "information gaps" mentioned earlier can be implemented, allowing students to have a more significant role in the interactional process.

SUMMARY

Asher's total physical response involves giving a series of commands to which the students respond physically. The students themselves remain silent until they are ready for oral production. At that time, they have the option of giving the commands. The students gradually develop their interlanguage, which becomes more and more like the language of their teacher. The main disadvantage, which becomes most apparent at later stages, is that the commands do not, except in some adaptations, adhere to a logical sequence based on experience.

Kusudo, Morain, and Elkins, while following the way led by Asher, enlarged upon the basic method by adding meaningful sequence. In addition, they considered their method to be an adjunct to a much larger program rather than the focus. A disadvantage may be that by recommending the use of a tape to give the commands, they take away some of the personalization and flexibility which seem to be an integral part of the Asher method.

In spite of their drawbacks, effective adaptations of either approach can pay large dividends in terms of student interest, spontaneity, and language development. Students' chances for becoming more proficient in their new language seem to increase when they are allowed to listen first, speak when ready, and be involved in the target language physically.

READINGS, REFLECTION, AND DISCUSSION

Suggested Readings and Reference Materials

Asher, J. (1982). *Learning another language through actions: The complete teachers' guidebook*. Los Gatos, CA: Sky Oaks. A must for anyone intending to use total physical response methodology in the classroom. Covers related research and discusses in depth the techniques themselves. The lessons can be readily adapted to teaching languages other than English.

Francois, L. (1983). *English in Action*. Southgate, CA: Linda Francois. Offers very explicit instructions on using the total physical response for teachers who have never experienced it before. Combines the total physical response with such activities as acting out, songs, and chants. Includes greetings, colors, shapes, body parts, time, numbers, the alphabet, directions.

Nelson, G., & Winters, T. (1980). *ESL operations: Techniques for learning while doing*. Rowley, MA: Newbury House. Through this book, students learn common, everyday operations by following simple commands. Making a paper hat, sharpening a pencil, pounding a nail, blowing up a balloon, playing concentration, making instant pudding, and writing a check are only a few of the activities offered.

Romijn, E., & Seely, C. (1980). *Live action English for foreign students (LAEFFS)*. San Francisco: Alemany. The book demonstrates how commands can be given in sequences within short, topically arranged units. Relevant topics such as using a pay phone or going swimming are included. Some of the sequences may need to be modified somewhat to make them more concrete and usable in the classroom.

Segal, B. (1984). *Teaching English as a second language: Shortcuts to success*. Paso Robles, CA: Bureau of Education and Research. Although Segal comes to questionable conclusions concerning right versus left brain function, she does offer helpful guidelines for teachers who want to develop units around total physical response lessons. She has created similar books for teaching Spanish, French, and German.

Questions for Reflection and Discussion

1. How serious is the problem of a lack of logical sequencing in the Asher method applied at later stages? Relate your answer to the arguments supporting the importance of predictability described in Chapter 4.

2. How might the total physical response foster lowered anxiety levels (refer to Chapter 5)? Discuss.

3. Kalivoda, Morain, and Elkins (1971) state, ''Careful structuring of the audio-motor units provides for reentry of materials at regular intervals.'' How might you incorporate reentries into a previous lesson from a present lesson? Create one or more examples of effective uses of this technique.

4. Prepare a 5-minute TPR or audio-motor unit lesson to try out on a small group of fellow students. If the commands are simple enough, you might want to demonstrate in a target language with which the group is unfamiliar. In what ways was the lesson successful? How can it be improved? Discuss with class members.

7

The Natural Approach
and Its Extensions

*The essence of language is human activity—activity on
the part of one individual to make himself understood,
and activity on the part of the other to understand what
was in the mind of the first.*

O. Jespersen, 1904

AN OVERVIEW

Terrell (1983) is careful to make no claim for the natural approach that other
methods could not match if they relied on real communication as their *modus
operandi*. Like Asher, he reminds us that students must acquire the second
language in much the same way that people acquire language in natural situations (therefore the term *"natural* approach"). Some argue that what is being
recommended is not really a method at all but is, in a more general sense an
approach. However, Krashen and Terrell (1983) develop the natural approach
as a method and so, for the purpose of discussion, that is the way it will be
presented here. They base their method on four principles.

The first principle states that *comprehension precedes production*. As in the
total physical response, the teacher must observe the need for a silent period.
During this time, the teacher must use the target language predominantly,
must focus on communicative situations, and must provide comprehensible
input which is roughly tuned to the students' proficiency levels.

Second, *production must be allowed to emerge in stages*. Responses will generally begin with nonverbal communication, progress to single words, then
to two- and three-word combinations, next to phrases and sentences, and
finally to complex discourse. Students speak when they are ready, and

speech errors are generally not corrected *directly*[1] unless they interfere with the intended meaning. Thus, the student's interlanguage is allowed to develop normally.

The third principle asserts that *the course syllabus must be based on communicative goals*. Grammatical sequencing as a focus is shunned in favor of a topical/situational organization. Discussion centers on items in the classroom, body parts, favorite vacation spots, and other topics of interest. It is felt that the grammar will be acquired mainly through the relevant communication.[2]

Fourth, *the activities themselves must be planned so that they will lower the affective filter* (see pages 24–25). A student who is engrossed in interesting ideas will be apt to have less anxiety than one who is focused mainly on form. In addition, the atmosphere must be friendly and accepting if the student is to have the best possible chance for acquiring the target language.

The natural approach and its extensions can be used in conjunction with many other methods and activities with which it is compatible (total physical response and the audio-motor unit, jazz chants, music, games, role play, storytelling, affective activities, and so forth). In fact, combining several of these methods and activities can produce extremely rich environments where concepts are reinforced through a variety of ways. The natural approach and all the methods with which it is used must blend to form a well-integrated program if it is to work. Concepts must be recycled in many different ways in order for them to be mastered.

Because the focus of the natural approach is on real communication, great demands are made upon the time and energy of the teacher. He or she must present a great deal of comprehensible input about concrete, relevant topics, especially at beginning levels. It is not unusual to see the natural approach language teacher trudging across campus with sacks filled with fruits to talk about and eat, dishes with which to set a table for an imaginary dinner, oversized clothes to put on over other clothes, and additional paraphernalia to demonstrate the notions involved. This teacher can no longer just ask students to open their books to a certain page, say ''repeat after me,'' or assign the students to endless exercises in rule application. According to Krashen and Terrell, the teacher's chief responsibility during class hours is to communicate with the students about things that are of interest and relevance to them.

Perhaps the following outline adapted from Krashen and Terrell (1983,

---

[1]While it is true that direct corrections are discouraged in the natural approach, indirect corrections are frequent and desirable in that they help to prevent early fossilization (see the example of negotiation for meaning on pages 95 and 204).

[2]Terrell (1987) appears to have modified his stand on this issue. He now argues that the explicit teaching of rules can be accomplished along with the natural approach. It may increase motivation in ''grammar-oriented'' adults and may help to make the input more readily comprehensible.

pp. 67–70) will be useful in planning units for beginning to low intermediate students.

Preliminary Unit: Learning to Understand

Topics

1. Names of students	5. Clothing
2. Descriptions of people	6. Colors
3. Family members	7. Objects in the classroom
4. Numbers	8. Parts of the body

Situations
1. Greetings
2. Classroom commands

I. Students in the Classroom

Topics
1. Personal identification (name, address, telephone number, age, sex, nationality, date of birth, marital status)
2. Description of school environment (identification, description, and location of people and objects in the classroom, description and location of buildings)
3. Classes
4. Telling time

Situations
1. Filling out forms
2. Getting around the school

II. Recreation and Leisure Activities

Topics

1. Favorite activities	6. Holiday activities
2. Sports and games	7. Parties
3. Climate and seasons	8. Abilities
4. Weather	9. Cultural and artistic interests
5. Seasonal activities	

Situations
1. Playing games, sports
2. Being a spectator
3. Chitchatting

III. Family, Friends, and Daily Activities

Topics

1. Family and relatives
2. Physical states
3. Emotional states
4. Daily activities
5. Holiday and vacation activities
6. Pets

Situations

1. Introductions, meeting people
2. Visiting relatives
3. Conversing on the phone

IV. Plans, Obligations, and Careers

Topics

1. Future plans
2. General future activities
3. Obligations
4. Hopes and desires
5. Careers and professions
6. Place of work
7. Work activities
8. Salary and money

Situations

1. Job interviewing
2. Talking on the job

V. Residence

Topics

1. Place of residence
2. Rooms of a house
3. Furniture
4. Activities at home
5. Household items
6. Amenities

Situations

1. Looking for a place to live
2. Moving
3. Shopping for the home

VI. Narrating Past Experiences

Topics

1. Immediate past events
2. Yesterday's activities
3. Weekend events
4. Holidays and parties
5. Trips and vacations
6. Other experiences

Situations

1. Friends recounting experiences
2. Making plans

VII. Health, Illnesses, and Emergencies

Topics
1. More body parts
2. Physical states
3. Mental states and moods
4. Health maintenance
5. Health professions
6. Medicines and diseases

Situations
1. Visiting the doctor
2. Hospitals
3. Health interviews
4. Buying medicines
5. Emergencies (accidents)

VIII. Eating

Topics
1. Foods
2. Beverages

Situations
1. Ordering a meal in a restaurant
2. Shopping in a supermarket
3. Preparing food from recipes

IX. Travel and Transportation

Topics
1. Geography
2. Modes of transportation
3. Vacations
4. Experiences on trips
5. Languages
6. Making reservations

Situations
1. Buying gasoline
2. Exchanging money
3. Clearing customs
4. Obtaining lodging
5. Buying tickets

X. Shopping and Buying

Topics
1. Money and prices
2. Fashions
3. Gifts
4. Products

Situations
1. Selling and buying
2. Shopping
3. Bargaining

XI. Youth

Topics
1. Childhood experiences
2. Primary school experiences
3. Teen years experiences
4. Adult expectations and activities

Situations
1. Reminiscing with friends
2. Sharing photo albums
3. Looking at school yearbooks

XII. Giving Directions and Instructions

Topics
1. Spatial concepts (north, south, east, west; up, down; right, left, center; parallel, perpendicular, etc.)
2. Time relationships (after, before, during, etc.)

Situations
1. Giving instructions
2. Following instructions
3. Reading maps
4. Finding locations
5. Following game instructions
6. Giving an invitation
7. Making appointments

XIII. Values

Topics
1. Family
2. Friendship
3. Love
4. Marriage
5. Sex roles and stereotypes
6. Goals
7. Religious beliefs

Situations
1. Making a variety of decisions based on one's values
2. Sharing and comparing values in a nonthreatening environment
3. Clarifying values

XIV. Issues and Current Events

Topics
1. Environmental problems
2. Economic issues
3. Education
4. Employment and careers
5. Ethical issues
6. Politics
7. Crime
8. Sports
9. Social events
10. Cultural events
11. Minority groups
12. Science and health

Situations
   1. Discussing last night's news broadcast
   2. Discussing a recent movie,
      etc.

The students move through three basic stages in the natural approach: (1) comprehension, (2) early speech production, and (3) speech emergence. Beyond speech emergence is a fourth stage now recognized by Terrell and others as "intermediate fluency," which is referred to in the Introduction as "toward full production" (see pages 4–5). The length of time spent in any one stage varies greatly depending upon the individual, upon the amount of comprehensible input received, and upon the degree to which the affective filter has been lowered. Some students begin speaking after just a couple of hours and others need several weeks. Children may need several months. The second stage, early speech production, may take anywhere from a few months to one year or longer. The third stage, speech emergence, can take up to three years but usually the student is reasonably fluent long before that if the input has been of high quality, if it was given in sufficient quantity, and if the student has been receptive to it. At first the teacher does most of the talking. However, as the students become more proficient, they take over and the teacher's role becomes predominantly that of an organizer and a facilitator.

THE COMPREHENSION STAGE

During this first stage the students are allowed to go through a silent period. They receive comprehensible input usually from the teacher or from peer teachers or lay assistants (see Chapter 12). Often the total physical response or versions of it are used. Although the students' main goal is to develop listening skills, many of the activities overlap into the next higher level, Early Speech Production. Simple responses to the comprehensible input may be made by gesturing, nodding, using the L1, answering yes or no, giving names of people or objects as answers to questions such as "Who has on a yellow dress?" (Kim) or "Do you want an apple or an orange?" (apple). A lot of visuals are used. The teacher's speech is a little slower than usual. The intonation is reasonably normal except that key words receive extra emphasis. Students are not called upon to respond individually. Instead, questions are directed to the whole group, and one or several can respond. Key terms can be written on the chalkboard, perhaps on the second or third time the students are exposed to them. If the student is exposed to written forms of the words too soon, he or she may experience a cognitive overloading which could interfere with acquisition.

Total physical response (TPR) activities may be used to get the students into some basic vocabulary. For example, students can acquire names ("Give the book to Hong''), descriptions (''Take the pencil to a person who has short hair''), numbers (''Pick up three pieces of chalk''), colors (''Find the blue book''), clothing (''Put on the raincoat''), parts of the body (''Scratch your left leg''), and many other concepts. Notice that aspects of the total physical response will be involved to some degree in almost every activity suggested for this level.

Once the student can identify some simple concepts, then the teacher can reinforce these and introduce some new ones by using a stream of comprehensible input: ''Look at Maria's feet. She is wearing shoes. Look at Jorge's feet. He is wearing shoes, too. His shoes are brown. Look at his hair. His hair is brown. How many students have brown hair?'' (nine) ''What is the name of the student with red hair?'' (Carolina) ''Who is behind the person with the red shirt?'' (Yung) ''Does Yung have on a shirt or a sweater?'' (sweater) ''What color is his sweater?'' (yellow) The teacher can carry on in this fashion about a wide variety of concrete subjects stimulated by a picture, an object, a map, a catalog, and so on.

Other sample activities, most of which are extensions of the natural approach, are described below:[3]

Where Does It Belong?

On a chalkboard, sketch and label the rooms of a house (See Figure 7.1). Then briefly talk about the house and the various rooms in it. (*Look at the house. It is big. It has many rooms. Here is the kitchen. Food is kept in the kitchen. People eat in the kitchen.* Etc.) A few typical household items including furniture can be roughly drawn in each of the rooms to help the students correctly identify them. Other household items can be cut from heavy paper, to be placed in the appropriate rooms. Pieces of Scotch tape can be rolled up and placed on the backs of the pictures to make them stick to the chalkboard. (Later the tape can be removed for reuse of the pictures.) Commands such as ''Put the stove in the kitchen'' or ''Put the dresser in the bedroom'' can be given.

An alternative might be to use a large doll house with miniature furniture for the same kind of activity.

Items typical of other places can be incorporated in similar activities. Simulated settings such as zoos, farm yards, hospitals, libraries, various work sites, cafeterias, and university campuses can be the focus.

Put It On!

Bring in a variety of oversized clothes. Talk about the clothes. (*These are pants. They are blue. See the pocket. Point to the pocket,* etc.) Have the students put the clothes on (over

---

[3]Many of these activities can be adapted to several age levels, provided students are cognitively able to deal with the tasks (see Chapter 12). They can also be adapted for teaching any language, second or foreign, and for most programs: English for Academic Purposes (EAP) (see those recommended for later stages), English for Special Purposes (ESP), and others.

Bedroom	Bathroom	Laundry
Garage	Kitchen	Living room

Figure 7.1

their own) according to the directions you give. The oversized clothes can be taken off using a similar procedure. A camera can come in handy for recording the highlights of this activity. The photos can be displayed in the classroom and used at a later stage to stimulate discussion.

A follow-up might be to provide the students with clothing catalogs, scissors, paste, and blank sheets of construction paper.[4] Then demonstrate the activity for the students. Take articles of clothing (which you have previously cut out) as well as a cut-out head, arms, and legs. Show the class how easy it is to create a figure by gluing these items to the construction paper. The figure will probably look very humorous, especially if you have chosen such things as enormous shoes, a little head, and a strange assortment of clothing. Have the students make their own funny figures. Through a cooperative effort, students locate the items each needs to complete a creation. In the process, the same words are repeated over and over, and a great deal of laughter is generated, lowering anxiety.

Guess What's in the Box[5]

Have a box filled with objects whose names are already familiar to the students. Describe a particular object and have the students guess which object is being described. Once the object has been correctly named, remove it from the box and give it to the student temporarily. Once all the objects have been handed out, you can then ask that the objects be returned: "Who has the rubber band?" and so forth.

Getting Around

For ESL students, make a large map of the campus or school using many strips of butcher paper taped together (an alternative might be to block off the various locations with masking tape placed on the floor). The total area should be large enough so the students can stand on it and walk from place to place. Label rooms, buildings, or whatever is appropriate. Make sure it is clear what the various rooms and buildings are. For example, you might place a picture of medicines in the clinic or pictures of food in the cafeteria. Using TPR, have students move around to various places. Take a tour of the campus or school itself, pointing out these same places. When the students feel familiar with the area, ask them to act as guides to new students of the same L1 backgrounds. In order to survive the first few days, new students need to know where things are before they are fluent enough to ask about them.

The People in Our School

Take photos of personnel within your school. Show them to your students, and talk about the job that each one does. You may want to act out the various roles: custodian, cafeteria helper, secretary, nurse, counselor, principal, teacher, baseball coach, orchestra direc-

---

[4]I wish to thank Teri Sandoval for the follow-up idea.

[5]Thanks to Esther Heise for introducing this idea to me.

tor. Have the students point to the picture of the custodian, the principal, and so on. Now ask the students to act out the roles. See if the others can guess which roles are being acted out. (See Chapter 9 for other role-play activities that would be appropriate to this level and would help reinforce concepts.)

Classifying Objects

Have each student make a classification booklet. Any categories can be used, depending upon the objectives you have in mind. For example, one page could be for household items, another for clothing, a third for sports or camping equipment. Give the students several magazines or catalogs and have them cut out pictures to be categorized. Then ask them to glue the items to the appropriate pages. You can provide comprehensible input about the pictures and can do some individual TPR with each student. (*Point to the _____. Name two objects that belong in a kitchen,* etc. Previously acquired concepts can be reinforced by this means.

Following a Process

Through a series of simple commands, students can learn to make things to eat (guacamole, onion and sour cream dip, sandwiches), items for play (kites, puppets, dolls, pictures), fascinating projects such as papier-mâché maps or miniature cities. You need to demonstrate first before taking the students through the step-by-step processes. Students are not expected to speak; they simply carry out the commands in TPR fashion.

Matching

Students can match pictures of objects with words placed on heavy paper and cut into puzzle pieces (Figure 7.2). Thus, the student can use the kinesthetic matching as a clue if necessary and the word itself will be more easily acquired. Or the student can use the word only and the matching of the puzzle pieces will simply reinforce the choice.

The above represent just a small sampling of the many activities that can be used with students at this stage. Of course, some are more applicable to certain ages than others. However, it has been my experience that activities that one might consider "childish" for older learners are often enjoyed by children and adults alike. A lot depends upon the degree of comfort the students feel in the setting the teacher has established.

Success in internalizing concepts is strongly influenced by the teacher's ability, not only to establish a freeing environment but also to reinforce concepts over and over again in different ways. In addition, the teacher needs to make optimal use of manipulative visuals; to act out, model, or demonstrate expected responses; to make full use of body language in order to clarify

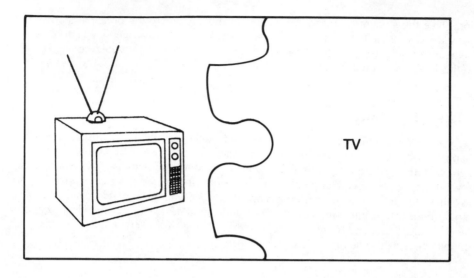

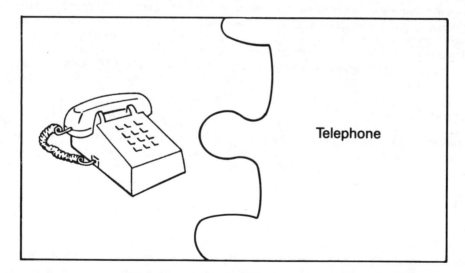

Figure 7.2

meaning; to use high-frequency vocabulary, short sentences, yes/no questions, either/or questions, and other questions that require only one-word answers; and to rely heavily on getting the students physically involved with the target language in order to facilitate its acquisition. At the same time, types of activities need to be varied within any given time period for two reasons: students' attention spans are often short and the teacher's stamina is limited.

THE EARLY SPEECH PRODUCTION STAGE

Getting into Speaking

The transition into the second stage generally begins with an extension of many of the activities used in the comprehension stage. The teacher gradually begins to see changes in the length of the responses. For example, to a question such as "Who has on a blue dress?" the teacher might get the answer, "Ashwaq has dress" instead of just "Ashwaq." Once the expansions begin to appear, they come naturally and abundantly, especially if the students are feeling comfortable with the teacher and the ambiance of the classroom. The speech at first will contain many errors which should be dealt with *only* indirectly. To the omission of words in the student's utterance above, the teacher might respond with "Yes, Ashwaq has on the dress" instead of "No, you should say, 'Ashwaq has on the dress'" (emphasizing *on* and *a*). If allowed to develop their interlanguage naturally, the students will continue to expand their utterances to include a wide variety of structures and eventually complex language.

Some of the activities that can be added to the teacher's repertoire at this stage are described below:

Charts and Other Visuals

Krashen and Terrell (1983) recommend the use of charts and other visuals that will make discussion easier and will serve as transitions into reading. The following can be written on the board as aids to conversation.

Numbers

How many students in the class have

rings _____
tennis shoes _____
belts _____
glasses _____

Clothing

Name of Student	Clothes
Carlos	jeans
Sung Hee	dress

Month of Birth

Month	Thang	Lammathet	Ellen	Franco
January				
February		X		
March				
April				
May			X	
June				
July				
August				
September	X			
October				
November				X
December				

Group Murals

Each student can be given a space on a huge piece of butcher paper that has been strung across a wall or two in the classroom. The students, who have been given pencils, rulers, wide felt-tip pens, paints, and brushes, can use their spaces to draw any pictures they wish. They are to put their signatures at the bottom of their pictures. The butcher paper is displayed for a week or two, then rolled up and saved. As the students progress in the target language, the butcher paper can be brought out for different kinds of activities. At first simple questions can be asked about each picture: "Look at Juan's picture. What color is the wagon?" (It's red.) "How many apples did Jenny paint?" (three) Later, when the students are into the stage of speech emergence and beyond, they can tell about their own pictures and those of their friends or they can make up an oral group story incorporating each picture in some way.

Open-Ended Sentences

Extend the streams of comprehensible input to include utterances which the student completes.

On Saturdays you _____.
Your family likes to _____.
Ho likes to eat _____.

Or students can bring in family photos to share. Using open-ended sentences, they can talk about their relatives pictured in the photos: My sister likes _____. My brother is _____. My cousins are _____.

Matrices

Open-ended sentences that are used in certain combinations for specific situations are called *matrices*. Below are a few situations in which they might be used:

First Meetings
Hi there, my name is _____.
Nice to meet you. I'm _____.
Are you a new student too?
Yes, I came from _____.

On the Telephone
Hola.
Hola. Soy _____. ¿ Con quién hablo? _____.
Con _____.

At an Office
May I help you?
My name is _____. I have an appointment with
_____.

The matrices should not be drilled in audiolingual style. Instead they should be used in role-playing situations in which a variety of responses can be given. Students simply use the matrices as aids and "starters" for as long as they need them (see Chapter 9 for more ideas). The matrices can be placed on cue cards, which can serve as transitions into reading (see page 198). The matrices can also be incorporated into jazz chants or lyrics (see Chapter 8).

Asking for the Facts

Students can be shown simple sale advertisements (Figure 7.3) from local newspapers (in second language classes) or foreign language newspapers (in foreign language classes). An alternative might be to show the students pictures of forms that have been filled out (a hospital record, an application for welfare, a passport); see Figure 7.4.

Pertinent questions can be asked about each:

Questions on the Sale Advertisement:

1. What is being sold?
2. How much was it?
3. How much is it now?
4. How much will you be saving?

Figure 7.3

Questions on the Job Application:

1. What is the person's last name?
2. What job does the person want?
3. Where does the person live?
4. What is the person's telephone number?
5. When was the person born?

Getting into Reading and Writing

Even though speaking is their major thrust, most of the above activities can be used as transitions into reading and writing. Key words written on the chalkboard, TPR commands which students may have listed in their notebooks, cue cards with matrices written on them, words on charts, and other visuals all lead to reading and writing in the target language. Of course, young children, nonliterate older learners, and students whose L1 writing system is vastly different from that of the target language will need special attention (see Chapter 12). However, the teaching should always be done through meaning rather than through a stringing together of isolated elements, such as phonemes, orthographic symbols, and the like. The natural approach itself is concerned mainly with oral communication skills. However, its advocates believe for the most part that skills—listening, speaking, reading, writing—should be taught simultaneously rather than as separate entities.

SAM'S HARDWARE STORE

Job Application Form

Name _Mohamed Abdullah_   Date _5 - 24 - 89_

Address _120 Maple Drive_
               (street)   Phone _(218) 543-7841_

         Minnesota   Sex (M or F) _M_
            (state)

    Mentor
      (city)

    _56702_
     (zip)

Birth date _3 - 20 - 53_   Social security number [4] [8] [0] [2] [2] [3] [9] [6] [7]

Position you are seeking _Clerk_

Figure 7.4

Listed below are several related activities that are particularly helpful in developing reading and writing skills (see also "Story Experience" in Chapter 9). These activities are compatible with the natural approach in that they begin with the student's own world and usually with language that the student already has acquired. They are valuable insofar as they provide more comprehensible input (in the case of reading) and in that they provide for further development of the ability to manipulate the target language (in the case of writing).

A Language Experience Adaption

In a procedure known as "language experience," prewriting activities are just as important as the writing itself; these can consist of activities such as a visit to the zoo or the park or exposure to a picture or object. At later stages, a poignant story, song, poem, or movie; a scene acted out (see Chapter 9); or an affective activity (see Chapter 11) can stimulate ideas for group and individual writing. Second language students can be eased into the process through group brainstorming followed by key-word listing (begun during the early speech production stage) and simple sentence creation (begun at the speech emergence stage). For example, you might display a picture of two boys and a dog on a picnic. The students are asked "What do you see here?" (two boys, a dog, a loaf of bread, a blanket, a basket, etc.) As the students talk about what they see, write down the items on the chalkboard. Then at later stages repeat the process with different pictures and this time ask the students to begin a story. As students begin to tell the story (very simple at first), write it down, making corrections *indirectly*[6] as the story unfolds. Then the students can read the story together out loud, perhaps repeating after you (a sort of palatable audiolingual technique). After this procedure, the students can be asked to copy the story in their notebooks. This activity can be repeated on several occasions, each following a different prewriting activity. When the students are ready, they can be asked to add to the stories on their own or create stories based on pictures or other experiences.

The People Hunt

Give the students the following list and ask them to find a person who

has shoelaces
wears glasses
is laughing

---

[6]An earlier version of the language experience method (Van Allen & Allen, 1967) included the writing down of student errors as they were given. However, I prefer to correct indirectly (see Chapter 3) and then write down the indirect correction without comment. If the students ask about a specific correction, I will explain the error simply and directly.

is wearing black socks

has on a plaid blouse or shirt

has five letters in his or her last name

has a 6 in his or her phone number

They must get the signature of a person in each category. As the students become more advanced (perhaps at the speech emergence stage), they can find a person who

has been to Hong Kong

has a sister who likes to eat cold spaghetti

hopes to be an actress

has seen *Gone with the Wind* on TV

Cartoons

As a transitional activity between this stage and the next, take several cartoons from the newspaper and cut out the words in the bubbles. Place the cartoons on a blank sheet of paper, providing a place for students to write their own very simple dialogues in the bubbles. They can exchange cartoons and end up with several versions of the action. (See Chapter 9 for more storytelling activities.)

THE SPEECH EMERGENCE STAGE AND BEYOND

Because speech has been emerging all along, to distinguish "speech emergence" as a separate stage seems artificial. Perhaps this is the reason Krashen and Terrell have replaced it with the term "extending production" in their book *The Natural Approach*. During this third stage, the utterances become longer and more complex. Many errors will still be made but, if enough comprehensible input has been internalized, they should gradually begin to decrease as the students move beyond this level toward full production. If undue attention has been paid to developmental errors, the process of acquiring correct grammatical forms in the new language could be impeded (see Chapter 3).

Also at this stage a large number of activities can be used that are somewhat more demanding and challenging but still within reach cognitively: music and poetry (Chapter 8), role play and drama (Chapter 9), affective activities (Chapter 11), and problem solving or debates at higher levels (Chapter 14). Many of the activities already recommended in this chapter for earlier stages can be extended to provide additional opportunities for development. For example, instead of simply answering questions about an application form, the students can now fill one out; instead of just following directions, they can begin to write their own sets of simple directions to see if others can follow them.

Following is a host of other activities that might be typical at this stage and beyond:

Draw This!

Divide the students into groups of four or five. Give one student per group a picture with simple lines and geometric shapes on it. Have each student give directions to his or her group so that they can reproduce the picture without seeing it. The student who comes closest to the original picture gives directions for the next picture. You may want to brief the group on the kinds of directions that will help by giving some words that may be key: horizontal, vertical, diagonal, perpendicular, parallel, a right angle, upper-left corner, lower right, etc. (see Figure 7.5). Pictures should become progressively more difficult as the students become more proficient (see another version of this activity on page 78).

Shopping Spree[7]

Set up one corner of the room as a grocery store. Stock the shelves with empty Jello-O boxes, egg cartons, milk bottles, cereal boxes, cleaning supplies, magazines, etc. Mark prices on the items. Have the students make out a shopping list (see Figure 7.6) and go shopping. Play money can be used. Students can take turns being the shoppers, salespersons, and cashier. Various situations can be set up to add variety to the shopping expeditions: A shopper may have to ask where a particular item is on the shelves, may need to exchange an item, may have been given the wrong change, and so forth. Similar public

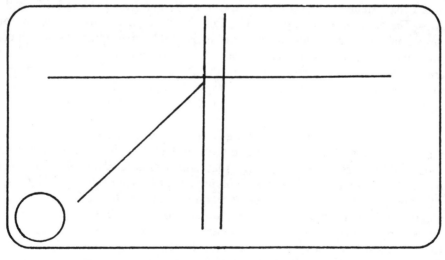

Figure 7.5

[7]Thanks to Cyndee Gustke, who introduced me to a similar idea.

Figure 7.6

places can be simulated: a doctor's office, a bank, the post office, a drug store, a clothing store, a garage. Various lists can be compiled, depending on each task. The situations can be an extension of matrices (see pages 97 and 138).

Whose Name Is It?

Write the name of a student in large letters on paper. Tape it on the back of a student volunteer. The volunteer needs to guess whose name is on his or her back by asking yes/no questions of the class (they are in on the secret). "Is the person a male or female?" (female) "Is she in the first desk?" (no) "Does she like to sing?" (yes) "Is it _____ ?'' (no) And on it goes until several volunteers get a chance. A variation of this activity is "Guess What's in the Box" described earlier in this chapter. One student could be given the box which would have only one object in it. The rest of the class would ask yes/no questions until the object is named. (See Chapter 10 for similar activities.)

Following Written Directions

Give students sets of simple directions to follow. The directions can be on many topics of interest: how to make a model car, how to make paper flowers, how to decoupage. See if the students can read the directions and follow them. Have students work in pairs on some projects and in larger groups on others. (See also "Following Recipes" in Chapter 6.)

Map Reading

This activity could be an extension of "Getting Around," described earlier in this chapter. Helpful phrases could be written on the chalkboard: turn right (left), go south (north, east, west), go around the corner (straight), on the right (left, north, south, east, west) side of the street, in the (middle, far corner) of the block, down (up) the street, until you see a mailbox (fire hydrant, bus stop), between the drug store and the bank, across from the hardware store, and so on. Give the students maps such as the one in Figure 7.7 and have them follow directions as you give them by tracing the route with a pencil. First do a demonstration with the class. Place the map on the overhead projector and trace a route while reading a set of directions out loud—for example, "Start at the bank, go north on Second Street until you get to Central Avenue, turn left, walk straight ahead to the gas station. It's between the grocery store and the bakery." Then divide the students into pairs and have them give each other directions while they trace the routes on their own maps.

An alternative might be to combine storytelling with the activities.[8] For example, create a story about a fugitive who moves from place to place in different ways: he walks, runs, darts, crawls, skips, and drives. The students trace the route on their individual maps as you read. Instead of drawing only straight lines, the students can draw broken lines for "walks" (--------------), zigzag lines for "runs" (ΛΛΛΛ), sideways carets for "darts" (>>>>>), wavy lines for "crawls" (∿∿∿∿), arches for "skips" (ⴖⴖⴖ), and a series of plus signs for "drives" (+ + + + + +).

Follow-ups could include having the students draw maps of sections of their own communities and write sets of directions to the various places within them. They may even want to write mini-stories to go with the directions. Eventually the students can participate in similar activities using real street maps of cities or highway maps of whole states or countries.

---

[8]I wish to thank Braden Cancilla for this idea.

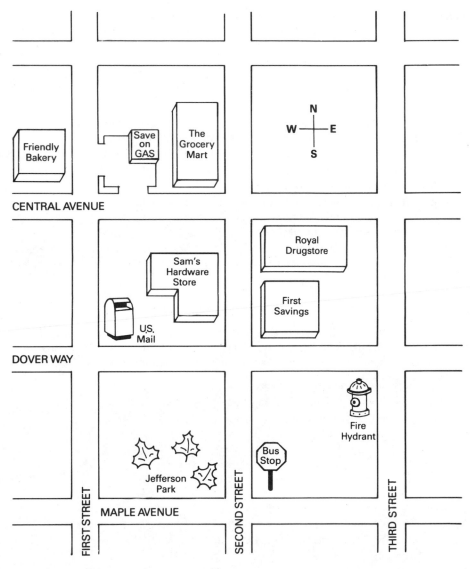

Figure 7.7

Sharing Books—the Classroom Library

Place several bean bag chairs in the corner of the classroom along with several bookcases set up at right angles to form a little library. Give students time to spend in this area where they can read individually, read to each other, and/or discuss books. Books might even be checked out through a system similar to that used in a public school or university library.[9] Students may even want to contribute their own books to the collection.

Writing Memos

Set up situations in which students can write memos. Some suggestions are below (see Figure 7.8):

> Your mother is at work. You are leaving for a basketball game. You and some of your friends want to go out after the game for a pizza. Write a memo to your mother to tape to the refrigerator door. Tell her you will be home a little late.

> You are at home. Someone has called for your brother. He is still at school. Write a memo asking him to return the call.

> You have a job as a receptionist. A salesman has come to sell paper products to your boss. Your boss is not in. The salesman asks you to leave a message. It should say that the salesman will be back later.

> You have an appointment with your professor. You must cancel it because your mother is coming to visit that day. Write a message to give to the secretary. Explain the situation.

Using Local or Foreign Language Newspapers[10]

1. Ask the students to find, cut out, and paste on butcher paper a sample of each of the following. Students can work in groups or individually. This kind of activity could begin at much earlier stages if the items are simple enough.

   the price of a pound of meat
   the low temperature in a major city
   a number greater than a thousand
   a face with glasses
   the picture or name of an animal
   a sports headline
   a letter to the editor
   the price of a used Ford Mustang
   a city within 50 miles of your own
   a movie that starts between 1:00 and 4:00 P.M.
   an angry word
   the picture of a happy person
   a ten-letter word
   the picture of a bride

2. Have the students go through the ads in a recent paper. Ask them to find three

---

[9]Cyndee Gustke suggested this idea.

[10]These activities have been adapted from the pamphlets "Newspapers in Education," *Albuquerque Journal/Tribune.*

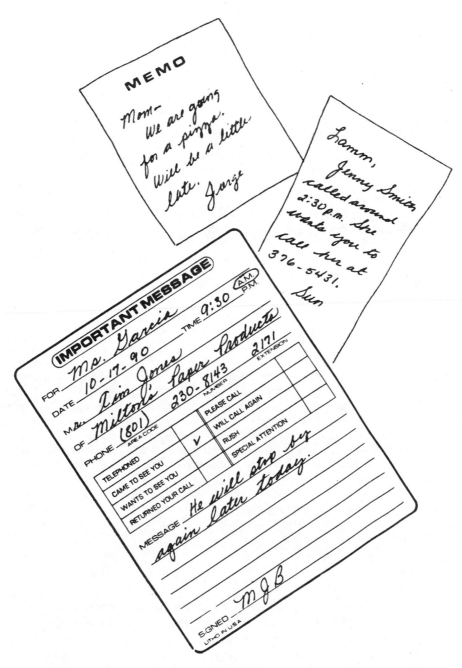

Figure 7.8

things that were produced in other countries. Ask them to find three things that were produced in the state or city in which they now live.

3. Students can look for suitable jobs, apartments, and other items of interest in the want ads. They can discuss what they have found and tell why the ones they have chosen fit their needs.

4. They can also look in the want ads to find items for sale. Have them play the roles of potential sellers and buyers. For example, the buyers can make "telephone calls" to the sellers to gather more information about the content of the ads. A fist held to the ear makes a good pretend phone.

   They can then write want ads advertising things they want to sell. They can even bring these items to class. Have them consider the following questions before writing: What do you want to sell? Who do you think will buy it? Why would someone want to buy it?

   Once they have written their ads (restrict number of words and dollar value), collect them, duplicate them, and distribute them among the class. Let them buy, sell, or trade at will.

5. Finding articles about interesting people in the news can be exciting. Students can plan a "celebrity" party and make a list of those they would like to invite. Have them tell why they would like to meet the ones they have selected.

6. Ask students to choose a headline and write an alternative story to go with it.

Pen Pals

Mainstream English classes or organizations within or outside of the school can write personal letters to ESL students. After several exchanges of letters have taken place, the groups might get together to meet for a party or outing.

In foreign language classes students can write to each other on a regular basis in the target language, they can write to students studying the same language in another school, or they can obtain pen pals in the countries where the target language is spoken.

You might want to establish a mailbox center in a quiet area of the classroom. Directions and information about the area can be displayed. A table with three or four chairs can be provided along with several types of paper, envelopes, and writing tools. To encourage letter writing, the teacher, teacher assistants, and advanced students can first write letters so that each student receives one. Then time can be scheduled regularly to receive, read, and respond to the letters as students become involved in writing to each other as well.[11]

SUMMARY

According to Krashen and Terrell, the foundation of the natural approach rests on four principles: (1) comprehension precedes production, (2) production must be allowed to emerge in stages, (3) the course syllabus must be based on communicative goals, and (4) the activities and classroom environment must work together to produce a lowered affective filter.

---

[11]Thanks to Cyndee Gustke, who shared this version of letter writing with me.

In order for the natural approach to work, it must be well organized and integrated with compatible methods. It must incorporate ways of continually reinforcing the concepts it introduces.

The natural approach and its extensions demand a great deal of teacher preparation. However, they can provide an extremely rich second language experience for those who are exposed to them. Under optimal conditions students can move with relative ease from comprehension, to early speech production, and into speech emergence and beyond.

READINGS, REFLECTION, AND DISCUSSION

Suggested Readings and Reference Materials

Bassano, S., & Christison, M. (1983). *Drawing out*. Hayward, CA: Alemany. Utilizes experiences in art to motivate oral and written language development. Contains examples of student work.

Byrne, D. (1967). *Progressive picture compositions*. New York: Longman. This series of picture books still holds its fascination for language students of all ages. The set includes very large pictures that are coordinated sequentially. Students place the pictures in the order in which they feel the actions occurred. Discussions and/or writing assignments can follow.

Christison, M., & Bassano, S. (1981). *Look who's talking*. San Francisco: Alemany. Adults and teens in the speech emergence phase and beyond can learn interaction techniques through the activities presented in this book. The suggested lessons, which include games and problem solving, begin with lower-risk kinds of activities and progress to more personal, higher-risk ones as the students become more proficient.

DLM teaching resources comprehensive catalog. Allen, TX: DLM Teaching Resources. Catalogs are not normally included in annotated reading lists such as this. However, because this particular catalog contains a wide variety of realia, I have included it even though not all of the materials contained therein are compatible with a natural approach. The following manipulatives, pictures, games, etc. are especially effective for language teaching: the colorful photo library sets; picture cards depicting opposites and categories of different kinds; sequence and spatial relation picture cards; map games; colored cubes for teaching cognitive skills; math games; plastic clocks; play coins and bills; association cards; and functional signs.

Krashen, S., & Terrell, T. (1983). *The natural approach: Language acquisition in the classroom*. Oxford: Pergamon. Essential reading for anyone planning to use the natural approach. The book clearly describes the method, offers theoretical justification for its use, and presents suggested activities for making it work.

Marino, E., Martini, M., Raley, C., & Terrell, T. (1984). *A rainbow collection: A natural approach to teaching English as a second language*. Norwalk, CA: Santillana. Activities in this collection are organized topically. They follow the stages of language acquisition according to the natural approach. The package is oriented to younger learners and contains a teacher's guide, a placement test, student assessment records, student progress reports, lesson activity cards, a picture card collection, wall charts, and a teacher training video.

Michener, D., & Muschlitz, B. (1979). *Teacher's gold mine.* Nashville, TN: Incentive. A diverse collection of story starters, game ideas, art projects, visuals for bulletin boards, and other realia. The activities can be easily adapted to a variety of age and proficiency levels.

Terrell, T. (1983). The natural approach to language teaching: an update. In Oller and Richard-Amato, *Methods that work,* pp. 267–283. Presents a convincing case for the natural approach. Includes an in-depth discussion of the stages of language instruction within this method.

Winn-Bell Olsen, J. (1977). *Communication starters and other activities for the ESL classroom.* Hayward, CA: Alemany. A handy "how-to" book for second language teachers. Informally written, it includes games, interviews, role play, journal writing, map activities, and many more.

Winn-Bell Olsen, J. (1984). *Look again pictures.* Hayward, CA: Alemany. The book contains 22 picture pairs (which can be duplicated) and student exercises to accompany them. Within each pair, one picture is different in eight ways from the other. Students are to search for the differences. The materials, which are designed for teenagers and adults, can stimulate a great deal of interaction.

Questions for Reflection and Discussion

1. Reflect on the process by which you became proficient in a second language. How closely did your progress approximate the stages described in the natural approach? Did your teachers appear to help or hinder your acquisition of the language? Explain.

2. Often listening, speaking, reading, and writing are treated as isolated skills by language teachers. How might you integrate them by using the natural approach? Give some specific activities as examples.

3. Create a 10-minute demonstration of the natural approach or an extension of it to try out on fellow students. The demonstration may be in a language unfamiliar to your group if it is simple enough. After your presentation, ask the group in what ways it was effective and in what ways it could be improved.

4. Terrell (1983) claims that one of the conditions that fosters acquisition is a low-anxiety environment. In what ways can the natural approach foster such an environment? Are there any situations in which anxiety might aid acquisition? Think of situations in which one might experience the anxiety associated with anger, for example. LaForge (1971) found in his experimental language classes that an overt display of anger seemed to make

students more uninhibited and freer in their communication. Thus, the acquisition process was actually helped by anxiety. Do you see this as being a possible refutation of Terrell's claim or only a surface discrepancy that can be explained through a deeper analysis of anxiety and its ramifications?

8

Jazz Chants, Music, and Poetry

Rhythm and rhyme, assonance and pun are not artificial creations, but vestigial echoes of primitive phases in the development of language, and of the even more primitive pulsations of living matter; hence our particular receptiveness for messages which arrive in rhythmic pattern.

A. Koestler, 1964

Second language learners, just like first language learners, should have the opportunity to play with language. Children and adults alike can receive considerable enjoyment from indulging in such frivolity. Through word/sound play, many "chunks" of useful language can be incorporated into the individual's linguistic repertoire at almost any age or level of proficiency. The use of prosodic elements, redundancy, and sometimes thoughtless repetition can produce lowered anxiety and greater ego permeability.[1] One might call the process a sort of "palatable audiolingualism." However, unlike audiolingualism, its rhythms and sound repetitions carry the student into sensually appealing activities that can go far beyond mere drill. The subject matter does not have to be frivolous but can be directly anchored in meaningful experience. The meanings can be rich and multileveled, and discussions can follow that would challenge even the most proficient among the group.

Second language students can be exposed to meaningful word/sound

---

[1]Guiora, Brannon, and Dull (1972) discuss the concept of *language ego*, which refers to the self-identity intricately involved with the risks of taking on a new language. It is responsible for boundaries which can make us extremely inhibited if too strong and impenetrable.

play through jazz chants, music, and poetry, all of which can provide them with a few tools for communication, especially valuable at beginning levels. Through these genres, students can internalize routines and patterns with or without consciously committing them to memory. Students do not even have to understand the meanings of the words within the chunks in order to use them to participate (albeit in a limited fashion) in social events and to encourage input from others. One possible drawback here is that others may at first assume that students are more fluent than they really are. However, it doesn't take long for these people to realize the approximate levels of second language students and adjust their speech accordingly.

The use of routines and patterns can provide a stopgap strategy that students can use to gain entry into the new culture before being considered "ready." Even though the process in developing routines and patterns is thought to be very different from that used in developing creative speech (Krashen, 1981b; Lamendella, 1979; see also Related Reading 4), they can become part of creative speech once the student's proficiency matches his or her need for communication.

JAZZ CHANTS

Jazz chants were developed by Carolyn Graham, an ESL teacher and jazz musician, in order to provide language learners with a rhythmic means for improving speaking and listening skills. Through the chants, students can be exposed to natural intonation patterns and idiomatic expressions in often provocative, sometimes humorous situations. Feelings are expressed in the playing out of the common rituals of everyday life. Because the chants are often in dialogue form, students can learn the cultural rules of turn-taking and appropriate ways to communicate specific needs in a variety of situations. The dialogues generally include three kinds of conversational patterns: question/response, command/response, and provocative statement/response.

Graham (1978) suggests that certain steps, summarized below, be taken:

1. The teacher needs to make sure that the students understand the situational context of the chant. Vocabulary items and cultural ramifications inherent in the situations themselves will need clear explanations.
2. Initially, the teacher in a normal conversational voice gives each line of the chant once or twice as needed and the students repeat in unison. Graham advises the teacher to stop at any point to correct pronunciation or intonation patterns.
3. The teacher then establishes a beat by snapping the fingers (students seem to prefer this means), counting, clapping, or using rhythm sticks. Step 2 is then repeated, but this time with a firm beat.
4. The teacher now divides the class into two parts (the numbers of students

in each part do not seem to matter). Using the beat established above, the teacher gives the lines. The two groups of students alternately repeat the lines as they are given.

5. The dialogue of the chant is then conducted between the teacher and the class. The teacher takes the first part in the dialogue, the students take the other (without the teacher to model). The teacher can use the tapes (optional) which accompany the jazz chants books (see Suggested Readings at the end of this chapter).

In my own experience with jazz chants, I have found it unnecessary to stop and correct students' pronunciation as Graham suggests. Students pick up the modeled pronunciation through the repetitions. In addition, stopping for corrections seems to place the focus on form rather than meaning.

Jazz chants can be used to help students internalize matrices (see Chapter 7) and, at the same time, reinforce specific vocabulary items. In the sample jazz chant excerpt below, sound play is embedded through the use of rhyme. The matrix includes various structures for offering and refusing food. Substitutions can be made to include the names of the common foods one wants reinforced. Follow-ups might include total physical response activities involving food preparation (see Chapter 6) or role play taking place at the dinner table (see Chapter 9).

Would you like
    a fried egg?
Would you like
    a fried egg?

        No thanks. I'm on a diet.
        Please don't fry it.
        Please don't fry it.

Jazz chants can also be used to introduce some of the topics recommended in the natural approach and its extensions (see Chapter 7). For example, the chant below was written to introduce a unit on sports events. Typical pictures of the events can accompany the chant. Follow-ups can include total physical response activities (involving basic actions of the sport), sports demonstrations, local news reporting of sports events, or a trip to a sporting event as part of a "Language Experience" activity (see Chapter 7). The matrix in the following chant offers a means for talking about sports. Word substitutions can easily be made to include a wide variety of events.

Where do you go? Where do you go?
Where do you go to see
a bail go in a basket,
a ball go in a basket?

Where do I go? Where do I go?
To a basketball game.
To a basketball game.
That's where I go to see
a ball go in a basket.

All you have to do is ask it.

Where do you go? Where do you go?
Where do you go to see
a ball kicked all around,
a ball kicked all around?

Where do I go? Where do I go?
To a soc-cer game,
To a soc-cer game.
That's where I go to see
a ball kicked all around.

You keep it on the ground.

Where do you go? Where do you go?
Where do you go to see
a girl fly through the air
a girl fly through the air?

Where do I go? Where do I go?
To a gym-nas-tics meet,
To a gym-nas-tics meet.
That's where I go to see
a girl fly through the air.

Would you do it on a dare?

There are many ways in which jazz chants can be orchestrated. The two parts can be used to pit males against females, those born in January through June against those born in July through December, those wearing green against the others, and so forth. To add variety, parts might be assigned to individuals who volunteer or to small groups of differing sizes.

Some chants can be partially improvised by the students. For example, in the following one, all the students sit in a circle on the floor.[2] A rhythm is set by the snapping of fingers. The teacher begins the chant with something like ''My name is _____. What's your name?'' The teacher looks at the student on the right, who responds, ''My name is _____.

---

[2]I wish to thank Linda Cobral for sharing this idea with me.

What's your name?'' The student looks at the next student on the right, who will be responding, and so on around the circle. Variations could follow that overlap into affective activities (see Chapter 11). ''My name is _____ and I like _____'' and ''My name is _____ and I feel _____'' are two examples of matrices that would lend themselves to this kind of activity.

Although the jazz chants above are oriented to beginning students, on pages 238–239 intermediate and advanced students are exposed to idiomatic expressions through this means. Subtle forms of humor, decisions about the appropriateness of utterances, and symbolic content are only a few of the things to which students at higher levels can be introduced. Through the cadences, the students' pronunciation and intonation can become more nativelike and natural without conscious drill.

MUSIC

Music, also, reduces anxiety and inhibition in second language students. Furthermore, it is a great motivator in that its lyrics are often fraught with meaningful input. Human emotions are frequently expressed in highly charged situations. Through music, language easily finds roots in the experience of students at any age or proficiency level. Often awareness is heightened through its prosodic elements. Kahlil Gibran once said, ''The reality of music is in that vibration that remains in the ear after the singer finishes his song and the player no longer plucks the strings.'' Music can break down barriers among those who share its rhythms and meaning. Its unifying effect can extend across time, nations, races, and individuals.

At beginning levels, music can be used to teach basic vocabulary. Colors, body parts, simple actions, clothes, and names of people are only a few of the concepts that can be taught through music. The teacher doesn't have to be talented in music to make it a memorable experience. A gravel voice can exude as much enthusiasm as a euphonious one. Records or cassettes can provide the accompaniment in some situations. Words can be created and students' names can be inserted into the stanzas that are coordinated with easy-to-learn melodies. For example, below are some lyrics that could be sung to ''You Are My Sunshine.''

> Your name is Car-los.
> Your name is Car-los.
> You come from Per-u,
> so far away.
> And now you're with us
> Until the summer.
> And it is here
> we want you to stay.

Your name is Sung Lee.
Your name is Sung Lee.
You're from Kor-e-a,
so far away.
And now you're with us
Maybe forever
Even after your hair turns
gray.

Your name is Ni-kom.
Your name is Ni-kom.
You come from La-os,
so far away.
And now you're with us
We are so happy.
We want to sing with you today.

Although Carlos, Sung Lee, and Nikom may not understand all the words the first few times they hear them, they will be highly motivated to find out what is being sung about them. Thus acquisition will be highly likely.

Specific matrices can be reinforced through music. Notice the lyrics of the following song, written to the tune of "Mary Had a Little Lamb."

Danella says, "Come on, let's go.
Come on, let's go. Come on, let's go."
Danella says, "Come on, let's go.
To the zoo on Friday."
Hung an-swers, "That's fine with me.
Fine with me. Fine with me."
Hung an-swers, "That's fine with me.
Let's go to the zoo on Friday."

Friday comes and off they go.
Off they go. Off they go.
Friday comes and off they go.
To see the an-i-mals.

First they see the el-e-phants.
El-e-phants. El-e-phants.
First they see the el-e-phants.
In the mud-dy waters.

Then they walk to the lion's den.
Lion's den. Lion's den.
Then they walk to the lion's den.
To find him pacing back and forth.

And on the song goes through as many stanzas as the teacher wants to create. Once students become more proficient, they can add their own stanzas. The words written down and duplicated along with pictures can aid the students' understanding. Total physical response can be used, with students pointing to the pictures of the animals while the song is being sung. A trip to the zoo can stimulate all sorts of additional meaningful experiences with the target language.

For those who prefer songs of a more "professional" nature, Hap Palmer[3] has provided several in a series of songbooks and records (see Suggested Readings at the end of the chapter). Figure 8.1 presents one that he wrote on body parts and actions for beginning students.

Although these songs are mainly of benefit to beginning students, there are many songs popular today that are particularly effective for intermediate to advanced students. Even the "top ten" can provide one or two. The lyrics should be duplicated so that each student can have his or her own copy. Students will probably want to take the words home so they can sing the songs to themselves or with their families and friends.

When a song is presented in class, it is usually a good idea to let the students just listen to the song first as it is played on the record or tape. Then hand out the words and play the song again. The third time the song is played, the students will no doubt sing along with you and the recording. Students should be given the opportunity to have words or phrases explained to them during the course of the activity. A discussion should follow in which the students can relate the song to their own lives and to the lives of others.

POETRY

Although poetic elements are contained in jazz chants and music lyrics, poetry can be treated as a separate category. Poems range in length anywhere from a few words to a whole book. They are generally concise, sometimes deceptively simple, and often highly charged with emotional content. They can be used at a variety of levels to reinforce ideas and introduce new ones.

The following poem by Jack Prelutsky[4] is a favorite, especially among elementary schoolchildren. It reinforces the names of concrete objects in the classroom as it presents a fantasy that we all may have had at one time or another.

---

[3]Thanks to Raquel Mireles for making me aware of these songbooks and records.

[4]From *The Random House Book of Poetry for Children* (1983). Thanks to Norma Ramirez, who introduced me to this poem.

Put Your Hands Up In The Air

Words and Music by Hap Palmer

Figure 8.1 (From Hap Palmer, 1971)

Put your hands in your lap.

Bow your head and take a nap.

Bow your head and take a nap.

Figure 8.1 *(Continued)*

The Creature in the Classroom

It appeared inside our classroom
at a quarter after ten,
it gobbled up the blackboard,
three erasers and a pen.
It gobbled teacher's apple
and it bopped her with the core.
"How dare you!" she responded.
"You must leave us . . . there's the door."

The Creature didn't listen
but described an arabesque
as it gobbled all her pencils,
seven notebooks and her desk.
Teacher stated very calmly,
"Sir! you simply cannot stay,
I'll report you to the principal
unless you go away!"

But the thing continued eating,
it ate paper, swallowed ink,
as it gobbled up our homework
I believe I saw it wink.
Teacher finally lost her temper.
"OUT!" she shouted at the creature.
The creature hopped beside her
and GLOPP . . . it swallowed teacher.

It is important to remember that poems such as this one may not at first be understood in their entirety. In fact, the students, when initially exposed to them, may understand only a few words. However, upon subsequent exposures to and discussion of the poems, the students will begin to understand more and more.

The next poem, by Edwin Arlington Robinson, is for students in university or adult programs. It can be used at high intermediate to advanced levels to reinforce various emotions such as happiness, love, envy, loneliness, and desperation and to teach literary devices such as symbolism and metaphor. The poem leads naturally into a discusson of Richard Cory's life and the seeming irony of his death. What was missing in his life that was essential to his happiness? The cultural ramifications and the social taboos concerning suicide might also be relevant to the discussion. A good follow-up to the poem is the narrative song of the same title from the Simon and Garfunkel album *Sounds of Silence* (1965, Eclectic Music Company). In the song, Richard Cory owns a factory and the narrator, who works for him, envies his lifestyle and is shocked at his death, just as we all are. Both poem and song are very powerful and can stimulate not only discussion but the writing of short papers as well.

Richard Cory

Whenever Richard Cory went down town,
We people on the pavement looked at him:
He was a gentleman from sole to crown,
Clean favored, and imperially slim.

And he was always quietly arrayed,
And he was always human when he talked;
But still he fluttered pulses when he said,
"Good-morning," and he glittered when he walked.

And he was rich—yes, richer than a king—
And admirably schooled in every grace:
In fine, we thought that he was everything
To make us wish that we were in his place.

So on we worked, and waited for the light,
And went without the meat, and cursed the bread;
And Richard Cory, one calm summer night,
Went home and put a bullet through his head.

In addition to listening to and reading poems written by others, the students who are ready may want to write some of their own even at beginning levels. Christison in her book *English through Poetry* (1982) recommends concrete poetry, formed from pictures and words. For example, students can be asked to draw large butterflies such as the one in Figure 8.2. Once the butterflies have been drawn, words and phrases such as "light," "flying," "beautiful," "in the air," "a dream" or whatever can be drawn on the wings or the bodies, following the forms of the butterflies. A butterfly for a student at an intermediate to advanced level might look something like the one in Figure 8.3.[5]

Also recommended for students at intermediate to advanced levels are verse forms such as word cinquain, Japanese tanka, or haiku. Below are examples, each followed by a summary of the structure that it contains.

Word Cinquain

A cat
Full of mischief
Charges, dances, pounces
Brightens my longest days
A wonder

1st line: a word or two to name the topic

2nd line: two or three words that describe the topic

3rd line: three or four words that express action

4th line: four or five words that express personal attitude

5th line: a word or two to rename the topic

---

[5]This poem and illustration are by Jane Decock and come from *Harbinger*, published by the Advanced Creative Writing Classes at Jefferson High School in Edgewater, Colorado, 1972.

Figure 8.2 (adapted from Christison, 1982)

Tanka

Drifting in the sky
Clouds come and go in patterns
I look to the sun
The darkness hovers around
Slowly rain begins to fall

1st line: 5 syllables
2nd line: 7 syllables
3rd line: 5 syllables
4th line: 7 syllables
5th line: 7 syllables

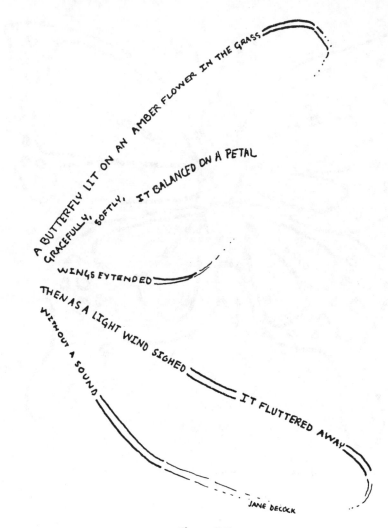

A BUTTERFLY LIT ON AN AMBER FLOWER IN THE GRASS

GRACEFULLY, SOFTLY, IT BALANCED ON A PETAL

WINGS EXTENDED

THEN AS A LIGHT WIND SIGHED

IT FLUTTERED AWAY

WITHOUT A SOUND

JANE DECOCK

Figure 8.3

Haiku

Flowers wave to me
  As I pass them in the field. . . .
Gentle, swirling wind

1st line: 5 syllables
2nd line: 7 syllables
3rd line: 5 syllables

(Note: There is generally a break in thought between the second
and third lines.)

The verses can be written at first in groups with the help of the teacher
or teacher assistants using pictures to stimulate ideas. Later the students may
want to try a few verses on their own.

Whether students are working in groups or individually, it is important
that they not be held to exact numbers of words or syllables for structured
verse unless they can be shown at the more advanced levels how a poem
might be improved by doing so.

Christison (1982) suggests that the events in the students' lives provide
some of the impetus for writing and sharing poetry of various kinds. For
example, greeting cards can be created to give to others for special occasions.
Birthdays, marriages, graduations, holidays, and other celebrations are ideal
times to write and/or illustrate poetry. If the students don't want to write
their own poetry, they can search in books for appropriate poems to put on
their cards, giving credit to their sources.

Another idea she recommends is to have students draw or paint pictures
and then find or write poems that seem to go with them. Activities such as
these can give the students important reasons for reading and writing poetry,
thus increasing their exposure to meaningful language.

SUMMARY

Jazz chants, music, and poetry often produce lowered anxiety and greater
ego permeability among second language learners. Beginners are often able
to internalize chunks of language which allow them to participate in social
situations early on. During initial stages of language development, students
often have the desire to communicate but do not have the necessary skills.
By having a repertoire of ways to be communicative (however limited), the
student is able to form a bond with native speakers and thus be in a position
to receive more input.

Intermediate and advanced students also gain benefits from jazz chants,
music, and poetry. Idiomatic expressions, subtle forms of humor, decisions
concerning appropriateness, and symbolic content can be internalized
through these media. Pronunciation and intonation patterns can take on a
more nativelike quality through use of word/sound play. Students can be
exposed to situations in which highly meaningful content can be dealt with
on many different levels.

READINGS, REFLECTION, AND DISCUSSION

Suggested Readings and Reference Materials

Christison, M. (1982). *English through poetry*. Hayward, CA: Alemany. Includes criteria for the selection, presentation, and creation of poetry in ESL classes. In addition, the incorporation of simple poetic forms, choral readings, and readers' theater is described. The book ends with several poems appropriate for second language students.

Graham, C. (1978). *Jazz chants*. New York: Oxford University. A collection of chants that teachers can use with beginners learning English as a second language. Especially effective for use with older children and adults. Often humorous dialogues are presented based on commonplace situations and events. Includes a cassette.

Graham, C. (1978). *Jazz chants for children*. New York: Oxford University. Oriented to young children learning English as a second language. Many feelings are portrayed in the chants: fear, anger, happiness, and joy. Pictures and games which children find very appealing accompany the chants. Includes a cassette.

Graham, C. (1986). *Small talk*. New York: Oxford University. The jazz chants presented in this latest book by Graham focus on specific tools for communication. Topics such as one might find in typical matrices (see pages 97 and 138) are in abundance. Greetings, introductions, saying goodbye, talking about food, money, and the weather are among the many relevant topics included. Available on cassettes.

Kind, U. (1980). *Tune in to English: Learning English through familiar melodies*. New York: Regents. Functions in English are taught by the use of familiar tunes. For example, ''I'm Glad to Meet You'' is sung to the tune ''La Cucaracha,'' ''My Father Has a Sister'' to ''Row, Row, Row Your Boat,'' and ''Where's My Key'' to ''Jingle Bells.'' A songbook and cassette are part of the package.

Osman, A., & McConochie, J. (1979). *If you feel like singing*. White Plains, NY: Longman. Contains the lyrics and music of old favorite songs including ''You Are My Sunshine,'' ''Where Have All the Flowers Gone,'' ''The Hammer Song,'' and ''We Shall Overcome.'' Each song is followed by a set of activities including crossword puzzles, word searches, cloze exercises, and matching words. A cassette accompanies this collection.

Palmer, H. (1971). *Songbook: Learning basic skills through music I*. Freeport, NY: Educational Activities. A record album accompanies this lively, action-packed book of songs. Although it is meant for teaching children, it can be used successfully with beginners of all ages. It includes such topics as colors, body parts, animals, numbers, clothes, names, and the alphabet. This particular volume is just part of a large collection of songbooks and records by Palmer on a wide variety of topics at many different levels.

The Random House book of poetry for children. (1983). New York: Random House. Presents poems that are highly appropriate to use with students learning English as a second language. Although the poems are meant for chidren, many would be enjoyed by students of all ages.

Silverstein, S. (1981). *A light in the attic*. New York: Harper & Row. This book of humorous poems with unexpected twists keeps students of all ages enthralled. A cassette tape is available.

Questions for Reflection and Discussion

1. Compare the use of repetition and imitation in the audiolingual method with the use of similar strategies in jazz chants, songs, and poetry. In what ways do the latter render the strategies more "palatable"? Consider the mapping-of-language-into-experience arguments found in Chapter 4. Consider also the prosodic elements involved in the content.

2. Krashen (1981b) argues that routines and patterns play a "minor, though significant role" in the second language acquisition process. Do you feel that a difference in the method of exposure to such prefabricated forms might make a difference in the role they play? Think about the level of proficiency at which the student might be exposed to them. Would the role of routines and patterns change in any way for an intermediate student? For an advanced student?

3. Choose a topic that you might wish to include while using the natural approach or an extension of it (see Chapter 7). Find a jazz chant, some lyrics set to a popular song, or a poem to introduce or reinforce some of the key concepts. You may write your own if you wish. Present it to a group of your fellow students. Inform them about what other activities you might use to reinforce the same concepts. Discuss with them the strengths of your presentation and ways in which you might improve it.

9

Storytelling, Role Play, and Drama

Drama is like the naughty child who climbs the high walls and ignores the "No Trespassing" sign. It does not allow us to define our territory so exclusively; it forces us to take as our starting-point life not language.

A. Maley & A. Duff, 1983

Second language students can easily become absorbed in the dramatic playing out of life's experiences and, through them, forget the self-consciousness often associated with learning another language. Drama-based activities can heighten the students' abilities to acquire. By losing themselves in the struggles and conflicts of others, they seem better able to make the target language part of their memory store (see Chapter 4).

In the results of a questionnaire given to UCLA teachers and students, Susan Stern found support for her theory that drama has a positive effect on second language learning by encouraging the operation of certain psychological factors which facilitate oral communication: heightened self-esteem, motivation, and spontaneity; increased capacity for empathy; lowered sensitivity to rejection (1983, p. 216). Storytelling, role play, and other forms of drama can be used in the second language classroom to help bring about such results. These activities allow students to explore their inner resources, empathize with others, and use their own experiences as scaffolds upon which to build credible action. As a result, each student may be able to improve his or her ability to produce the target language, lower anxiety, acquire many of the nonverbal nuances of the language, and improve the ability to work cooperatively in group situations.

Before the teacher involves the students in the main body of activities presented in this chapter, a series of warm-ups is recommended to reduce anxiety and to create a warm, active environment.

WARM-UPS

The warm-ups included here require almost no verbal language and therefore can be used with rank beginners. In addition to the benefits mentioned above, they help to establish trust and understanding among the group members and to lower their inhibitions. The teacher may want to begin with a series of simple exercises involving stretching, bending, and the tightening and relaxing of specific muscle groups before proceeding to the activities below (see similar activities on page 237).

Circle Mimics

Students form a circle. The first student is asked to make some sort of movement such as hopping on one foot. The second student repeats the movement and adds a new one such as shaking a fist in the air. The third student hops on one foot, shakes a fist in the air, and adds a third movement and so on around the circle.

Baseball Mime

Throw a make-believe ball across the room to one of your students. After the student "catches" it, motion to the student to join you in a game of catch. Then throw the ball to other students and motion to them to join you also. The game can remain simply a game of catch or it can develop into a full baseball game if the students are familiar with it. Give one student a make-believe bat and station the others around the room at pretend bases. Let the students take over the game.

Once students have worked out tension and seem to have lowered inhibitions, they may be ready to attempt storytelling.

STORYTELLING

Stories have traditionally been used to teach, to entertain, and to explain the unknown. The activities offered here can be coordinated with several of the methods recommended in this book (total physical response, the audio-motor unit, the natural approach, etc.) Some of the activities are more appropriate to beginners; others, to more advanced levels. Most can be adapted to any age level provided they are within the students' range cognitively.

Allowing students to be exposed to a story before fully understanding the words is highly motivating for beginners at any age.[1] The same story can be used from time to time in different ways until a full understanding is achieved over a period of perhaps several months. Activities such as those presented below enable the students to participate in the language *before* actually becoming proficient in it, just as children do when they are being read to in their first language. Through these activities, curiosity in the target language is stimulated.

Story Experience[2]
Level: Beginning

Have the students form a large circle. Choose a story or a narrative poem such as the one below (this particular one is oriented to children although adults have been found to enjoy it too). Pick out the concrete words that can be easily acted out. Assign to each student a word to act out. Help the students understand what the word means by demonstrating its meaning or by showing a picture to illustrate. Then read the story aloud with much feeling. Each student is to listen carefully for his or her word. When the word is read, the student is to go across the circle acting it out as he or she moves across. Students on the other side will have to make room as the actors come across. For the following story excerpt, the teacher will need these words acted out: a fly, a spider, a bird, a cat, a dog, a cow, and a horse.

Excerpt from *There was an Old Lady Who Swallowed a Fly*[3]

There was an old lady who swallowed a *fly*.
I don't know why she swallowed a *fly*.
Perhaps she'll die.

There was an old lady who swallowed a *spider,*
That wriggled and wriggled and jiggled inside her.
She swallowed the *spider* to catch the *fly*.
I don't know why she swallowed a *fly*.
Perhaps she'll die.

There was an old lady who swallowed a *bird*.
How absurd, to swallow a *bird*!
She swallowed the *bird* to catch the *spider*.

---

[1]Note that this recommendation appears to fly in the face of the arguments favoring comprehensible input. It is true that if the story were simply read aloud with little expression of feeling and if there were no physical involvement on the part of the student, then it probably would be as meaningless as most other input that is not understood.

[2]This activity has been adapted from one presented by the Barzak Institute of San Francisco at a workshop done for the Jefferson County Public Schools of Colorado in 1979.

[3]Those who would like the story in its entirety can refer to the version by Ruth Bonne, illustrated by Pam Adams, and published by Child's Play (International). I wish to thank Ernestine Saldivar for introducing me to this version.

There was an old lady who swallowed a *cat.*
Well, fancy that, she swallowed a *cat!*
She swallowed the cat to catch the *bird.*

There was an old lady who swallowed a *dog.*
What a hog, to swallow a *dog!*
She swallowed the *dog* to catch the *cat.*

There was an old lady who swallowed a *cow.*
I don't know how she swallowed a *cow!*
She swallowed the *cow* to catch the *dog.*
She swallowed the *dog* to catch the *cat.*
She swallowed the *cat* to catch the *bird.*
She swallowed the *bird* to catch the *spider,*
That wriggled and wriggled and jiggled inside her.
She swallowed the *spider* to catch the *fly.*
I don't know why she swallowed a *fly.*
Perhaps she'll die.

There was an old lady who swallowed a *horse.*
She's dead of course.

The next story experience activity is oriented toward teenagers and adults. This time the students in the circle are to hold cards of various colors: red, blue, green, orange, and so on. Work with the students to make sure they are able to associate the words with the particular colors each has been assigned. They are to listen very carefully to the words as the story is read. When the names of their colors are read, they are to walk across the circle holding up the colored card. More than one student may have the same color. The number of students holding each color will depend upon how many persons the teacher would like to involve at any given time.

A Spring Day

The door opens wide. It is Sasha. Sasha comes to my house every morning at 6 o'clock. We walk to work together.

Today is a warm day. We walk on the long, *gray* sidewalk. A *yellow* sun peeks through the trees. It is spring. The flowers are opening up—*red* flowers, *yellow* flowers, *blue* flowers. Their *green* leaves are wet. We see a man in the street. He is riding a *red* bicycle. He is wearing *black* boots and a *blue* hat. He stops riding. He asks, ''Have you seen a *brown* and *white* sweater? My child left it here yesterday.'' He points to the *green* grass behind us. We look at the grass. Then at each other.

''No, we haven't,'' we say at the same time. ''Sorry.'' He gets back on his bicycle. He rides away. ''Wait,'' I yell. ''I see something here . . . behind the tree. It's *brown* . . . and *white.*'' I pick it up. He turns around and comes back.

''Oh, I thank you very much.'' He takes the sweater and rides away. We walk again. A *gray* car comes by. Then a *white* one. The town is waking up.

We turn the corner. A *black* door is in front of us. We open the door and walk in. It's time for work.

Once the students are familiar with the colors and feel comfortable with the activity, they can pretend to be the objects as they go across the circle. One can, for example, be the sun, others can be flowers, and so forth. Even the characters and main actions of the story can be acted out once a fuller understanding is achieved.

Sound Effects
Level: Beginning

Demonstrate the sound effects that accompany the following story.[4] Beginning students only have to listen for the words that cue the appropriate effect (blanks have been inserted where the sound effects should go). Once the students understand the whole story (perhaps at an intermediate level), they can act it out. If they want, they can change the ending or rewrite it compeletly.

Rosita's Night to Remember

Rosita is alone in the house. Outside she hears the wind blow through the trees _____ (hooing noises). Rain begins to fall _____ (patting of fingertips on the desks). There is a scratching at the door _____ (light touch of fingernails scratching on desks). Maybe it is a lion _____ (roaring). Maybe it is a mouse _____ (squeaking). Maybe it is a monster _____ (howling). She is scared. She turns on the radio to drown out the scratching _____. The radio is playing a song _____ (singing—it doesn't have to be a particular tune). She turns it low _____ (the singing softens), high _____ (it becomes very loud), off _____ (it stops). At the door the scratching continues _____ . She opens the door _____ (creaking). Her dog comes in, jumps up, and gives her a big kiss _____ (kissing sound).

As the students become more proficient, they can write their own scenarios complete with sound effects. At advanced stages the mini-dramas can even become part of full-blown radio shows complete with commercials and newsbreaks.

Identifying Objects in Stories
Level: Beginning

Ask advance-level volunteers, peer teachers, or lay assistants (see pages 190–192) to read very simple stories with lots of pictures in them to small groups of beginners (two or three in a group). Have the readers stop reading aloud from time to time and ask students to point to various specific objects in the pictures. Some of the volunteers or assistants might want to make up their own stories centering around a series of pictures. A book corner could be set up in your room where students can go to read stories aloud to small groups (see also Sharing Books—the Classroom Library).

---

[4]This story is an adaptation of one shared with me by Sylvia Pena.

Story Act-out
Level: Beginning to Intermediate

Read a favorite story aloud while the students listen. Give students a chance to ask questions, then read the story again. Ask for volunteers to take the parts of the characters. Pin a sign with the character's name on each volunteer. Read the story a third time as students act it out, action by action. Then give other volunteers a chance to be the actors.

What's the Title?
Level: Intermediate

Read a story to students but leave out the title. Once the students understand the story, let them make up a title for it. Eventually the author's title can be revealed and discussed in relation to the meaning of the story.

Spinning Stories[5]
Level: Intermediate

Take a ball of yarn and tie knots in it at varying intervals. Some knots will be close together, others far apart. Tape a stimulating picture with people in it to the wall. After placing students in a circle, ask them what they see in the picture. Write the words on the chalkboard as they give them to you so that they will have some starters. Have students make up names and short biographical sketches for the people. Give the ball of yarn to one student in the circle. Ask him or her to begin a story about the picture while unraveling the ball of yarn. The student continues to tell the story until he or she reaches the first knot. Then the ball of yarn is passed to the next person, who continues the story until reaching the next knot. The activity continues until every student in the circle has had a chance to contribute.

Group Story
Level: Intermediate

Using a language-experience type of activity (see page 100), have the students create a group story. As each student makes his or her contribution, write the utterances on the board, making any necessary corrections indirectly. The stories will probably be very brief at first but will evolve into longer and more complex plots as the students gain proficiency. A series of pictures can be used to stimulate ideas.

Silly Stories[6]
Level: Intermediate to Advanced

You and your students can create a story together while a teacher assistant writes it on the chalkboard. Begin by offering the first half of a sentence and have a volunteer student finish it. Other sentences can be produced in the same fashion. For example:

---

[5]Adapted from an activity shared with me by Esther Heise.

[6]This idea has been adapted from Wright, Betteridge, and Buckby (1984, p. 99).

TEACHER: The elephant knocked at . . .
STUDENT 1: . . . the door to my house.
TEACHER: He asked . . .
STUDENT 2: . . . "Can I borrow a cup of straw?"
etc.

Ghost Stories by Candlelight
Level: Intermediate to Advanced

Ask each student to bring a scary story to tell the class in the target language. Have the students sit in a circle on the floor. Light a candle, place it in the middle of the circle, and turn off the lights. Students are told that they can volunteer by taking the candle from the center and placing it in front of them so it lights up their faces. Then they proceed to tell their stories. The candle is returned to the center as each student finishes his or her story. The teacher should demonstrate the procedure first. Background music, the volume of which can easily be adjusted to fit the situation, can be used to fill the silence between volunteers while adding to the mood. Because this activity may be a little too frightening for young children, you will probably want to limit its use to older children, teens, and adults. A flashlight may be used to substitute for a candle as a safety measure, especially for preadolescents.[7]

Finish the Story
Level: Intermediate to Advanced

Present part of a story, and have students finish it orally and/or in writing. At first most of the story can be given. Later only a few lines such as the following may be necessary to launch students into building a climax followed by the denouement.

The boys see a dark shadow fall across the sidewalk. They look up and see. . . .
The first day of her trip went well. Then she opened her suitcase. She discovered. . . .

Tape a Story[8]
Level: Intermediate to Advanced

Choose a short paperback book. Record half of the story on a cassette tape (stop at a high point). End the recording with the words "Continue to read on your own. . . . " Place the cassette and the book in a folder with pockets and make it available to your students along with a cassette player and headset.

Story Interpretation
Level: Intermediate to Advanced

The following story is one that is sure to interest ESL students in particular because it involves the mixed feelings that seem to accompany returning to one's homeland.

---

[7] I want to thank Cesar Montes for suggesting this precaution to me.

[8] Adapted from Michener and Muschlitz (1979, p. 208).

At first it is necessary to motivate the students to read the story by offering what I call "mind grabbers." Questions about their own longings to return home or about what they think it might be like to return home will serve well in preparing them for the experience in store for them. Following the story are relevant activities that can heighten its impact.

Excerpt from "Blue Winds Dancing," by Thomas S. Whitecloud

Morning. I spend the day cleaning up and buying some presents for my family with what is left of my money. Nothing much, but a gift is a gift, if a man buys it with his last quarter. I wait until evening, then start up the track toward home.

Christmas Eve comes in on a north wind. Snow clouds hang over the pines, the night comes early. Walking along the railroad bed, I feel the calm peace of snowbound forests on either side of me. I take my time; I am back in a world where time does not mean so much now.

I am alone—alone but not nearly so lonely as I was back on the campus at school. Those are never lonely who love the snow and the pines, never lonely when the pines are wearing white shawls and snow crunches coldly underfoot. . . .

Just as a light snow begins to fall, I cross the reservation boundary. Somehow it seems as though I have stepped into another world. Deep woods in a white-and-black winter night. A faint trail leading to the village.

The railroad on which I stand comes from a city sprawled by a lake—a city with a million people who walk around without seeing one another; a city sucking the life from all the country around; a city with stores and police and intellectuals and criminals and movies and apartment houses; a city with its politics and libraries and zoos.

Laughing, I go into the woods. As I cross a frozen lake, I begin to hear the drums. Soft in the night the drums beat. It is like the pulse of the world. The white line of the lake ends at a black forest, and above the trees the blue winds are dancing.

I come to the outlying houses of the village. Simple box houses, etched black in the night. From one or two windows soft lamplight falls on the snow. Christmas is here, too, but it does not mean much—not much in the way of parties and presents. Joe Sky will get drunk. Alex Bodidash will buy his children red mittens and a new sled. . . . The village is not a sight to instill pride, yet I am not ashamed. One can never be ashamed of his own people when he knows they have dreams as beautiful as white snow on a tall pine.

Father and my brother and sister are seated around the table as I walk in. Father stares at me for a moment. Then I am in his arms, crying on his shoulder. I give them the presents I have brought, and my throat tightens as I watch my sister save carefully bits of red string from the packages. I hide my feelings by wrestling with my brother when he strikes my shoulder in token of affection. Father looks at me, and I know he has many questions, but he seems to know why I have come. He tells me to go on alone to the lodge, and he will follow.

I follow the trail to the lodge. My feet are light, my heart seems to sing to the music, and I hold my head high. Across white snow fields blue winds are dancing.

Before the lodge door I stop, afraid. I wonder if my people will remember me. I wonder—"Am I Indian, or am I white?" I stand before the door a long time. I hear the ice groan on the lake, and remember the story of the old woman who is under the ice, trying to get out, so she can punish some runaway lovers. . . .

Inside the lodge there are many Indians. Some sit on benches around the walls. Others dance in the center of the floor around a drum. Nobody seems to notice me. It seems as though I were among a people I have never seen before. . . . I look at the old men. Straight, dressed in dark trousers and beaded velvet vests, wearing soft moccasins. Dark, lined faces intent on the music. I wonder if I am at all like them. They dance on, lifting their feet to the rhythm of the drums. . . .

The dance stops. The men walk back to the walls and talk in low tones or with their hands. There is little conversation, yet everyone seems to be sharing some secret . . . they are sharing a mood. Everyone is happy . . . the night is beautiful outside, and the music is beautiful.

I try hard to forget school and white people, and be one of these—my people . . . we are all a part of something universal. I watch eyes and see now that the old people are speaking to me. They nod slightly, imperceptibly, and their eyes laugh into mine. I look around the room. All the eyes are friendly; they all laugh. No one questions my being here. The drums begin to beat again, and I catch the invitation in the eyes of the old men. My feet begin to lift to the rhythm, and I look out beyond the walls into the night and see the lights. I am happy. It is beautiful. I am home.

Follow-up Activities to "Blue Winds Dancing"

1. First ask the students if there are any words or phrases that they do not understand. Ask them to guess at the meanings. Discuss.
2. Have volunteers retell the story to a guest who is not already familiar with it (you may want to invite someone in for this purpose).
3. Divide the students into pairs. Have one person take the part of the Indian who comes home and the other the part of one of the older Indians who is at the lodge. Have them make up a dialogue, write it down, and practice it. Ask volunteers to share their scenes with the class.
4. Divide ESL students into groups of three. Have them speculate about what it would be like to return to their homelands. Encourage them to share the problems they might have as well as the delights.

Story Writing
Level: Advanced

Students can be given time to write and share their own stories. They may want to make their stories autobiographical, biographical, or fictional. As a culminating activity, they may want to put copies of all the stories together in a book with illustrations and a table of contents. The books can be shared with other classes or placed in the school's library to be checked out by anyone who wants to read them.

ROLE PLAY

Role play has high appeal for students because it allows them to be creative and to put themselves in another person's place for a while. As Atticus says in Harper Lee's *To Kill a Mockingbird*, "You never really understand a person until you consider things from his point of view—until you climb into his skin and walk around in it.'' Role play can be just ''play'' or it can have serious social implications, such as in sociodrama.

Scarcella (1983) defines sociodrama as being student oriented rather than teacher oriented. Students act out solutions to social problems, generally defining their own roles and determining their own courses of action. The enactment is open-ended but centers around a clearly stated conflict which is relevant to the students. Only those students who demonstrate a special interest in particular roles are chosen to play them. The steps, which she adapts from Shaftel and Shaftel (1967), include introducing a topic, stimulating student interest, presenting new vocabulary, reading a story which clearly identifies a problem, stopping the story at the climax, discussing the dilemma, selecting students to play the roles, preparing the audience to listen and later offer advice, acting out the rest of the story, discussing alternative ways of dealing with the problem, and replaying the drama using new strategies if necessary. Some sample mini-sociodramas (one might call them simply ''role-play situations'') are below.

For Adults or Teenagers

Sun Kim comes home from school all excited. Jeff, an Anglo-American boy, has asked her for a date. She tells her mother. Her mother is very upset.

"In Korea you do not do such thing,'' her mother reminds her.

"But, Mother, this is not Korea. This is America.''

"But we are Korean,'' her mother insists. ''You are Korean. This is not what we do. The time will be ready. Your father and I arrange a nice Korean man for you. We will not let you go alone with man.''

"Oh, Mother . . . but. . . . I''

For Preadolescents

"Look. I'm as big as you,'' Anita says to her brother John. She stretches up on her tiptoes. ''Why can't I go to the movie with you?''

"Look, Squirt, you stay home this time, okay. The movie is not for you because. . . .''

For Young Children

"Mom. Come here. Come here. The cat is stuck up in the tree. He won't come down. Come quick.''

Mother sticks her head around the door. ''Now just a minute, Sally. Don't panic. The first thing we'll do is. . . .''

It's important that the students be gradually worked into the above role-play situations. The teacher can get them into their roles by asking questions such as, "How old are you, Anita? What kinds of movies do your parents want you to see?" When the students seem to feel comfortable in their roles, the teacher can reread the situation and let the actors take it at the point where the story leaves off.

Another activity for the more proficient students which can be adapted to various age groups is acting out roles of characters from literature. Literature can come alive when students play the role of a character with which they are familiar. For example, if they have just read *The Pearl* by John Steinbeck (1947), one student may want to play Juana and another Kino. The characters could be interviewed as they might be on the Johnny Carson show or they might be part of a panel discussion on what money and greed can do to one's life. In addition, people from history might be brought back to life for a day or two. For example, one student might play Abraham Lincoln and another Susan B. Anthony. After students read up on their lives and times, these characters can be brought together for a TV show such as Steve Allen's "Meeting of the Minds," popular during the 1970s. Other characters from history could be pitted against each other in a debate about a current topic. It would be interesting to see how Henry VIII might feel about divorce or how Joan of Arc might react to women's liberation issues.

Mid-beginners also can participate in role play. Tools for communication can be taught through role-play situations. Students can be given matrices on index cards to be used as cues. Short scenes can begin with total-physical-response activities in which the teacher plays the role of the director and directs students in their parts (move to the right, sit down, walk to the table, say, "Are you ready to order?"—see also page 79). Matrices such as those below can be tailored to fit different situations. It is suggested that similar matrices first be incorporated into jazz chants and lyrics (see Chapter 8).

In a restaurant:

(Menus are given to two customers by the waiter.)
Are you ready to order?
Yes, I will have the _____.
And you? (looks at the second person)
I will have the _____.

At a produce store:

(A clerk is setting out baskets of strawberries. A customer approaches from behind.)
Excuse me. Can you please tell me where the _____ is/are?
Oh, yes. It's/they're by the _____.
Thank you.

Typical greetings, simple compliments, frequently asked questions, and often-used comments can be introduced or reinforced in this manner. Other public places can be simulated to serve as settings (a post office, a doctor's office, a library, a hospital). Eventually the students can simply be given an oral description of a situation (no cue cards this time) to which they can respond through role play.

You are in a restaurant. The waiter comes to take your order. You look at the menu and tell the waiter what you want.

You are in a produce store. You can't find what you want to buy. You ask the clerk for help.

The most beneficial kind of role play, however, is that in which the *teacher plays a key role*. For example, if the teacher *is* the waiter in the restaurant or the clerk in the produce store, he or she can provide comprehensible input to extend the conversation. The teacher can prompt, expand, or offer help as needed. By this means groups of mixed abilities can be included in the same role-play situation. Starters are offered to some, explanations provided to others, and others are given no help at all if they don't need it. Below is an illustration to show how this can work.

At a produce store— (The students have been given play money and have had prior experience counting it.)

Pedro stands in front of the strawberries.

TEACHER (or teacher assistant) playing the role of the clerk: Strawberries? For you, Pedro? (She holds up a basket of them.)

PEDRO: aaa . . . Straw . . .

TEACHER: Strawberries? Do you want strawberries?

PEDRO: . . . Strawberries . . . (nods his head)

TEACHER (offering the basket to him): Do you want *to buy* the strawberries? Yes? (points to some play money in the box which serves as a cash register)

PEDRO: Yes . . . buy.

TEACHER: One dollar. Give me one dollar. (Pedro takes some play money from his pocket but looks puzzled.)

TEACHER: One dollar (points to a dollar bill in his hand).

PEDRO: One dollar (gives the teacher the dollar bill).

TEACHER: Thank you (takes the money and gives him the basket).

PEDRO: Thank you.

TEACHER (turning to the next customer): Do you want some strawberries, Nor?

NOR: I want oranges.

TEACHER: Oranges, huh (moves to the oranges). I've got juicy ones for you.

NOR: Juicy?

TEACHER: Yes. Juicy. Lots of sweet juice (squeezes one to show its softness).

NOR: Oh, yes. Juice.

TEACHER: They cost $1.50 a bag. Do you want a bag?

NOR: Yes. I'll take bag (gives the teacher the money and takes the oranges).

Thus the teacher is able to adjust the input to fit the approximate level of each student. *No cue cards are needed.* With sufficient input the students will begin to acquire the structures through the interaction.

DRAMA

To some it may seem artificial to make drama a separate category since it is an integral part of storytelling and role play. However, for the sake of clarity we will use this term for activities with roles, plots, and dialogues that are written down in play form to be memorized and acted out on the stage or read aloud. Some of the introductory activities recommended here can be used as warm-ups for storytelling and role play as well.

At beginning levels students can first be introduced to the simple emotions involved in dramatic action. The teacher or teacher assistant can model the emotions, using exaggerated facial expressions and other movements to illustrate words such as joy, anger, fear, sadness, and doubt. Students can model the emotions themselves as a group (see also "Identifying Emotions" in the Total Physical Response section of Chapter 6). They can refine their abilities to recognize and reproduce emotions by learning to draw them. (See Figure 9.1.) For further reinforcement, they can find pictures in magazines of people expressing specific feelings. The pictures may be cut out and pasted in a book of emotions (one page can be labeled "Joy," another "Fear," another "Anger," and so forth).

Later when the students are a little more proficient, each can be asked to write the name of an emotion on a piece of paper to be put into a grab bag. Each student will then take an emotion from the grab bag and act it out while the rest of the class guesses which emotion is being portrayed. At another time the names of specific activities can be written on pieces of paper, and students can pantomime the activities while the class guesses what is being acted out.

Yet another technique is to choose a segment of a TV soap opera to put on videotape. Find one that you feel will interest your students. Show it without sound and let the students decide the emotions that the actors are feeling. Later you can show the same segment, again without sound, and let your

Figure 9.1 (adapted from Evans & Moore, 1982)

students figure out what they think is happening just from facial expressions and actions. Then replay the same segment and listen to the words. How close did the students come to guessing the reality? Discuss it with them. It is not necessary that they understand all the words this time. You may play it again in a few months and let them write and act out additional segments. Eventually, they may want to write and stage their own soap operas.

Students, particularly younger ones, can each make a puppet out of heavy construction paper and a tongue depressor, see Figure 9.2.[9] For the head, they can cut out two identical shapes from construction paper and staple the edges together, leaving an opening at the neck. Placing a small wad of newspaper inside gives the puppet a three-dimensional effect. They can then place the tongue depressor where the neck should be and staple the paper to it. Yarn can be used for hair. Eyes, a nose, and a mouth can be drawn with a felt-tip pen. The puppet can be given a name and can become part of a series of dramas or mini-scenarios which the students write and act out.

---

[9]This idea came from a handout distributed at a presentation by Susan Andrews during the Spring COTESOL Conference 1980, Denver, Colorado.

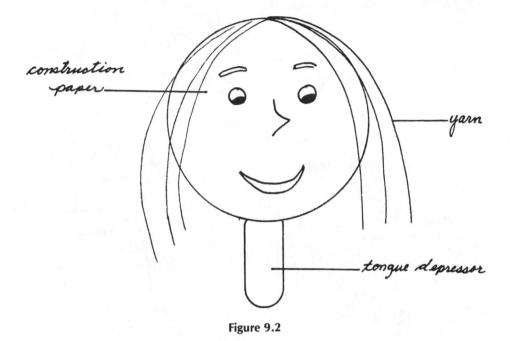

Figure 9.2

One alternative might be to have the students make flannel board characters to move about on a large flannel board.

Another activity (this one can be used during the upper elementary grades and later) is an adaptation of an idea called "The Prop Box," which comes from Winn-Bell Olsen.[10] Each student is asked to bring something from home that isn't wanted anymore. It can be from any room in the house but it must be something that the teacher can keep. All the items should be placed in a large box (the prop box). The class should be divided into groups of two, three, or four students. Each student is asked to reach into the prop box without looking and draw out an item. The groups then write short dramas or skits that incorporate all the items as props. The plays can be rehearsed with the help of peer teachers or lay assistants (see Chapter 12) and presented to the whole class.

Finally, Goodman and Tenney (1979) recommend readers' theater as a vehicle for acquiring a second language. The name "readers' theater" comes from the fact that the actors hold their scripts and read from them with expression and feeling. The actors and the narrator generally sit on tall stools

---

[10]She gives credit to the Creative Environment Center, SFUSD workshop for this suggestion. Prop boxes can be used to teach other lessons, particularly in conjunction with with the natural approach (see Chapter 7). For example, one box could include household items, another camping equipment, and so forth.

arranged in a semicircle in front of the audience. It might help them to imagine that the wall in back of the audience is a mirror. The actors talk directly to the ''images'' of the other characters rather than address them directly. In fact, they more or less ignore the presence of the other characters except as they appear in the ''mirror.'' Characters who are supposed to be offstage also sit on stools, but keep their backs to the audience, facing the audience only upon their entrances. The narrator, who addresses the audience directly, plays a large role: he or she sets the scene, introduces the characters, and gives running comments about actions, feelings, and moods. In other words, the narrator provides the glue that holds the dialogue together and makes it comprehensible.

Because readers' theater involves a great deal of repetition as students are rehearsing a presentation, the words become part of the students' repertoires without conscious memorization. The whole class, even the audience, begins to internalize the lines. Reading also can be enhanced if members of the audience are able to look at the scripts as the lines are being read. Goodman and Tenney feel that creating a script and putting on a play can be a good culminating activity for almost any unit of study. Through it, concepts and structures can be acquired or reinforced. However, they recommend teaching the techniques of readers' theater through a prepared script first. Below is a sample.

An Unusual Birthday Celebration

NARRATOR: It is midafternoon. Two elderly women and a dog are on the sidewalk. They are in front of the ice cream store on Twenty-second Street.

MABEL: Well, Nettie, what will we get today?

NARRATOR: She smiles at Nettie. Their eyes are dancing.

NETTIE: I want something very special today . . . something new.

NARRATOR: Nettie tugs at her dog's leash.

NETTIE: Now you be a good boy and lie down.

NARRATOR: She points to the sidewalk in front of the glass door. The dog lies down obediently. The two women go into the store.

MABEL: Something new? You're going to try something new? You always want the same old thing. A chocolate cone with one scoop. You always get that.

NETTIE: But today I want something special. Today is my birthday, you know. Seventy-six years old.

NARRATOR: She looks at all the pictures on the wall. There are ice cream sundaes everywhere. Chocolate and caramel drip from them. They are covered with nuts, whipped cream, and cherries. Her mouth waters. Mabel says. . . .

MABEL: Did you hear from your son today? Did he wish you a happy birthday?

NARRATOR: Mabel's hands flutter in the air. Nettie's smile fades.

NETTIE: No. I'm afraid he hasn't. . . .

CLERK: What will you have, Ma'am?

NETTIE: I think I'll have that. . . .

NARRATOR: She points to a caramel sundae.

NETTIE: I'll have . . . that caramel sundae . . . with whipped cream and nuts. No cherry, please. I'm allergic to cherries. They give me hives.

CLERK: Yes, Ma'am. Right away.

NARRATOR: She turns to look at Mabel. She catches a glimpse of the glass door and the sidewalk outside. Something is wrong. Her eyes open very wide. She screams. . . .

NETTIE: My dog. Where's my dog?

NARRATOR: She runs out the door. She looks up and down the street. But she can't find him. She calls and calls. . . .

NETTIE: He-re Lad-die. He-re Lad-die.

NARRATOR: . . . in a high voice. A stranger comes out from behind the building.

STRANGER: Ma'am, is this the dog you're looking for? He's right here eating ice cream. A little boy dropped his cone. . . .

NARRATOR: Nettie runs around to the side of the building. Sure enough, there in front of her is the dog. He is lapping up the last bit of ice cream from the ground. He makes slurping sounds. Nettie is overcome with joy. She says. . . .

NETTIE: Oh, my Laddie. Thank goodness he's safe.

NARRATOR: She rushes over and hugs him. The dog is now licking his chops. Mabel is right behind her.

NETTIE: Oh, my sweet Laddie.

MABEL: I guess he wants something special on your birthday too. Just like a dog, you know. They all think they're people. Come on, let's get our ice cream. I don't have all day, you know.

NARRATOR: The three of them head back to the door of the ice cream store.

Goodman and Tenney suggest that the teacher first have selected students read the dialogue aloud and then ask the audience what they think was especially effective about the way it was read. Then the teacher can discuss the drama with the students to create interest in the problems of the characters. The teacher as director should model the roles with much enthusiasm to encourage the students to put aside some of their own inhibitions. Then the students should read the parts one more time with added expression and feeling. The audience might then be called on for suggestions which might include the addition of various sound effects or other elements. All the students should be made to feel that they are part of the drama in some way.

Later, students might be encouraged to write and perform their own scripts based on pictures or other forms of mental stimulation (musical lyrics, poetry, television shows, etc.). The productions can then become whole-class projects from beginning to end.

SUMMARY

Storytelling, role play, and drama, through their attention to human experience, can involve students in highly motivating activity. Because students can lose themselves in the characters, plots, and situations, they are more apt to receive the benefits of reduced anxiety levels, increased self-confidence and esteem, and heightened awareness.

Even beginning students can enjoy the pleasures of dramatic action right from the start. They can join in on the prelanguage activities or warm-ups, "Story Experience" and various other physical responses, sound effect production, or simple recognition of emotional states.

As they progress, the students can improve their abilities to comprehend and later produce the target language, and can learn to work cooperatively in group situations toward mutual goals. Eventually students can spin their own tales, interpret stories, deal with problems through sociodrama, and write, read aloud, and even produce mini-dramas.

READINGS, REFLECTION, AND DISCUSSION

Suggested Readings and Reference Materials

Lewis, S. (1985). *One-minute favorite fairy tales*. Garden City, NY: Doubleday. These short versions of well-known fairy tales maintain their original appeal to youngsters, in particular. "Sleeping Beauty," "Little Red Riding Hood," "Rapunzel," and "Snow White and the Seven Dwarfs" are among the stories in the collection.

Maley, A., & Duff, A. (1983). *Drama techniques in language learning: A resource book of communication activities for language teachers.* Cambridge: Cambridge University. Presents a useful selection of dramatic activities for the language classroom. The authors are careful to point out that their book is not about putting on plays for audiences. In fact, many of the activities appear to have little to do with dramatic performance. Instead, they are dramatic in that they pique our curiosity and interest by capitalizing on the unpredictable events that can occur when people are placed in contact with one another.

Markstein, L., & Grunbaum, D. (1981). *What's the story?* New York: Longman. Each of the twelve picture sets (four pictures per set) included in this package can be arranged to tell many stories. The way each story evolves depends upon how the pictures are arranged and upon the imaginations of the students writing or telling the story.

Scarcella, R. (1983). Sociodrama for social interaction. In Oller and Richard-Amato, *Methods that work,* pp. 239–245. A discussion of the ways in which sociodrama can be used to teach the target language. Activities include the enactment of solutions to social problems.

Questions for Reflection and Discussion

1. How might dramatic experiences help to make the ego more "permeable" in the sense that Guiora uses the term? (See Chapter 5.)

2. What might be some advantages to the language acquisition process of drama that has been improvised by the students over drama written by playwrights to be memorized by actors (the students)? Any disadvantages? What about advantages and disadvantages of preparation for an actual performance before audiences? Is it better, for example, for the students simply to perform for themselves and each other?

3. DiPietro (1983) points out that a scenario that is appropriate in one culture may be inappropriate in another. What role should cultural constraints play in your selection of content? What might be the consequences if such constraints are ignored? Give examples.

4. Plan a lesson using storytelling, role play, or drama. Be specific about the age levels and proficiency levels of the students with whom you might use it (beginning, intermediate, or advanced). Share the lesson with members of your class and get their feedback.

10

Games

Game playing, having apparently originated as a form of instruction, now appears again to be coming into its own as an instructional activity.

T. Rodgers, 1978

Games are often associated with fun. While it is true that games *are* usually fun, one must not lose sight of their pedagogical value, particularly in second language teaching. Like most of the other activities recommended in this book, games can lower anxiety, thus making the acquisition of input more likely. In addition, they are often highly motivating, relevant, interesting, and comprehensible.

Games are sometimes used in classrooms to develop and reinforce concepts (e.g., colors, shapes, numbers, word definitions), to add diversion to the regular classroom activities, and even to break the ice, particularly in the case of rank beginners. Occasionally they are used to introduce new ideas. Perhaps their most important function, however, is to give practice in communication skills. Although some are quiet, contemplative games, others are noisy and require much verbal or physical involvement. Some are meant for small groups, others for large groups. Often classes can be divided into smaller units and several games can be played simultaneously. The teacher, peer teachers, or lay assistants (see Chapter 12) can facilitate in the individual groups.

The games recommended here may involve a certain amount of group competition, but competition is generally not the focus (except perhaps in some of the nonverbal games). Games in which individuals may be singled out and embarrassed in front of large groups of peers are avoided.

It is important that the rules of the games be very few and clearly explained. In some cases students can begin the games and have the rules explained as the game progresses. Demonstrations also can be very helpful.

Most of the games discussed below can be adapted to any age level, provided students are cognitively able to handle the content. In addition, most can be adapted to several proficiency levels (beginning, intermediate, or advanced) according to the difficulty of the tasks involved. None of the games requires large outlays of money. Usually the materials needed can be easily collected or made by the teacher or an assistant.

Even though the categories often overlap, the games are divided into the following types depending on their emphasis: nonverbal games, board-advancing games, word-focus games, treasure hunts, and guessing games.

NONVERBAL GAMES

Games such as relays or musical chairs can help students become acquainted with each other, even before they can speak. Used sparingly, they can serve as ice breakers and can be used to bring together students of mixed levels. After hearing the directions for a specific game given in the target language, the more proficient students of various language backgrounds might be able to translate the directions into the L1 of other, less proficient students.

Nonverbal games can also be used to form groups for other games and activities. For example, at Christmas time, trees may be made of construction paper and cut into puzzle pieces to be matched (Figure 10.1). The number of trees will depend on how many groups are necessary for the game that is to follow and on how many students are in the class. For example, if the class is going to play classroom scrabble (described later in this chapter) and 14 students need to be divided into four teams, four trees will be necessary (two trees will be cut into three puzzle pieces and two into four puzzle pieces). The students will each draw a puzzle piece out of the grab bag and find the students who have the missing pieces to make a complete tree. Thus a group is formed. The same can be done with hearts on Valentine's Day, pumpkins on Halloween, shamrocks on St. Patrick's Day, and so on. Another alternative is to cut several pictures (one for each group desired) into puzzle pieces, mix them up, and have each student take one piece and find the other people with the pieces that will complete the picture. (For more ideas about forming groups, see pages 76 and 161–162.)

BOARD-ADVANCING GAMES

Using game pieces (such as buttons or little plastic cars) to represent the players, students can perform certain tasks or simply roll the dice to move forward

Figure 10.1

a certain number of spaces. The board itself can be as imaginative and colorful as the teacher wants to make it. The spaces must form some sort of pathway from a starter point to an end point which is the goal, as in Figure 10.2.

Students might also take turns drawing cards with specific commands on them (jump three times, write your name on the chalkboard, sing a song from your country). Once the student has completed the task (other students can help in interpreting and carrying out the command), he or she can move forward the number of spaces indicated on the card. Additional tasks can include giving synonyms or antonyms for specific words, identifying objects on pictures, doing simple math computations, or any kind of task that will reinforce what the teacher wants the students to learn. The "winner" is the one who reaches the goal first.

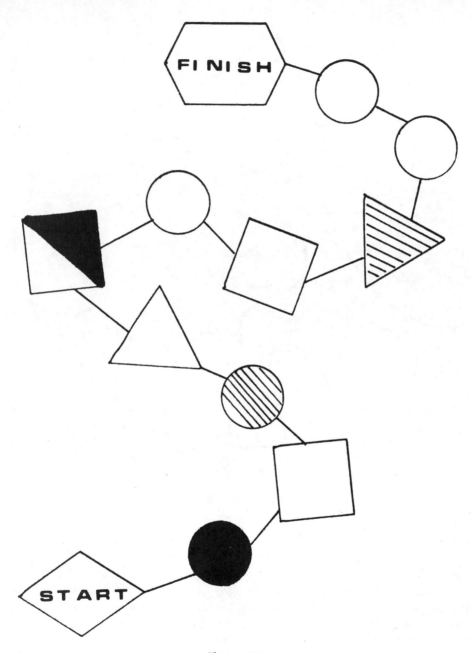

Figure 10.2

WORD-FOCUS GAMES

Students can be given words to see how many other words they can make from them. For example, the following words can be made from the word *teacher:* ear, her, teach, reach, cheer, each, hear, here, arch, tea, eat, and so forth. By working with others in a team situation, the student can learn new words from the other members in the group. Group competition to see which group can make the most words in a certain time period may add to the excitement and probably will not raise anxiety levels since no individuals are put on the spot.

An alternative activity is to have teams of students see how many words they can make from a letter grid such as the one shown in Figure 10.3. Students must move along the connecting lines without skipping any letters. A single letter cannot be used twice in succession but can be returned to if there

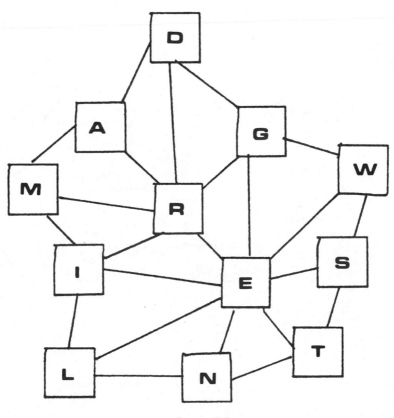

Figure 10.3

is an intervening letter. For example, in Figure 10.3 *regret* is acceptable but *greet* is not.

The bean bag toss suggested by Evans and Moore (1979) can be adapted to teach antonyms, synonyms, or categories of words. They suggest that the teacher make a large playing area on tagboard with a felt tip pen. The teacher draws circles all over the area, and puts one word in each circle (see Figure 10.4). The teacher should make sure that each word has its opposite (if work-

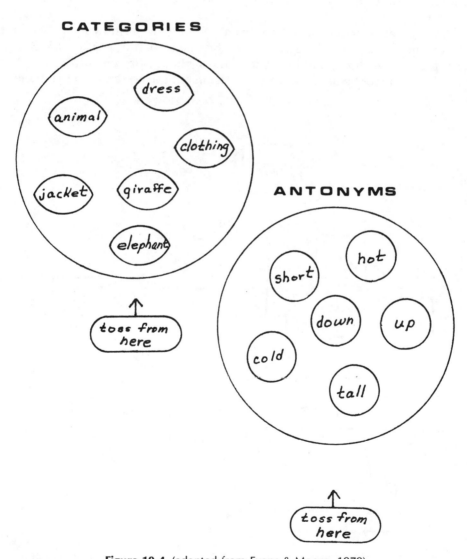

Figure 10.4 (adapted from Evans & Moore, 1979)

ing on antonyms), that each word has a corresponding word that means the same thing (if working on synonyms), or that each word has a corresponding category to which it belongs (if working on categories). The student stands behind a line that has been marked with masking tape and tosses a bean bag. After reading the word on which the bag lands, the student takes a second bean bag and tries to toss it so it will land on the antonym, synonym, or a category member.

Classroom scrabble[1] is a particularly effective word-focus game. Students are divided into teams, three to four students per team. A scrabble board is drawn on the chalkboard (see Figure 10.5). Notice that some squares have been shaded in; letters placed on the shaded areas receive double their normal count. Two to four teams are given letters cut from index cards (four consonants and three vowels per team), on which point values have been written—lower point values for frequently used letters, higher point values for the rest. The teacher begins by writing a message in the middle of the board, such as "Peace." The students must build their words off the letters in the message. Scotch tape is rolled up and put behind each letter to make it stick to the chalkboard (later the tape can be removed so the same letters can be used again). The teams take turns, making as many words as they can. All words must connect to a word already on the board, either horizontally or vertically. Each team's letters are replaced after the turns, a vowel for a vowel and a consonant for a consonant. They are drawn at random by a team mem-

Figure 10.5

---

[1] I wish to thank Deborah Floyd for this game idea.

ber from a reserve guarded by the teacher. To keep the game moving, it is a good idea to place a time limit of about two or three minutes to complete a turn.

One commonly used word-focus game that I choose to avoid is "scrambled word." The students are given words with the letters scrambled. They are supposed to unscramble them to form the intended word. For example, "cesenic" can be unscrambled to form "science." Although native speakers might find this fun, second language students tend to find such games frustrating. To most of them, the language may appear to be "scrambled" to begin with, so it seems senseless to cause them additional anxiety.

TREASURE HUNTS

A treasure hunt is a favorite game among second language learners. It allows them to work cooperatively in a group effort to find the items required. At the same time communicative competence can be increased. Often the items will call for a group consensus. For example, the students may have to find something beautiful, so they have to agree on what is beautiful. Condon (1983) suggests that the following steps (paraphrased below) be taken in organizing a treasure hunt. The hunt can take anywhere from ten minutes to an entire day, depending on the number and kinds of items listed.

1. Divide the class into groups of from three to six members.
2. Give an identical list of treasures to each group.
3. Read the items aloud for children or less proficient students to make sure they understand the vocabulary.
4. A time limit should be given.
5. Say "Go" to indicate when the groups can begin their searches.
6. At the end of the time limit, or when the first group returns, everyone gets together to check each item, giving points (five points are suggested) for each completed item. Points are taken away for incompleted ones.

Here are a few of the more interesting tasks in which Condon involves her students.

1. List five countries the members of your group would like to visit.
2. What is the largest shoe size in your group?
3. Find something useless.
4. Make a dinner menu in English.
5. Find a photograph.
6. Collect the autographs of three people not in your group.

7. Find something that smells good.
8. Make a crazy hat for your teacher.
9. Write down six ways of making people laugh.
10. Find a picture of something good to eat.

GUESSING GAMES

Guessing games can be painless ways to develop or reinforce any number of concepts. "Guess What I Am" or "Guess Who I Am," for example, can be used to teach about animals, professions, or people in different age groups (baby, child, teenager, young adult, middle-aged adult, elderly person). Each student can pantomime a particular role, and the class guesses which role is being acted out. The student who guesses the role correctly is "it" and takes the next turn. A time limit should be set so not too much attention is devoted to any one person.

"Guess What I'm Doing" can be used to teach recognition in the target language of activities such as taking a bath, going fishing, doing homework, and so forth. "Guess What I Have" is even more focused on verbalization. The student gives verbal hints as to what object is being described, or the students ask questions about the object (as in "Twenty Questions"). The object may be hidden or in full view. It is important that the class not know the name of the object beforehand.

Alternatives include "Whose Name Is It?" or "What Am I?" In either case, one person is "it," and a sign, which the person cannot see, is placed on his or her back. On the sign has been written the name of a classmate (see page 103) or the name of a specific occupation. The person with the sign asks "yes or no" questions of the class until the correct response is arrived at. (Do I wear a hat? Do I climb ladders?) The students take turns being "it."

Games come in many different forms and can be gathered from a variety of sources: books on the subject, young people's magazines, department store game sections. However, one important source that must not be overlooked is the second language students themselves. Having students share games from their countries or cultural backgrounds can be a very exciting experience for everyone and can provide many opportunities for practice with the target language.

SUMMARY

Games can be used to develop or reinforce concepts, to add diversion to the regular classroom activities, or just to break the ice. However, their most important function is to give practice in communication.

It is recommended that competition be downplayed for most games, that the rules be few, and that they be clearly explained and demonstrated where possible.

Although the categories can overlap, the games offered here are divided basically into the following types depending on their emphasis: nonverbal games, board-advancing games, word-focus games, treasure hunts, and guessing games.

Various sources for game ideas are mentioned, but teachers are reminded that one of the best sources is the students themselves.

READINGS, REFLECTION, AND DISCUSSION

Suggested Readings and Reference Materials

Grunfeld, F. (Ed.). (1975). *Games of the world*. Versailles, KY: Rand McNally. A colorful collection of illustrated games from a variety of cultures. Contains information on the history of the games and on how to create the necessary game pieces and materials. Includes Chinese "Rope-kicking," Japanese "Go," and many others. Some are suitable for the classroom; others require space out of doors.

McCallum, G. (1980). *101 word games*. Oxford: Oxford University. This explicit, easy-to-use book includes word games that can aid students in developing proficiency in the target language. Activities involve listening practice, conversation, spelling, and vocabulary building. Helpful suggestions accompany the game descriptions.

Oller, J., & Richard-Amato, P. (Eds.). (1983). Fun and games (Part VI). In *Methods that work*. Rowley, MA: Newbury House. Additional games not included in this chapter are described: Berkeley-Wykes' jigsaw reading, Leong's debate activity, and Rinvolucri's action mazes.

Wright, A., Betteridge, D., & Buckby, M. (1984). *Games for language learning*. Cambridge: Cambridge University. A wide array of language games is presented that can be used to teach many different target languages and can be quite easily adapted to various age levels.

Questions for Reflection and Discussion

1. Form a set of criteria that you might use in the selection of a game for classroom use. Give examples of games that might or might not fit particular situations based on the criteria you have developed.

2. How can a game such as a treasure hunt be used to reinforce the teaching of a story? Choose a particular story, describe the story, and tell what "treasures" you might incorporate in order to reinforce the concepts.

3. Recall a favorite game that you played as a child. How might it be adapted to a second language class?

4. Select several topics for use with the natural approach or its extensions (see Chapter 7). Find and adapt, or create, two or three games that you could use to reinforce each topic. Try one game out on members of your class. To what extent was it successful?

11

Affective Activities

When given the opportunity to talk about themselves in personally relevant ways, students tend to become much more motivated. The result is that they want to be able to express their feelings and ideas more in the target language. They want *to communicate. When this happens, growth becomes a reciprocal process: enhancing personal growth enhances growth in the foreign language.*

G. Moskowitz, 1978

BACKGROUND INFORMATION AND DESCRIPTION

Many of the affective activities found in this chapter have grown, either directly or indirectly, from an earlier interest in values clarification. Raths, Merrill, and Simon (1966) asserted that valuing is made up of three categories of subprocesses: prizing beliefs and behaviors, choosing beliefs and behaviors, and acting on beliefs. The approach that they recommended did not include the inculcation of any specific set of values. Instead the aim was to help students work through the process of valuing in order to reach a clarification of what it was that gave meaning to their lives. It was felt that exploring beliefs that had already formed and those that were emerging could be a very rewarding experience for students of all ages and could greatly enhance their self-esteem and confidence.

Many teachers today feel that, for second language learners, especially those at intermediate to advanced proficiency levels, affective activities (including values clarification) can add another dimension to the language learning process. If used appropriately by an impartial, accepting teacher, such activities not only can provide meaningful dialogue in the target language, but can serve as an important means of bonding between students. This can be particularly important in ESL classes in which many different values systems are brought together (see Chapter 5). An environment that fosters an appreciation of differences tends to encourage individual growth and decrease hostility.

It must be pointed out, however, that in spite of their potential benefits, affective activities are not for everyone. They are not for the teacher who feels uncomfortable with sharing feelings and opinions. They are not for the teacher who wants to treat them as therapy sessions, although, as Moskowitz (1978) points out, they may be therapeutic. And they are certainly not for the teacher who wants to use them as a way to change the beliefs of others.

If they are to be effective for language teaching, they must be used by a teacher who has read in depth (see suggested readings) or who has completed a training program. Moreover, the activities chosen must be compatible with the students' age and proficiency levels, and they must be appropriate to the cultural environment in which they are to be used. In some cultures it is considered offensive to reveal oneself or to probe the thoughts of others.

For the teacher who decides to implement affective activities, Moskowitz lays down a few ground rules: students must be given the right to pass, meaning they must not be forced to answer questions or contribute; they must have the right to be heard; and they must have the right to see their own opinions respected (no put-downs are allowed). She recommends further that the students have a chance to express afterwards how they felt about specific activities and what they learned from them.

In addition Moskowitz advises that the activities accentuate the positive and that they be of low risk so that the teacher and students will not feel threatened by them. In other words, instead of asking students what they dislike about themselves, ask them what they like; rather then asking them what they feel guilty about, ask them what makes them feel proud. Of course, negative feelings cannot be denied when they do arise. They should be treated like any other feelings, unless, of course, they are used to diminish someone else. At the same time, it must be remembered that not all the items in the activities can be positive in all respects. For example, we may want to ask students what they would want changed in the world or how something might be made better in their lives. What Moskowitz is saying, I believe, is that the overall focus should be positive in that it is constructive.

Although there appears to be some disagreement in the literature (Simon, Howe, & Kirschenbaum, 1972; Galyean, 1976, 1982; Moskowitz, 1978) as to the role of the teacher in the affective activities, all seem to agree that the chief duty is one of facilitator. As facilitator, the teacher needs to encourage honest responses, to establish an aura of trust, to listen with genuine interest to what the students say, and to invite sharing but only what students want

to share. Furthermore, the teacher should clarify what they say by responding with questions such as "Is this what you're saying?" and by paraphrasing
what has been said with statements such as "I think your saying. . . . " In
addition, the authors all seem to agree that the teacher should be free to reveal his or her feelings and opinions in the discussions. However, Simon,
Howe, and Kirschenbaum believe that these revelations should occur only at
certain times.

> The best time for the teacher to give his view is toward the end, after the
> students have had a chance to think things through for themselves and to
> express their own points of view. The teacher should present himself as a
> person with values (and often with values confusion) of his own. Thus the
> teacher shares his values, but does not impose them. In this way, he presents
> the class with a model of an adult who prizes, chooses and acts according to
> the valuing process. The teacher gets a chance to share his actual values as
> does any other member of the class. The particular content of his values holds
> no more weight than would anyone else's (1972, pp. 26–27).

On the basis of my own experience with affective activities, I agree that
it is important for the students to realize that teachers,[1] like other people, are
engaged in the valuing process themselves. However, it may be naive to think
that the teacher's point of view can be downplayed to the extent that it holds
no more weight than anyone else's, particularly when the teacher is acting
as a facilitator. The problem then appears to be how teachers can make it
known that they are developing and refining their own values without their
belief systems' having an undue influence on the students. Perhaps the answer lies in how we view a *facilitator's role* as opposed to a *participant's role.*
It is my opinion that the teacher should not attempt to be a facilitator *and* a
participant simultaneously. As a facilitator, the teacher should remain objective throughout the activity. It is the facilitator's job to prepare and lead the
students into a particular activity, to enforce the ground rules, to listen
thoughtfully and nonjudgmentally, to clarify, to accept each student as he or
she wants to be accepted, and to provide transitions as well as closures at the
end of each activity.

The participant's role also includes listening thoughtfully and nonjudgmentally, clarifying others' ideas, and accepting others on their own ground,
but it does not require that one remain impartial. A participant has the right
to state his or her opinions and feelings about the subject as long as others'
rights to opinions are respected.

In order for the teacher to be in a position where his or her ideas can find
expression without being given undue weight, a switching of roles generally
needs to take place. The teacher can become a participant on occasion and

---

[1] When I use the word *teachers* here, I also mean peer teachers and lay assistants if they are
included in the program (see Chapter 12).

volunteer students can become facilitators (somewhat akin to the dialectical relationship between student and teacher described by Freire in Chapter 3). This role switch provides a chance for teachers and students to maximize the benefits of the activities and creates a great deal of excitement and motivation for students when they realize that they too can take on the responsibility of being facilitators.

There are also other ways in which a teacher can express opinions without being overly imposing. For example, the teacher can step down from the role of facilitator without reversing roles. However, it may be prudent to do this only when the students ask for the teacher's opinion on a certain issue of interest and only *after* students have had a chance to express themselves fully, as Simon, Howe, and Kirschenbaum suggest. The teacher also may want to use himself or herself as an example in a demonstration as part of the preliminary instructions, especially if the issue involved is not a controversial one.

Affective activities can be used in the classroom at almost any time. However, there are some situations in which they can be particularly beneficial. On days when students are feeling especially tense or somewhat down emotionally, such activities can have comforting effects. For example, when tensions seem to be very high, before final exams or other somewhat threatening events, the teacher can attempt an overt enhancement of self-concepts. Seating the students in a circle and having them concentrate on one person at a time, each member of the group including the teacher can say one thing they especially like about that person. During the session someone (perhaps an advanced student) can record on separate sheets of paper what is said about each person so that the students can go home at the end of the day with the comments in writing (Richard-Amato, 1983).

On lighter occasions the teacher may want to center on a theme such as ''exploring career options'' with teenagers and adults or ''choosing a pet'' with children. In addition there are times when a particular activity is very compatible with what is being discussed in reaction to a story, song, or poem (described later in this chapter). For instance, if a character in a story being studied has to decide between marrying for love and marrying for money, an affective activity on related choices might be in order. In this way the content of the various genres can be related to the lives of the students. Flexibility helps the teacher recognize these moments and take advantage of them in a way that will maximize the benefits of each activity. Particularly at advanced levels, the teacher may want to use several activities to stimulate thought for writing assignments. Similar activities may also serve as appropriate means for culminating library research.

Most of the activities presented in this chapter are for small groups (two, three, or any number up to ten). Groups can be formed by many different means. Students can be grouped sociometrically. The teacher can have students write down the names of students with whom they feel most comfortable. After collecting their papers, the teacher can plan what might be some workable groups. In an ESL class the teacher might want to have the various cultures represented in each group. In addition, the teacher might want to make the act of grouping an affective activity in itself by setting up groups on the basis of favorite colors, seasons, foods, and the like. For example, the teacher might say, "Today we will have four groups. The group to which you belong will be determined by your favorite season of the year. All people who like fall come to this table; spring to that table. . . . "Or random units might be formed by simply having the students number off. The method used for forming groups depends on the activity chosen, the number of groups needed for the activity, the number of students in the class, and/or whether or not the groups need to be of equal numbers (see also pages 76 and 148).

Most of the activities suggested in this chapter are intended for intermediate to advanced levels although some, particularly those recommended in the next section, can be accomplished with beginners. It should be kept in mind that most of the activities can be modified to accommodate several different proficiency levels and can quite easily be adapted to various age groups simply by changing the content (see Chapter 12). Many of the questions and statements used as examples in the exercises that follow are oriented toward the interests of teenagers and adults. However, they can be changed to reflect the interests of children. Topics appropriate to children might include: animals, toys, being the youngest or oldest in the family, discipline at home, holidays such as Halloween and Valentine's Day, TV cartoons, allowances, what you want to be when you grow up, and so forth. The activities must always be tailored to the needs, interests, and capabilities of the students. In addition, they must be activities with which the teacher feels comfortable.

PREPARATION OF THE STUDENTS

It is important at beginning stages of langauge development to expose students to some of the basic vocabulary that will be particularly useful for the affective activities later on: emotions, feelings, favorite things to do, preferences in foods, colors, clothing, occupations, classes, and so forth. These can be taught through several of the methods presented in previous chapters. For example, using the total physical response, students can be introduced to emotions by having them demonstrated and by being asked to display them (to cry, to laugh, etc.); to foods by preparing various foods according to directions; to clothing by putting on and taking off sweaters, jackets, and other garments; to colors by manipulating objects of various colors. Through discussion, students can hear and talk about these same concepts. During warm-ups for role play, they can have similar notions reinforced.

As the students move into the early speech production stage, they can begin to express feelings and preferences through an activity such as one of the jazz chants described in Chapter 8. The students can be asked to supply the missing words. Once the beat has been established by snapping of the fingers, the teacher begins and the students follow suit: "My name is _____, and I feel _____ (happy, sad, tired, etc.)" or "My name is _____ and I like _____ (apples, pizza, movies, dancing, to read, etc.)."

Eventually, as the student begins to move into the speech emergence stage, the vocabulary becomes a little more sophisticated. Words such as *beautiful, stubborn, smart, safe,* and *selfish* may have become part of the student's repertoire, although several of these words may have appeared sooner. As the student approaches full communication, he or she may pick up such words and phrases as *self-confident, self-conscious, ridiculous, secure, spiteful, stimulated, enthusiastic, open-minded, to know oneself,* and *to lay it on the line.* Many similar words and structures commonly used in expressing feelings and opinions will come naturally through participation in the affective activities themselves. There may be times, however, when the teacher may want to provide supplementary vocabulary and perhaps even some open-ended sentences (Moskowitz calls them "stems") to reinforce certain vocabulary and structures by building exercises around them:

> If I were older, I would. . . .
> One thing I do well is. . . .
> I want my friends to. . . .
> I wonder if. . . .
> I like you because. . . .
> My brother (sister) makes me feel. . . .
> People seem to respect me when I. . . .
> People can't force me to. . . .
> One thing I like about my family is that. . . .
> When people tease me, I. . . .
> If I could have one wish come true, I would wish for. . . .

In addition, students should be encouraged to get assistance when attempting to share something that is temporarily beyond them rather than simply to pass. Thus they will expand their repertoires even more. Students should be invited to consult with more proficient peers or with the teacher. Thus, others can serve as counselors similar to those used in conjunction with Curran's counseling learning approach.[2]

---

[2]Curran (1972) describes an approach whereby the teacher or others proficient in the target language serve as counselors and linguistic models for the students (see pages 371–372 in the Related Readings). At the beginning the students are completely dependent on the counselors, who help them translate their utterances from L1 to L2. As they become more and more proficient in the new language, they eventually reach complete independence.

If intermediate to advanced students seem reluctant to use affective activities, it may be a good idea to start with activities involving characters in literature. For instance, one might have the students read a story with well-developed characters and have them role-play the characters, revealing what they think the character's values might be. It is easy then to slip into a "and what would you have chosen in this situation?" kind of activity. For example, the students may be reading about a couple who fight because one wants to buy an expensive home, own a flashy car, and take frequent trips to Europe whereas the other would rather live moderately, drive a simple car that runs well, and vacation in the Sierras in a camper. Students can participate in affective activities while role-playing the characters. Once comfortable in pretend situations, they may be ready to do the same activities without role play. An alternative might be to have the students make up a story about the people in a picture shown to them and then role-play those characters while using appropriate affective activities. Once the students feel at ease when expressing feelings and preferences that belong to someone else, it may not seem so difficult to express their own.

Another aid for reluctant students (all students may be a little reluctant at first) is to warm up for each activity by beginning with issues not very close to the heart. For example, instead of asking, "Describe a moment when you were really embarrassed," the teacher might begin with something less personal, such as "Tell us about your favorite movie." Several of the ideas presented below may also serve as warm-ups to the other activities.

ACTIVITIES

Values Survey[3]

Students are asked questions and are given three or four choices from which to select the answer. Place the items on a ditto and distribute to the class. When giving the instructions, stress that *there are no right or wrong answers.*

Which would you rather be?
_____ an astronaut
_____ a business person
_____ a teacher
_____ a mechanic
_____ a social worker

---

[3]Adapted from Simon, Howe, and Kirschenbaum (1972, pp. 58–93).

If you had $2,000, what would you do with it?

_____ give most of it to some worthy cause

_____ put it in the bank or invest it

_____ buy a nice present for yourself

Where would you like to spend your vacation?

_____ by the ocean

_____ in New York City

_____ at a ski resort

_____ on a camping trip

Which is most important in choosing a spouse?

_____ looks

_____ personality

_____ interests

_____ values

What kind of gift do you prefer?

_____ something someone made

_____ money so you can buy something you want

_____ a gift that somebody buys for you

How would you most like to spend an afternoon with a friend?

_____ on a picnic in the mountains

_____ at the movies

_____ bowling

Which do you like least?

_____ a person who is loud and obnoxious

_____ a person who is dishonest

_____ a person who gossips

What would you most like to do alone?

_____ eat at a restaurant

_____ attend a party

_____ go to a movie

_____ visit the zoo

Which car would you buy if you could?

_____ a small, compact car

_____ a sports car

_____ a medium-sized, comfortable car

_____ a pickup truck

Which is most important to you?

_____ to plan for your future

_____ to show others that you care about them

_____ to get all the possessions you can

It is interesting to the students to complete the same survey several months later to see if their values have changed over the months.

The Search[4]

Place the following on a ditto and distribute to the students (see "The People Hunt" in Chapter 7 for a similar activity):

Find someone who . . . (write the name of the person in the blank following each item).

likes to go to libraries _____

has eaten okra _____

as been to a water polo game _____

would like to have a cat as a pet _____

saw a funny movie in the last week _____

is trying to break a habit _____

would like to be an actor _____

wants to take a trip to Mars some day _____

plays a guitar _____

went swimming recently _____

likes to tell jokes _____

owns a computer _____

can tap dance _____

Give the students about 5 minutes and then call time. Ask the whole class questions such as the following: Who likes to go to libraries? Who has eaten okra? and so forth.

An alternative might be to have the students take similar search sheets home to use with family members, neighbors, or friends.

Values Voting[5]

One sure way to get all the students involved in affective issues is to use this rapid-fire activity. Begin with the question "How many of you _____?" The blank can be filled in with items such as those below. Students raise their hands if the phrase is true of them.

have a dog

are afraid of storms

think parents should be stricter with their kids

do not like movies

enjoy loud music

---

[4]Adapted from Moskowitz (1978, pp. 50–52).

[5]Adapted from Simon, Howe, and Kirschenbaum (1972, pp. 38–57).

plan to go to college
have ever been in love
wear seat belts in the car
like to eat chocolate
disapprove of smoking cigarettes
want to end all wars
think school is exciting
work part time
want to get better grades in school
like to sing

My Favorite Possession

Have the students decide which objects in their households are the most valuable. Tell them to imagine that their houses are about to be destroyed by a natural disaster (earthquake, tornado, hurricane, or fire) and that they are each allowed to save only one thing (all humans and animals are already out of danger). What one thing would they save and why? Have them talk about their answers in small groups.

A Collage about Me

Give students several magazines out of which they can cut pictures. Have them paste pictures together on individual poster boards of things that are particularly revealing about themselves. Items can include favorite activities, colors, foods, clothes, products, sayings, poems, jokes, and so on. After dividing the students into groups of about six, have them talk about their collages and what each item reveals. The collages can then be hung around the room for all to see.

An interesting follow-up might be to have students find someone else's collage that comes closest to revealing their own values.

My Own Space

If the room is large enough, you might want to give each student (especially younger ones) some bulletin board space. Free-standing bulletin boards work well for this purpose. Each student can use the space for things that are important to him or her but that could be replaced if lost or damaged: favorite sayings, reprints of family pictures, art work, compositions, poetry, pictures from magazines. Students may want to rearrange their spaces from time to time and put up new things.

Pretend Pen Pals

Ask the students to pretend they are writing to pen pals for the first time. In the letters have them talk about such topics as their physical appearance, family, pastimes, favorite classes, and activities. Ask them to include questions they want to ask the person with whom they are corresponding. Divide them into groups of four, and have them share their letters. The group might want to suggest additions to each letter. A follow-up could be the real ''pen pal'' activity suggested in Chapter 7.

An alternative might be to have the students (particularly teenagers) describe themselves to a ''blind date.'' This could be done orally in small groups.

A Helping Hand[6]

With your assistance, the students can make two separate lists: one for the things they know how to do that they can teach others, the second for the things with which they want help (Figure 11.1). Collect these lists, choose those tasks that can be worked on in

Figure 11.1

[6]Adapted from Farnette, Forte, and Loss (1977, p. 25).

class, and give the students time to help and be helped as appropriate. The activity could be repeated at various times throughout the year and could involve many different tasks.

Students can follow up the activities by answering these questions:

What is one new thing I learned today?

Who helped me?

What would I like to learn tomorrow?

Who can help me?

What did I help someone do today?

You can get into the act if you wish. Learning from the students such things as how to fold paper birds Japanese style or how to count in Korean can be very challenging and exciting.

Dear Abiwail[7]

Tell the students to pretend that they are assistants to the famous personal advisor, Abiwail. Have them write answers to the following letters (these particular letters are oriented toward teenagers).

Dear Abiwail,

I can't seem to get this boy at school to talk to me. I try to get his attention by wearing clothes I think he will like and by saying things to attract him. Nothing seems to work. I did catch him staring at me one day but when I am near him, he ignores me. What can I do? I think I am in love with him.

Love Sick

Dear Abiwail,

Last week I did a terrible thing and I feel very guilty. In fact, I can't do my school work. I just think about what I did all the time. When I was in the hardware store near my house, I was looking at some tools. The next thing I knew, I put a small wrench in my pocket and walked out with it. No one saw me do it, but I feel just awful. My parents always taught me never to steal. How can I make myself feel better?

Guilty in Memphis

---

[7]Adapted from Farnette, Forte, and Loss (1977, p. 59).

Dear Abiwail,

I can't seem to make any friends. Everyone around me has many
friends and they laugh and talk all the time. But, me, I'm alone. I think
maybe I'm boring. I just can't think of anything interesting to talk about
when I'm with someone. I try to act cool so no one will know what I'm
really feeling. I think I'll go crazy if I can't have at least one friend.
Help me please.

Only the Lonely

The Most Influential Person

Have students decide which persons have affected their lives the most. Ask them to write
about these people and include information such as descriptions (they may have pictures
to share), how long they have known these people, and what these people did that made
such an impact. Divide them into groups to share their writings.

Reaching the Goal

Ask students to decide on a goal (either academic or social) and map their approach to
it, trying to anticipate possible obstacles (see Figure 11.2). Work out one to use as an
example. When the students have completed the exercise, divide them into small groups
for a discussion of their goals and the steps they will take to overcome the obstacles.

A Quote to Live By[8]

Have students choose a favorite quotation such as "To have a friend, you must be a
friend" or "If you love something, you must set it free." Provide a few books of quota-
tions from which the students can select their sayings, or give them the option of creating
their own. Make available felt tip pens with which to illustrate the sayings they have
chosen. Give each student a poster board which can later be displayed in the room.
Divide the class into small groups to discuss the meanings of their sayings. At the high
school or university level, the teacher might ask the students to develop effective paragraphs or essays using the quotes as topics (see also pages 202–204 for ways in which this
and similar activities might be carried out).

Journal Keeping

Daily journal entries are one means by which reactions, feelings, and experiences can
be recorded in the target language. Encourage the students to make "I" statements, such
as "I was angry when I found out that . . ." or "Today I knew that . . . ." From time to
time the students can hand in their journals for your reaction. It is recommended that

---

[8]Adapted from Moskowitz (1978, pp. 232–234).

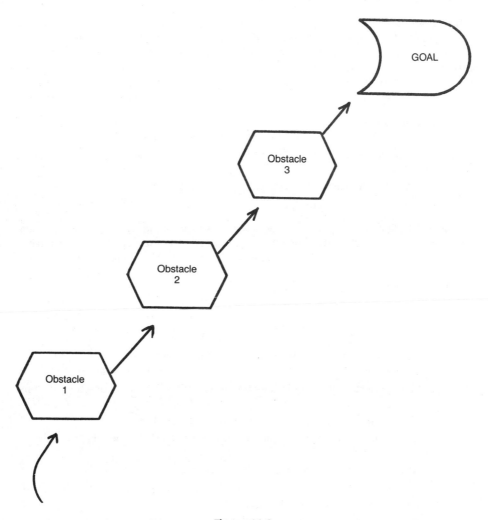

Figure 11.2

the journals not be corrected for mechanical errors. However, space should be provided for you or your assistants to write positive and encouraging comments.

Getting to Know You through Interview

Below are listed a few interviewing situations which can be used to provide practice with the target language and to aid students in the process of clarifying values. Remind students of their right to pass.

1. Even though most of the students in the class may already be acquainted, new students who are at intermediate or advanced levels come in from time to time and need

to be introduced. One effective way to do this is to write questions on cards (one or two per card) and distribute them. Pair the students up and have them briefly interview each other, allowing about 3 minutes for each member of the pair. During the interview, the students can include the questions on the card. Then have each student introduce the person he or she interviewed and tell about the answer that was given to the questions on the cards as well as other information received. Below are some sample questions:

What place do you like to go to when you're all alone? Describe it.

What person do you admire most? Tell about that person's qualities.

If you could choose any time period in which to live, which would you choose? Give your reasons.

Where would you like to take your next vacation? Explain your choice.

Which famous person would you like to have as a personal friend? Why?

2. Ask students to bring to class questions to ask each other (you can provide them with a list of sample questions to help them get started). On the day of the interviewing, place the students in a circle and have one volunteer begin by asking a question. Allow people to volunteer to give an answer. The person who volunteers to answer then has the privilege of asking the next question.

3. Have two volunteers go to the front of the room to be interviewed. Either one or both can answer the questions as they are asked by the teacher. It is important that the questions be reasonably nonthreatening in nature.[9] Here are a few possibilities:

Who is your favorite female athlete? Explain your choice.

What do you think is the best thing one person can give to another person?

What kind of person do you usually choose as a friend? What characteristics must he or she have?

What is the funniest situation you've ever found yourself in?

Out of all the people in the world, past and present, who is the one you most admire? Why?

Have you ever made a choice that surprised everyone? What was it?

Do you have any advice to give us that you think would be good for us to hear?

Which has been your best year in school? Why?

Has any news in the paper or on TV really worried you lately? If so, what was it and why did it disturb you?

How would you change this school if you could?

If you could have one question answered about life, what would your question be?

It is important before going on to the next question to follow up answers with other appropriate questions or react by simply repeating what the students say in order to

---

[9]It must be pointed out that what might seem nonthreatening to one student may not be to another. Sometimes even an innocent question such as "Where does your mother work?" might bring tears to one who has just lost a mother. The teacher simply has to use his or her best judgment and encourage the students to do the same in asking questions. As teachers and other facilitators become more experienced and skillful in using affective activities, they may want to take higher risks in some situations in order to maximize the results.

ensure that the intended meaning comes across. Once you complete the interview, the class should have a chance to ask questions also.

An alternative might be to have the volunteers select topics about which they would like to be interviewed. You might post a list somewhere in the room to suggest possible categories: sports, movies, vacation, school, dating, and so on.

4. Invite students, teachers, and administrators (who speak the target language) from outside the class to come in to be interviewed. Students, with your help, can prepare questions beforehand. Other questions will grow out of the interviews themselves.

5. Send the students out into the school or university campus to interview other students (this is especially appropriate for an ESL class). Have them form the questions beforehand and return to report the most interesting answers they received.

One alternative is to have students write up an opinion poll and ask students outside of class to respond orally while their opinions are recorded. Questions calling for a "yes," "no," or "maybe" answer, such as "Do you think most drugs should be legalized?" would be the easiest to tabulate. The results can be tallied once the students return to class.

Stand Up and Be Counted![10]

Place five large signs around the room far enough apart so groups have room to form by them without crowding. Label the signs "Strongly Agree," "Agree Somewhat," "Neutral," "Disagree Somewhat," and "Strongly Disagree." Read a statement. The students move to the sign that best describes their reaction. Then volunteer spokespersons from each group tell the whole class why they have chosen that particular position. Each group is heard out fully before a verbal exchange among groups is allowed. Only one person should talk at a time and all the ground rules mentioned previously must be adhered to. Below are sample statements to which students can react:

Childhood is the happiest time of life.

Men and women should share equally the chores of running a household.

Grades in school should be outlawed.

Pets should be allowed in homes for the elderly.

Most people are dishonest when given the chance.

This activity could be followed up with advanced writing activities and in many cases library research, particularly if the issues are ones about which a great deal has been written.

Concentric Circles[11]

Students sit on the floor in two concentric circles with equal numbers in each circle. The members of the inner circle face outward toward corresponding members of the outer circle, who face inward. The activity begins with a question such as "What do you find

---

[10]Adapted from Simon, Howe, and Kirschenbaum (1972, pp. 252–254).

[11]I first heard of this activity from another teacher (whose name is unknown to me) at a workshop several years ago. Later I came across a version of it in Moskowitz (1978, pp. 78–79).

especially difficult about learning a second language?" The students in the outer circle answer the question first, and as soon as a lull in the conversation becomes apparent (after a minute or so),[12] the students in the inner circle answer the same question. Then the inner circle remains stationary while the outer circle rotates clockwise until each student is aligned with the next person to the left. A different question is asked. This time the inner circle answers first, and after those in the outer circle answer also, the inner circle rotates counterclockwise to the next person, and so on.

An alternative, with somewhat different interpersonal dynamics, uses groups of three. One person in each group answers the question while the others listen. When time is called, the second member of each group answers the same question, and then the third member.

Below are a few sample questions:

Describe one thing you would like to learn to do well.

Is there anyone in the world with whom you would like to change places? Explain your answer.

If you could run this school or university, what would you change about it?

What do you really like about the person (or people) sitting across from you?

What is the biggest problem faced by the younger generation living at home?

If you were the President of the United States, what is the first thing you would try to do?

What was the nicest thing anyone ever did for you?

What is one thing you wish you had the courage to do?

Problem Posing

The following is an adaptation of Wallerstein's (1983) approach to language teaching based on Freire's philosophy (see Chapter 3). She presents the activity as a means of developing critical thinking through group dynamics. However, it can also be used as a means of clarifying values. Begin by listening to the students to discover what issues seem to be important to them. Then attempt to find a codification (a story, a dialogue, a photograph, a picture) to tap into what is truly meaningful. For example, the students in an advanced ESL class may have recently been discussing the difficulties they faced when first coming to this country. As a codification for a problem posing activity, you might show the students a picture of a lone woman waiting with her suitcases near the departing taxis at an international airport in the United States. She is dressed in native garments from India. Ask a series of inductive questions about the codification to try to pinpoint the problem as the students see it:

What is happening here?

Is there a problem?

---

[12]During some affective activities, time is called after each response to indicate that it is now someone else's turn to react. The turn should stay with only one person until the facilitator says that time is up. If that person finishes his or her response early, the group can either use the remaining time to ask questions to clarify or its members can simply reflect silently until it is the next person's turn.

Have you or someone you have known experienced a similar problem?

To what causes can you attribute this problem?

What can we do?

In answering the questions, the students decide that the woman, who speaks no English, has been forgotten by those who were to meet her. She must survive on her own, at least for a while. A discussion ensues about the students' own experiences in similar situations and about the causes of such dilemmas. They decide, as a group, that they can do something to help others who find themselves in similar predicaments. They outline some steps for preparing pamphlets in a variety of languages to place at an international airport in the area. The pamphlets will clearly explain important procedures (finding the restrooms—a map of the airport will be included, converting one's money into dollars, using the telephone, finding a hotel or alternative lodging, taking a taxi or a shuttle bus, and so on).

Problem posing, as a process, has three major components: listening, dialogue, and action. It is important that only one problem be the focus at a time so that the issues do not become clouded. In addition, care must be taken to flow with the students when pinpointing the problem rather than lead them to one that has been predetermined. Issues can be dealt with on several different fronts: personal, school, community, nation or state, world. Actions can run the gamut from speaking frankly with those who are in charge on the local level to writing letters to members of Congress or leaders of countries. The teacher and the students need to determine what actions would be effective and appropriate in each situation. Problem posing may require considerably more time than the teacher anticipates, but the benefits of increased student interest and the subsequent gains in language acquisition can make it very worthwhile.

SUMMARY

One important reason for using affective activities in the classroom is to help students reach an understanding of those beliefs and behaviors that give meaning to their lives. At the same time, these activities can provide motivating dialogue in the target language and serve as a way to bring individuals and groups closer together.

Although many benefits can accrue from use of affective activities, they are not suited to everyone. Teachers who are not comfortable sharing feelings and opinions, teachers who want to turn them into therapy and/or sensitivity training sessions, or teachers who are interested in imposing their own belief systems on others are not good candidates. Before attempting to use them, teachers should be familiar with the literature and, if possible, be specially trained in the techniques.

The activities themselves must be appropriate to the proficiency and age levels of the students as well as to the cultural environments in which they are used. They should be nonthreatening and generally positive in nature. Certain ground rules must be adhered to concerning the right to pass, the right to be heard, and the right to have one's opinion respected. If the classroom atmosphere is warm and accepting and the teacher wise and caring, affective activities can carry the students far in the language acquisition process.

READINGS, REFLECTION, AND DISCUSSION

Suggested Readings and Reference Materials

Byrd, D., & Clemente-Cabetas, I. (1980). *React interact: Situations for communication.* New York: Regents. Affective activities and storytelling are interwoven into an effective combination for intermediate students. A typical lesson includes a compelling story, oral interaction about the story (involving group decision making), written reactions exploring values, and vocabulary development.

Galyean, B. (1982). A confluent design for language teaching. In R. Blair (Ed.), *Innovative approaches to language teaching* (pp. 176–188). Rowley, MA: Newbury House. Galyean calls for a merging of subject skill mastery and humanistic goals. Although her approach may be too grammar oriented for some, she does offer several ideas that can be adapted in the second language classroom.

Green, K. (1983). Values clarification theory in ESL and bilingual education. In J. Oller and P. Richard-Amato, *Methods that work*, pp. 179–189. Includes a working definition of values clarification and shows how the techniques can be applied in college-level ESL and in bilingual education for elementary students.

Hooker, D., & Gallagher, R. (1984). *I am gifted, creative, and talented.* New York: Educational Design. EDI 331. A collection of self-development activities centering around self-awareness, working with others, sharpening mental gifts, creativity, and talents (teens–adults). Includes activities on personal opinions, family expectations, dreams, fears, peer-group influence, trusting others, and much more.

Moskowitz, G. (1978). *Caring and sharing in the foreign language class.* Rowley, MA: Newbury House. A sourcebook on humanistic methods. Presents a wide array of ideas on relating to others, discovering the self, expressing feelings, and sharing values. Is included as suggested reading for Chapter 5 as well.

Simon, S., Howe, L., & Kirschenbaum, H. (1972). *Values clarification: A handbook of practical strategies for teachers and students.* New York: Hart. Contains a series of activities and explains how to use them for furthering the process of values clarification. Includes decision making, problem solving, and many other means for confirming and developing values. Even though a few of the topics suggested in this book may be a little high risk for most teachers and students, many of the activities lend themselves readily to successful language teaching.

Questions for Reflection and Discussion

1. To what extent do you feel our values are culturally determined? Is there a set of values basic to all cultures? Explain. What role does individual experience seem to play in the process of the development of a values system?

2. Green (1983) stresses the characteristics of a successful values clarification teacher.

   > Use of values clarification in the classroom requires a teacher who (1) is willing to examine his or her own values; (2) can accept opinions different from his or her own; (3) encourages a classroom atmosphere of honesty and respect; and (4) is a good listener (1983, p. 180).

   What might be the consequences in the classroom for the teacher who tries to use values clarification but who lacks even one of these characteristics?

3. What are several situations in your own teaching for which affective activities could be adapted? Plan in detail a few such activities for at least two situations. You might consider using them as part of a literature or history unit of some kind, as a follow-up to the study of the lyrics of a song, as a unit to commemorate a special holiday, or for any other situation in which such activities might be appropriate.

4. Choose one of the affective activities planned above and try it out with the members of your class. State clearly the situation, the proficiency and age levels for which it is intended, and the possible follow-ups you would use. Give the class members a chance to express their feelings about it afterwards. In what ways was it successful? How can it be improved?

PART III

Some Practical Issues

It is the teacher in the classroom who has the task of putting it all together and making it work. No book can dictate a program or a methodology. What may be good for one group of learners in one particular setting may not be appropriate for those in other situations. The following types of programs and a few of their implications are presented below for your consideration (see Chapter 14 for a fuller description of these types in relation to bilingual education and/or sheltered classes).

SECOND LANGUAGE PROGRAMS

Second language programs were referred to in the Introduction (see footnote 1) as programs in which the target language is the dominant language in the area where it is being taught. Generally, students in such programs are interested in learning to survive physically, socially, and often academically in the new culture. They are, in most cases, surrounded by the target language in the community, the workplace, and the school or university campus. Sometimes, however, second language students live in communities in which their first language and culture is predominant. This means that, although they have the advantages of L1 language and cultural maintenance, they may lack the target language input available to those in more integrated situations. For them, having considerable contact with native or nativelike speakers as part of the curriculum would be especially important to their interlanguage development.

FOREIGN LANGUAGE PROGRAMS

Foreign language programs were referred to in the Introduction as programs in which the target language is not the dominant language in the area where it is being taught. Students have a variety of reasons for being in these programs. Sometimes their goals are integrative ones; for example, they may want to communicate with people from another language group or survive in another culture. Often their goals are instrumental; for example, they may want to get a job which requires that they be bilingual. Other times, the goal is simply personal enrichment. The environment outside of the classroom, however, does not usually give foreign language students the opportunity to be immersed in the target language. They are in special need of meaningful interaction since the classroom may be their only source. On the other hand, because they may not receive a sufficient quantity of high-quality input in the classroom to become proficient (many foreign language classes meet only one hour a day), they may find a formal application of rules to be necessary in facilitating the acquisition process. This presents the teacher with somewhat of a dilemma. Other factors come into play as well. The culture of the students may prevent some methods or activities from being as effective as they might be in other circumstances. For example, in many Asian cultures it is considered rude to talk of oneself. In such cultures affective activities such as those found in Chapter 11 may be highly inappropriate.

Additional foreign language programs have their own implications for curriculum planning. For example, instrumental programs that are offered strictly for a single academic purpose (e.g., interpreting research findings in another language) or for other specific purposes (e.g., becoming acquainted with a new medical procedure used in another culture) may not include the development of communication skills at all. In these programs learning to read and being familiar with a certain technical vocabulary may be all that is necessary.

12

Classroom Management

Just as there is no one set of ideal teaching materials, so there is no universal teaching method suited to the many contexts of language learning. . . . The most effective programs will be those that involve the whole learner in the experience of language as a network of relations between people, things, and events. The balance of features in a curriculum will and should vary from one program to the next, depending on the particular learning context of which it is a part.

S. Savignon, 1983

A single method by itself will probably not provide an adequate language teaching program. Neither will the concatenation of several methods and activities. What we need is an interweaving of courses of action, each providing what is required at the moment, all working together to form a highly integrated curriculum. There will be times when activities most typically related to the total physical response and the natural approach are well suited, other times when jazz chants and role play are more appropriate, and still others when affective activities fit the situation best. Grammar exercises may have their place, once students have enough competence to benefit from grammatical analysis. Much depends on whether the goals are integrative and/or instrumental (see Chapter 5), what concepts and proficiencies are needed, and what the learning and teaching preferences are, cultural factors, and age and competency levels of the students. No longer can a teacher depend upon a single book or a single course of action to get the job done.

INTEGRATION OF METHODS AND ACTIVITIES

A program utilizing an integration of methods and activities could be organized at beginning stages around basic topics and situations similar to those suggested by Krashen and Terrell (1983) (body parts, physical actions, clothing, occupations, emotions, recreation, going shopping, etc). Gradually the program might ease into subject-area concepts and themes, including their related proficiencies.[1] The subject areas might include art, math, business, computer processing, physical education, social and natural sciences, and literature. Whatever the content, it must be relevant to the students and their needs. In addition, it must include areas of knowledge in which the teacher has expertise.

Students might at first be introduced to many key concepts during a comprehension stage, through aspects of the total physical response or the audio-motor unit (Chapter 6). The *same* concepts could be reinforced while new ones are introduced through activities typical of the natural approach and its extensions (Chapter 7). Toward the end of the comprehension stage and as a transition to early speech production, jazz chants, simple poetry, and/or music lyrics (Chapter 8) could be added and used occasionally either to introduce a set of concepts or to reinforce them. During this transitional period, techniques from storytelling, role play, and drama (Chapter 9) can be highly motivating while providing the many passes through the material necessary for acquisition to occur. Games (Chapter 10) can be effective if played occasionally to develop or reinforce concepts or to teach the vocabulary and structures of game playing itself. During the speech emergence to full production stages, the teacher may want to involve the students to a greater extent in the planning process. At this level the teacher could introduce and reinforce concepts through affective activities (Chapter 11) and through more advanced applications of the above methods. All the while, the necessary proficiencies could be taught in an integrated fashion rather than as separate sets of skills and subskills (see rationale beginning on page 196 later in this chapter).

Various methods and activities can also be combined on a much smaller scale, either within a unit (several lessons about the same topic) or within a single lesson. In the two examples following, we have several methods and activities merged *within a unit*.

Susan Ashby, a teacher in the Alhambra School District of California, illustrates how storytelling, music, affective activities, and poetry can be integrated with aspects of the total physical response and the natural approach. All can work together to produce a unified whole—in this case a subject-area unit on birds. She suggests that the unit (intended for use with children at

---

[1]Most of the suggestions here are applicable in all second and foreign language teaching situations in which subject-area content is the focus (see Chapter 14 and Related Reading 9).

intermediate levels) begin with the Mexican folk tale, "The Pájaro-cu." It is the story of a bird who, at the beginning of the world, appeared before the eagle (the king) stark naked because he had no feathers. The eagle was so offended that he sent the featherless bird into exile. A dove took pity on him and began a campaign to clothe him. Each bird willingly contributed a feather. The result was a bird so colorful and beautiful that he became vain and would have nothing to do with the other birds. He decided to leave the country. The other birds were sent to look for him. In their search, the various birds began to sing out the different calls by which they are now known. Although the lost bird (called the *pájaro-cu*) has never been found, the other birds still sing their characteristic songs but no longer expect an answer.

By using an extension of the natural approach, the teacher and students discuss the meaning of the story. In addition, the teacher displays a series of colored pictures of birds and talks with the students about the different types and the features that most birds have in common. By including elements of the total physical response, the teacher has the students pantomime to the beat of a drum the movements of various birds: big birds, delicate birds, birds that run, walk, and soar. Using movements to music (see Chapter 8), the children dance, playing the roles of different types of birds. The teacher then asks them to pretend that *National Geographic* has commissioned the class to paint a picture of the missing pájaro-cu. Following a lesson in watercolor (again using aspects of the total physical response), the students sketch and paint the bird, perhaps combining crayons and watercolors to give the hues a jewel-like appearance. An affective activity comes into play when the students are asked to find sayings such as "Birds of a feather flock together" and "A bird in the hand is worth two in the bush." After discussing the meanings of the sayings, the students can use them to label their pictures. Ashby suggests a poetry lesson as a follow-up. One poem she finds particularly effective and stimulating for discussion is "Gooloo" by Shel Silverstein.

> The Gooloo bird
> She has no feet,
> She cannot walk
> Upon the street.
> She cannot build
> Herself a nest,
> She cannot land
> And take a rest.
> Through rain and snow
> And thunderous skies,
> She weeps forever
> As she flies,
> And lays her eggs
> High over town,

And prays that they
Fall safely down.

The second example of an integrated unit is provided by Heather Robertson, an instructor in the American Culture and Language Program at California State University, Los Angeles. It combines affective activities and role play to provide a cultural awareness unit for English as a Second Language students in a course entitled "Readings in Sociology." The course is intended for advanced students who will soon be seeking admission to the university.

In the first lesson, the students are given a mini-lecture on how appropriateness of behavior is judged in many cultures. Students are asked to listen and take notes. They are then given a quiz during which they are encouraged to use their notes. As homework for that evening, they are to read a section from a college-level sociology text reinforcing the same concepts. During the next lesson, students discuss what sorts of behaviors are considered appropriate in their cultures but not appropriate in the United States. They share opinions on how native speakers might react to persons deviating from the norm. Homework for the second evening consists of coming up with situations in which specific behaviors are incorporated for the purpose of bringing about overt or subtle reactions among native speakers. The behaviors might include such actions as facing the "wrong" way in an elevator and standing "too close" to someone while speaking.

On the third day the students decide which situations they would like to act out at various spots around the campus. The students who feel uncomfortable with being actors can volunteer to be observers and recorders of the reactions of native speakers. Once the roles have been decided, the students predict the kinds of responses they expect to get and how the responses might make them feel. The observers and recorders are told to watch the native speakers carefully and record in writing their reactions. Even a wry smile or raised eyebrow should be noted.

The last day is reserved for reporting the results and for a discussion aimed at achieving some sort of perspective. Did the native speakers react as predicted? What were the feelings of the actors? The observers? Had they been in similar situations before? How had they reacted the first time? Through a sharing of such responses, students seem better able to deal with the feelings, whatever they might be.

In the next example, Sandy Nevarez, a resource teacher in the ABC Unified School District of California, combines characteristics of several approaches *into a single lesson* which is part of a subject-area unit on insects or bugs. She incorporates the natural approach, total physical response, and some elements from poetry to produce a "soup fit for toads." She tells the students (primary children at beginning levels) that they are about to prepare a real delicacy—toad soup. Prior to the activity, the students are introduced to the names of various insects or other bugs and are given small pictures of them (run off on a ditto and cut out). The teacher has provided a pot in which to make the soup, along with the various ingredients needed: a raw egg, water, honey, cooked spaghetti noodles, and sand filled with small rocks. Each ingredient should be kept out of view until it is needed, thus increasing anticipation. The dialogue can go somewhat like this:

TEACHER: What are some bugs that toads like? Put them in the pot. (The teacher looks at each picture and says its name as the students put them in the pot.) Very good. Now we have many bugs in the pot. We have spiders, bees, flies, mosquitoes, ladybugs, and many others. The soup should be very good, don't you think? (The students nod but with some doubt.) Could our soup use a raw egg? (She breaks an egg into the soup, adds water, and stirs the mixture around with her hand.) Ooooooh, it feels slimy. It feels sliiiimy. (She lets the students feel in the pot.) How does it feel? Does it feel slimy?

STUDENTS: (muttering while grimacing) Slimy. Slimy.

TEACHER: Okay. Could our soup use some noodles? Yes, it could use some noodles. (She dumps in a fistful of noodles and stirs it around, again with her hand.) Squishy. It feels squishy and ishy and soooo slimy. (Again she lets the students feel.) How does it feel? Squishy and ishy?

STUDENTS: Yes.

TEACHER: Slimy?

STUDENTS: Yes.

TEACHER: Sooooo squishy and ishy and slimy. (The students make faces to indicate their disgust.)

The teacher continues in this manner adding the other ingredients and using other rhyming words: sticky, icky (for honey), and lumpy, bumpy (for sand with rocks). Through the highly comprehensible input, the physical involvement, and the sensual quality of the words and actions, the students become completely absorbed in the activity, making acquisition highly probable.

PLANNING LESSONS

It is important to ensure that the same concepts will be reinforced over and over using different methods in different situations. This is particularly crucial at beginning to intermediate levels. Too often inexperienced teachers present concepts once and then let them drop, never to be returned to again.

In the example above, the rhyming words could be reinforced through the following jazz chant constructed by the teacher and used as a follow-up:

How does the toad stew feel?
Slimy and sticky?

              Yes!
              Slimy and sticky.

Squishy and icky?

              Yes!
              Squishy and icky.

Is that how it feels?
Is that how it feels?

              Yes!
              That's how it feels.
              That's how it feels.

Students clap or snap their fingers to the beat.

In another activity, pictures of insects could be taped to the walls and the students could write a group paragraph, language experience style (see page 100). Much later, students might create simple poetry about insects, using the rhyming words (see Chapter 8).

It is important that teachers remain flexible in planning the content of their units. Some of the best lessons teachers have will be those spontaneous ones that grow out of a special need or interest that presents itself at the moment.

Concerning the structure of lessons, Wong-Fillmore (1985) concludes that teacher lessons that are consistent, are well-organized, and have similar formats with clear beginnings and endings appear to be most effective. Familiar routines provide a sort of ''scaffold'' for the learning of new materials.[2]

The routine outlined below is similar to the plan described by Madelyn Hunter and Douglas Russell (1977) for classroom lessons but with important differences.

1. Perspective (opening)

Address the following questions when appropriate:

What have you learned to do? (previous activity)
What concepts have you learned? (previous activity)

---

[2]Her conclusion is based on a study she did with colleagues at the University of California at Berkeley. They observed the input given in 30 kindergarten through fifth-grade classrooms over a five-year period. In addition, she observed and recorded teachers in another ten classrooms in which there were Limited English Proficient (LEP) students.

How does it make you feel? Proud of yourself?
More confident?

Give a preview of possibilities for the new lesson.

2. Stimulation

The following are a few options:

Pose a question to get students thinking about the coming activity.

Help the students to relate the activity to their lives.

Begin with an attention grabber: an anecdote, a little scene acted out by peer teachers or lay assistants (see pages 190–192), a picture, a song. Use it as a lead into the activity.

3. Instruction/Participation Phase (teacher/student contributions)

Below are examples:

Read and discuss the story or poem, sing the song or have it sung, do the jazz chant, search for the issues, agree upon expectations, check for understanding, divide into groups, and so on. Encourage student involvement to the largest extent possible, depending on the students' emerging capabilities in the target language.

4. Closure

Address these questions when they are appropriate:

What did you learn?
How did you feel about doing the activities?

Give a preview of the possibilities for future lessons. Get student input.

5. Follow-up

Use other activities to reinforce the same concepts and introduce new ones.
Give students the opportunity to do independent work in class or as homework.

Whereas the original Hunter-Russell model appeared to be highly teacher centered and teacher controlled, this model allows for greater student input and participation.[3] As the students gain competence, they can gradually take

---

[3]The same type of plan can be used by peer teachers and lay assistants (see section later in this chapter) for their work with small groups and individuals.

on a larger role in choosing the content and even in the structure of the lessons themselves.

Note that some elements of the lessons will be downplayed and others emphasized depending upon the situation and upon the proficiency levels of the students. For instance, a full development of the Perspective would probably not be appropriate for preproduction students because not much of it would be understood unless it were given in the primary language. Nor would it be appropriate for young children. Simple statements such as, "I think you know what watercolors are. It will be fun to see what you do with them," would be sufficient. On the other hand, fully developed, highly comprehensible instructions during the Instruction/Participation Phase would be very appropriate for preproduction students and young children. Furthermore, the teacher should keep in mind that students will probably at first not understand every word in the lesson. Nor should they expect to understand every word. It takes time and many passes through similar structures and concepts to acquire the target language.

ADAPTING THE CONTENT

Most of the activities recommended in this book can be adapted to almost any age level. Following is an example of how an affective activity (see Chapter 11) developed for use with adults can be modified for use with children. At both levels the students are grouped into pairs. The responses are timed so all students have a chance to express themselves on each item.

Describe how you feel when. . . .

For adults (late speech emergence stage)

. . . someone gives you a compliment.

. . . you are late for a meeting at which you are the speaker.

. . . your boss asks you to work four extra hours and you are very tired.

. . . you receive an all-expense-paid vacation to the Bahamas.

Adapted for children (late speech emergence stage)

. . . your friend says you have a nice smile.

. . . your teacher scolds you for coming late to class.

. . . your favorite movie is on TV and your mother tells you to go to bed.

. . . someone offers to treat you to a chocolate sundae.

Some activities can be easily modified for different proficiency levels. For example, in the activity below the students are going on a treasure hunt through the local newspaper. The first group of treasures is for students in the early speech production stage; the second is for students in late speech emergence.

Early Speech Production

Directions (should be given orally and demonstrated): *You are going on a treasure hunt. You will use the pictures in a newspaper. See how many pictures of these things you can find. Cut out the pictures.*

Find something . . .
    small
    soft
    made of glass
    square
    short
    narrow
    heavy
    sticky
    longer than a pencil

Late Speech Emergence

Directions (can be given orally, in written form, or both): *Go on a treasure hunt in the local newspaper. Find pictures of the items and cut them out. Paste them on a piece of paper. Write the name of the category above each picture. For example, you are asked to find something that looks comfortable. You might cut out the picture of a bed. Paste it on your paper. Write the words "something that looks comfortable" above it.*

Find something . . .
    that tastes good
    that has a pleasing smell
    that can be harmful or even dangerous
    that is a good buy
    that is used. . . .
        to beautify something
        to control something
        to change something
    that is durable
    that is accurate
    that you would like to buy

In the first version of the activity, the items are very concrete and simple; in the second version they are more abstract. Modifications can also be made in the content depending upon various interests, backgrounds, goals, and so forth.

UTILIZING PEER TEACHERS AND LAY ASSISTANTS

An ideal teaching situation would be one in which each student receives

1. An adequate amount of meaningful, relevant input aimed roughly at the $i + 1$ or the Zone of Proximal Development (see Chapter 3)
2. A sufficient number of opportunities to enhance the self-image and develop positive attitudes
3. Regular encouragement, motivation, and challenge
4. Plenty of opportunity for output
5. Continual feedback
6. Proper linguistic models (native or near-native speakers of the target language are best)

The quantity or amount of each of these necessary to the acquisition of the target language depends on the individual student and on each situation.

Peer teachers and/or lay assistants may prove to be necessary adjuncts to the program in order to help meet the students' individual needs in the above areas. They, like the teacher, can facilitate communication through a negotiation for meaning, offer comprehensible input, and give encouragement and feedback. They can provide a social link to the rest of the students in the school and to the community. In addition, they can serve as linguistic models to help prevent early fossilization. Potential peer teachers who are fluent in the target language are usually available within the schools themselves. For example, in the foreign language class one can draw from the advanced students in the language; in ESL at the junior and senior high schools and at universities, one can draw from the student body at large; in elementary schools, from the upper grades except in cases in which the tasks are not very demanding cognitively. In those cases, peer teachers can be much younger. (However, younger peer teachers will require a lot more supervision from the teacher than will older ones.) In adult programs, one can draw from the community (see Chapter 15). Lay assistants who are fluent in the target language can be invaluable at all levels. They are often an overlooked community resource.

Peer teachers and lay assistants should meet certain qualifications: they must have the necessary skills, enjoy aiding others, have a lot of patience, be supportive, and be willing to work hard. In addition they will need training workshops (especially effective at secondary and adult levels) to aid them in the following areas:

1. Development of cultural sensitivity (see also Chapter 5)
2. Knowledge of the instructional procedures the teacher chooses to use
3. Familiarity with the methods and materials with which they will be working (role play might help here—they can gain practice in the techniques by trying them out on each other)
4. Pertinent background information on the students with whom they will be working—cultural information, common problems, and so on
5. Strategies for creating friendly, supportive relationships

Below is a collection of strategies for helping others which could be discussed at a training workshop.

Strategies for Helping Others

1. Become familiar with the student's name and use it frequently.
2. Have an easy smile.
3. Be friendly. Get to know the student.
4. Be a good listener. Encourage the student to talk. Ask questions to find out more or to clarify what the student is saying.
5. Show recognition of and enthusiasm for the student's accomplishments no matter how small. Praise genuinely. Make it as specific as possible. Try to build intrinsic motivation by getting the student to reflect on what he or she has done. Questions such as "How does it make you feel to have _____?" or "You must be very proud of _____" encourage the student to be self-motivating.
6. Find out about the student's culture.
7. Be accepting of the person's right to his or her own opinions and beliefs. Avoid put-downs.
8. When asking questions, give the student enough time to respond. Be patient.
9. Give the student sufficient time to work at his or her own pace without feeling hurried.
10. Instead of responding with a flat "No, that's wrong," say something more encouraging such as "You're giving it a good try. But maybe we should look at it in a little different way. . . . "
11. If the student does not understand a concept after several attempts, go to something that you know the student can do with success. Later when you return to the more difficult task, it may come more easily.
12. If the student is obviously troubled or upset, give him or her a chance to talk to you about it. The task at hand can wait.
13. Use language that the student can understand. Repeat frequently. Use pictures and/or act out concepts whenever necessary.
14. Keep your directions short and simple.
15. Be honest with the student. If you don't know the answer to a ques-

tion you have been asked, be willing to admit it. Often you and the student can pursue information about an area of mutual interest together.

16. Remember that the teacher is there to help you when you need it. Do not hesitate to ask for assistance when there is something you can't handle.

In addition to training workshops, the peer teachers and lay assistants need to meet with the teacher regularly to make flexible lesson plans and to talk about possible problems and various approaches. The following is an evaluation checklist to ensure frequent communication between the teacher and peer teacher or lay assistant concerning the progress of the students.

EVALUATION CHECKLIST

Name of peer teacher or lay assistant _____

Name of student __ _____

Date _____

1. What did the student accomplish today?

2. Were there any problems?

3. What activities will you work on tomorrow?

4. Can the teacher help you in any way?

Comments:

The task of organizing a program utilizing peer teachers and lay assistants may at first appear overwhelming. However, once they are trained in the methods that the teacher chooses to use and are assigned to workable groups (perhaps three or four students of similar proficiency levels), the program seems to take on a momentum of its own (see Chapter 15). At that point, the time and talents of the teacher can be put to optimal use. The teacher is able to concentrate on students needing special help, peer teachers and lay assistants wanting additional guidance, whole-class activities, and overall structural concerns.

COOPERATIVE LEARNING
AS A MANAGEMENT TECHNIQUE[4]

In cooperative learning, students help other students within groups of four to five persons in an effort to reach goals. Adaptations of cooperative learning can be effective at many age levels from the late elementary grades up through adult levels. It can be used in both second and foreign language teaching situations.

In cooperative learning there is an *interdependence* established among the students in each group as they strive for the achievement of group or individual objectives. This technique draws from both behaviorism and humanism. On the one hand, it frequently offers group rewards (in the form of points or grades) as its prime motivation; on the other, it urges students to develop more fully their own individual identities while respecting those of others. It must be remembered, however, that the students should be cognitively able to handle its challenges in whatever situations the teacher wishes to incorporate it.

The results of studies done on cooperative learning (Slavin, 1983) indicate great potential for some aspects of the method to produce academic success, especially in classes of mixed ethnicity. In almost all the studies (89 percent) in which group rewards were based on individual achievement, there were noted achievement gains. On the other hand, in studies in which only individual grades were given, or a group grade was given based on a group product, achievement was roughly the same as that found in the control classes. Moreover, several studies indicated that medium to low achievers seem to benefit most and that their accomplishments were not made to the detriment of high achievers (Martino & Johnson, 1979; Armstrong, Johnson, & Balow, 1981).

One drawback of cooperative learning, if it is used extensively at beginning to intermediate levels with second or foreign language students, is the possibility of early fossilization (see Chapters 3 and 5). Wong-Fillmore (1985) reports that students who are not proficient in the target language do not provide adequate models for each other. This was true also in the immersion programs. This is not to say, however, that all non-native peer grouping should be avoided. On the contrary, such groups can provide comfortable environments in which the students can practice giving output and negotiating for meaning (see Long & Porter, 1984; Pica & Doughty, 1985; Porter, 1986). The danger, it would seem, comes when non-native peers are the *major*

---

[4]I wish to thank Carole Cromwell, Linda Sasser, and Leslie Jo Adams for sharing their ideas about cooperative learning with me. However, it is improbable that each will agree with every one of my conclusions.

source of input during the language acquisition process. Perhaps it is Porter who sums it up best:

> though learners cannot provide each other with the accurate grammatical and sociolinguistic input that native speakers can provide them, learners can offer each other genuine communicative practice, including the negotiations for meaning that may aid second language acquisition (1986, p. 220).

Versions of cooperative learning can be incorporated very successfully in almost any subject area, especially in intermediate to advanced language classes and in mainstream content-area classes. It is particularly effective in the latter, where ESL students can be grouped with native or near-native speakers.

Kagan (1981) describes five distinct types of cooperative learning which I have briefly summarized below. The examples for possible use are mine. Types 2–5 seem to work best when groups of mixed ethnicity (in the case of ESL) and mixed ability levels are created. It should be noted that there are many other versions of these basic types that have evolved over the past few years.

1. *Peer Tutoring*. Teammates teach each other simple concepts. This type is often used for math or language arts. It would be particularly applicable in a mainstream content-area class that includes ESL students.
2. *Jigsaw*. Each member of the group is given the chief responsibility for a specific portion of the learning unit. These members work with the members of other groups who have been given the same assignment. They form ''expert groups.'' However, eventually each member must learn the whole unit by sharing information with the others in the group. This type of cooperative learning is often used in the mastery of text material in social sciences. For example, a unit on the contributions of women in America might be studied by each group. One group member might be responsible for women's contributions to science, another on their contributions to literature, a third on their contributions to politics, and so forth. Each student is graded individually on his or her understanding of the whole unit.
3. *Cooperative Projects*. The members of the group work together to complete a group project such as a presentation, a composition, or an art project. Members receive individual grades based on the evaluation of the group product.
4. *Cooperative/Individualized*. Students work alone on a particular assignment or project but their progress contributes to a group grade. They may help each other so that each can achieve the best possible results.
5. *Cooperative Interaction*. Students work as a unit to learn. However, there is no group grade received. Each member of the group is graded

individually even though completion of the unit (e.g., a lab experiment, a panel discussion, a dramatic presentation) requires a cooperative effort.

Although the above suggestions are mainly for long-term projects, some very simple applications of cooperative learning can be incorporated in short-term activities at any level for which the specific content is appropriate. Following are some examples:

1. In a version of the activity commonly known as "numbered heads together," the class is divided into several groups of four or five and each student is given a number within the group. Each student (depending upon the number assigned) does one small portion of the group's work. For example, if a class in adult basic education is studying cultures, the teacher might give the groups several short passages, each describing an important custom in the United States. The person who is assigned the number 4 in each group could be responsible for reading the passage about how late one can be to a dinner party without being considered rude. The same person is then responsible for sharing this information with the others. The person assigned to number 3 could do the same for a passage describing who is expected to pay when one is asked to go to a movie, and so forth. Any number of topics can be handled in this manner.

2. The members of each group can study together for a test or work together to complete an assignment.

3. The group can complete a short-term group project such as a brief skit, a description of a scene, a collage, or a small-group discussion. Each member receives a group grade.

Kagan (1985) in his book *Cooperative Learning: Resources for Teachers* describes a highly structured cooperative learning system consisting of team building, management techniques, and rewards based on a fairly complex system of points. However, some teachers might prefer to downplay behavioristic goals (points and other extrinsic motivational devices) and concentrate on humanistic goals (personal development and respect for others). In spite of the claims made for cooperative learning in its unadulterated forms, it has been my experience that similar results can be had by focusing on the development of intrinsic motivation through the natural reward of a simple smile or a genuine compliment.

However, those who wish to use cooperative learning as Kagan intended would be wise first to read the literature (see Kagan, 1985, and his references) and perhaps participate in training workshops when they are available.

APPROACHING THE BASIC SKILLS

An effective program makes it possible for the students to move gradually from cognitively undemanding tasks for which the materials are heavily context embedded, offering many clues, to cognitively demanding tasks for which the materials are context reduced, offering few clues (see Cummins in Related Reading 9).

Listening, speaking, reading, and writing can be integrated in such a program provided that it focuses on meaning. All four skills can develop naturally if allowed to, even for the student whose L1 writing system is vastly different from that of the target language. It is when these abilities are treated as separate sets of skills and subskills to be learned that students often run into difficulty. For example, learning to read in a first or second language is not a matter of stringing phonemes into words and words into phrases and sentences and so on. It is also not a matter of practicing such skills as scanning and skimming. K. Goodman in his article entitled "Acquiring Literacy Is Natural: Who Skilled Cock Robin" asserts:

> There is a comfort and orderliness that appeals to teachers in sequential skill hierarchies. They particularly lend themselves to very formal and structured classrooms. But the emptiness of such hierarchies and irrelevance to actual development in reading is observable in any skill oriented classroom. In such classrooms, there are always two kinds of learners; one kind do well on the skill drills because they have enough control of the reading process to deal with the parts within the wholes. They don't need the skill instruction. The second kind have great difficulty with the sequenced skills because they are dealing with them as abstractions outside of the meaningful language process. Such learners can't profit from skill instruction unless they can transcend it and find their way to meaning on their own (1982, p. 247).

Learning to read in a first or second language is generally a matter of wanting to know what someone has to say about some area of interest. A few readers may have to be reminded that they need not understand every word and that trying to do so may interfere with their grasping the overall meaning. However, under normal conditions the reader is not even consciously aware that he or she is skimming or scanning or reading intensively. These are strategies that come naturally as the situation demands. Yet many exercises require that the reader learn the skills additively even if it means putting off a search for meaning until later. As F. Smith so aptly put it, "Programmed instruction can often be viewed as the systematic deprivation of information" (1978, p. 187). It is important to remember that reading is as much a part of the natural communication process as speaking and writing. Like listening, however, it is a receptive process as opposed to an expressive one. As Goodman reminds us:

If you understand and respect language, if you understand that language is rule governed, that the most remarkable thing about human beings is that they learn a finite set of rules that nobody can teach, making it possible for them to say an infinite number of things, then it is also necessary to understand that you cannot chop language up into little bits and pieces and think that you can spoon feed it as you would feed pellets to a pigeon or a rat. . . . Language doesn't work that way. . . . We have learned a lot of things. One of those things is that language is learned from whole to part. . . . It is when you take the language away from its use, when you chop it up and break it into pieces, that it becomes abstract and hard to learn (1982, p. 238).

Integrating the four skills is not difficult.[5] It should come as naturally for the teacher as it does for the students. When one is listening, opportunities for writing evolve. When one is reading, opportunities for speaking make themselves felt. Flowing with these opportunities involves the kind of flexibility necessary to allow the skills to grow naturally. Often impetus for skill development comes from a need of the moment. For example, students may find themselves in situations in which writing is required to fulfill immediate obligations. For the foreign language student in the later elementary grades or beyond, it may be that a response to a letter from a foreign pen pal is urgent. For an ESL student at the secondary level it may be a job application that must be filled out in the target language. In these situations, the student cannot wait until the early speech production stage is over and speech emergence appears. The teacher, peer teachers, and lay assistants can aid the students in fulfilling these obligations. With guidance, students will frequently find themselves performing far above levels for which they are supposed to be "ready."

The teacher can begin integrating almost right from the beginning without causing an undue overload on the students' mental capabilities. Even during the comprehension stage, literacy in the new language can be introduced to ESL students who need to survive in school settings and on the street. Labels on various rooms throughout the school can be made clear, especially the words designating males and females on the lavatory doors. Words for the street are even more important: "stop," "danger," "keep out," and similar ones are crucial for survival. In the foreign language classroom, labels can be placed on common objects around the room after their oral forms have been acquired or partially acquired. Story experience (see Chapter 9) can be highly motivating for beginners at any age, since it allows students to participate in a rich language environment even before they can utter a word in the target language. Later simple stories with accompanying pictures (see the same chapter) can be read in both ESL and foreign language

---

[5]The assumption is made here that the goal of any particular language program is to promote proficiency in all four skills. It should be noted, however, that not all language programs have this as a goal; some may be concerned with only one or two of the skills.

classes. Speech development may be accelerated simply through the excitement of involvement in someone else's conflict. Natural curiosity may push the student into higher and higher levels of communication incorporating all the skills of which the student is capable. If we or our peer teachers and lay assistants are there to take advantage of the *natural curiosity phenomenon*, we can guide the student far beyond what might have been considered possible in the traditional teacher-oriented, inflexibly structured classroom.

As students reach the early speech production stage, they will already have begun their transition into literacy through their exposure to labels and other pieces of written language necessary for survival. At this point, it is important to let the reading and writing skills come from the students' own experiences and through the vocabulary and structures with which they are already familiar. One method that seems to work particularly well with students of all ages who are cognitively able to handle literacy is called the "language experience approach" (see Chapter 7). It begins with a planned or spontaneous experience that the students all have in common (a story, a song, a picture, a trip to the local shopping center). After the experience, the students brainstorm while the teacher writes key words on the board. Each student then contributes to a group story or paragraph which is written on the chalkboard by the teacher, peer teacher, or lay assistant. Students can then read what has been written aloud as a group and copy it into their notebooks. After many exposures to this technique over a period of time, students can begin to read and write simple, short texts somewhat independently as they move through the speech emergence stage. Other helpful transitions are the matrices (see page 97), charts (see pages 95–96), and other activities that involve the comprehension of written messages in the target language.

There may be times when students need practice in specific skill areas such as the following: sound-letter correspondences (often a problem in English), word and/or phrase recognition, the formation of written symbols, guessing meaning from context, and so on. However, such practice, in most circumstances, should be related to meaningful text and should never be the major focus of a reading program.

Nonliterates in ESL classes need special attention during the early stages. If possible, they should develop their literacy skills in their primary languages first (if their languages have written traditions) and then transfer this knowledge to the second language.[6] It has been my experience that the more similar the first language and culture are to those of the target group, the more likely will be the transfer of specific as well as general reading skills. For example, if the L1 is a European language using the Roman alphabet and the L2 is English, specific transfer will probably involve many similarities in sound

---

[6]Note that this probably would not be true for a student in an immersion foreign language situation (see Related Reading 9).

combinations, the written symbols, punctuation, the movement of the eyes from left to right while reading, and so forth. On the meaning level, specific transfer might involve cognates, organizational patterns, shared cultural knowledge, experiences, and expectancies.

On the other hand, when the language and culture are very different, the transfer appears to be more general. For example, if the L1 is an Asian language using an ideographic writing system, the transfer would tend to be limited to more general elements such as sensory-motor skills; the symbolic nature of written language; attitudes toward the reading process itself; general comprehension skills such as predicting, finding main ideas, inferencing, coming to conclusions, etc. (see also Thonis, 1984). However, it must be remembered that *learned concepts* in the content areas are always transferable across languages, regardless of the languages involved.

Learning to read in the first language is particularly important for children, in order that their cognitive development not be arrested while they are trying to learn a new language system (Cummins, 1981). Nonliterates for whom an L1 mastery of literacy skills is impossible for whatever reason need to be introduced to the written form of their second language in much the same way that the other students are introduced to it, except that more preliminary work is necessary. The students need first to focus on the symbolic nature of language through such activities as role play (see Chapter 9) or game playing (see Chapter 10). During the course of these activities, objects can be made to represent people or things. The symbols are arbitrary, just as the words on the printed page are arbitrary representations of concepts. In addition, nonliterate students may need considerable exposure to multisensory input in order to develop a rich visual and kinesthetic representational system before they can be eased into literacy. Story experience and charts (both mentioned above), pictures to be labeled, maps, graphs, and actions associated eventually with the written word (such as one finds in the total physical response and the audio-motor unit) all form important preliminary steps leading into literacy at any age.

At later stages, all students (previous nonliterates included) can continue to work on their literacy skills through activities especially oriented to their development and improvement.

In reading in both ESL and foreign language classes at almost any age level, the teacher can provide motivation by having students make predictions about what they are going to read and by asking questions that relate the main ideas to their own lives. Experiences can be provided to give the students a greater familiarity with new concepts involved in the reading selections. In the later elementary grades and beyond, the teacher can aid understanding by helping the students to map out the main ideas, particularly while reading expository texts, thus giving the content a graphic dimension. For relatively uncomplicated contexts, a clustering device such as that developed by Gabrielle Rico at San Jose State University might prove an effective tool. See Figure 12.1. For a more complex networking of ideas, the tree structure shown in Figure 12.2 might be appropriate. To further aid understanding, questions can be asked that call for reflection and inference. Rather than asking mainly questions requiring factual answers, teachers can ask opinion questions such as those found in the interdependent categories below. These particular questions are intended for adolescents or adults at intermediate to advanced levels.

1. Predicting content and outcomes
   a) What do you think the story (essay, poem, etc.) will be about? (Refer students to the title, pictures, subheadings, or other clues.)

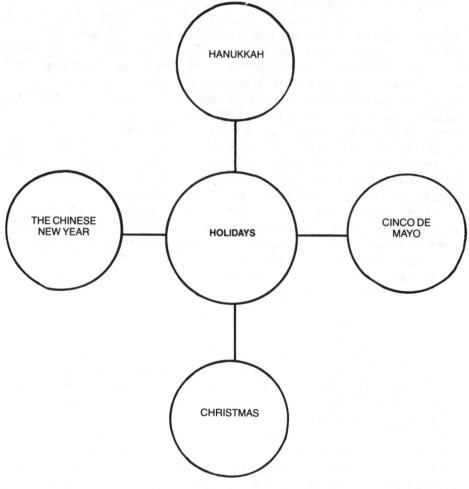

Figure 12.1

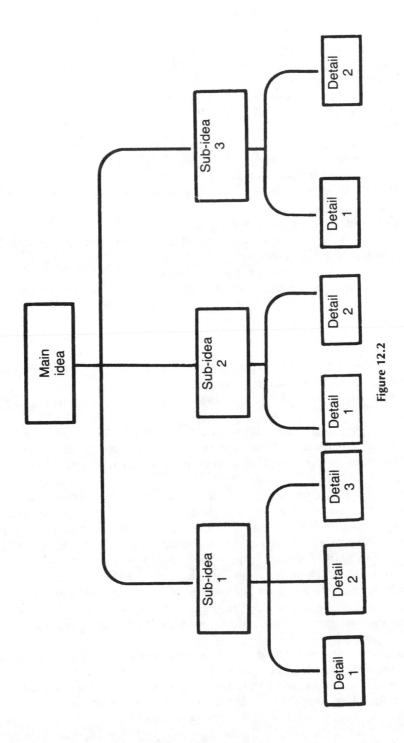

Figure 12.2

   b) In what sorts of dilemmas do you think the characters might find them-
      selves?
   c) What will happen?
2. Relating the text to prior knowledge
   a) What does the author claim are the reasons for the occurrences of this
      incident (effect)?
      —Can you think of other examples in which similar incidents (effects)
        occurred?
      —What caused them to take place?
   b) Are there alternative courses of actions that the author (character)
      might have pursued?
3. Making inferences and supporting conclusions
   a) What is the author attempting to tell us here? (Refer to a specific line,
      paragraph, event, etc.)
   b) How do you think the character (author) feels?
   c) Why is the character (author) happy (angry, doubtful, relieved, etc.)?
   d) Upon what evidence do you base your conclusions?
4. Relating to self and one's culture
   a) What would you have done had you been in a similar situation (di-
      lemma)?
   b) Are similar situations (dilemmas) prevalent in your culture? If so, in
      what manner are they approached?
   c) Does this event (fact, opinion) make you angry (glad, fearful)? Explain.

Additional questions can be asked about organizational strategies and patterns, use of literary devices, and whatever else is appropriate to the situation. The students can be asked to generate their own questions to ask one
another.

Small-group discussions of readings can allow the students to share ideas
and, by doing so, develop their own hypotheses about the meaning. By
bouncing their opinions off others in the group, they can either verify their
own interpretations or reread and then modify them. Peer teachers and lay
assistants can help facilitate the process by asking relevant questions of the
small groups with whom they are working.

Another consideration for all classes is the materials themselves (see
pages 208–210). They must be of interest and they must be comprehensible
semantically and syntactically, with some elements that are a little beyond the
students' present levels.

When students are writing, motivation can come from numerous sources
in ESL and foreign language classes. Experiences with music, poetry, storytelling, role play, drama, and affective activities often provide motivation and
can lead into some highly relevant, exciting topics. Students need to begin
the writing process with a certain amount of confidence, which can come in
part from their exposure to the language experience approach described

previously. The writing itself can be very subjective (letters to pen pals, journal entries, simple poetry) or more objective (lists of various kinds, forms, charts, maps, compositions). The kinds of writing done will depend to a large extent upon the student's ages, needs, and proficiency levels. However, it is generally best to begin with short pieces of writing before proceeding to longer ones.

In all writing, students need to concentrate on the *process* as well as the *product*. Murray explains: "You don't teach anything. You let the students write. . . . Writing must be experienced to be learned" (1982, pp. 115–116). At intermediate to advanced levels in the later grades and beyond, the writing process itself involves brainstorming for topics of interest, gathering information, allowing that information to settle into some sort of overall plan (the clustering and tree formations described above might be useful in planning), putting the words down on paper, and revising.

Revisions are particularly important to the writing process at these levels. According to Murray, they provide opportunities for the student to "stand back from the work the way any craftsman does to see what has been done . . . the most important discoveries are made during the process of revision" (1982, pp. 121–122). Because the effective writer frequently has to pause, go back, reread, rethink, rewrite, and write some more, he or she must be able to concentrate intensely on the composition without interference from the teacher or others who might want to help. Help may be needed before the actual writing begins in order to stimulate thinking, and again later once the student has had a chance to hammer out at least part of the piece alone. At that point the teacher, peer teacher, or lay assistant can consult with the student as needed. At first, suggestions should be made only in reference to meaning. What points are coming across clearly? Questions can be asked to confirm meaning and to stimulate further development of ideas. What portions are not readily understood? Strategies can be discussed in an attempt to redress breakdowns in communication. Students then need a chance to reshape the writing if it has not communicated what was intended or if they feel challenged to move in other directions. Dialoguing with peers also can generate a great deal of enthusiasm for the writing process and can motivate thoughts and feelings that might otherwise remain unexplored.

Students need to be reminded that errors are perfectly normal during the writing process not only for L2 students developing an interlanguage but for native writers as well. An inductive approach to errors is often the most effective way to attack them. The teacher might underline or lightly circle the word or phrase in which a problem appears and ask the student to try to identify it. Most errors can be related to meaning. The teacher can guide by asking pertinent questions. For example, in responding to an error in verb tense the teacher might simply ask "*When* did this occur?" Often the students will recognize the error themselves without any lengthy explanation or further probing. In addition, if the teacher or the students quietly read aloud the writing during the individual conference sessions, the errors often become more salient and can be corrected more easily. However, sometimes brief explanations are needed in further dialogue with the students to lead them to a better understanding of their errors. Errors should be treated in a matter-of-fact way so that the students don't associate them with the quality of the ideas themselves. In addition it is best not to focus on too many errors at once; much depends on what the students might be ready for at any given time.

Error correction may sometimes be handled indirectly in writing just as it is with oral production, particularly for composition of a more personal nature. For example, after students hand in their journals, instead of marking errors, the teacher may simply react to the entry in the margin by repeating the words that the student has used, but in correct form. Thus, the teacher's comment serves as a model. For example, if the student writes "On Tuesday my mother sick," the teacher might respond with "I'm sorry your mother was sick."

It is a good idea to keep a folder for each student in which work can be saved so that all concerned can keep abreast of the progress that is taking place. For some students, specific activities on recurring errors might help; for others, rewriting and a simple discussion of strategies may be enough.

The teacher at times may want to demonstrate the writing process. By this means, the students can experience vicariously the frustrations and joys that go into writing and at the same time be exposed to the forms and conventions of various types of composition. For example, watching the teacher execute a well-developed paragraph on the chalkboard can be highly motivating as well as instructive. The teacher will have to choose a topic (the students may want to make topic suggestions), brainstorm for ideas, map out the organization, begin a first draft, provide transitions, erase, move materials, modify, rewrite, and use the dictionary. If the teacher does his or her thinking out loud during the process, the students will more fully realize that even the teacher has to struggle to communicate.

EVALUATING STUDENTS

By keeping individual folders, the ESL or foreign language teacher can assess improvement in written skills over whatever length of time constitutes a grading period. An appropriate test, similar to a placement test (see pages 210–214), can help to determine progress in the other skills and in the content areas where appropriate. Often students can be rated informally by teachers who are familiar with their proficiencies. By using the list of typical behaviors found in Table 13.1 on pages 212–213 as a guide, the teacher can, with experience, be reasonably accurate in making determinations not only about evaluations, but about the students' levels of operation.[7] Reclassifications may be necessary in many cases.

In determining grades, both progress and effort should be important factors. It would be unfair to base the evaluation only on a score received on a discrete point test unless the teaching has been of the discrete point nature. Although the student may score very well, such a test could not be considered an adequate means of determining to what extent the student can communicate in the target language or how well the student has absorbed the content.

One highly motivating and satisfying activity during the later elementary grades and beyond in both ESL and foreign language classrooms is for the teacher, peer teacher, or lay assistant to sit down with each student at the end of every grading period and discuss the gains made and to review the goals for the next grading period. Students are usually very pleased and sometimes surprised at the progress they have made.

SUMMARY

Developing a methodology for both ESL and foreign language classrooms involves the synthesis of theory and practice into a program that works. It generally means drawing from several methods and approaches in order to create an integrated curriculum that will meet the needs of the students and the situation. Integrative and/or instrumental goals, the particular concepts being taught, learning and teaching preferences, cultural factors, and age and competency levels of the students are all important considerations.

Lessons need to be structured in such a way that students will receive optimal exposure to important concepts. The lessons should be well organized and contain familiar routines in order to serve adequately as vehicles for new information. Content needs to be modified to be appropriate for various age and proficiency levels.

Peer teachers and lay assistants can be trained to help the teacher provide sufficient amounts of comprehensible input, self-image enhancement, encouragement, motivation, and opportunity for negotiating meaning. At the same time, they can serve as linguistic models to help prevent early fossilization. In addition, the peer teachers and lay assistants can help make it possible for students to move from cognitively undemanding tasks to more de-

---

[7]Although limited to orally assessing skills, an instrument similar to the SOLOM (Student Oral Language Observation Matrix) developed by the California State Department of Education can be used. It allows teachers informally to evaluate their students' performance in five areas: comprehension, fluency, vocabulary, pronunciation, and syntactical usage.

manding ones and to integrate the four skill areas as they flow with the students' needs and interests.

Versions of cooperative learning also can serve as effective classroom management tools, particularly in intermediate to advanced second language classes or in mainstream content-area classes in which ESL students are included. Students can make substantial strides in communicative and academic competence through cooperative efforts.

Evaluation of students should be an ongoing process, regardless of the methods or content chosen. Effort as well as progress in the target language should be considered in determining a grade. Individual conferences with students about their progress can be very effective in motivating students toward greater achievements.

READINGS, REFLECTION, AND DISCUSSION

Suggested Readings and Reference Materials

Dixon, C., & Nessel, D. (1983). *Language experience approach to reading (and writing)*. Hayward, CA: Alemany. Presents an extensive literacy program for ESL students based on the language experience approach. Combines theoretical and practical ideas for teachers.

Kagan, S. (1981). Cooperative learning and sociocultural factors in schooling. In *Beyond language: Social and cultural factors in schooling language minority students* (pp. 231–298). Los Angeles: Evaluation, Dissemination and Assessment Center, California State University. An overview of cooperative learning and a report of its results. Good background reading for anyone planning to use this management technique.

Murray, D. (1982). *Learning by teaching: Selected articles on writing and teaching*. Upper Montclair, NJ: Boynton Cook. Although this book is intended for teaching writing to native speakers of English, many of its suggestions are applicable to teaching writing in a second language. Among the topics covered are giving students the experiences writers need to be productive, teaching revision as a motivating force, and helping students find what they want to say.

Oller, J., Jr., & Richard-Amato, P. (Eds.). (1983). *Methods that work*. Rowley, MA: Newbury House. A collection of current methods for teaching second languages. Includes Asher's total physical response, Gattegno's silent way, Lozanov's suggestopedia, Curran's counseling–learning, Raths's values clarification, Freire's problem–posing, Stern's drama, Terrell's natural approach, Graham's jazz chants, and Rassias's histrionics, to name a few.

Savignon, S. (1983). *Communicative competence: Theory and classroom practice: Texts and contexts in second language learning*. Reading, MA: Addison-Wesley. A broadly based discussion of the theory of communicative competence and its applications to the classroom.

Questions for Reflection and Discussion

1. Find or create a lesson that is oriented to a particular age group and adapt it to another age group. Doing the same for proficiency level, modify a lesson intended for one proficiency level (beginning, intermediate, or advanced) to make it appropriate for another. What problems needed to be considered in completing each task?

2. Plan a workshop for a small group of peer teachers and lay assistants. What important training will you want them to have?

3. Can you think of a few units for which you might want to incorporate some version of cooperative learning? Briefly describe how these units might be organized.

4. Develop a complete unit for a hypothetical or real second language classroom situation.[8] After considering your students' goals, decide what major concepts you will teach and reinforce throughout. Describe the unit, including a few lessons in which several methods and activities are integrated. Develop fully one of the lessons utilizing a structure similar to that outlined on pages 186–188. Try it out with the members of your class. Make sure you state clearly the situation, the proficiency and age levels for which it is intended, and how it fits into your unit. Ask the members of your class for feedback.

---

[8]Situations might be one of the following: an elementary, secondary, or university second or foreign language program, an adult basic education program, or a language program for special purposes such as preparing students for specific technical occupations, and so forth.

13

Tools of the Trade: Textbooks, Placement Tests, and Computer Programs

> *. . . part of the task of selection, then, becomes the selection of segments of real world knowledge and experience . . .*
>
> R. Crymes, 1979

Many different kinds of materials have been suggested throughout this book. Most of them have been materials not specifically intended for second language teaching such as television programs on videotape; newspapers and periodicals, stories and other pieces of literature; catalogs; games; reference books of several kinds; lyrics to popular songs; maps; pictures; and others. They have included both teacher- and student-made materials. Commercial products especially designed for second language teaching can be just as useful if chosen carefully.

It is not the purpose of this chapter to advocate specific textbooks, placement tests, or computer programs. Rather the chapter will emphasize the considerations that must be taken into account in making prudent decisions concerning these teaching tools.

TEXTBOOKS

Some teachers and many publishers long for the days when one set of materials (complete with student texts, cassettes, workbooks, and teacher manuals) was considered to be the answer to language teaching needs. Today, although many still cling to that dream, most realize the inadequacy of such an approach to language teaching. Because of the shift in emphasis to an interactional approach, pressure is being placed on publishers to provide the kinds of materials that are more supplemental in nature, that require a larger, more active and creative role on the part of teachers and students, and that focus on relevant, meaningful content. Some teachers are even turning entre-preneur and publishing their own materials in an attempt to fill the gap.

Below are some important questions to ask when examining textbooks, supplemental or otherwise. It is assumed here that the main goal is to learn and communicate in the target language.

1. Is the target language generally considered the *means for learning and com-municating* about some topic of interest, or is the language itself predomi-nantly the *content* to be studied and analyzed? If the language *is* the main content, then you might want to look for something more motivating and more comprehensible, especially at beginning to intermediate levels.
2. Are the grammatical structures allowed to exist naturally as a result of the content or is the content determined by which grammatical structure is being studied (see Chapter 4)?
3. To what extent are the students encouraged to relate the content to their own lives?
4. Are the materials appropriate to the language needs, age, and interests of the students with whom they are to be used? Consider content, illus-trations, activities, formality of the language, and so on.
5. Is the discourse motivated and logical according to human experience (see Chapter 4)?
6. Is the input comprehensible? Consider here the proficiency levels of the students with whom the materials will be used. Does the input gradually become more complex?
7. Are concepts recycled several times or are they introduced and quickly forgotten?
8. Do the materials foster reduced anxiety and a positive self-image?
   a. Are students allowed to develop their interlanguage normally (through the use of indirect correction) or are they expected to pro-duce correct language right from the beginning? This is particularly important for activities involving oral production.
   b. Are the directions clearly presented to prevent needless frustration?
   c. Will the activities enhance self-concepts and boost confidence?
   d. Do the materials promote positive attitudes toward the various cul-tures, including the target language culture?
   e. Are the materials relatively free of sexual bias?
9. Do the activities encourage use of creative language and negotiated meaning in a variety of situations?
10. Are the skill areas integrated to a large extent or do they seem to be ap-proached as separate entities? (See Chapter 12.)

11. Do the activities involve a wide variety of tasks appropriate to the objectives of the students?
12. Do the questions intended for high beginning to advanced students call for thinking and reflection or are they usually probes for factual, often irrelevant detail?
13. Do the materials intended for intermediate to advanced students become increasingly more challenging academically?

Sometimes the titles of textbooks are misleading and can lure one into believing that the content is generally communicative in nature. Catchy titles, those that imply a cast of characters, and those containing the words "communicative" or "communication" are not always what they appear to be. Often these books are grammar- or function-based texts disguised to look communicative. It pays to scrutinize them carefully before ordering them for student use.

PLACEMENT TESTS

Student placement is at best an onerous task. Teachers often have difficulty locating tests that will adequately determine at which levels the students are operating in the target language as well as in the primary language (knowing the latter is necessary for placement in bilingual programs). The choice of procedure has particularly important implications for the student's emotional well-being and linguistic development. Many times students find themselves misplaced simply because of their scores on a single standardized test.

Oller (1979) describes the differences between two kinds of tests: discrete point and integrative (see Related Reading 8). *Discrete point tests* examine the knowledge of specific elements in phonology, grammar, and vocabulary in order to determine proficiency in the isolated skill areas of listening, reading, speaking, and writing. Can the student auditorally distinguish between "pill" and "bill"? Can the student recognize a past tense form or use the present progressive? Does the student know the meaning of "chair" or "hippopotamus"? *Integrative tests*, on the other hand, examine the student's ability to use many skills simultaneously when accomplishing a task. Can the student answer a question that is typical of normal conversation? Can the student determine the meaning of a certain passage? Can the student tell a story that can be understood? Can the student write an effective letter? The two kinds of tests are not dichotomous in nature but rather at two extremes on a continuum. Some tests are thought to be more discrete point, others more integrative. To complicate matters, a test may be integrative in task but discrete point in evaluation. For example, the student may be required to write an essay (integrative in task), but it may be evaluated on specific errors in grammar and vocabulary (discrete point in evaluation). Generally speaking, tests that are integrative both in task and in evaluation probably tell us more about the proficiency levels of the students, mainly because they test communicative competence.

Oller describes yet a third kind of test—*a pragmatic test*, which he defines as a type of integrative test meeting two naturalness criteria. First, it must require that the student be able "to utilize normal contextual constraints on sequences in the language" and, second, it must require "comprehension (and possibly production also) of meaningful sequences of elements in the language in relation to extralinguistic contexts" (1979, p. 70).[1] Pragmatic tests, according to Oller, include dictation (the teacher dictates sentences; the students write them down as they are being read), cloze procedures (passages are given in which every *n*th word is deleted; students are to supply the missing words), paraphrase recognition, question answering, oral interviews, essay writing, narration, and translation. It is interesting to note that pragmatic tests (even those of very different types) tend to correlate more highly with each other than they do with other tests. In other words, students who tend to do well on one pragmatic test will also tend to do well on others. Oller concludes that "at present, pragmatic testing seems to provide the most promise as a reliable, valid, and usable approach to the measurement of language ability" (1979, p. 71).

When choosing what kind of pragmatic test to use, it might be wise to carry Oller's definition of such a test one step further. If we say that *the test tasks themselves have to approximate "normal classroom communication situations,"* then we would have to eliminate some of the pragmatic tests listed above except for certain kinds of question-answering tasks, oral interviews, essay writing, paraphrasing, and narration. This is not to say that cloze activities and dictation have no value. On the contrary, they do. But they may not be as valuable in determining placement as several of the other tasks. If our goal is to divide students roughly according to proficiency levels into beginning, intermediate, and advanced classes (see definitions on pages 4–5), then perhaps the combination of a listening comprehension task (with perhaps some simple total-physical-response activities), oral interview (pictures may be referred to), some informal writing, and a reading interpretation or paraphrasing section might be all that are needed to make a reasonable determination. Once the teacher has reached the student's level of operation in each area, it is important to terminate the testing at that point and move on to the next area.

It should be kept in mind that there will be a great deal of overlap between one placement level and the next and that the levels may vary depending on the tasks. However, this should not be disturbing, because when deal-

---

[1]An example of an integrative test that is not pragmatic might be the writing of isolated sentences to demonstrate the use of a rule in the target language. The task is highly integrative in that many skills are called for simultaneously but it is not pragmatic for two reasons: (1) the sentences lack a normal sequential context and (2) extralinguistic data such as our perceptions of life, relationships between people, and so forth are not relevant.

ing with human beings one can never get a completely homogeneous unit. Even though the groups themselves will be fairly diverse, they will still be workable in that the "net" of input cast out will generally cover a fairly wide range of levels. This will be true particularly for the interactional classroom in which meaningful communication about some content of interest is the focus.

Although there are tests on the market that may yield a more detailed diagnosis than most teacher-made tests, unless they are pragmatic they often lead to a focus on discrete point teaching in separate skill and subskill areas. In addition, the tests on the market are often expensive and longer than necessary. Teacher-made tests, on the other hand, may be somewhat crude and highly subjective, but they are usually short, easy to use, and flexible. Furthermore, they can include exactly those items that are appropriate to a specific situation and thus be quite effective for the initial placement (and later reassessments) of students. The list in Table 13.1 may be of help in creating tests to place the students in workable groups. Similar to the ACTFL (Ameri-

TABLE 13.1. TYPICAL LANGUAGE BEHAVIORS OF STUDENTS AT VARIOUS LEVELS OF PROFICIENCY DURING THE NATURAL PROCESS OF LANGUAGE ACQUISITION IN THE CLASSROOM

Beginning Student	Typical Behaviors
	Low
	Depends almost entirely upon gestures, facial expressions, objects, pictures, a good phrase dictionary, and often a translator in an attempt to understand and to be understood
	Occasionally comprehends words and phrases
	Mid
	Begins to comprehend more, but only when speaker provides gestural clues, speaks slowly, uses concrete referents, and repeats
	Speaks very haltingly, if at all
	Shows some recognition of written segments
	May even be able to write short utterances
	High
	Is comprehending more and more in social conversation, but with difficulty
	Speaks in an attempt to meet basic needs, but remains hesitant; makes frequent errors in grammar, vocabulary, and pronunciation; often falls into silence
	Can read very simple text
	Can write a little, but very restricted in structuring and vocabulary

Intermediate Student

Low

(same as high beginning above)

Mid

May experience dramatic increase in vocabulary recognition, both oral and written

Has difficulty with idioms

Often knows what he or she wants to say but gropes for acceptable utterances

Makes frequent errors in grammar, vocabulary, and pronunciation

Is often asked to repeat and is frequently misunderstood

High

Is beginning to comprehend substantial parts of normal conversation but often requires repetitions, particularly in academic discourse spoken at normal rates

Is beginning to gain confidence in speaking ability; errors are common but less frequent

Can read and write text that contains more complex vocabulary · and structures; experiences difficulty with abstract language

Advanced Student

Low

(same as high-intermediate above)

Mid

Comprehends much conversational and academic discourse spoken at normal rates; sometimes requires repetition; idioms still present difficulty

Speaks more fluently but makes occasional errors; meaning is usually clear; at times uses vocabulary or structures inappropriately

Reads and writes with less difficulty materials that are commensurate with his or her cognitive development; demonstrates some problems in grasping intended meaning

---

High

Comprehends normal conversational and academic discourse with little difficulty; most idioms are understood

Speaks fluently in most situations with fewer errors; meaning is generally clear but experiences some regression at times

Reads and writes both concrete and abstract materials; is able to manipulate the language with relative ease

can Council on the Teaching of Foreign Languages) list of proficiency guidelines, it contains language behaviors typical of students at various levels of proficiency. Unlike the ACTFL list, it is fairly concise and easy to use, and the items within it are expressed positively. In other words, it focuses on what the students can do at each level rather than on what they can't do.

Teachers might want to set up a rating scale by which to judge students in the various proficiencies. If each student is rated by three or more judges, an even more accurate placement may be possible. This will be especially true once the judges have had adequate experience in assessing performance.[2]

In addition to testing for language competency, teachers should also test for competency in the content areas. Generally, the most valid tests of this kind for newcomers are those given in the students' first languages unless the program is an early immersion foreign language program. Such tests can be of great help, particularly in the placement of ESL students into sheltered and bilingual classes (see Chapter 14). If no appropriate tests of this kind are available, then tutors from the various language backgrounds who are proficient in the content areas in question can be asked to give informal evaluations based on performance during specific tasks. When students appear to be functioning at advanced levels, it is important to make sure that they have developed a sufficient amount of Cognitive Academic Learning Proficiency (CALP) in the target language before they are placed in academically-oriented mainstream classes (see Related Reading 9). Content area tests in the target language are readily available for most subject areas.

COMPUTER PROGRAMS

Much of the software used in computer-assisted language learning (CALL) programs has been of the drill and test variety. The computer plays the role of the "teacher" and imparts information. The students generally apply the information (often a rule) and then are tested. Those who fail to make the right choices on the test are cycled back for further instruction and application. The teacher may wish to use an authoring system, which makes it possible to set up similar lessons by learning special commands for that purpose. The teacher may choose to use the already established content or may opt for making additions or other modifications by selecting items from a series of possible choices. He or she also may have the option of creating new content for the program.

Although such programs may be appropriate at times, they can simply become one more means for perpetuating the dreariness of discrete point

---

[2]Some commercial tests that utilize similar procedures might be worth exploring. See, for example, the Foreign Service Institute Oral Interview.

exercises, confining the student to endless branching menus of boredom. Papert (1980), Jamieson and Chapelle (1984), and Canale and Barker (1986) are among those who stress the importance of using computer programs that instead have a highly integrative rather than discrete-point focus. For example, there are simulation programs in which students can take fantasy trips and choose, from among many options, where to go, what to eat, and so forth. There are interfacing programs in which students can hear prerecorded messages and interact with the computer by pressing particular keys or touching certain areas of the screen. There are programs in which the students are asked questions to clarify their thinking about essays that are in the planning stages. There are programs in which the students can create and illustrate stories by using graphics. There are programs that enable students to write poetry, sometimes with line-by-line assistance for special patterns (rhymes, limericks, haiku, etc.). And there are programs featuring test-taking and problem-solving strategies.

Canale and Barker suggest that by incorporating integrative programs, the computers can serve the same purposes for which language itself is used. Such programs can be used as tools for thought (self-directed language), tools for social interaction (other-directed language), and tools for play and art in which the emphasis is on self-expression. They are convinced that the activities should be intrinsically motivating, provide for the autonomy of the language student, and involve problem solving in many different situations.

Perhaps the most readily available integrative programs on the market today involve word processors, games, programming/problem-solving tools, and videodiscs.

Word Processors

Writing on a word processor is sometimes frustrating, often exhilarating, and always challenging to the second language student. Perhaps the best time for the students to begin is at late beginner/early intermediate levels. At that point they have acquired a repertoire (however limited) of language structures and vocabulary. Children, too, provided they can handle the experience cognitively, are able to work on word processors, especially if the programs are designed with them in mind. Some programs use extra large characters on the screen and the menu choices are pictorial in order that they be more easily comprehended.

Students seem to learn best when they are eased into the process gradually with the aid of the teacher, peer teachers, lay assistants, or other students. One way to begin, especially for a student who has never been introduced to a computer before, is to type something on the keyboard about the student that he or she can comprehend. The student's name might be used in the message. The student can then respond verbally while the teacher or aide types the words as they are said. The student can eventually proceed from the comprehending and writing of very short messages to fully developed text. The necessary commands can be learned gradually over a period of time.

Some programs, usually called "writing aids," are specifically designed to guide the writer through the preliminary stages of writing. For example, a few programs ask a series of questions to aid the students in targeting the purpose for a specific composition. Other programs enable students to exchange information and react to one another's ideas through a networking system called "electronic mail." Caution should be taken, however, with programs that give general reactions to student efforts such as "How interesting!" or "Nice job!" regardless of what has actually been written. Other programs to be wary of are those that accuse students of being "wordy" if the sentences are too long or of being "unclear" if the ratio of nouns to verbs is too high. Parkhurst (1984) feels that such programs may focus the student on mechanics at the expense of meaning or may make the student overly concerned with sentence length as opposed to clarity.

In most programs, files can be created in which ideas are stored. In some systems these files can be brought into full view on one part of the screen while the students are composing on the remaining area.

Being able to delete material, move whole passages to other parts of a document, select and change formats at will, write and send messages, and perform numerous other functions does much to facilitate the writing process.

Games

Often the best language teaching tools are computer programs that are intended for other purposes. Some games fit into this category. Computer games, although not usually meant for second language teaching per se, are one means for providing the language learners with challenges in the target language. They can present simulations that call for the students to make decisions and they can require interaction with others involved in the game. Computer games are currently available in many areas: math, science, language arts, and so forth. For example, one company puts out a math program which introduces children to the concepts of number lines, number pairs, and graph plotting. The students are asked to plot their own designs. Another program takes students on a simulated safari journey through a grid-like environment where they decipher clues in order to find the hiding place of a "mystery" animal. In the process they get practice in making inferences, creating tactics, and collecting and organizing clues. Other kinds of computer games include chess, word games, memory games, teasers with missing numbers, and many more.

Programming/Problem-Solving Tools

Some programs immerse the learner in a wide variety of problem-solving strategies. Some even have features that allow the student to "teach the computer" to complete a task. For example, there is the popular "turtle graphics" using Logo, a computer language first developed as a means by which children could discover concepts, especially in math and geometry. The tasks involve programming the behavior of a small triangle (the "turtle"). The turtle can be taught to draw different shapes and objects through a series of simple commands. Students are stimulated to interact as they discuss, write out, and modify their plans.

Canale and Barker see today's Logo programs mainly as prototypes of the more intelligent systems to come. Among the drawbacks of many of the versions of Logo currently available are a limited working memory, lack of a help-menu feature, difficult error messages, and low operating speed. However, they feel that even with the limitations, the programs are well suited to the needs of second language learners.

Videodiscs

Charles Findley of the Digital Equipment Corporation says, "Like no other medium, interactive videodiscs bring together the emotional, affective power of television with the processing power of the computer" (1986, p. 10). The system requires a videodisc player and a computer setup that includes a monitor, a keyboard for giving input, and a microcomputer. In addition, an interface is needed to connect the videodisc player to the computer.

Among its more meaningful uses is its ability to show real people in compelling scenarios that enable the learner to have input. For example, a married couple on the screen may be engrossed in an argument about whether or not their teenaged daughter should take a trip to Lake Tahoe with a girl friend. Arguments fly back and forth. Finally, one of the characters turns to the student and asks for help in forming a solution. Several choices are flashed on the monitor, and the student has to press the button representing his or her choice. The character then comments on the advice and the scenario continues. If all else fails, the character may even seek advice from the "expert tutor" who is part of the computer program.

Another use Findley mentions is to teach the listening skills necessary for academic success. A videodisc lecture is presented on some topic of interest. The student presses a key whenever he or she hears what appears to be a main idea. At the end of the lecture, all the main ideas are printed on the monitor and the student is asked to form questions using the ideas. As soon as a question is formed, the program returns to the speaker, who answers the question. Of course, one problem that seems apparent is the matching of questions to answers. There is a strong possibility that the student will want to ask questions for which the speaker has no answers.

Finally, Findley speaks of the videodisc as a dictionary. All the student needs to do is type a word onto the keyboard. The computer first checks for spelling and perhaps presents the student with alternative words from which to choose if there has been an error. On the videodisc, a speaker then demonstrates the use of the word in a context. In addition, the word is printed on the screen in a sample sentence.

These are only a few of the possible uses of a videodisc. Many programs are just now being developed for second language students and should be on the market soon.

SUMMARY

The selection of textbooks, placement tests, and computer programs is not a task that should be treated lightly. In order for these tools to be maximally useful, their substance and the activities they promote must reflect the basic philosophy of the teacher and the goals of the students. If the students' main goals are to communicate effectively and to learn subject matter in the target language, then tools must be chosen that are consistent with those objectives. This means that the materials must allow for active participation on the part of the learner and that the tasks must involve the use of natural language in meaningful contexts.

READINGS, REFLECTION, AND DISCUSSION

Suggested Readings and Reference Materials

The best from Sunburst. Pleasantville, NY: Sunburst Communications. This is a catalog containing award-winning educational courseware for the following computers: Apple; Atari; Commodore 64; IBM PC, PCjr; TRS-80 III, 4, Color; Tandy 1000. Strategies in problem solving seem to be the main thrust of its programs which are oriented toward the following subject areas: math, social and natural sciences, language arts, and many more. A word processing program called the "Magic Slate" (for the Apple) is included. At the lowest level in this system, the characters on the screen are very large and the commands are pictorial, making it particularly appropriate for second language students. The programs are in English only and are intended for preschool through adult students.

Gessler: The foreign language experts. New York: Gessler Educational Software. Language teaching software in French, Spanish, German, Italian, Latin, and English is made available through this catalog. Games, simulations, crossword puzzles, and the more traditional grammar-focused programs are included.

Oller, J., Jr. (1979). *Language tests at school: A pragmatic approach.* London: Longman. Focuses on creating, giving, and interpreting the results of pragmatic language tests. Stresses the importance of having the test reflect the teacher's general teaching philosophy (see excerpt in Related Readings on pages 372–381).

Savignon, S. (1983). Testing. In *Communicative competence: Theory and classroom practice* (pp. 231–278). Reading, MA: Addison-Wesley. A comprehensive treatment of many aspects of testing in general and second language testing in particular.

Questions for Reflection and Discussion

1. Locate at least three second language or foreign language textbooks and/ or supplementary materials. Analyze them using appropriate criteria from the list presented at the beginning of this chapter. Which materials would you select for use in a hypothetical or real teaching situation see footnote on page 207? Justify your choices.

2. Discuss how the following considerations might affect the teacher's choice of textbooks and other materials?
   a. the culture in which the materials are to be used
   b. size of the class
   c. experience of the teacher in teaching a second language
   d. proficiency level of the teacher in the target language

3. How might you incorporate the types of materials listed below into the classroom? Several suggestions for use have been mentioned throughout this book. You can probably think of many additional means for incorporation. Give specific examples.
   a. teacher-made materials
   b. student-made materials
   c. magazines and newspapers
   d. catalogs
   e. pictures and photographs
   f. television and/or radio shows

4. Create a short test that would be useful to you in placing students in a language program. Explain how you would use it to determine levels. How might you use another version of it to evaluate students at the end of a grading period?

5. If you have access to computers and computer software, select four programs for preview (they need not have been created specifically for language teaching). Which of the four would you select to use with your students? Justify your choices and explain how each might fit into your program, hypothetical or real.

14

Teaching Through the Content Areas

The immersion programs have provided us with ample evidence that it is possible to develop academic and second language skills simultaneously. . . .

L. Wong-Fillmore, 1985

Cognitive Academic Language Proficiency (CALP) and Basic Interpersonal Communication Skills (BICS) (see Related Reading 9) are both important to the second language student if he or she is to succeed in an academic environment. Doing well in academic or social settings in which students interact with and are accepted by educated people requires effective communication about a variety of subjects. The student must eventually have a command of the new language as it pertains to abstract thinking and problem solving. Whether the related skills are taught in self-contained classrooms in which a variety of subject areas are covered or in classrooms set up for the purpose of teaching specific subject matter, the lessons must be increasingly challenging academically and the environment must foster high self-esteem to be maximally effective.

Teachers of ESL and foreign languages can teach the target language through basic academic content using many of the methods and activities advocated in previous chapters. For example, total physical response might be used to teach math skills (Draw an octagon. Divide it in half with a vertical line) or to teach the commands associated with physical education (Line up. Count off by fours). The natural approach and its extensions can be used to demonstrate how to prepare a specific food for a meal or how to blend various colored paints for an art project. Jazz chants can be written about famous people in history or about concepts related to various sports. Here again the activities must make greater and greater cognitive demands upon the students in order that they may gain academic competence.

Once students are ready for higher levels within the content areas, they can be introduced to more difficult concepts through concrete approaches and can later progress to more abstract ones. For example, students might first be required to comprehend the intricacies involved in a science experiment by watching the teacher demonstrate and explain it. Following the demonstration, the students can be given specific oral directions (reminiscent of the total physical response) and do the experiment themselves. At an intermediate stage, students might be asked to perform experiments by using only written directions. Much later the students may be required to visualize similar experiments and write about what the results might be under various conditions.

It must be noted, before proceeding, that foreign language classes are usually independent of the other subject areas in the public school or university and are limited to specific time slots unless, of course, they are part of immersion programs. On the other hand, English as a Second Language classes are often taught in conjunction with one or more content-area programs: a submersion program; an immersion program consisting of sheltered content-area classes; and/or a bilingual program.

SUBMERSION

Students whose first language is different from that of the school and community are often "submerged" in content-area classes in which they are a minority among native speakers. In submersion classrooms they find themselves at a disadvantage in not being given the comprehensible input they need, and they are often treated as intellectual inferiors. The teachers generally do not understand their languages and know very little about their cultures. A first language may be regarded as a hindrance (subtractive)[1] to a mastery of the second. The students may or may not have the opportunity to be tutored individually. Sometimes the students who have the option of being tutored are placed in what are known as "pull-out" programs[2] which frequently put them at an even greater disadvantage. They may miss concepts simply because they were not in class when the concepts were introduced. Submersion

---

[1] Lambert (1974) identifies two treatments of primary languages within a second language environment: subtractive and additive. A language is said to be *subtractive* when it is considered detrimental to the learning of the second language and *additive* when it is thought a beneficial adjunct.

[2] A pull-out program is one in which the students are taken out of their regular classes for certain portions of the day in order to receive special help with the target language.

programs as a whole can be dangerous, especially for children, whose overall cognitive development may suffer as a result.

Mainstreaming for ESL students is a form of submersion but with a difference. Students are first placed in an ESL class. Once they become more socially and academically proficient in the target language, gradual transition is made to the regular content-area classes. Before they are mainstreamed into a regular class, the students are usually considered ready for entry by the ESL teacher and the content-area teacher into whose class they will be mainstreamed. They should have been introduced to the basic concepts involved and should have the skills necessary to function in the new environment. At first they may be placed in such classes as physical education, art, music, and math and later in the natural and social sciences. The subject matter for beginners during initial stages of transitioning is generally cognitively undemanding, the materials are context embedded, the content-area teacher is aware of the students' need for comprehensible input, and the atmosphere is one of acceptance rather than rejection.

IMMERSION

In immersion programs, students are placed in content-area classes in which the target language is the medium for communication. However, unlike submersion, all of the students are at *similar levels of proficiency* in the target language and the teacher is usually familiar with their first language and has a knowledge of their culture. If the new language is a foreign language (as opposed to a second language), it is additive and generally has the support of the parents and the community (see the early immersion program described in Chapter 16).

Another type of immersion program consists of *sheltered classes* taught in conjunction with a second language program such as ESL (see example in Chapter 15). At least some of the content-area subjects are taught in the second language to students who are of approximately the same proficiency levels. A sheltered-English program differs from other immersion programs in that the students usually come from several different linguistic and cultural backgrounds. Even though the teacher probably does not speak the various languages, he or she is usually well trained in current ESL methodology and is at least somewhat familiar with the various cultural backgrounds of the students. ESL itself is an example of immersion. However, it is usually taught with more basic social and academic goals in mind.

One of the problems that may occur as a result of an immersion program of any type is the fossilization of interlanguage forms due to a lack of sufficient contact with native speakers of the target language. However, the continued exposure to peer teachers, lay assistants, and native-speaking or near native-speaking peers from outside the classroom will do much to prevent early fossilization from being a major problem.

BILINGUAL EDUCATION

Bilingual education can be used in conjunction with any of the above kinds of programs (see Related Reading 9). Bilingual education involves teaching the students in some combination of their first and second languages. There are basically three types of bilingual education: transitional, maintenance, and enrichment. In *transitional* programs, students learn most of the subject matter in L1 until it is determined that they are ready (e.g., after considerable time spent in the ESL component of the program) to be gradually transitioned to all-English classes. In *maintenance* programs, students continue throughout their schooling to learn a portion of the subject matter in their L1 in order to continue improving their L1 skills. *Enrichment* programs are foreign language programs in which a portion of the subject matter is taught in L2, not for the purpose of immediate survival, but to broaden cultural horizons or in anticipation of some future move or visit to another culture.

Unfortunately, most of the bilingual education in the United States today is transitional. In other words, once the students have acquired a sufficient amount of the target language to survive, the bilingual component of their schooling is dropped. This is unfortunate for two reasons: (1) the students often are not ready for academic mainstreaming, since their academic skills are not yet highly developed in the target language, and (2) they will not be able to function with maximal effectiveness in our multicultural society, a society which *needs* people who are highly literate in more than one language.

Language maintenance programs (as opposed to transitional ones) would enable us to take advantage of our tremendous language resource. Ironically, we as a nation spend much time and energy improving and expanding our enrichment language programs so that our citizens will be "cultured," and yet we almost daily discourage the natural resource that many of our students already possess but need to develop—their first languages.

According to Cummins, an important goal of any second language program should be to develop proficient bilinguals (see the Threshold Hypothesis[3]). He reports:

---

[3]The Threshold Hypothesis argues that being proficient in one language facilitates being proficient in another. There are really two thresholds involved: (1) a higher threshold dividing the *proficient bilingual* (one who has obtained high levels of proficiency in both languages) from the *partial bilingual* (one who is proficient in one of the languages) and (2) the lower threshold dividing the partial bilingual from the *limited bilingual* (one who has only low-level skills in both languages).

. . . studies were carried out with language minority children whose L1 was gradually being replaced by a more dominant and prestigious L2. Under these conditions, these children developed relatively low levels of academic proficiency in both languages. In contrast, the majority of studies that have reported cognitive advantages associated with bilingualism have involved students whose L1 proficiency has continued to develop while L2 is being acquired. Consequently, these students have been characterized by relatively high levels of proficiency in both languages (1981, p. 38).

Cummins further says that one of the major successes of bilingual programs in elementary schools in particular is that they encourage students to take pride in their native languages and cultures, a necessity if the students are to have positive attitudes not only toward themselves but toward the target language and the people who speak it.

One of the problems facing maintenance bilingual education associated with ESL programs in particular is that there may be only one or two students speaking any given language within a particular school. Most school districts require that there be a minimum number of students in order to make the hiring of a bilingual teacher feasible. Yet another problem is finding qualified teachers, especially in the languages for which there are fewer speakers. For most of the languages it is possible to hire classroom tutors who are fluent, but unfortunately these people often cannot do much more than aid in transitional bilingual situations. For some teachers the only option available is to encourage students to maintain their first languages by not discouraging their use and by emphasizing the advantages and opportunities for those who become proficient bilinguals.

AN OPTIMAL PROGRAM FOR ESL STUDENTS

Perhaps the optimal program for ESL students would be one in which ESL is combined with mainstreaming, sheltered classes, and maintenance bilingual education. I especially like the one outlined in Table 14.1, adapted from Krashen, 1984.

TABLE 14.1. PROGRAM FOR ESL STUDENTS (adapted from Krashen, 1984)

Level	Mainstream	Sheltered	First Language
beginning	art, music, physical education	ESL	all core subjects
intermediate	art, music, physical education	ESL, math	social and natural sciences
advanced	art, music, physical education, math	ESL, social and natural sciences	enrichment
mainstream	all subjects	—	enrichment

Students at *beginning* levels would be mainstreamed into subject areas in which the concepts are generally concrete and less demanding cognitively. For some students (especially those in high school), home economics and industrial arts might be added as additional mainstream electives. Students would study all the core subjects in the first language. During *intermediate* levels, the same students might add typing to their mainstream course selections. Sheltered mathematics would be offered. The remainder of the core subjects would be taught in the first language. At *advanced* levels, students would be mainstreamed in most subjects except the social and natural sciences, which would be taught in sheltered environments. The first language would be used mainly for enrichment.[4] Notice that ESL would be taken throughout the program until the students were completely mainstreamed. The amount of time spent in ESL at each level would depend on the particular needs of each student. If teaching the core subjects in the first language were not possible through the intermediate levels, then these subjects would be taught in the second language within sheltered classes beginning at intermediate levels.

Teachers of mainstream and sheltered classes in the various content areas can do much to lower the cognitive and affective burdens of the ESL students. They can modify their teaching to meet three basic objectives: (1) to integrate the student (in the case of mainstream classes), (2) to communicate effectively with the student, and (3) to teach the subject matter in a manner conducive to acquisition. Below are some suggestions to help the content-area teachers meet these goals. Although the majority of ideas can be adapted to almost any situation, there may be a few that are not relevant. Their relevance will usually depend on the age levels, proficiency levels, and cognitive development of the students with whom they are to be used.

For Mainstream Teachers

1. *Provide a warm environment in which help is readily available to the student.* One way to do this is to set up a "buddy" system in which native English-speaking students are paired with ESL students. Another useful technique is peer teaching, in which a native English speaker teaches one or more ESL students. Group work, in general, increases the chances that the student will receive the necessary help. In addition, it increases the amount of interaction and comprehensible input received (see sections on peer teachers and lay assistants and on cooperative learning in Chapter 12).

---

[4]The term "enrichment" may imply a sort of token treatment of L1. The importance given to it will depend upon those operating the program. It is hoped that L1 will be used for academic as well as social communication in situations that really matter. Program directors might want to consider using L1 for a portion of the subject matter teaching provided that adequate teaching staff and materials are available.

2. *If possible, use a "satisfactory/unsatisfactory" grade option until the ESL student is able to compete successfully with native speakers.* Students may be ready sooner than expected, since many of them adapt very rapidly. It is important to remember that often the students, particularly those who are older, will already have a high level of academic understanding in the first language and may even surpass native speakers once they have proficiency in the new language.

3. *Record your lectures or talks on tape.* Students need to be able to listen to them as many times as necessary for understanding.

4. *Ask some of your native-speaking students to simplify the textbook by rewriting the chapters.* The job can be made as easy as possible by giving each native-speaking student just a few pages to simplify. The simplified materials not only aid ESL students but other students who may find the regular text too difficult. The students who do the rewriting benefit also in that the task serves as a review for them.

5. *Choose native-speaking students who take effective, comprehensible notes to duplicate them for ESL students.* By this means, the latter can be provided with study aids.

For Mainstream and Sheltered-Class Teachers

1. *Plan lessons that are related to the students' lives, utilize a lot of visuals, and provide for "hands on" kinds of involvement.* For example, drawing, coloring, and labeling maps in geography and pinpointing where the students came from is far more valuable than simply listening to a talk about maps.

2. *Communicate individually with the ESL students as much as time permits.* Avoid using complicated words or complex sentences. Speak slowly but keep the volume and intonation as normal as possible. Use few idioms. Incorporate a lot of body language. These strategies will be used subconsciously, for the most part, by those whose main goal is to communicate.

3. *Avoid forcing students to speak.* Allow them to speak when they are ready, in other words, when they volunteer. Students' right to a "silent period" (see Chapter 3) needs to be respected, especially when they are being introduced to new concepts.

4. *Reassure the students that their own languages are acceptable and important.* If other students from the same language group are present, do not insist that they use only English in class. No matter how good the intentions of the teacher, refusing to allow students to speak in their first languages is in essence saying that their languages are not good enough. Of course, students may need to be reminded that first languages should not be used to exclude others from discussion.

5. *Make all corrections indirectly by repeating what the students have said in correct form.* For example, suppose an ESL student says, "My book home"; the teacher can repeat, "I see. Your book is at home." It must be remembered, that simplified (ungrammatical) forms are to be regarded as normal while the student is progressing toward more complete competence in English. When the student is ready to move to another level, the indirect correction will probably be picked up and internalized after it is heard several times in a variety of situations. In written production, a few suggestions can be made for improvement as long as they are balanced with positive comments. Keep suggestions simple and offer only what you think each student can handle at his or her proficiency level.

6. *Try to answer all questions that the students ask but avoid overly detailed explanation.* Simple answers which get right to the point will be understood best. If possible, point to objects and pictures, or demonstrate actions to help get the meaning across.

7. *If you are in a situation in which lectures are appropriate, try to make them as comprehensible as possible.* Emphasize key words and phrases through intonation and repetition. Write them on the chalkboard or on an overhead transparency as you are talking. Give concrete examples. Use pictures and charts, map out ideas (see pages 200–201), use gestures, acting out, simplifications, expansion of ideas, or whatever is necessary to ensure understanding. Definitions, comparisons, and the like can be incorporated in the lectures to clarify new words and concepts. For example, in a history lesson you might say, "The government's funds were depleted. It was almost out of money. Thus the phrase "funds were depleted" is made more comprehensible.

8. *Check to see that what you are saying is understood.* Frequently ask questions such as, "Do you understand?" or "Do you have any questions?" and be very aware of the feedback you are getting. Blank stares or puzzled looks are sure signs that you are not being understood. Often it is better to ask more specific questions directly related to the preceding utterance. For example, after saying, "In Arizona rainfall is minimal during most of the year," you might check for understanding by asking, "Does it rain much in Arizona?" Asking a question such as this to confirm interpretation is yet another means by which students can be exposed to new words and concepts without losing the meaning of the message.

9. *Encourage students to use their bilingual dictionaries when necessary or to ask questions when they don't understand important concepts.* Help them to guess at meanings first by using the context. Assure them that they do not have to understand every word to comprehend the main idea.

10. *Reinforce key concepts over and over in a variety of situations and activities.*

Hearing about the concepts once or twice is not enough. Students need to be exposed to them several times through a wide range of experiences in order for internalization to take place.

11. *Whenever possible, utilize tutors who speak the native languages of the students.* Such help is especially important to students operating at beginning to intermediate stages.

12. *Request that appropriate content-area books be ordered for the library in the students' native languages.* These can be particularly useful to students in comprehending the concepts while the second language is being mastered. They also provide the students with a means for maintaining and developing skills in the native language.

13. *Become informed as much as possible on the various cultures represented by your students.* Knowing how particular students might react to classroom events and being able to interpret nonverbal symbols could help prevent misunderstanding and confusion.

14. *Acknowledge and incorporate the students' cultures whenever possible.* For instance, differing number systems can be introduced in math, customs and traditions in social science, various medicines in natural science, native dances and games in physical education, songs in music, ethnic calendars in art, haiku in literature, and so on. In addition, holidays can be celebrated, languages can be demonstrated for appreciation, and literature with translations can be shared.

15. *Prepare the students for your lessons and reading assignments.* You might ask them what they already know about the subject. Encourage them to look for main ideas by giving them a framework or outline beforehand. Ask them to predict outcomes and then to verify their predictions.

16. *Increase possibilities for success.* Alternating difficult activities with easier ones allows the ESL students to experience early successes. For example, in natural science one activity might be to create a diary that Neil Armstrong might have kept on his trip to the moon; the next assignment might be to make a list of the personal items including food that he might have taken with him. Of course, the tasks as a whole should gradually become more academically challenging as the students become more proficient.

AN OPTIMAL PROGRAM FOR
FOREIGN LANGUAGE STUDENTS

Immersion appears to be an optimal program for foreign language students. Note, for example, the successes of the French immersion programs in Canada and the Spanish immersion program in Culver City, California (see Chapter 2). Immersion programs are usually combined with maintenance bilingual education to ensure that students are developing skills in their first language even though it is also being fostered at home and in the community. Through immersion, students of approximately the same proficiency and age levels are given comprehensible input in the various subject areas (see the description of an early immersion program in Chapter 16).

Unfortunately, most foreign language programs involve students in the target language for only a small portion of each day. Because the classroom will probably be the only source of input for the student, it is *vitally* important that the class time be spent mainly on meaningful communication through interaction (see the high school foreign language program in Chapter 16). However, because the students may not receive a sufficient amount of input, even though the focus is on interaction, they will probably need some formal instruction in order to facilitate the acquisition process, especially those students who are cognitively able to use rule application.

SUMMARY

If we are to succeed in producing individuals who can function with maximum effectiveness in a pluralistic society, we must be concerned not only with their development of interpersonal skills but with their academic language skills as well. There are three basic approaches to content-area teaching: submersion, immersion, and bilingual education. Often these approaches are mixed. The optimal ESL program combines ESL with mainstreaming (a positive type of submersion), sheltered classes (a kind of immersion), and maintenance bilingual education.

Immersion programs have proven to be optimal for foreign language teaching as long as there are enough native-speaking or near native-speaking linguistic models present to help prevent early fossilization. However, most foreign language programs consist of brief daily time slots set aside for the teaching of the target language, making meaningful interaction in class even more important.

READINGS, REFLECTION, AND DISCUSSION

Suggested Readings and Reference Materials

Beyond language: Social and cultural factors in schooling language minority students. (1986). Office of Bilingual Bicultural Education, California State Department of Education, Sacramento. Los Angeles: Evaluation, Dissemination and Assessment Center, California State University. A collection of timely articles written to inform teachers about the problems facing minority students in the U.S. public schools. Suggestions and perspectives are presented so that students may be aided in their struggle to meet academic challenges.

Cummins, J. (1979b). Linguistic interdependence and the educational development of bilingual children. *Review of Educational Research, 49*(2): 222–251. Investigates the factors involved in explaining why there are marked differences in outcomes of immersion programs for the majority child and submersion programs for the minority child. Looks at such variables as community background factors, educational input factors, student input factors, and instructional treatments.

Enright, D. S., & McCloskey, M. L. (1985). Yes, talking!: Organizing the classroom to promote second language acquisition. *TESOL Quarterly, 19*(3), 431–453. This article advocates group work as a means for providing interactional opportunities. It discusses a communicative model and its uses in ESL and content-area classrooms.

The immersion phenomenon. (1984). *Language and Society* (12). This entire issue is devoted to the remarkable success of immersion in Canada. Articles such as "For My Kids, It's French without Tears" by Gibson; "School Systems Make It Work" by McGillivray; "Research Update" by Lapkin and Swain; and "Immersion: Why It Works and What It Has Taught Us" by Krashen.

Stanford, G. (1977). *Developing effective classroom groups.* New York: Hart. Presents ways of structuring groups for a variety of academic experiences. Offers methods for creating groups to bring about maximal interactional benefits.

Questions for Reflection and Discussion

1. What might be the ideal time for introducing students to a second language? Consider submersion and immersion differences and how they might affect children in the lower grades. Discuss other factors that would be relevant (see Cummins in the Suggested Readings above).

2. Find out as much as possible about the cultures that might be represented in a hypothetical or real classroom for which you might be responsible (see footnote on page 207). How can the various cultures be incorporated in some of your lessons? What specific problems might your students have with the subject matter due to cultural factors (see also Chapter 5)? What will you do to help them overcome these difficulties?

3. One of the suggestions for mainstream and sheltered-class teachers is to keep success within each student's reach by alternating difficult activities with easy ones, all the while increasing the academic challenges as the student grows in the new language. Plan a series of activities for one or two lessons of your choice in which you would increase chances for success by this means.

4. Choose additional ideas from the suggestions for mainstream and sheltered-class teachers in this chapter and apply them to a specific situation in which academic skills are taught. To a group of class members, demonstrate the use of one or more of your applications. Ask the group for feedback.

PART IV

Programs in Action

Reading about a variety of programs can give teachers a wealth of ideas about how to create and implement methods, activities, and methodologies (including decisions about content, how and when to correct, how to incorporate a silent period, and so forth). Seeing the ways in which vital questions are answered by others and being exposed to the direct application of various methods and activities can give real insights into what might work in certain situations, with specific groups of learners.

The programs here have been divided into ESL programs (Chapter 15) and foreign language programs (Chapter 16). Several different levels are represented—elementary through university, including adult basic education. Some are districtwide programs, others take place in a single school setting. An immersion foreign language program, a sheltered English program, a life-skills program using community resources, and a university language institute are only a few of the many presented here.

15

ESL Programs

As was stated in Chapter 14, an optimal program for ESL students might be one in which ESL is combined with mainstreaming, sheltered classes, and maintenance bilingual education. Although none of the programs described in this chapter claims to be optimal, several have features at which we may want to take a closer look. The programs include an ESL Intensive Learning Center[1] (Alameda High School in Lakewood, Colorado), a sheltered English model (Artesia High School in Artesia, California), a kindergarten ESL program within a Spanish bilingual school (Loma Vista Elementary in Maywood, California), a life-skills adult basic education program (the North Hollywood Adult Learning Center in Hollywood), and a university English language institute (the University of Michigan in Ann Arbor).

Some of the descriptions focus on the overall design of the programs, others on specific elements within them. Although the programs have been developed for specific age groups and purposes, the basic designs and activities need not be used exclusively in these situations. An imaginative teacher can probably see many ways in which most can be adapted for other educational settings (see Chapter 12).

---

[1]This program is summarized from Chapter 32 of *Methods That Work*, Oller and Richard-Amato (Newbury House, 1983). Because the students were of diverse language backgrounds (nine different languages were represented), a bilingual program was not considered feasible by the school district. However, sheltered classes (see Chapter 14) were provided in social studies and math. Tutors who spoke the various languages were available upon request.

A SECONDARY ESL
INTENSIVE LEARNING CENTER

This program was an emergency effort to meet the needs of adolescent refugees and other newcomers who found themselves going through language and culture shock (see Chapter 5).[2]

In the fall of 1979 the ESL Intensive Learning Center (ILC) was established by the Jefferson County Schools at Alameda High School in Lakewood, Colorado. The center served 41 students from eight different countries: Vietnam, Laos, Korea, Taiwan, Somalia, Romania, Colombia, and the Philippines. Altogether they spoke nine languages, including two dialects of Chinese. Seventy-eight percent were refugees from Southeast Asia. Nearly all of them planned to make the United States their home.

In preparation for the center, a cultural awareness program was established for the school's student body and staff. Retreats and inservices provided the settings for learning more about the cultures of the students and for becoming more sensitive to their needs. The inservicing eventually evolved into an ongoing attempt to remain informed, to solve problems, and to share ideas, concerning not only ESL students but the improvement of the school in general.

As the director of the center, my objectives were threefold: to help the students acquire English but at the same time maintain their own languages and as much of their cultures as possible; to prepare them for mainstreaming, both academically and socially; and to help them function effectively as members of a multicultural society in the United States.

Placement

By using oral interviews and writing samples (similar to those discussed in Chapter 12), I examined each student's interlanguage to determine roughly his or her approximate level. I divided the students into the traditional categories of beginning, intermediate, and advanced, but held no illusions about clear-cut boundaries between one level and another, realizing that overlap would occur.

The *beginning students* were typically in the center most of the day for one or two weeks and then were gradually transitioned to content-area classes for part of the day. At first they needed to develop survival skills. Finding an apartment for themselves or their parents and helping with the shopping were among the first challenges. In addition preparation was made for entry into mainstream classes such as art, physical education, and music, and eventually into sheltered math and social studies.

Most *intermediate students* needed one to two hours a day in the center

[2]I am grateful to the Jefferson County Public School District, to my students and colleagues at Alameda High School, and to my collaborator on *Methods That Work*, John Oller, who first encouraged me to develop an in-depth description of the center.

to develop language skills through interaction before certain interlanguage elements had fossilized. By the time they had reached the end of this stage, most students were into a full schedule of content-area classes except for regular English.

Advanced students required at least one hour in the center a day to continue developing communicative competence and to work in specific skill areas in preparation for regular English classes. Although much of the work was individualized at this level, there was a lot of opportunity for interaction.

Classroom Activities

To create positive attitudes toward the general environment, decrease inhibitions, and avoid the necessity of verbal responses, the beginning students at first were involved in purely physical activities such as the following (see also the warm-ups in Chapter 9).

1. The students joined hands in a circle. I guided them to move (with hands still joined) until the group was all tangled up and didn't look like a circle anymore. A student who had been sent out of the room came back to untangle the group. The activity was repeated until all volunteers had had a chance to go out and come back to restore the circle.

2. Mirror dancing was used once the students felt fairly comfortable with one another. Following a demonstration of the activity, I divided the students into pairs and had the members of each pair stand opposite each other. Rock music was played. One member of each group danced while the other member mirrored every move. Then they switched roles. This activity provided a way of communicating without verbalizing.

At beginning levels, the principal activities relied heavily on Asher's total physical response and the audio-motor unit (see Chapter 6) and on the natural approach and its extensions (see Chapter 7). The techniques were integrated to facilitate mini-dramas (see Chapter 9), in which I acted as the director and the students were, at first, mute actors and actresses.

Perhaps the method that helped most to establish a secure environment once the students reached high beginning levels was a version of "Suggestopedia" (Lozanov, 1978). While soft music played in the background, students were asked to close their eyes, breathe deeply, and exhale slowly but completely while tensing and relaxing specific muscle groups. Then they were told something like: "Try to remember when you were a child. You were sitting very close to someone who was reading to you . . . maybe it was your mother or your father or an older sister or brother. You felt very warm and secure. You knew you could learn just about anything at that moment."

Through this suggestive technique, students were reminded of a comfortable childlike state at a time when they were presumably highly capable learners. Even though they may not have understood all the words, just the tone of voice seemed to soothe them. Again they were taken through the deep breathing. They then were asked to open their eyes. Pictures of objects were displayed one by one, as the names of the objects were read dramatically. The vocabulary items selected were suggested by the content-area teachers who would eventually have these students in sheltered or mainstream classes. Although the procedure itself falls far short of real communication, it worked well, presumably because the students were instrumentally motivated to learn just those items in order to get into the relevant content-area classes later on.

Throughout the entire process of teaching ESL, I was always attempting to help the students make progress toward full communication. I tried to create situations in which the students were taken through the natural process of language acquisition, from TPR and mini-drama, to games, to chants, and subsequently to increasingly demanding communication.

What I hoped to do in the ESL classroom was to appeal to the univeral interest, curiosity, and uninhibited spirit associated with first language acquisition. One means for accomplishing this was to use jazz chants (see Chapter 8). With student input, I even wrote my own jazz chants. Although such exercises were often written for beginning levels, the following one was written for a group of intermediate to advanced students as a means of teaching idiomatic expressions. A sheet of paper was placed on the door on which the students could list phrases that they heard in the halls but didn't understand. Using these phrases, the following jazz chant was constructed:[3]

What do you say when your friend's sad and blue?

> Hang in there!
> Hang in there!

What do you say when your love's not true?

> I'm feeling down.
> I'm feeling down.

What do you say when your friend's been in a fight?

> Keep cool.
> Keep cool.

What do you say when you don't do something right?

> I blew it.
> I blew it.

What do you say when your sister misbehaves?

> Don't mess around!
> Don't mess around!

---

[3]Some of the idiomatic expressions incorporated in the chant are regional. However, teachers desiring to use this chant may want to replace some of the expressions with ones that are current and appropriate to their own areas.

What do you say when you feel like slaves?

> We're fed up!
> We're fed up!

What do you do when someone is shy?

> Break the ice!
> Break the ice!

What have you done when you can't remember why?

> I've spaced it out!
> I've spaced it out!

Students would snap their fingers to the rhythm of the words as they read them aloud.

Moving toward more challenging production, I created situations in which one student had vital information that another did not have but needed. I employed a version of the *information gap* (see page 78). For example, one student gave directions on how to reproduce a specific drawing while another tried to follow the directions. This activity generated much comprehensible input and TPR type mappings of utterances to actions.

Perhaps the most effective communication, however, was the one-to-one interaction that occurred for the major portion of each day. Peer teachers and lay assistants were instrumental in this process. Fortunately, qualified peer teachers (see also Chapter 12) were in ample supply at Alameda High School as they are in most schools. English-speaking students with native or near native competence were selected from regular English classes on the basis of teacher recommendations and individual interviews. These students were trained in two four-hour workshops which included orientations to the various cultures represented and discussions on how to interact with others to encourage, motivate, and communicate effectively. Then within the first two weeks in the semester they attended two more workshops, which lasted two hours each. During this time the peer teachers observed and became acquainted with those groups or individuals whom they would eventually be teaching. During these sessions the peer teachers became familiar with the materials and the methods they would be expected to use. They spent part of the time in role play using the materials and methods on each other as they alternately took on the roles of teachers and students. Thereafter, they attended one two-hour workshop every month or so to share successes and to discuss problems.

In addition to the peer teachers, two adult lay assistants were hired from the community by the school district. They also participated in the workshops. I met with each of the lay assistants and peer teachers at least once a week. These sessions centered on discussing student progress and on making flexible lesson plans, week by week.

At the beginning- to lower-intermediate levels, the peer teachers, the lay assistants, and I worked with small groups of three or four students. With the high-intermediate to advanced levels, the work was often individualized. We reacted to written work by providing positive feedback and asking relevant questions. We encouraged frequent revisions. Pictures were often used to stimulate ideas for stories and expository paragraphs, and a topic box was made available out of which students could draw ideas, similar to the topics found in Chapter 11. Students who chose topics of their own often wrote about their most poignant memories. One student, for example, wrote about how the people on a boat from Vietnam gathered rain water on a plastic sheet in order to have enough to stay alive. Another wrote about being a nurse in a Thai refugee camp where at the age of 13 he delivered babies.

In addition to the individualized work, we were able to lead our respective groups in activities such as writing short scenarios, reading or acting out stories, writing expository paragraphs, discussing relevant topics, and in general doing any sort of activity that would result in comprehensible input through interaction.

Affective activities were also used to strengthen self-concepts and further the development of communication skills. Interviewing (see pages 171–173) seemed to be particularly popular, since it brought the students in contact with many people outside the classroom, including students, teachers, counselors, and the principal.

Mock telephone conversations also provided situations for relevant communication. I would pretend to hold a telephone up to my ear and would say, for example, "Hello, is Carlos there?" Carlos would pretend to answer and a conversation would ensue. After a weekend or a vacation we often used this method to get in touch with the students again. When we had visitors in the classroom, bringing them into the game was a way to get to know them. This procedure seemed to relieve the tensions often associated with classroom performance. Although the student was "on the spot," so to speak, there was still the freedom to contribute without fear of having one's surface form evaluated, since corrections were usually done indirectly. When tensions seemed particularly high, such as after a pep assembly, before final exams, or after an unpleasant incident, we sometimes used relaxation techniques similar to those described earlier for suggestopedia. In the case of an unpleasant incident, we would take time out to discuss it, emphasizing that other, less important things could wait. Students might even role-play stressful situations (see Chapter 9). For example, if someone had been shoved in the hall, or if someone had been teased, taking time out in this manner was important to the teaching of coping strategies and alternative approaches to conflict resolution.

Yet another tension-reducing technique was the use of music (see Chapter 8). Music seemed to foster the building of self-esteem, sensitivity to others and their problems, and the development of communicative skills. Paul Simon's "Bridge over Troubled Water," Carol King's "You've Got a Friend," and other old favorites stimulated a lot of conversation. Music provided one means by which the ESL students could deal with nostalgia and the inevitable feelings of depression and loneliness. We realized that repression of such feelings could only be detrimental. We did not pressure anyone to talk about the past, but we did try to provide an open atmosphere in which they could discuss feelings when the need arose.

Evaluation of the Students

To evaluate the students, we looked at progress and effort made in the development of basic skills. We used speech samples and writing samples taken at nine-week intervals (similar to the diagnostic procedure mentioned earlier). At the end of every nine-week period, we held individual conferences with each student to emphasize gains made during the previous nine weeks and to discuss and obtain feedback concerning the work for the coming nine weeks.

Mainstreaming

To effect a smooth transition from the relatively protective environment of the center into the mainstream, we tried to involve as many people in the process as possible. The idea was to move the students rapidly and comfortably toward full participation in the school at large.

Teachers in the school invited the students to share in family outings; peer teachers invited them to movies, sports events, and other activities; clubs and organizations involved them in parties and retreats. Even the members of the Alameda High School Student Government volunteered to write personal letters to them. These personal letters were especially appreciated, as they were received and answered every few weeks. Some of the ESL students became close friends with their ''pen pals.''

The Native Language and Culture

An effort was made to encourage language and cultural maintenance. We stressed the advantages of being multilingual and multicultural in a global society. We also compared cultures a lot. One activity which was especially useful in this connection was for each cultural group to choose a national holiday to celebrate. Students planned for these events weeks and even months in advance. They invited people from the community, content-area teachers, administrators, counselors, and friends to join them. During the festivities of each special event, the students shared their customs, dances, songs (in their own languages), games, and food.

Some Reflections and Recommendations

Obviously, a brief overview of a program that extended over several years can cover only the barest essentials. Therefore, it seems reasonable to include some thoughts and conclusions drawn from the overall picture that might be of use to teachers in training or to others who might one day find themselves in the position of having to set up a similar program. In that vein, here are listed some elements of the ESL Intensive Learning Center (ILC) which one might want to include.

Staff

The following staff members are needed:

1. *A full-time ESL teacher* to (a) manage the ILC each day; (b) be responsible for curriculum planning; (c) make decisions on academic mainstreaming; (d) coordinate programming for individual students with content-area teachers and other personnel; (e) provide inservice training for lay assistants, peer teachers, and content-area teachers; and (f) order materials, supplies, and equipment.
2. *Two part-time lay assistants* (each at four hours per day) and *one peer teacher* for every four to five students (one period each per day) who would be responsible for (a) participating in workshops in order to become familiar with methods and materials; (b) teaching on a one-to-one basis; (c) playing a facilitative teacher role in small-group situations; (d) assisting in student evaluation; and (e) helping the teacher in materials preparation.
3. *Resource persons* to help out in a variety of ways that should be more or less obvious according to category: (a) a reading teacher, (b) one or more counselors, (c) a librarian, (d) a media specialist, (e) a school psychologist, and (f) one or more social workers. In addition, the school administrators should be apprised of and sensitized to the special needs of Limited English-speaking students.

The Room and Furnishings

To allow space for multiple simultaneous activities, the room should be fairly large, about 25 by 35 feet. To accommodate the physical activities, it should be well ventilated and attractively decorated, preferably with movable furniture (see Figure 15.1).

It should include the following items:

Furniture: tables, comfortable chairs, bookshelves (used for partitioning as well as for shelving books), listening stations, bulletin boards, chalkboards, files, and enclosed cupboards.

Equipment: tape recorders, cassette players, listening stations with headsets (for private listening), record players, an overhead projector, and one or more typewriters.

Materials: folders for student work, a topic box with topic ideas for writing

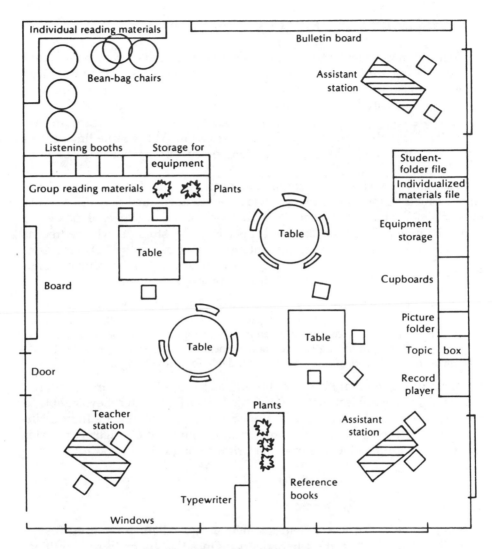

Figure 15.1. A Floor Plan of the ILC

and discussion, a picture folder to stimulate ideas for writing and discussion, audiovisual aids (hand-manipulated clocks, maps, telephone dials, picture cards, etc.), records to provide music for many purposes (background music, music to promote discussion, etc.), games, magazines, and current newspapers.

Student reference books: dictionaries in various languages, subject matter books from the content-area teachers, idiom dictionaries, simplified dictionaries, special-interest books (how to get a job, colleges and universities, etc.).

A SECONDARY SHELTERED ENGLISH MODEL[4]

We learned in Chapter 14 that a sheltered class is a kind of immersion situation in that the students are at similar levels of proficiency in the target language. We also learned that the teacher may be familiar with their first languages and usually has a knowledge of their cultures. A sheltered class can provide the comprehensible input necessary for the student to acquire the target language through conte.it-based instruction. At the same time, it can serve as a surrogate family of sorts or a temporary buffer between the student and the mainstream.

Artesia High School in Artesia, California, is one of the schools in the ABC Unified School District which has a highly developed network of sheltered classes. The school offers 36 sections of ESL and sheltered classes to approximately 350 Limited English Proficient (LEP) students who represent 21 different languages. All the students in what is called the "Diverse Language Program" (ESL only) are eligible to take the special courses. Pam Branch, the school's program coordinator, reports:

> What immersion has taught us is that comprehensible subject matter teaching *is* language teaching; students can profit a great deal from subject matter classes in which the conscious focus is on the topic and not on language. Classes are taught in English, but native speakers are excluded in order to make the teacher's input more understandable for limited-English students.

Students in this program begin with two periods of ESL and three sheltered classes in specific subject-matter areas (see Figure 15.2). Later they are able to add other sheltered classes (see Figure 15.3). Gradually they are fully mainstreamed, first in those areas that require less command of English and later in all subjects. Bilingual aides provide primary language support for the students.

Identification and Evaluation

A home language survey and supplementary questionnaire is used first to identify LEP students in the school district. Once the student is so identified, he or she receives the Language Assessment Scale (LAS) test and, when appropriate, a battery of other tests, including subtests of the Comprehensive Test of Basic Skills (CTBS) and an informal writing sample. Each student is then rated on an oral language observation matrix which is similar to the ACTFL (American Council on the Teaching of Foreign Languages, 1982) proficiency levels 1–5. On the basis of these measures, students are placed in either Level I, II, or III.

---

[4]I wish to thank Pam Branch, Lilia Stapleton, Marie Takagaki, Ted Marquez, and many others with the ABC Unified School District who made it possible for me to observe their sheltered class program and include it in this chapter.

Description of Each Level

Level I (akin to the beginning stages described on page 212) includes two periods of ESL: Skills I and Conversation I. At this level, the students can also choose from among several sheltered courses (see Figure 15.2).

Skills I focuses on survival skills such as telling time, using the telephone, filling out application forms, and so forth. *Conversation I* emphasizes various topics of interest such as those recommended by Krashen and Terrell (see Chapter 7). In both classes the total physical response and the natural approach are relied upon to foster low anxiety and provide sufficient comprehensible input. The sheltered classes at this level require tasks that are cognitively undemanding and heavily context embedded. For example in *Art* the students are given a wide variety of art experiences in which they can express themselves freely while they study composition and color as these are used in drawing, painting, and making three-dimensional objects. *Geography* also relies on concrete concepts for which pictures, maps, and globes can be used. Drawing maps or making papier-mâché ones in relief can provide a great deal of hands-on activity. *Horticulture* finds students planting and caring for a garden after diagraming and labeling the plants in a basic plan. The course not only helps students acquire the language through here and now tasks but may even open up some possible jobs for the future. *Piano* offers individualized instruction on the use of electric keyboards with headsets. If the students wish, they may elect to continue Piano into the next level. Students are placed

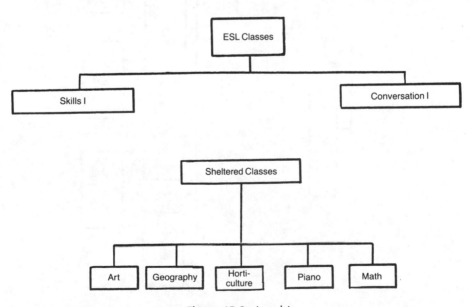

Figure 15.2. Level I

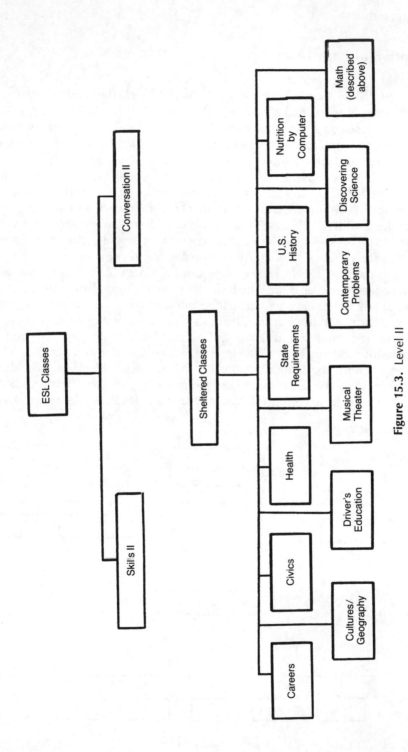

Figure 15.3. Level II

in *Math* (in Levels I and II) according to math ability rather than level of proficiency in English. Problems are worked out on the chalkboard, and vocabulary banks are used to help students remember words already learned and to add new words for future work. Because word problems remain a continuing difficulty, the teacher helps students to break down the problems into various steps, making the tasks more manageable.

Level II (akin to the intermediate stages described on page 213) includes two periods of ESL: Skills II and Conversation II. At this level, the students have even more choices from among sheltered classes (see Figure 15.3).

Skills II and *Conversation II*, like their counterparts at Level I, extend survival skills through a topical organization, adding vocabulary appropriate to the students' needs. At this level the tasks are more cognitively demanding but are still highly context embedded. *Careers* looks at various vocational possibilities and helps the students to discover their own strengths and weaknesses. It makes an effort to find what kinds of jobs are best suited to each individual. The students receive practice in interview technique by role playing (see Chapter 9). *Cultures/Geography* helps students to gain an appreciation of many different cultures in relation to their geographical advantages and constraints. *Civics* takes a historical approach to the American governmental system, its organization, and the ramifications of its tenets. *Driver's Education* gives the students an opportunity to prepare for the written portion of the driver's exam and presents a reading task for which the students are already highly motivated (later they can enroll in the driver's training course, which teaches them how to actually drive a car). *Health* covers the human body and emphasizes the prevention and control of common diseases. *Musical Theater* presents American culture as depicted through Hollywood's version of Broadway musicals. *State Requirements* includes a variety of units mandated by the state of California: mental health, first aid (students receive a certificate upon completion of the unit), fire and accident prevention. *Contemporary Problems* is also a sort of catch-all course highlighting issues on consumerism and interpersonal relations. Topics covered include money management, credit, insurance, self-awareness, alternative lifestyles, sexuality, and parenting. *U.S. History* is taught through frequent dramatizations of events, bringing the past alive and making it meaningful to the students. *Discovering Science* includes experiments and a lot of realia to explain physical phenomena. *Nutrition by Computer* exposes students to the benefits of a balanced diet and at the same time introduces them to computers, a rather unusual but effective combination. Students chart daily food intake, categorize foods into groups, and plan well-balanced meals.

Mainstream classes are gradually added beginning at Level II. Students are required to take mainstream physical education and can elect to take other mainstream courses such as typing or home economics.

Level III (akin to the advanced stages described on page 213) is tailored for advanced students who are into a full schedule of mainstream courses except for regular English. Literature is at the core of the program, and the basic skills (listening, speaking, reading, writing) are integrated into the activities evolving out of it. Students are eventually reclassified from Level III ESL once they demonstrate through a variety of means (similar to the initial battery of tests) that they are ready to move on to more challenging activities.

Staff Development

One reason for the apparent success of Artesia's program in helping students to acquire English is the emphasis the school places on staff development. In fact, this was one of the qualities cited when Artesia High School was given national recognition as an Exemplary School in 1983–84 by the Department of Education. All seventeen of the ESL/content-area teachers have received special training in giving effective comprehensible input and in correcting through modeling and expansion. This special training is part of a series of after-school inservices provided by the district's ESL resource teachers. In addition, Krashen has consulted with the district on several occasions, offering its teachers practical applications of his theories.

Alfredo Schifini and other language arts and reading consultants from the Los Angeles County Office of Education have conducted inservices in writing/reading activities. Schifini stresses that introducing the main points of a lesson increases the use of contextual clues for comprehension of the material. Recapping the major points on the chalkboard or an overhead also increases the possibility of acquisition. He feels that lectures laden with jargon are inappropriate in a sheltered class. Instead, oral interaction should be used extensively. Students can be engaged in small group tasks such as science experiments, map making, creating murals, preparing skits, and similar activities. It is the teacher's job to demonstrate or model the task for the students to then carry out. He advises teachers, when choosing textbooks, to consider the readability, print size, paragraph length, and types of illustrations used. He recommends mapping or other kinds of graphic organization (see pages 200–201) as useful techniques for helping students obtain meaning from the materials. About sheltered classes, he reminds the teachers:

> Sheltered English classrooms do not involve any magical approach to teaching. Certainly there is no "quick fix". . . . The potential exists with the sheltered model to provide truly meaningful instruction for a wide range of LEP students. It is important to restate that sheltered English should not be viewed as a substitute for bilingual education, but rather as a component in a carefully planned out developmental program designed to facilitate academic success.[5]

---

[5]Here it should be noted that the school discontinued its bilingual program in Spanish, some think to its detriment (see Chapter 14), when it began the sheltered model program.

In addition to the inservicing provided by the ABC Unified School District, several of the staff members at Artesia are in the master's degree program in teaching second languages offered through a joint effort between the district and California State University, Los Angeles. All the courses in the program are taught locally to make them even more attractive to the teachers.

Staff members working in the program have come to the conclusion that the sheltered class model is an effective means for teaching the target language to diverse primary language groups for whom bilingual education is not currently considered a possibility.

A KINDERGARTEN ESL PROGRAM
WITHIN A SPANISH BILINGUAL SCHOOL

At Loma Vista Elementary School in the heart of Maywood, California, a Spanish-speaking community, every class has two components: ESL and Spanish bilingual education.[6] The kindergarten is no exception.

Beverly McNeilly, a teacher of the ESL component of the kindergarten program, takes a holistic approach to teaching English to her 31 children. In her class, English is the vehicle by which the students are exposed to stories, films, songs, games, and other items of interest. Structured ESL lessons represent only a small portion of the program; they are the first to go if any spontaneous opportunity presents itself. For example, one day the class abandoned a lesson to watch the tree trimmers as they sawed off the limbs of an old tree outside the window.

The Subject Matter, Activities,
and Classroom Management

The subject matter itself is integrated into a variety of skill areas. Target vocabulary words are generally presented in an introductory lesson and then used again and again throughout the day, whether in math, science, art, physical education, or music. The words will be reinforced naturally in the course of events. For example, in a unit on ocean life the children, as part of an art project, create starfish and coral for a mural. In math they choose which of several drawings are "true octopi" (the ones with eight legs). Music finds the children dancing to aquatic sounds on a recording as they imagine how a shark, a crab, a whale, or a dolphin might move. The reading lesson for the day consists of a game in which the children use magnets to "catch" fish on which letters of the alphabet have been written. A science display (see display area in Figure 15.4) features shells and sand for the children to explore. The

---

[6]Loma Vista Elementary School is in the Los Angeles Unified School District.

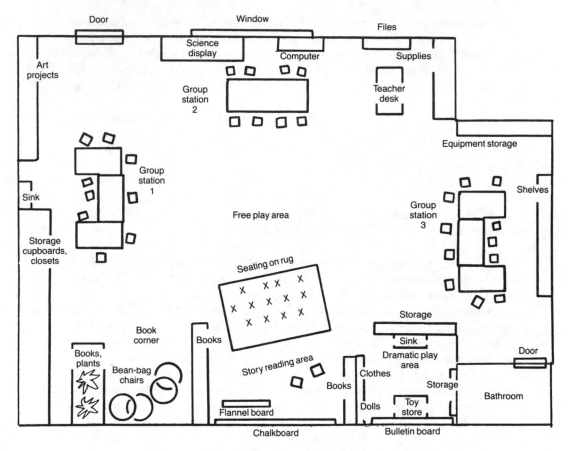

Figure 15.4. A Floor Plan of the ESL Kindergarten.

entire room environment reflects the topic in other ways with pictures, bulletin boards created by the children, and books on the theme.

The teacher and her assistants, including one or two peer teachers from the fifth grade, manage a variety of activities for small group participation. Group size varies from six to nine members depending on the task at hand and on the number of assistants available. Instead of rigidly defined groups and timetables, fluid grouping is used. Several centers are set up each day which focus on related concepts. For example, one day during the study of mathematics, the children were divided into groups to participate in some of the activities from *Mathematics Their Way* by Lorton (1976). One group found how many designs they could make with only three Tinker Toys. Another group explored the different ways of separating six cubes into two piles. Other groups made geometric shapes with rubber bands and sequential patterns with rocks and shells. The amount of time needed to complete a task depended on each individual. Ongoing informal evaluation and periodic pre- and post-testing of key objectives provided evidence that children were mastering the concepts.

For the above lessons, the groups were formed based on a placement test which accompanies the Lorton book. However, usually the small group activities are not sequentially organized and the children are allowed to select their own groups. Because they are allowed the freedom of choice, interest and curiosity remain at high levels. There are times when the group into which a student wants to go is full (all the chairs are taken). In that case, the student has two choices. He or she either can move to another activity or can participate in free or dramatic play in the areas designated for those purposes (see Figure 15.4). It is in these areas that the child can reinforce concepts just learned or pursue other goals of immediate interest.

The teacher claims that she is often heartened to see the themes with which they have been working reflected in their choices of play activity. She reported:

> When we discussed transportation, block play produced trains and rocket ships. When we were concentrating on body parts, the table in the dramatic play area was an operating table, as amateur doctors came out with appropriate original language. To me, having a child produce "I'm a doctor. What's the problem? Let me see your leg"—a combination of words that had never been taught her—is so much more rewarding than having little parrots.

Total physical response (Chapter 6) is combined with drama (Chapter 9) and songs and poetry (Chapter 8) to reinforce concepts. Props and pictures are used to aid understanding. For example, a skit about a firefighter's day includes the following song, which is sung to the tune of "Frère Jacques." The children act out the words as they sing the song.

> Are you sleeping? Are you sleeping?
> Firefighters, firefighters.
> Alarm bells are ringing, alarm bells are ringing.
> Ring, ring, ring . . . ring, ring, ring.

Because the lyrics are accompanied by action, even rank beginners can respond to the cues after observing their more advanced classmates. Children who are in the early speech production stage begin to sing along with the words. Thus, children at all levels are accommodated in this activity.

The teacher frequently reads aloud stories related to the units. Some of the children "read" the stories to each other later in the book corner (see Figure 15.4), prompted only by the pictures. One of McNeilly's favorite stories to read to the children is Esphyr Slobodkina's *Caps for Sale* (1984) during a unit on clothing. She generally simplifies the story to ensure understanding. She reports that because she often repeats the same story several times in a row, she is not surprised to hear expressions from it used by the children in other situations. For instance, "Hats for sale! Does anybody want to buy a hat?" the next day became "Pencils for sale!" when one of the students was handing out the pencils.

Nursery rhymes also are used. One day she exposed the children to "Baa, baa, black sheep," and the next day she asked if they could remember it. In unison they said, "Baa, baa, black sheep, you have any wool?" This made more sense to them than the original syntax, indicating that they were focused more on meaning than on form. Other nursery rhymes such as "Pat-a-cake" and "Pease porridge hot" are introduced as they relate to the topics at hand. The rhymes are memorized by the children and seem to serve a function similar to jazz chants (Chapter 8), appealing to the senses through their rhythmic and other poetic qualities.

McNeilly's attitude toward error correction is that "only global errors that impede communication" should be corrected. She accepts most surface form errors and primary language responses which she considers to be perfectly healthy and normal. She feels that if the children are not overly corrected, they will be able to develop the self-confidence they need to acquire the language naturally.

To build self-esteem, the children also are given responsibilities to make the classroom function successfully. Even the rituals that begin the class each day are handled almost entirely by children, including the flag salute and attendance procedures. Children are given center stage whenever possible. On some occasions they hold the book from which the teacher is reading aloud; on other days they steady the flannel graph so it won't fall over while others are sticking figures to it, illustrating a story that is being read. In addition, the children's own drawings are mimeographed and made into booklets for the book corner.

Following is one of the integrated units the teacher likes to use.

Topic: Food

Whole Class Activities

Introduce vocabulary with real objects

Use a grab bag of fruits and vegetables

Have a fruit-tasting party

Play the song "Alice's Restaurant" (See H. Palmer in references. Children are asked to hold pictures of food and respond to the verbal cues.)

Make vegetable soup from items brought from home

Small Group Follow-up Activities

Make macaroni collages

Use cookie cutters in dough made of clay

Put illustrated cookbooks in the book corner

Make collages, gluing pictures of food onto paper plates

Fingerpaint in chocolate pudding

Practice writing in thin layers of Jell-O® crystals placed in trays

String popcorn

Bake cookies

Set up a supermarket in the play area with food boxes, cans, etc.; have the children "go shopping"

A Typical Day

11:25–11:45 A.M.

1. Greeting. The teacher greets the students and they greet her back.
2. Calendar coloring takes place. Today's numeral on a large calendar at the front of the room is colored in by a child volunteer. The teacher and students sing the song "What is the day to be happy?" which cues the answer to the question "What day is it today?"
3. Attendance. Children are learning to respond to visual cues. The teacher holds up flash cards and asks, "Is the person with this last name here today?"
4. Quick review of this week's concepts through the use of a picture dictionary.
5. Large group ESL lesson. With use of posters and other realia, the Chinese New Year, which is coming soon, is discussed. Comparisons between the Chinese New Year and holidays that the children celebrate with their families are drawn.

11:45–12:25 P.M.

Small group activities. Children choose one or more of the following:

Make paper firecrackers for the Chinese New Year

Play a game involving guessing how many pennies are in "red packets" (made previously in preparation for the Chinese New Year)

Listen to "The Story about Ping" by Marjorie Flack as it is being read in the book corner

Decorate paper plates with water colors; plates will later be assembled into a giant dragon for the Chinese New Year parade

Dramatic free play

12:25–12:35 P.M.

Cleanup and nursery rhymes. All the children participate in the cleanup. Then the children retire to the rug (see Figure 15.4). The "teacher of the day" (a child volunteer) leads in a chanting of some of the nursery rhymes the children have learned to date.

12:35–12:55 P.M.

Recess. Outdoor free play with sand toys, balance beams, and climbing apparatus for psychomotor and large muscle development. At this time the children are transitioned to the Spanish component of the program. The Spanish bilingual teacher is also on the playground with her group of children. When recess is over, the teachers return to their respective rooms, each with a different group.

A LIFE-SKILLS ADULT
BASIC EDUCATION PROGRAM[7]

In attempting to meet the needs of adults who are struggling not only with a new langauge but with providing a living for themselves and their families, the North Hollywood Adult Learning Center has made the community its classroom.

The coordinator of the program, Sandra Brown, reports, ''By making use of community resources and related classroom strategies, the teacher of adult ESL students can make the curriculum a vital and relevant one, focusing on real situations encountered by the students in their everyday lives'' (1979, p. 48).

The 500 students who are enrolled in the program represent many different cultural groups from around the world: Hispanic (70 percent), Asian (12 percent), Middle Eastern (9 percent), and European (4 percent). The remaining 5 percent are native English speakers who are taking courses outside of the basic ESL program. The curriculum itself consists of six levels of ESL, running from beginning to advanced; a reading lab for students with special problems in reading; a language skills lab which emphasizes writing, spelling, and grammar; and a high school lab for those desiring a GED Certificate or a high school diploma. In the latter three, the ESL and native-speaking students are mixed.

Incorporating Community Resources

Every month the activities are built around specific life-skills topics such as the following:

Community Resources	*Mental and Physical Health*
the community and its members	medical care
autobiographical data	nutrition
cultural–social integration	personal hygiene
the world around us	dental care
police–fire–paramedic services	safety and home
the telephone	
the post office	

[7]I would like to thank the following people at the North Hollywood Adult Learning Center for sharing their program with me: Sandra Brown, Harriet Fisher, Rheta Goldman, Roberto Martinez, Ethel Schwartz, Katie Treibach, and the many others I talked with during my observation.

Community Resources

leisure-time activities
  athletic activities
  entertainment activities
  recreational activities
educational services
  schools
  libraries

Occupational Knowledge

vocational training/counseling
  job searches
  the interview
  on-the-job skills

Government and the Law

vehicles and the law
law and legal services
government
taxes
current issues

Consumer Economics

individual/family economy
  physical concerns
  financial services
consumer rights
insurance
consumerism
  general shopping skills
  food shopping
  meals
  clothing shopping
  housing

These topics and the information related to them serve as an important part of the content through which the structures, vocabulary, and pronunciation of English are taught. Integral to these units are the trips that the students at all levels take to city government offices, occupational centers, markets, companies, factories, music/arts centers, libraries, museums, parks, hospitals, and many other places in and around the city.

On one such trip to the Farmers' Market, Rheta Goldman, a teacher of intermediate ESL, asked her students to search out the answers to the following questions:

What animals are in the window of the pet shop?

Find the post office. What shops are next to the post office?

What's the name of a store where you can get shoes repaired?

Go to the Farmers' Market newspaper stand. Can you buy a newspaper in your native language?

How much does it cost?

What kind of food can you buy at the shop *next* to Gill's Ice Cream Shop?

Find the glassblower. Write the names of four glass animals you can buy there.

How much does a fresh-baked pie from Du-Bar's Bakery cost?

What kinds of pies do they have today? Name three.

In addition to the trips and related activities, the students are exposed to films, real-life materials, and a stream of representatives from the community: an immigration attorney to give advice on becoming citizens; a speaker from the Red Cross to help the students be better prepared in the event of a major earthquake; a representative from the Department of Consumer Affairs to inform them of their rights as consumers; police officers to make them aware of strategies to use in protecting themselves from crime, to name a few. Also in connection with the units, the students participate in activities in their classes such as role play, dialogues, conversations, discussions, and writing activities commensurate with their proficiency levels.

To aid other teachers in setting up similar programs, the coordinator and teachers at North Hollywood have compiled extensive lists of ideas in several areas: community services, consumer education, cultural awareness, employment, family life, government/citizenship/law, health, and recreation (see S. Brown, 1979). Below is an example.

Community Services

Real-life materials/transparencies:

1. *Post office* forms; telephone directory pages of zip code maps
2. *Bank* forms, statements, checks, travelers' checks
3. *Telephone* directory pages of emergency telephone numbers; emergency number stickers for the telephone; telephone bills
4. *Telegram* form
5. *Driver's license* application form, test, change of address form
6. *Traffic* signs; parking/traffic citation forms; bus, train, airline schedules; bus maps from local bus company; road maps (from oil company, local Chamber of Commerce)
7. *School* (elementary, secondary, adult) enrollment forms; school report card; announcement of school activity
8. *Library* card applications

Brochures:
   Police Department (home protection, self-defense, drugs, etc.); *Fire Department* (fire prevention); *automobile club and National Safety Council* (traffic safety); state *Department of Motor Vehicles* (vehicle code booklet to prepare for driver's test); *library*; city *Building and Safety Department* (earthquake safety); *adult school* schedule of classes; *city councilman, state assemblyman* (booklets on local agencies and services)
Audiovisuals:
   Recorded tapes of telephone conversations (tell them prior to hearing the tapes that they are only simulations) with police and fire departments, telephone operator, directory assistance, Western Union; bus, train, taxi, and airline personnel; *taped conversations in the community,* at the post office, bank, with child's teacher, etc.; *taped telephone recordings* of weather, time, numbers, disconnected telephones, etc. *Teletrainers*—actual telephones with a control unit (on loan from telephone company)/free films

Speakers:
> *Police officer* (home protection or self-defense, with film and demonstration); *fire-man* (with film on fire safety and exit procedures); *paramedics* with demonstration of life-saving equipment and techniques; *AAA and National Safety Council representatives* with films on traffic safety; *library aide; elementary, secondary and/or adult school principal; telephone company representative* with film on use of telephone; *city councilman* on community services; *United Way representative*

Trips:
> Fire station; police department; post office; bank (before it opens); library; telephone company; local elementary school; airport

Subjects for discussion, dialogue, role playing, and other activities:
> *At the post office;* sending, insuring, picking up packages; buying stamps, airletters, money orders; correctly addressing letters, etc.
>
> *At the bank:* savings/checking; deposit/withdrawal; travelers' checks, safe deposit boxes, etc.
>
> *Emergency services:* the role of police—home and self-protection; fire prevention; reporting a fire, a prowler, a break-in, an auto accident, calling the paramedics, etc.; what to do in case of a fire, earthquake, break-in, rape attempt; experiences with and attitudes toward police
>
> *Telephone:* emergency calls; long distance calls; directory assistance; wrong number; out of order; telegrams; taking messages; weather report; using the telephone directory; social and business calls
>
> *Transportation:* car, taxi, bus, train, airline schedules; map reading activities; locating local services; geography of local areas; traffic safety; dangers of hitchhiking; obtaining a driver's license; at the gas station, garage; asking directions
>
> *Education:* registering child/self in school; conference with child's teacher, counselor, principal, nurse; participation in child's school activities; report cards; education in U.S. compared with education in other countries; levels and types of education; special education; private schools; new approaches to education; admission requirements to colleges and universities.
>
> *Library:* card application; Dewey Decimal System; overdue books; reserving books; foreign language books; using children's books
>
> *Philanthropic organizations:* becoming involved in volunteer activities; charities; charity drives; animal protection agencies

Community Volunteers

One of the most interesting aspects of the program is its utilization of volunteers from the community. Eighteen community workers arrive every week to assist the teachers in classrooms, to tutor students, or to help out wherever they are needed. They come primarily from the ranks of housewives and retirees. Although they receive no monetary rewards for their time, they do receive numerous rewards of a different kind. Their individual birthdays are celebrated, articles in school papers are written to honor their accomplishments, and special days are set aside to recognize the work they do. Ranging in age from 26 to 82, they form a dependable resource. Some are there only one or two hours a week; others are there 15 to 20. The volunteers determine,

in advance, their own schedules and sign contracts confirming the agreement
(see the sample contract, Figure 15.5).

Once officially accepted as part of the staff, the volunteers are given mail-
boxes and their names are added to the check-in sheets. Then they receive

North Hollywood Adult Learning Center
VOLUNTEER JOB DESCRIPTION

POSITION TITLE: Adult Basic Education Tutor
PLACE: _____ Reading Lab   _____ High School Lab

_____ Language Skills Lab   _____ English as a Second
                                                                Language

PROGRAM OBJECTIVES: To assist students who want to learn or improve their basic
                                        skills in English as a Second Language or to earn a GED cer-
                                        tificate or a high school diploma.

TIME COMMITMENT: Days _____ Hours _____

_____   _____

RESPONSIBILITIES: • To work under the guidance and supervision of the teacher to
                                whom you have been assigned
                            • To work with either individuals or groups according to the needs
                                of the teacher and students
                            • To follow the teacher's plans for each session
                            • To assist the teacher in any way the teacher feels will be of benefit
                                to the students
                            • To be reliable and on time on regularly scheduled days
                            • To sign in and out on the sign-in sheet
                            • To inform the office or teacher if you must be absent
                                (The volunteer does not: diagnose student needs, prescribe in-
                                struction, select materials, evaluate student progress, or counsel
                                students.)

QUALIFICATIONS: • A positive attitude, interest and enthusiasm in working with adult
                            basic education students
                        • Ability to work cooperatively with school personnel and other vol-
                            unteers
                        • Adequate communication skills
                        • Dedication to fulfill all of the obligations of the position

TRAINING: BY THE TEACHER TO WHOM YOU ARE ASSIGNED

I have read and understand the above and agree to conscientiously carry out the responsibilities as described.

x _____

Figure 15.5

an orientation and off they go to their assigned classrooms, where they are trained by the teacher with whom they will be working. In addition to the orientation and training, the volunteers are given suggestions in writing concerning general strategies to use when working with students (see pages 191–192 for a similar list intended for peer teacher and lay assistant training). They also receive self-evaluation checklists containing items about cooperation with others, following the teacher's directions, being friendly and encouraging, and so forth.

A UNIVERSITY ENGLISH LANGUAGE INSTITUTE

One of the oldest and most highly acclaimed university-level language programs is the English Language Institute (ELI) at the University of Michigan.[8] The 45-year-old program has survived so long because of its ability to change with the times and with the needs of its students. In addition, the Institute has remained aware of the dynamic role it has to play in relation to the campus community of which it is a part. In recent years enrollment in its intensive program has been adversely affected by several factors: a general tendency to migrate to warmer climates; an increase in the number of competing intensive programs, some of which have carried on extensive advertising campaigns; and the strict admission requirements of the university itself. Because of the decline in enrollment and the coincidental need for increased language support on campus, the intensive program is currently being phased out.

New Directions

In response to the above factors, the Institute has hastened its diversification and expansion into other areas of influence. One of the first steps taken has been to extend and/or develop programs intended for international students and teaching assistants already enrolled in the univerity. Through a cooperative effort with other departments, the instructional staff of the ELI is involving itself more and more with colleagues across subject areas to address the special needs of foreign students in specific academic fields. In order to meet new challenges, the staff members are willing to develop the additional specialized skills necessary for implementing courses in the area of English for Academic/Special Purposes. One manifestation of this movement has been the creation of a Pre M.B.A. program for foreign graduate students entering

---

[8]Much of the information presented here is summarized with permission from Carolyn Madden and John Swales (Eds.), 1986. I am grateful to them for sharing the description with me and to the others who also contributed to its development: Patricia Aldridge, Josh Ard, Moya Brennan, Sarah Briggs, Rod Fraser, Susan Gass, Stephen Guice, Stan Jones, Joan Morley, Sue Rienhart, Larry Selinker, Ann Sinsheimer, Betsy Soden, and Mary Spaan.

the School of Business Administration. This interdepartmental program has been designed to meet the students' special needs and will include courses such as Language and Communication in the Business World, Principles of Management, Introduction to Handling Case Studies, and Business English Tutorial.

Other proposed changes include increasing support of second language acquisition on the Institute's research agenda, and expanding its testing role to include the evaluation of the English proficiency of potential teaching assistants from foreign countries and the reevaluation of some of the foreign students. Additional plans include giving input into the use of computer and video facilities on campus, marketing tests for the screening of foreign teaching assistants, and evaluating the English proficiency levels of foreign graduate students.

Current Programs and Services

The Intensive Program

At the present time the foreign students, most of whom will be moving over into academic programs, are able to take six levels of courses in ESL: two beginning (110 and 120), two intermediate (130 and 140), and two advanced (150 and 160). In addition, two programs for advanced students are offered in the summer. The first is the MBA program mentioned above. The second is the Academic Entry English Program, which teaches the skills needed for comprehending lectures, researching, and otherwise functioning in a university classroom. This program includes a course in one of the major fields with which the students will be involved. Both programs are available primarily to students who have already been admitted to the university.

Beginning courses in the ELI assume that the students have some prior knowledge of English, its structure, and its vocabulary but that they lack proficiency in their ability to communicate. In the beginning courses the students participate in classroom activities in which they gain experience using English in situations such as those found in a mainstream university environment. Interaction through a negotiation of meaning is the emphasis. The teacher's role is that of facilitator as the students attempt to solve problems, gather information, and share tasks. The focus is on the goals to be reached as part of the tasks rather than on language itself. Language is simply the *means* by which the goals are achieved.

Core A (see Figure 15.6) concentrates on activities such as interpreting schedules, giving and receiving directions, and conversing about topics having to do with medical concerns, school and community survival situations, entertainment, and so forth. In Core B the students' abilities to converse is extended to more complicated and subtle social situations with the aid of video and audio tapes. While interaction and negotiation of meaning are still stressed, supplementary exercises are added which direct the students' atten-

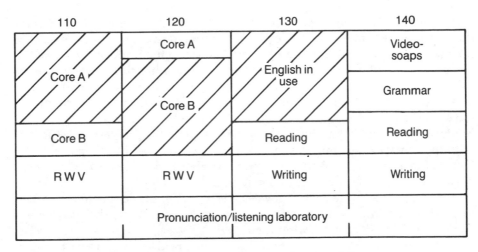

Figure 15.6. Beginning and Intermediate Level Courses

tion to accuracy in form. The Reading, Writing, and Vocabulary (RWV) courses can serve to reinforce the concepts and skills introduced in the Core courses or they can launch into new territory. The vocabulary items chosen for inclusion are related to the tasks in the Core courses, while the Core courses integrate reading and writing into their curricula. In the RWV courses, the students are exposed to longer passages for reading comprehension, strategies for paragraph development, word study skills, introduction to library skills, and so forth. Pronunciation classes are available at all levels in the program.

At the low intermediate level (see 130 in Figure 15.6) students spend most of their time in task-based activities and in courses in reading and writing. Carolyn Madden describes it this way: "Up to this point in the curriculum, one might say, the goal is to work students into a frenzy of English, that is, to involve the students in activities to enhance their active participation in the learning process and to dampen a tendency to be overly concerned with the accurate use of English" (Madden & Swales, 1986, p. 6). She goes on to say, however, that at the 140 level a balance between fluency and accuracy is the goal. Here the students spend five hours a week in a grammar course, which concentrates on accuracy in form. However, the students continue to improve fluency through communication in speaking and listening and they continue to work on reading comprehension, composition, editing skills, and so forth. In addition to these areas of concentration, the students take an experimental course in video-soap operas.

This experimental course integrates listening, speaking, and reading with advanced grammar in what Larry Selinker refers to as "real time." He feels that soap operas appear to be an excellent source of input and can be used effectively as a tool for learning English. For example, the students and the teacher watch two videotaped episodes a week of *The Young and the Restless* the day after each appears on television. This one-day delay gives the teacher time to prepare a transcript and worksheet to aid in the understanding of the episode. Many of the students are able to see the other three episodes each week as well and many of them report that they continue to watch the soap after the course is over, attesting to the strong appeal that such programs have. In the episodes that are watched together, the teacher turns the sound off during commercials and uses that time to explain the plot, aid the students with their own oral summaries, and ask for opinions. Selinker reports, "The fact that students are asked their opinions about the often-exciting events seems to be especially popular and may be important to the apparent learning which takes place" (Madden & Swales, 1986, p. 22). Students are also asked to predict outcomes in the story lines and to ask questions that can be answered only by actually viewing the tape.

The classes also look at rhetorical and conversational recurring forms in the soap opera, particularly those involved in summarizing, an activity frequently indulged in by the characters. Knowing how to summarize information is an important tool in language use, Selinker feels. Other recurring forms given attention are polite and impolite forms, ways of agreeing, disagreeing, denying, asking for information, ending a conversation, and other functional structures often associated with the notional/functional approach to language teaching. Idiomatic language, too, has been incorporated into the discussions and practice activities. By this means, colloquial expressions are internalized or appear to "stick in the memory" of those exposed to them in real time.

At the upper levels, the ELI has incorporated an elective program. Students can select four courses from the following list:

Current Events	Language and Culture
Test-Taking and Grammar	Speaking/Listening
Advanced Reading	Principles of Business Management
American Literature	Business Communication
Advanced Grammar	Classroom and Research Skills
Pronunciation	Writing
Microcomputer Lab	Music
Reading, Speaking, and Listening	

Some of the electives appear to be surface-form oriented (e.g., Advanced Grammar, Pronunciation). Others are skill oriented (e.g., Classroom and Research Skills, Speaking/Listening). Still others are content oriented (e.g., Principles of Business Management, American Literature). However, the trend seems to be toward exposing the students in a "sheltered" setting to the content relevant to an academic environment.

Courses for Enrolled Students

According to Betsy Soden (Madden & Swales, 1986), the ELI began offering six one-semester mini-courses in the fall of 1985 for students already enrolled in the university. These courses, which meet during fall and winter terms for 90 minutes once a week, are available to both graduate and undergraduate students. They focus on the academic proficiency in English needed across disciplines: the humanities, the social and physical sciences, architecture, business, and law. They include the following areas:

Writing for Academic Purposes. Activities focus on writing for special purposes: descriptions, extended definitions, literature reviews, technical reports, and abstracts, to name a few. Students spend much time making revisions in cooperation with peer editors, tutors, or the instructor. Students do most of the writing tasks related to their particular fields outside of class so that in-class time can be spent in group or pair work.

Term Paper Writing. After an introduction to the resources in the library, the students work on selecting and focusing topics, taking notes on their reading, paraphrasing, summarizing, organizing, outlining, documenting, revising, and so on. Students may want to work on a paper to which they have been assigned in another course. After regular individual conferences with their instructors, students are expected to complete a six- to ten-page typed paper by the end of the term. Students may use the word processors available to them at the university.

Text Processing and Academic Vocabulary. Students learn strategies useful for approaching academic texts, unfamiliar lexical terms, and the structure of academic vocabulary. Morphology, word analysis (prefixes, stems, suffixes), semantic fields, and superordinates are among the items covered.

Lecture Comprehension. This course stresses listening skills in academic situations. The students first concentrate generally on lecture comprehension and note taking. Later they develop the same skills as related to their own areas of study by using modular materials which are field specific. They are trained to listen for organizational signals and paralinguistic cues to meaning. They use their notes later for discussion or summary writing. Sometimes typical interactions between professors and students are role played.

Pronunciation. Students are given diagnostic speech tests and video interviews, assignments in an audio and video laboratory/classroom, individual self-access, self-study activities, small-group practice sessions and video presentations, and individual practice and presentation. The main goal is to improve intelligibility, communicative competence, and self-confidence.

During half of the spring term the students are offered a more intensive multi-focus course which meets twice a week for 90 minutes. This course aids students in the skills involved in academic writing, listening to lectures, taking notes, and giving oral presentations.

It should be pointed out that graduates receive no credit for these courses; undergraduates are awarded one credit per course. Any student on campus can enroll in these mini-courses. They are also open to Foreign Teaching Assistants, who may be required to enroll as a result of their performance on the evaluation mentioned earlier.

Testing and Evaluation

The ELI English Placement Test (an abbreviated version of the MELAB—the Michigan English Language Assessment Battery) is given to incoming students in order to place them initially. The test measures listening, grammar, vocabulary, and reading. In addition the students have to write and be interviewed orally for placement at the lower levels.

Students who have already been admitted to the university after scoring high on the MELAB or on the TOEFL are given the Academic English Evaluation, a test of reading, writing, and listening abilities designed for local use at the University of Michigan. It also is an abbreviated version of the MELAB. In addition, they are given an oral interview. The students are then counseled into the mini-courses described above according to their demonstrated written and oral skills. Students are evaluated regularly by the instructors and, as of 1987, will receive letter grades and a recommendation such as "no further work needed," "further work strongly recommended," "lightly recommended," and so on. Students needing additional work in a specific area can sign up for another course the following term.

Evaluation within the classes themselves is determined by the individual instructors. In the lower level classes many task-based tests have been developed and shared by the instructors and, according to Steven Guice, they "more accurately reflect what has been taught in the class than a standardized grammar test would" (Madden & Swales, 1986, p. 13). The tests often include tasks such as reading map directions and marking a specific location or reading two resumes and deciding which candidate is more qualified for a specified job.

The Audio/Video Laboratory Setting

Joan Morley, who is in charge of the pronunciation strand of the curriculum, likes to avoid the term "language laboratory," because of its association with what she calls the "sleep-inducing stimulus-response models of the fifties and sixties" (Madden & Swales, 1986, p. 18). She deemphasizes the traditional learner objectives of "perfect pronunciation" and "near-native" mastery. Instead she stresses the following goals:

1. Improving intelligibility (so that speech is relatively easy to understand and is not distracting to listeners).
2. Developing communicative competence (at a level that meets the individual student's needs).
3. Developing self-confidence in using oral English.

Three components are offered in the program in varying combinations: group classes consisting of 10 to 15 students meeting for two to three hours per week; tutorial/small-group sessions meeting for one to two hours per week; and self-study, including prerecorded self-study laboratory work, oral practice, and self-recording. The activities are of three types: imitative practice, both choral and individual (teacher dependent); guided self-practice (partially independent); and independent self-practice and self-monitoring (completely independent). Self-access, self-study listening programs are available in skill areas such as comprehending, pronouncing, and self-testing.

Other Programs and Services
In addition to the programs and services already described, the University of Michigan offers help to the foreign student in several areas:

1. The Office of Student Services begins each term with an orientation for new students. The foreign students are provided with handbooks dealing with the attendance policy, housing, and other campus and community survival issues. In addition they are given a description of the ELI program, its methodology and content. It is expected that a few of the students will be able to survive on their own, but the majority of foreign students will need the ELI to aid them in the transition to mainstream university life.
2. The ELI's own library has a self-access area where students can use video cassettes, microcomputers, a word processor, language-instructive games, three daily newspapers, a collection of college catalogs, travel information, and books and journals about a variety of subjects.
3. A free six-week course is open to all nonnative speakers of English living in the area. Susan Gass describes the kind of student most likely to take advantage of this free program: "The foreign students enrolled in this course range from spouses of students to students in professional schools to business people in the community." She says that approximately 100–150 foreign students attend this session each year (Madden & Swales, 1986, p. 23). The course is organized and implemented by students enrolled in the M.A. Program in ESL under the guidance of the ELI instructional staff. It provides a training ground for the graduate students after they have completed courses in linguistics, second language acquisition, and ESL theory and before they are expected to complete an internship at the ELI.

16

Foreign Language Programs

Many foreign language students are finding that they can indeed acquire a second language in the classroom, particularly if interactional strategies are employed. The three programs selected for illustration in this chapter were chosen because they contain combinations of features that may be of special interest to foreign language teachers.

The first program to be examined represents Jefferson County's approach to teaching foreign languages in Lakewood, Colorado. Students there are supplementing their classroom experiences with foreign language camps and a districtwide "springfest internationale." In the same school district young children are acquiring foreign languages through an extracurricular parent-sponsored effort. The second program to be examined is a Spanish program at Artesia High School in Artesia, California. There the students are acquiring the target language mainly through classroom interaction, in the traditional one-period-a-day mode. The third is an early immersion program in four elementary schools in Thunder Bay, Ontario, Canada, where children are acquiring French through exposure to the various subject-matter areas.

In this chapter, as in the previous one, the descriptions focus on the more salient characteristics of each program, sometimes on the overall organization and other times on specific activities. Although the programs are designed for particular age groups and specific purposes, it must again be kept in mind that most of the ideas can be readily adapted to other age levels and other kinds of programs.

ONE DISTRICT'S APPROACH
TO FOREIGN LANGUAGE TEACHING[1]

Lorenzo Trujillo, Coordinator of Second Language Education for the Jefferson County Public Schools in Lakewood, Colorado, is calling the renewed interest in foreign language study within his school district a "renaissance." At the high school level alone, the enrollment in foreign language classes has grown 12 percent in the last four years. Over 21,000 students, K–12 (approximately 26 percent of the total school population), have signed up for one of the district's many foreign language classes, including French, German, Latin, Russian, and Spanish. The classroom teachers are strongly encouraged to emphasize oral skills (except in Latin) through a variety of activities including role play, games, singing, dancing, ethnic food preparation, interacting with native-speaking guests, field trips, and so forth. In addition to recommending these kinds of activities for the classes themselves, the district feels that the apparent revitalization has been due, at least in part, to a few innovations that have become integral aspects of the program. It is these innovations that will be the focus here.

Language Camps

The camps began in 1970 when a group of high school Russian teachers transformed a mountain ranch complex owned by the school district into the "ancient Russian village" of Sosnovka. Russian menus, typical Russian activities, traditional costumes, Russian language signs, make-believe passports, and radio-broadcast tapes were prepared for the events, which were scheduled to last through the weekend. The students, who arrived by bus, were first stopped for an inspection at a road block (the local police cooperated in this activity). The visitors were asked by pretend Russian border guards, dressed in rented costumes, to show their passports and open all their luggage for inspection. Only Russian was spoken. After several good-natured hassles over the luggage and paperwork, the students were officially welcomed to Sosnovka by the newly appointed commissar, who gave a rather lengthy and dramatic speech.

Today similar procedures are used to welcome newcomers to El Pinar

---

[1]Thanks to the Jefferson County Public Schools for giving me permission to summarize their foreign language program and related activities. Special thanks go to the people who helped supply the details upon which this summary is based: Lorenzo Trujillo, Patsy Jaynes, Martha Quiat, Xavier Valenzuela, and Jennie Green (the former Coordinator of Second Language Education).

(Spanish), Tannenbaum (German), and Val-les-Pins (French), in addition to Sosnovka. Each camp is visited by approximately 150 students, 20 to 30 teachers, and 10 to 20 native speakers. The native speakers usually play the largest roles (commissars, mayors, or police chiefs) and the teachers sometimes are the gendarmes, priests, or other village personalities.

A typical day at the camp might include rap sessions with group leaders or activities such as dancing, singing, watching skits, movies, and other programs. Each visitor is given plenty of time to soak up the ambiance and browse through the many colorful shops featuring perfumes, arts and crafts (made by the schools' language clubs), and souvenirs (usually imported). Play currency is created and an exchange rate established to provide the students with the experience of dealing with foreign money. Cafes sell pastries, espresso, piroski, allouette sans tete, paella, auschnit, and other foreign delicacies. At any given moment there may be seven to fifteen different activities to choose from, all being carried out in the target language. For example, there may be lessons in macrame, lectures on various subjects of "local" interest, games, Ukrainian Easter egg painting, weaving, baking, candle dipping, or silk-screen painting, to name a few. The village of Val-les-Pins even has an artist-in-residence who does caricatures. In some of the village's night spots, a piano player is often on hand with foreign language songsheets for those who wish to sing along.

For the participants, the cost of the weekend is minimal, usually running about thirty dollars. Participation is voluntary. Anyone, regardless of proficiency level, who is in a foreign language class in one of the district's secondary schools is eligible to attend.

Concerning the effectiveness of the program, one of the students sums it up best, "I really want to go to Spain now that I have tried El Pinar."

A Springfest Internationale

An event with features similar to those of the language camps is the Springfest Internationale, which occurs every three years. All foreign language and English as a Second Language students K–12 are involved in the one-day celebration of multiple languages. The day begins with much pomp and circumstance. A parade of about 50 units, representing the various schools in the county, marches through the city. Included are international flags and banners, floats, Roman chariots, children attired in traditional ethnic costumes, and other entries of interest. Even the members of the Board of Education and other school/community groups and individuals participate in the parade. Ribbons and medals are given to what are judged to be the outstanding units entered in the competition.

After the parade arrives at the location for the day's activities, faculty members give welcoming speeches in six languages. Then there is the lighting of the Springfest Internationale flame, reminiscent of the Olympics. The children dressed in ethnic costumes place flowers into a bouquet of many colors, signifying the coming together of nations and languages. Balloons are released as the throngs of people enter the many language villages to begin the day's cultural and competitive activities.

Competitions include trivia bowls, speeches, skits, and many other events in all the target languages. Athletic games include relays, tugs-of-war, volleyball, soccer, and many others.

The buildings at the chosen site are all decorated in streamers, posters, and other paraphernalia to represent the different villages. Each building has its share of booths, cafes, game areas, stages for presentations, and display sections to simulate each country's culture. In order to play the games and buy food items and souvenirs, the students exchange their money for "quichees" (the common currency) at the International Bank. Profits are used to pay the expenses of the fest, and whatever is left over is divided among the schools to help purchase supplementary materials for the language classes.

Foreign Languages in the Elementary Schools (FLES)

The district's FLES program began as a grass roots movement sponsored by several local parent, teacher, and student groups. The sponsors were motivated by the notion that children gain many advantages by becoming bilingual at an early age. The parents thought that their children would perhaps experience a higher degree of creativity and cognitive flexibility due to the additional challenge that acquiring a second language brings. In addition, they felt that learning a second language would be just plain fun.

The children (K–6) now meet every day either before or after school to learn Spanish, German, French, Latin, Modern Greek, or Russian. The teachers, who have been hired by a parent group, must be fluent in the target language, work well with children, have a communicative philosophy, and be able to maintain a high level of excitement in the classroom. However, it is not required that they be certified as teachers. Once hired, they must be trained in natural methods at workshops provided by the school district. It is interesting to note that many parents also participate in the workshops to learn ways in which they can encourage and provide assistance to their children at home.

The four-year-old program already encompasses 48 elementary schools in the district and it is still expanding. About 3,000 of the district's elementary students are enrolled. Each school has from one to four FLES teachers, who are paid according to the number of students registered. In order to allow for meaningful interaction, only 10 to 15 students are allowed in a class. The cost of participation is approximately fifty dollars per child for each semester; this pays for materials and the teacher's salary. The school district and the FLES

Committee, consisting mainly of parents elected from 48 schools, aid in the entire process. They survey community needs, assist new schools where parents want programs, and make recommendations concerning hiring procedures and other organizational decisions. However, each school designs and is in charge of its own program. A volunteer parent in each school serves as the program's coordinator and acts as a liaison between the school and the community.

A HIGH SCHOOL SPANISH PROGRAM[2]

Although working against odds common to many high school foreign language programs, Christina Rivera uses natural methods as much as possible in her Levels I and II (first and second year) Spanish classes at Artesia High School in Artesia, California. One of the constraints under which she works is that she must cover a certain amount of formal grammar so that the students will be ready for what is expected at subsequent levels. A second constraint is that she is able to meet with her students only one period a day, five days a week. Yet a third constraint is that, as in other California schools, the students are in foreign languages classes not always by choice. Often they are there to satisfy graduation or college entrance requirements. Thus, many of her students bring to her classes less than positive attitudes.

Nevertheless, it is her hope that by the end of the program the students will be able to communicate effectively and appropriately in the target langauge. It is also her hope that students will become more sensitive to cultural differences. Activities in her classes, for the most part, center around her students' world: their objectives, their personal attempts to deal with uncertainties, and their efforts to comprehend and speak another language.

Level I

Before beginning the instruction in Spanish, Rivera takes time to educate the students in the theories upon which her methods are predicated. She feels that as a result of her doing so, the students are less apt to find her methods "strange" and are more apt to try.

Using an outline similar to what Krashen and Terrell suggest (see pages 85–88), she works on receptive skills first with Level I students. Body language, gestures, facial expressions, and tone of voice are all important in the initial stages. Through total physical response (see Chapter 6), students learn colors by manipulating pieces of colored paper. They learn about the objects in their immediate environment, foods, clothing, and many other relevant

---

[2]Artesia High School is part of the ABC Unified School District.

concepts by manipulation of various items. Pictures and props are used to act out scenes. Familiar stories are told as visuals are shown. And because it does not require students to respond orally, bingo is played, reinforcing concepts related to the topics covered. Simple treasure hunts (see pages 154–155) are designed requiring students to find objects of certain colors or that have other specific characteristics.

The following activities combining the natural approach and total physical response are typical:

1. Describe a picture from a current magazine and follow up by making statements or giving commands.

    Example: *This is a picture of some skirts. Notice the colors. This one* (points to a skirt) *is green. Jane* (a student in class) *is wearing a skirt. Her skirt is green. This one* (points to another skirt) *is pink. Point to the pink skirt,* etc.

    Follow up: (Thumbs up means "yes"; thumbs down means "no.") *This skirt* (points to a pink skirt) *is green* (thumbs should be pointed down). *This skirt* (points again to the pink skirt) *is pink* (thumbs should be pointed up), and so forth.

2. Ask students to draw or cut out pictures of items in a category (food, clothing, kitchen utensils, etc.). Ask them to hold up pictures of specific items. Have them take specific pictures to various places around the room.

3. Using pictures, facial expressions, and gestures, introduce the students to some of the more common emotions: happy, sad, angry, bored, fearful, etc. Hold up cue cards on which the names of the different emotions have been written. Have the students point to the picture that clearly expresses the specific emotion indicated.

4. Using numbered pictures, ask the students to say the number of the picture described by the teacher.

5. Have the students make "self" collages with items that they feel best express themselves. Later in the year they will be discussing these with class members in the target language.

As the students progress to early speech production, mass media are relied upon because of their relevance and contextuality. Rivera finds commercials particularly effective. Students act out the commercials with props as the teacher gives commands. Much later, students will be writing and acting out their own commercials. Other activities she feels are appropriate to this stage are described below:

1. Using a real suitcase and real clothing and other items for travel, students prepare for an imaginary trip. The teacher asks the students to place the items in the suitcase that they would take to Acapulco, Aspen, etc.

2. The students are shown a picture from a magazine. They are asked to name what they see. A list of the items mentioned is written on the chalkboard.

3. Students make a chart consisting of several of their names, the clothes they are wearing, and the color of each item (see a similar activity on pages 95–96).

4. Matrices such as the following are used as starters for scenarios:

¿Cuánto cuesta el ————————————— ?
Está de venta. Le cuesta ————————————— ?
¡Qué bueno! (¡Qué malo!)

Necesito un ————————————— .
Por qué no vas a ————————————— ?
¿Cuánto cuesta?
Cuesta ————————————— mas o menos.

5. Students write in a journal each day using the target langauge. The teacher guides them at first. They begin by writing down their favorite colors and favorite items of clothing. At later stages the writing becomes freer as students write their feelings and thoughts.

The study of culture also is included as the students progress. Discussions are conducted entirely in the target language aided by props, maps, and a lot of visuals. Cultural information is frequently woven into other activities such as listening to music and game playing.

Grammar is introduced at early stages. However, the concepts are those that are generally easily learned and applied. Many of the grammar activities are assigned as homework.

Level II

Level II students (those in their second year of language study) are usually somewhere in the early production stage. Rivera feels that many of them regress over the summer since they have had almost no exposure to the target language then. However, after spending a few weeks doing activities similar to those described above, the students will soon move into speech emergence. Students at this level are expected to listen to Spanish-language broadcasts during a part of each day for several days in sequence.[3] They may hear traffic reports, time/temperature/weather reports, commercials, horoscope readings, song dedications, listener call-ins, interviews, sports reports, the news, or lyrics to music. They are encouraged to tape the broadcasts for repeated listening experiences. They are asked to write down what items they understand from each report. As they listen to the same reports from time to time, they are pleased to find that they understand more and more of the

---

[3]Credit for this idea is given to Lynne La Fleur.

broadcasts. Through this process students are exposed to native speakers using contemporary, idiomatic speech. They learn to take advantage of cognates, intonation, and other clues to meaning.

Affective activities (see Chapter 11) are favorites among Rivera's students at this level. It must be kept in mind that the students have spent some time preparing for humanistic activities all along. At earlier stages, emotions were identified through the natural approach and total physical response. The journals allowed students to express their likes and dislikes and their attitudes in general. In addition, the collages contributed to their willingness to reveal themselves in low-risk situations.

Below are a few of the activities used:

1. To reinforce the terminology describing human emotions, the teacher reads a soap opera melodramatically. The cue cards (mentioned above) with the names of various emotions can be held up by the teacher or an assistant as the story is being read. The students as a group can act out the emotion that is being displayed.

2. Students are asked in the target language to draw a happy baby, mad father, and so forth. Then they are instructed to draw the following:
   a. a father who has just heard that his teenager has smashed the family car
   b. a mother seeing an "A" on her child's report card
   c. a girl seeing her boy friend with her best friend
   d. a cheerleader after falling off the human "pyramid"

3. Students hold up small cue cards with the names of emotions written on them. Each card is held up in response to statements in the target language made by the teacher. Below are some examples.
   a. When someone is mean to me, I feel. . . .
   b. At a party I feel. . . .
   c. Before a test, I feel. . . .
   d. With my family I feel. . . .
   e. At the doctor's office I feel. . . .

4. Students are asked to name songs that make them feel happy, sad, like dancing, etc.

5. Students draw and label pictures about their favorite activities. They then interview each other about the activities depicted.

Eventually the students are able to discuss problems, goals, and everyday matters in the target language. Although they may not be able to converse in perfect Spanish by the end of the second year, they seem to communicate with a minimum of anxiety.

Rivera insists that her main goal throughout the stages is to create as natural a learning environment as possible. She feels that she still has a long way to go to create an optimal classroom. However, she admits modestly that she is coming closer to her vision with each passing year.

A FRENCH IMMERSION MODEL
FOR ELEMENTARY STUDENTS[4]

Background

Two out of three English-speaking Canadians want their children to learn French to "improve their career options and broaden their horizons."[5] Hence it is not surprising that a group of Thunder Bay, Ontario, parents (of mainly Finnish or Italian origin) approached the Lakehead Board of Education in the spring of 1977 to request a French *immersion* program for their children. Why did they choose an immersion program over one of the more traditional ones? They believed, as do many parents in Canada, that immersion does in fact produce bilinguals. Their views were compatible with those of the Ontario Ministry of Education, which concluded that immersion is an optimal means for achieving a high level of competency in French. Immersion programs (see Chapter 14) involve a far more extensive and meaningful experience with French than can be provided by the more traditional *core* programs, in which students study French for one period each day, or the more recently developed *extended* programs in which at least one content-area class is taught in French in addition to the core.

While their children are learning the subject matter in French, the parents feel assured that the skills in the first language will not be adversely affected. According to Lapkin and Swain (1984), any fears that may be present concerning this issue have no basis in reality. This is at least partially due to the fact that the children belong to the majority culture (in the case of Thunder Bay, only 3 percent of the households claim French as the home language) and that English dominates their lives outside of the school environment. Lapkin and Swain report:

> The English achievement results for students in the early total-immersion programme indicate that, although initially behind students in unilingual English programmes in literacy skills, within a year of the introduction of an English Language Arts component into the curriculum, the immersion students perform equivalently on standardized tests of English achievement to students in the English-only programme (1984, p. 50).

---

[4]I wish to thank the following for sharing information about their programs with me and for allowing me to observe French immersion classes in their respective schools: Ken Cressman, Nicole Gaudet, George Rendall, Lise Bagdon, Colette Aubry, John Brusset, Carol Nabarra, Glenn Coriveau, and Roy Fossum. My thanks also to Wendy Hansen for providing transportation and lodging.

[5]From "Making Choices Campaign" (1986). In *Canadian Parents for French*, 24; p. 8. The statistics are based on the results of a Gallup Poll taken for the Canadian Parents for French organization.

They claim that this is true even for students who are not introduced to English until grade 3 or 4. They point out, too, that after grade 4, French immersion students sometimes outperform their English-only peers in some aspects of English language skills. Their achievement in the subject areas (math, science, social studies, etc.) is also comparable to that of their English-only peers (see Krashen, 1984).

In addition, parents are convinced that their children do not need particularly high IQs to be successful in French immersion programs (see also Related Reading 9). On this issue, Lapkin and Swain assert that IQ is not any more predictive of success in French immersion programs than it is in regular English-only programs. Students of below-average intelligence are not at a greater disadvantage in immersion programs. In fact, being bilingual may boost their confidence and have other positive results affectively.

In general, most students can expect to reach native-like levels in French intake skills (listening and reading) by the time they finish elementary school. However, in the output skills (speaking and writing), they are often less native-like until they have had considerable contact with native French speakers or Francophones. The only children found by the organization of Canadian Parents of French to be less than adequate candidates for immersion programs are those who exhibit a lack of ability in auditory discrimination or auditory memory. Problems in these areas are usually detected in the first year of kindergarten and the students having them can be steered early on into English-only programs.

Because of the efforts of those first parent advocates of French immersion in Thunder Bay and those parents, teachers, and other educators who were to follow, the program has mushroomed. It began with 36 students in one elementary school and now boasts of having 647 students in four elementary schools, one of which has a program extending from the second year of kindergarten (for five-year-olds) all the way through grade 8. The programs, which are allowed to grow with the students, increase by one grade level at a time as the students become older, until all the programs extend at least through grade 8. However, the school board is currently considering the incorporation of French immersion into the secondary curriculum beginning with grade 9. Future plans also include the establishment of a French Immersion Center (where the regular English-only program would be dropped) at Redwood Public School, should the current enrollments continue. For the past two years, 16 to 17 percent of all second year kindergarten children have been enrolled in French immersion programs throughout the district.

Enrollment and Transportation

Enrollment is on a first come, first served basis, and transfers from other immersion programs are accepted provided there is room. Transportation is generally available for those accepted into the program, making it possible for a larger number of students to be involved. The students within the urban area are bused from designated neighborhood pick-up points to the schools, and for those in the rural areas transportation arrangements can be made at a reasonable cost.

Support Services

Every school in which a French immersion program is located attempts to maintain an ever-expanding collection of books and reference materials in French. The teachers are now looking for materials oriented to the needs of immersion students in particular. In addition, audiovisual resources appear to be in ample supply and new ones are ordered yearly.

Assistance is available for enrichment or remediation from a bilingual resource teacher or a qualified special education resource teacher. Parents of children with severe problems will be counseled and recommendations will be given depending upon the type of problem and upon the resources available at each school.

The home itself can be considered a "support service." Nicole Gaudet, an education officer for the district, reports, "Because the parents have made a decision about the education of their children to be in French immersion programs, they are more involved in their children's education." Parents seem more than happy to read stories in English to their children at home, work with teachers to provide experiences with Francophones whenever possible, take their children to French cultural events, and volunteer to aid in classroom ventures.

Program Description

In the first two years of the program, the language for instruction is 100 percent French (except in emergency situations). In addition, all communication within the classroom is in French. In the second, third, fourth, and fifth grades, English is added but is limited to 75 minutes per day of English Language Arts. French is the language for instruction 75 percent of the time, English 25 percent of the time. During grades 6, 7, and 8, 50 percent of the instruction is in French and 50 percent in English. By the end of the eighth grade the students will have studied history, geography, math, science, and other subjects in both languages. The subjects cover a wide range of content areas at each level (see Table 16.1).

The concepts to which the students are exposed in the French immersion program are comparable to those to which they are exposed in the regular English-only classroom.[6] In listening, the goals include helping children to

---

[6]The concepts listed here are paraphrased from the *Core Language Guide* (1985) made available by the Lakehead Board of Education. No attempt is made to list all of the goals set down by the board. A few of the more typical ones have been selected for inclusion.

TABLE 16.1. FRENCH IMMERSION CURRICULUM

Grade	K	1	2	3	4	5	6	7	8
French	X	X	X	X	X	X	X	X	X
Math	X	X	X	X	X	X	*	X	*
Environmental Studies	X	X	X	X	X	X	X		
Science								*	X
Music	X	X	X	X	X	X	*X	*X	*X
Physical Education	X	X	X	X	X	X	*X	*X	*X
Art	X	X	X	X	X	X	*X	*X	*X
History								X	*
Geography								*	X
English			*	*	*	*	*	*	*

Code: * subjects taught in English
X subjects taught in French

Adapted from *Programme d'Immersion Précoce*, The Lakehead Board of Education, 1985.

listen with interest and selectivity at appropriate levels in a variety of experiences. They are taught to judge validity, make comparisons, make inferences, draw conclusions, generalize, and understand intent. During speaking, children learn to articulate their ideas and feelings confidently in a supportive environment, extend and synthesize various speaking skills (drama, role playing, conversation, discussion, oral reading, and others), and develop opinions through interaction with the teacher and peers. They learn to tell stories, interpret pictures, name and describe objects, explain events, evaluate, and question using verbal as well as nonverbal clues. Reading skills and processes involve exposing students to a variety of reading materials (legends, myths, folktales, poems, plays, cartoons, novels, biographies, magazine articles, recipes, directions, newspapers), enabling them to respond to print within the environment (e.g., names, labels, signs, initials), comprehend and respond to ideas, relate pictures to print, recall details, sequence events, recognize plot, understand relationships, follow directions, make judgments, distinguish fact from fantasy and fact from opinion, check for bias, predict outcomes, and so forth. Writing involves being able to label components on maps and diagrams; record personal experiences in their own words; adapt style to intended purpose; write from dictation; and create stories, poetry, diaries, letters, sets of directions, expositions, and reports. Even by the end of kindergarten, children have acquired a fairly extensive vocabulary in French; they are able to follow instructions and to comprehend simple stories. They can answer questions appropriately, participate effectively in drama, and sing a number of songs.

Because the immersion classes focus on the subject matter rather than on the target language itself, it is important that the teachers have an adequate knowledge of the subject areas they teach and that they be native speakers of French or have native-like fluency. It is also important for the students to associate specific teachers with French and others with English. For this reason, the school district always assigns teachers to classes taught in the same language. This is especially important when there is a possibility that the same students will be present in more than one class taught by the same teacher.

Strengths and Weaknesses of the Program

Ken Cressman, the principal of Redwood Public School, feels that the French immersion program in his school has benefited the entire student body. When French cultural events are arranged, they are planned not only for the French immersion students but for everyone. It is his feeling that any cultural activity, even one in another language, can be enriching for all the students, be it singing, mime, or drama. In addition, he has observed that the French immersion students have improved the ambiance of the school in general in that they tend to be more tolerant of other cultures and differences among people. When asked if one segment of the school has benefited more than others from the immersion program, he targeted the core French program as having perhaps received the most advantages. Although the students in this program take French for only one period a day, they profit from exposure to French immersion students with whom they can sometimes converse in a limited fashion and from whom they can often receive help with their homework.

Nicole Gaudet also is convinced that French immersion has been a real boon to the environments of all the schools of which it is a part. Because of the increased parental support and interest of the parents of these children, the schools' parent associations thrive and the atmospheres of the schools are becoming more positive.

However, both Cressman and Gaudet agree that improvements can be made. Lack of materials appropriate to French immersion was one of the problems mentioned. Currently, most of the materials come from Francophone programs and are intended for native French speakers. However, teachers are busy creating their own materials and translating the ones intended for the English-only programs. Another problem mentioned was recruiting enough teachers with expertise and fluency to meet the growing needs. In addition, developing a long-range plan for inservicing was felt to be a necessary means for helping the teachers to keep current once they have been hired.

Because these weaknesses are not inherent in the immersion programs themselves, both administrators are of the opinion that they can be overcome with additional funds and further effort on the part of everyone involved with the programs.

Conclusion

There is a solid theoretical foundation for an interactional approach to second language teaching with far-reaching implications for the classroom. Programs that involve the students in real communication about interesting, relevant subject matter in low-anxiety environments appear to be the most effective avenues to acquisition in the classroom.

This does not mean that there is never any value in grammar exercises, drills of various sorts, translating, or other such activities. On the contrary, all of these may have a place depending upon the objectives, age and proficiency levels, and cognitive development of the learner. However, it is when such relatively noncommunicative activities become the focus of the curriculum that they can be deterimental to the progression of second language students in programs in which communication is a goal.

Organizing interactional activities related to content, providing for a silent period, and allowing for the natural development of interlanguage require creativity, flexibility, and patience on the part of teachers. For those willing to accept the challenge, the feelings of satisfaction are great once they find their students growing in the target language, whatever that language may be.

PART V

Related Readings

This section presents a collection of edited readings from various people in fields related directly or indirectly to second language teaching: Chomsky, Widdowson, Breen and Candlin, Ellis, Krashen, Vygotsky, H. D. Brown, Oller, and Cummins.

The Related Readings, which are referred to frequently throughout the book, are intended mainly for those desiring supplemental materials. This section may be particularly useful in the teaching of theory or methods courses, in which the readings might be assigned in preparation for subsequent class discussions (see also the questions that end each chapter in Parts I, II, and III).

It must be noted that only a few readings could be presented here. The ones selected seemed to be most appropriate in that they expanded the book's implications and provided additional areas for reflection and discussion.

HOW LANGUAGE IS SHAPED: An Interview

Noam Chomsky (interviewed by J. Gliedman)

In 1953 a rickety old tub that had been sunk by the Germans and later salvaged was plodding its way across the Atlantic on the first voyage of its new life. Aboard that listing ship, a seasick young Philadelphian hit on an idea that would make him an internationally known scholar and would radically alter the way linguists view language.

"I remember exactly the moment when I finally felt convinced," Noam Chomsky recalls of the crossing. Sure of himself, he set about emphasizing the role of the mind, outlining the unconscious mechanisms that make human speech possible and insisting that a genetically programmed "language organ" in the brain primed the human infant to master the intricacies of his mother tongue. This language organ allows for the gift of speech that sets humans apart from the other animals. But it also defines and delimits the characteristics of all human languages, from Urdu to Navajo.

Before Chomsky's breakthrough in the mid-Fifties, American linguists did not believe that brain structure played any significant role in shaping language. They viewed the young child's mind as a blank slate, capable of learning virtually *any* conceivable kind of language. They had no concept then that certain languages might exist almost beyond human comprehension, just as X rays and ultraviolet radiation are invisible to the naked human eye.

Many of these linguists were searching for purely mechanical procedures—"discovery procedures"—that would objectively describe the structure of any human language. Chomsky himself started out as a structural linguist and published a technical paper on discovery procedures while he was a junior fellow at Harvard, in the early Fifties. He considered this work to be real linguistics, although he was exploring alternative ideas.

But by the time he set out on that fateful ocean voyage, he was ready to concede that "several years of intense effort devoted to improving discovery procedures had come to naught." His other efforts, carried out in almost complete isolation, were yielding consistently interesting results. This was Chomsky's pioneering research in generative grammars and explanatory theory.

From "Interview (with Noam Chomsky)," *Omni*, 6 (2): November, 1983.

Chomsky expanded the definition of *grammar* to include all the elements and rules of each language that the child assimilates as he learns to speak and understand what is said to him, as well as the linguist's theory of what goes on in the speaker's/hearer's brain.

Chomsky believes that language, along with most other human abilities, depends upon genetically programmed mental structures. In other words, language learning during childhood is part of the body's preprogrammed pattern of growth. Just as heredity endows each infant with a heart and lungs that continue to develop after birth, it provides each newborn with a highly complex language organ. The accidents of evolution have shaped this language organ so that it is capable of learning only those languages within a relatively narrow range of logical structures. Other languages, no less suitable for intelligent communication but lacking these human hallmarks, would be virtually unlearnable, even for the most gifted linguist. Chomsky foresees the day when scientists will have constructed a kind of linguistic analogue to Mendeleyev's periodic table—a list of the linguistic "atoms" and their permissible combinations that defines *every possible* human language. . . .

Chomsky once said that "anybody who teaches at age fifty what he was teaching at age twenty-five had better find another profession." Over the last 25 years, his own linguistic theory has passed through four main stages, each differing in major ways from its predecessor. Chomsky is unique among contemporary scientists in that most of his opponents defend theories he either originated or profoundly influenced. Today he is a professor in the department of linguistics and philosophy at the Massachusetts Institute of Technology.

Psychologist and science journalist John Gliedman, who studied Chomsky's theories in the late Sixties at MIT, discussed ideas about language and mind in the linguist's austere campus office.

OMNI: Why do you believe that language behavior critically depends on the existence of a genetically preprogrammed language organ in the brain?

CHOMSKY: There's a lot of linguistic evidence to support this contention. But even in advance of detailed linguistic research, we should expect heredity to play a major role in language because there is really no other way to account for the fact that children learn to speak in the first place.

OMNI: What do you mean?

CHOMSKY: Consider something that everyone agrees is due to heredity— the fact that humans develop arms rather than wings. Why do we believe this? Well, since nothing in the fetal environments of the human or bird embryo can account for the differences between birds and men, we assume that heredity must be responsible. In fact, if someone came along and said that a bird embryo is somehow "trained" to grow wings, people would just laugh, even though embryologists lack anything like detailed understanding of how genes regulate embryological development.

OMNI: Is the role of heredity as important for language as it is for embry-ology?

CHOMSKY: I think so. You have to laugh at claims that heredity plays no significant role in language learning, because exactly the same kinds of ge-netic arguments hold for language learning as hold for embryological devel-opment.

I'm very much interested in embryology, but I've got just a layman's knowledge of it. I think that recent work, primarily in molecular biology, how-ever, is seeking to discover the ways that genes regulate embryological devel-opment. The gene-control problem is conceptually similar to the problem of accounting for language growth. In fact, language development really ought to be called language *growth*, because the language organ grows like any other body organ.

OMNI: Is there a special place in the brain and a particular kind of neuro-logical structure that comprises the language organ?

CHOMSKY: Little enough is known about cognitive systems and their neu-rological basis, so caution is necessary in making any direct claims. But it does seem that the representation and use of language involve specific neural structures, though their nature is not well understood.

OMNI: But clearly, environment plays *some* role in language development. What's the relationship between heredity and environment for human lan-guage?

CHOMSKY: The language organ interacts with early experience and ma-tures into the grammar of the language that the child speaks. If a human being with this fixed endowment grows up in Philadelphia, as I did, his brain will encode knowledge of the Philadelphia dialect of English. If that brain had grown up in Tokyo, it would have encoded the Tokyo dialect of Japanese. The brain's different linguistic experience—English versus Japanese—would modify the language organ's structure.

Roughly the same thing goes on in animal experiments, showing that different kinds of early visual experience can modify the part of the brain that processes visual information. As you may know, cats, monkeys, and humans have hierarchically organized brain-cell networks connected to the retina in such a way that certain cells fire only when there is a horizontal line in the visual field; other hierarchies respond only to vertical lines. But early experi-ence can apparently change the relative numbers of horizontal- and vertical-line detectors. MIT psychologists Richard Held and Alan Hein showed some time ago, for example, that a kitten raised in a cage with walls covered by bold, black vertical lines will display good sensitivity to vertical lines as an adult but poor horizontal-line sensitivity. Lack of stimulation apparently causes the horizontal-line detectors to atrophy.

An even closer analogy exists between language growth and the growth that occurs in human beings *after* birth—for example, the onset of puberty. If someone came along and said, "Kids are trained to undergo puberty because they see other people," once again everybody would laugh. Would we laugh because we know in great detail the gene mechanisms that determine puberty? As far as I can tell, no one knows much of anything about that. Yet we all assume that puberty is genetically determined.

OMNI: Still, as your own example shows, environmental factors do play a major role in physiological growth.

CHOMSKY: And it goes without saying that the onset of puberty may well vary over quite a range depending on childhood diet and all kinds of other environmental influences. Nonetheless, everyone takes for granted that the fundamental processes controlling puberty are genetically programmed. This is probably true of death as well. You may be genetically programmed to die at roughly a certain point; it's a reasonable theory.

Look, all through an organism's existence, from birth to death, it passes through a series of genetically programmed changes. Plainly language growth is simply one of these predetermined changes. Language depends upon a genetic endowment that's on a par with the ones that specify the structure of our visual or circulatory systems, or determine that we have arms instead of wings.

OMNI: What about the linguistic evidence? What have you learned from studying human languages to corroborate your biological viewpoint?

CHOMSKY: The best evidence involves those aspects of a language's grammar that are so obvious, so intuitively self-evident to everyone, that they are quite rightly never mentioned in traditional grammars.

OMNI: You mean that school grammars fill in the gaps left by heredity? They teach everything about French or Russian, for example, that can't be taken for granted by virtue of the fact that you're a human?

CHOMSKY: That's right. It is precisely what seems self-evident that is most likely to be part of our hereditary baggage. Some of the oddities of English pronoun behavior illustrate what I mean. Take the sentence, "John believes he is intelligent." Okay, we all know that *he* can refer either to John or to someone else, so the sentence is ambiguous. It can mean either that John thinks he, John, is intelligent, or that someone else is intelligent. In contrast, consider the sentence, "John believes him to be intelligent." Here the pronoun *him* can't refer to John; it can refer only to someone else.

Now, did anyone teach us this peculiarity about English pronouns when we were children? It would be hard to even imagine a training procedure that would convey such information to a person. Nevertheless, everybody knows it—knows it without experience, without training, and at quite an early age. There are any number of other examples that show that we humans have explicit and highly articulate linguistic knowledge that simply has no basis in linguistic experience.

OMNI: There's just no way that children can pick up this kind of information by listening to the grown-ups around them?

CHOMSKY: Precisely. But let me give you another example. English contains grammatical constructions that are called parasitic gaps. In these constructions, you can drop a pronoun and still understand the sentence in the same way as when the sentence contains a pronoun. Consider the sentence, "Which article did you file without reading it?" Notice that you can drop the pronoun *it* without changing meaning or grammaticality. You can say, "Which article did you file without reading?" But you can't say, "John was killed by a rock falling on," when you mean, "John was killed by a rock falling on him." This time omitting the pronoun destroys both meaning and grammaticality.

Constructions of this type—where you can or cannot drop the pronoun—are very rare. In fact, they are so rare that it is quite likely that during the period a child masters his native language (the first five or six years of life), he never hears any of these constructions, or he hears them very sporadically. Nonetheless, every native speaker of English knows flawlessly when you can and can't drop pronouns in these kinds of sentences.

OMNI: So we're faced with a mystery. How could anyone possibly learn enough about the English language to possess the rich and exotic grammatical knowledge that we all seem to possess by the time we are five or six years old?

CHOMSKY: There's an obvious answer to that: The knowledge is built in. You and I can learn English, as well as any other language, with all its richness because we are designed to learn languages based upon a common set of principles, which we may call universal grammar.

OMNI: What is univeral grammar?

CHOMSKY: It is the sum total of all the immutable principles that heredity builds into the language organ. These principles cover grammar, speech sounds, and meaning. Put differently, universal grammar is the inherited genetic endowment that makes it possible for us to speak and learn human languages.

OMNI: Suppose that somewhere else in the universe intelligent life has evolved. Could we, with our specialized language organ, learn the aliens' language if we made contact with them?

CHOMSKY: Not if their language violated the principles of our universal grammar, which, given the myriad ways that languages can be organized, strikes me as highly likely.

OMNI: Maybe we shouldn't call it *universal*, then. But please explain what you mean.

CHOMSKY: The same structures that make it possible to learn a human language make it impossible for us to learn a language that violates the principles of univeral grammar. If a Martian landed from outer space and spoke a language that violated universal grammar, we simply would not be able to learn that language the way that we learn a human language like English or Swahili. We would have to approach the alien's language slowly and laboriously—the way that scientists study physics, where it takes generation after generation of labor to gain new understanding and to make significant prog- ress. We're designed by nature for English, Chinese, and every other possible human language, but we're not designed to learn perfectly usable languages that violate universal grammar. These languages would simply *not* be within our range of abilities.

OMNI: How would you assess current research about universal gram- mar?

CHOMSKY: In the last three or four years there's been a major conceptual change in the underlying theory. We now assume that universal grammar consists of a collection of preprogrammed subsystems that include, for exam- ple, one responsible for meaning, another responsible for stringing together phrases in a sentence, a third one that deals, among other things, with the kinds of relationships between nouns and pronouns that I discussed earlier. And there are a number of others.

These subsystems are not genetically preprogrammed down to the last detail. If they were, there would be only one human language. But heredity does set rather narrow limits on the possible ways that the rules governing each subsystem's function can vary. Languages like English and Italian, for example, differ in their choice of genetically permitted variations that exist as options in the universal grammar. You can think of these options as a kind of linguistic menu containing mutually exclusive grammatical possibilities.

For example, languages like Italian have chosen the "null subject" option from the universal-grammar menu. In Italian you can say *left* when you mean "He left" or "She left." English and French have passed up this option and chosen instead a rule that requires explicit mention of the subject.

OMNI: What are some other grammatical options on the universal- grammar menu?

CHOMSKY: In English the most important element in every major gram- matical category comes first in its phrase. In simple sentences, for example, we say *John hit Bill*, not *John Bill hit*. With adjectives we say *proud of John*, not *John of proud*; with nouns we say *habit of drinking wine*, not *drinking wine of habit*, and with prepositions we say *to John*, not *John to*. Because heads of grammatical categories always come first, English is what is called a head- initial language.

Japanese is a head-final language. In Japanese you say *John Bill hit*. And instead of prepositions, there are postpositions that follow nouns: *John to*, rather than *to John*. So here's another parameter the child's got to learn from experience: Is the language head-initial or head-final?

These grammatical parameters are interconnected. You can't pick them any more freely than, say, a wine fanatic who insists on white wine with fish and red wine with meat is free to choose any main dish once he's decided on his wine. But grammars are even more sensitive than this culinary example might suggest. A slight change in just one of the universal grammar's param-

eters can have enormous repercussions throughout the language. It can produce an entirely different language.

Again, there's a close parallel to embryology, where a slight shift in the
gene mechanisms regulating growth may be all that separates a fertilized egg
from developing into a lion rather than a whale.

OMNI: So what exactly would you say *is* the grammar of English?

CHOMSKY: The grammar of English is the collection of choices—head-
initial rather than head-final, and null subject forbidden, for example—that
define one of a limited number of genetically permitted selections from the
universal-grammar menu of grammatical options. And of course there are all
the lexical facts. You just have to learn your language's vocabulary. The universal grammar doesn't tell you that *tree* means "tree" in English.

But once you've learned the vocabulary items and fixed the grammatical
parameters for English, the whole system is in place. And the general principles genetically programmed into the langauge organ just churn away to
yield all the particular facts about English grammar.

OMNI: It sounds as if your present research goal is to reach the point
where you can define every human language's grammar simply by specifying
its choices from the universal grammar's menu of options.

CHOMSKY: That's the kind of work you would hope would soon be done:
to take a theory of universal grammar, fix the parameters one way or another,
and then deduce from these parameters the grammar of a real human language—Japanese, Swahili, English, or whatnot.

This goal is not on the horizon. But I think that it is within our conceptual
grasp. Undoubtedly the principles of universal grammar that we currently
theorize are wrong. It would be a miracle if we were right this early along.
But the principles *are* of the right type, and we can now begin to test our
present system with complex examples to see what is wrong and to make
changes that will improve our theory. . . .

OMNI: Moving on to another controversial area in the behavioral sciences,
how do you think your views differ from B. F. Skinner's behaviorist theory
of language, learning, and mind?

CHOMSKY: Skinner used to take a relatively extreme position. At one point
he held that, apart from the most rudimentary functions, essentially nothing
of importance was genetically programmed in the human brain. Skinner
agreed that humans were genetically programmed to see and hear, but that's
about all. Accordingly he argued that all human behavior was simply a reflection of training and experience. This view can't possibly be correct. And, in
fact, Skinner's approach has led absolutely nowhere in this area. It has
yielded no theoretical knowledge, no nontrivial principles as far as I am
aware—thus far, at any rate.

OMNI: Why is that?

CHOMSKY: Because Skinnerian behaviorism is off the wall. It's as hopeless
a project as trying to explain that the onset of puberty results from social

training. But I really don't know whether Skinner still maintains this extreme position. [*He has since modified it.—Ed.*]

OMNI: What about the late Jean Piaget? Where do you stand on his theories of the child's mental development?

CHOMSKY: Piaget's position is different; it's more complex than Skinner's. Piaget held that the child passes through cognitive states. According to my understanding of the Piagetian literature, Piaget and his supporters were never really clear about what produced a new stage of cognitive development. What they could have said—though they seemed to shy away from it—is that cognitive development is a genetically determined maturational process like puberty, for example. That's what the Piagetians *ought* to say. They don't like this formulation, but it seems right to me.

OMNI: In other words, Piagetians place much more emphasis on the role of experience in cognitive development than you do. Are there other differences as well?

CHOMSKY: Yes. Piagetians maintain that the mind develops as a whole rather than as a modular structure with specific capacities developing in their own ways. This is a possible hypothesis, but in fact it seems to be extremely wrong.

OMNI: How do you mean?

CHOMSKY: Well, consider the properties that determine the reference of pronouns that we talked about earlier. Once you ferret out these rules of pronouns, they seem to have nothing in common with the logical operations that Piagetians single out as being typical of the early stages of the child's mental development.

OMNI: In other words, a four-year-old who may not realize that the amount of water stays the same when you pour the contents of a low, wide glass into a tall, thin container nevertheless displays sophisticated logical abilities in his grasp of the complex rules of English grammar?

CHOMSKY: Yes. And these abilities are independent of the logical capacities measured by tests. There's just no resemblance between what a child does with blocks and the kind of knowledge that he displays of English grammar at the same age. In fact, I think it's sort of quixotic to expect tight interconnections between language development and growth in other mental domains. By and large, body systems develop in their own ways at their own rates. They interact, but the circulatory system doesn't wait until the visual system reaches a certain stage of organization before proceeding to imitate the visual system's organizational complexity. Cognitive growth shouldn't be different in this respect either. As far as we know, it isn't. . . .

RELATED READING 2

THE NOTIONAL SYLLABUS:
Does It Lead to Communicative Competence?

H. G. Widdowson

Notional syllabuses are represented by their proponents as an alternative to, and an improvement on, structural syllabuses. How do they differ? And what are the grounds for believing them to be better?

The two types of syllabus differ most obviously in the manner in which the language content is defined. In the structural syllabus it is defined in *formal* terms, as lexical items and grammatical patterns *manifesting* the system of English. In the notional syllabus, language content is defined in *functional* terms, as notions which are *realized* by formal items. In both cases the essential design is an inventory of language units in isolation and in abstraction. In the structural syllabus the inventory is ordered by reference to grading criteria. In the notional syllabus it is not.

The question then arises: what are the grounds for favouring a functional rather than a formal definition of language content? We can, I think, discern two arguments in the supporting literature. One refers to linguistic description. The other to learner needs.

The first argument rests on the assumption that descriptions provided by linguists capture the 'real' nature of language so that units for teaching should correspond with units of linguistic description.

The structural syllabus was developed at a time when linguists conceived of language in terms of the distributional properties of surface forms. So the subject matter for teaching language was similarly defined. The notional syllabus is being developed at a time when linguistic interest has shifted to the communicative properties of language, when meaning has moved to the centre of the stage with speech acts, presuppositions, case categories, conversational implicatures, and what have you all dancing attendance. It looks as if linguists have now decided that language is 'really' communication. As before the syllabus designer follows the fashion.

If you do not believe that we progress towards the truth of things by recurrent revelations, or if you do not believe that there should be a necessary correspondence between units of linguistic analysis and units for language teaching, then you will not be impressed by the fact that the notional syllabus can drum up current linguistic support. So we will turn to the second argument: the one relating to learner needs. The question to consider here is this:

From H. G. Widdowson, *Explorations in Applied Linguistics* (Oxford: Oxford University Press, 1979), pp. 247–250.

what kind of knowledge or behaviour does a learner need to have acquired at the end of a course of instruction?

Proponents of the structural syllabus will argue that the learner needs a basic knowledge of the language system, of lexical and grammatical forms constituting a core linguistic competence, and that this will provide the essential basis for communicative behaviour when the learner finds himself in a situation which requires him to use the language to communicate. The belief here is that what has to be *taught* is a knowledge of the language system: its exploitation for communicative purposes can be left to the learner.

Proponents of the notional syllabus will argue that the learner needs to learn appropriate behaviour *during* his course since one cannot count on him learning it later simply by reference to his linguistic knowledge. The belief here is that communicative competence needs to be expressly taught: the learner cannot be left to his own devices in developing an ability to communicate.

Both types of syllabus recognize that the learner's goal should be the ability to communicate. They differ in the assumption of what needs to be actually taught for this ability to be acquired. In both cases there is a gap between what is taught and what is learnt, both leave something for the learner to find out for himself. They differ again in their awareness of this fact.

The structural syllabus quite openly—brazenly, you might say—leaves the learner to realize his linguistic competence as communicative behaviour when the occasion arises. A tall order.

The notional syllabus, it is claimed, develops the ability to do this by accounting for communicative competence within the actual design of the syllabus itself. This is a delusion because the notional syllabus presents language as an inventory of units, of items for accumulation and storage. They are notional rather than structural isolates, but they are isolates all the same. What such a syllabus does not do—or has not done to date (an important proviso)—is to represent language as discourse, and since it does not it cannot possibly in its present form account for communicative competence—because communicative competence is not a compilation of items in memory, but a set of strategies or creative procedures for realizing the value of linguistic elements in contexts of use, an ability to *make* sense as a participant in discourse, whether spoken or written, by the skillful deployment of shared knowledge of code resources and rules of language use. The notional syllabus leaves the learner to develop these creative strategies on his own: it deals with the *components* of discourse, not with discourse itself. As such it derives from an analyst's and not a participant's view of language, as does the structural syllabus. Neither is centered on the language user.

The focus of attention in the notional syllabus, then, is on items, not strategies, on components of discourse, not the process of its creation, and in this respect it does not differ essentially from the structural syllabus, which also deals in items and components. In both cases what is missing is an appeal to cognition, to the language processing ability of the learner. For example, in a notional syllabus functions of different kinds are correlated with various linguistic forms. But the relationship between function and form is not just fortuitous: the form itself has what Halliday refers to as 'meaning potential' and it is this which is realized on particular communicative occasions. This realization of meaning potential depends on a knowledge of the conventional code meanings of linguistic items *and* of the ways in which these meanings can be conditioned by context. A notional syllabus presents certain common formal realizations of a range of communicative functions but does so *statically* without any indication of the dynamic process of interpretation that is involved. There is no demonstration of the *relationship* between form and function, of the meaning potential in the language forms which are presented. And so there is no attempt to develop an awareness of how this potential is realized by interpretative procedures which provide linguistic items with appropriate communicative value. But what is important for the learner is not to know what correlations are common between certain forms and functions, but *how* such correlations and innumerable others can be established and interpreted in the actual business of communicative interaction.

It seems to me, then, that the focus of the notional syllabus is still on the accumulation of language items rather than on the development of strategies for dealing with language in use. And in practice once you start writing materials or applying teaching procedures it may turn out not to make much difference whether you define these items as forms or functions.

I have spent most of my time pointing out what I see as the deficiencies of the notional syllabus, as it has been developed to date. I want to end on a more positive note. What the work on notional syllabuses has done, I think, is to sharpen our perception of what is required of a syllabus if it is to develop communicative competence in learners. It is an attempt to look afresh at the principles of syllabus design and it thus directs us to a reappraisal of these principles. I have said, for example, that the notional syllabus, in its present form, does not develop an awareness of meaning potential. But then how does one go about developing such an awareness? This question might then take us back to the structural syllabus to find out if there are not ways of reforming it, so that there is an emphasis on the meaning potential of forms and the varied ways in which this is realized in contexts of use.

We can now return to the two questions I posed at the beginning. How does the notional syllabus differ? Its proponents represent it as an alternative to the structural syllabus, so forcing us into taking sides. This is unfortunate. The work on notional syllabuses can best be seen, I think, as a means of developing the structural syllabus rather than replacing it, and if it were seen in this light, the extent of difference between the two would become clear and we would be less likely to be deluded by false visions, which we are all rather prone to be. How far are notional syllabuses an improvement? In the attempt rather than the deed, I think. They are the first serious consideration of what is involved in incorporating communicative properties in a syllabus. We must give full credit for that. Work on the notional syllabus, properly interpreted, opens up the horizons and does not confine us to a creed. It indicates a direction to follow and ground to explore. But it is a starting point, not a destination.

RELATED READING 3

THE ROLES OF THE TEACHER, THE LEARNERS, AND THE CONTENT WITHIN A COMMUNICATIVE METHODOLOGY

Michael Breen and Christopher Candlin

THE TEACHER

Within a communicative methodology the teacher has two main roles. The first role is to facilitate the communicative process between all participants in the classroom, and between these participants and the various activities and texts. The second role is to act as an *interdependent* participant within the learning-teaching group. This latter role is closely related to the objective of the first role and it arises from it. These roles imply a set of secondary roles for the teacher: first, as an organiser of resources and as a resource himself. Second, as a guide within the classroom procedures and activities. In this role the teacher endeavours to make clear to the learners what they need to do in order to achieve some specific activity or task, if they indicate that such guidance is necessary. This guidance role is ongoing and largely unpredictable, so the teacher needs to share it with other learners. Related to this, the teacher—and other learners—can offer and seek feedback at appropriate moments in learning-teaching activities. In guiding and monitoring the teacher needs to be a 'seer of potential' with the aim of facilitating and shaping individual and group knowledge and exploitation of abilities during learning. In this way the teacher will be concentrating on the process competences of the learners.

A third role for the teacher is that of researcher and learner—with much to contribute in terms of appropriate knowledge and abilities, actual and observed experience of the nature of learning, and organisational capabilities. As a participant-observer, the teacher has the opportunity to 'step back' and monitor the communicative process of learning-teaching.

From Michael Breen and Christopher Candlin, "The Essentials of a Communicative Curriculum in Language Teaching," *Applied Linguistics* 1 (2) (Oxford: Oxford University Press, 1979), pp. 99–104.

As an interdependent participant in the process, the teacher needs to actively share the responsibility for learning and teaching with the learners. This sharing can provide the basis for joint negotiation which itself releases the teacher to become a co-participant. Perceiving the learners as having important contributions to make—in terms of initial competence and a range of various and changing expectations—can enable the teacher to continually seek potential and exploit it. A requirement on the teacher must be that he distinguish between learning and the performance of what is being learned. The teacher must assume that the performance within any target repertoire is separable from the means to the achievement of that repertoire. Also, he must assume that learners are capable of arriving at a particular objective through diverse routes. The teacher needs to recognise learning as an interpersonal undertaking over which no single person can have full control, and that there will be differences between ongoing learning processes. The teacher has to accept that different learners learn different things in different ways at different times, and he needs to be patiently aware that some learners, for example, will enter periods when it seems that little or no progress is being made and that, sometimes, learning is typified by silent reflection.[1]

THE LEARNER

Regardless of the curriculum in which they work and regardless of whether or not they are being taught, all learners of a language are confronted by the task of discovering *how to learn* the language. All learners will start with differing expectations about the actual learning, but each individual learner will be required to adapt and continually readapt in the process of relating himself to what is being learned. The knowledge will be redefined as the learner uncovers it, and, in constructing and reconstructing his own curriculum, the learner may discover that earlier strategies in the use of his abilities need to be replaced by other strategies. Thus, all learners—in their own ways—have to adopt the role of negotiation between themselves, their learning process, and the gradually revealed object of learning.

A communicative methodology is characterised by making this negotiative role—this learning how to learn—a public as well as a private undertaking. Within the context of the classroom group, this role is shared and, thereby, made interpersonal. If we recognise that any knowledge which we ourselves have mastered is always shared knowledge and that we always seek confirmation that we 'know' something by communicating with other people, we have to conclude that knowledge of anything and the learning of anything is an interpersonal matter. Also, if we recognise that real knowledge is always set in a context and this context is both psychological and social—what is known will always be contextualised with other knowledge in our minds and will always carry with it elements of the social context in which it was experienced—then we also have to conclude that a significant part of our learning is, in fact, socially constructed. These justifications for a genuinely interpersonal methodology are quite independent of the nature of what is to be learned. If the object of learning is itself communication, then the motivation to enable the learner to adopt an interpersonal means to that learning is doubly justified. Quite simply, in order to learn to communicate within a selected target repertoire, the learner must be encouraged to communicate—to communicate about the learning process, and to communicate about the changing object of learning on the basis of accepting that 'learning how to learn' is a problem shared, and solved, by other learners.

Within a communicative methodology, the role of learner as negotiator—between the self, the learning process, and the object of learning—emerges from and interacts with the role of joint negotiator within the group and within the classroom procedures and activities which the group undertakes. The implication for the learner is that he should contribute as much as he gains, and thereby learn in an interdependent way. The learner can achieve interdependence by recognising responsibility for his own learning and by sharing that responsibility with other learners and the teacher. A further implication is that the learner must commit himself to undertake communicative and metacommunicative acts while working with other participants in the group, and while working upon activities and texts. This commitment can be initiated and supported by a milieu in which the learner's own contributions—interpretations, expressions, and efforts to negotiate—are recognised as valid and valuable. Such a context would be typified by the acceptance of ongoing success *and failure* as necessary prerequisites towards some ultimate achievement, where it is assumed that learners inevitably bring with them 'mixed abilities' and that such a 'mixture' is, in fact, positively useful to the group as a whole. Commitment to communication on the learner's part need not be regarded as something unattainable or threatening—even for the 'beginning' learner—because he is expected to rely on and develop that which is familiar: his own process competence and experience of communication.

As an interdependent participant in a cooperative milieu where the learner's contributions are valued and used, the individual learner is potentially rewarded by having his own subjective expectations and decisions informed and guided by others. In a context where different contributions and differential learning are positively encouraged, the learner is allowed to depend on other learners and on the teacher when the need arises, and also enabled to be independent at appropriate moments of the learning. He can feel free to exploit independent strategies in order to learn, to maintain and develop personal affective motivations for learning, and to decide on different routes and means which become available during learning. The paradox here, of course, is that genuine independence arises only to the extent that it is interdependently granted *and* interdependently accepted. Learning seen as totally a personal and subjective matter is seeing learning in a vacuum; indeed we may wonder whether such learning is ever possible.

Learners also have an important monitoring role in addition to the degree of monitoring which they may apply subjectively to their own learning. The learner can be a provider of feedback to others concerning his own interpretation of the specific purposes of the curriculum, and the appropriateness of methodology to his own learning experiences and achievements. In expression and negotiation, the learner adopts the dual role of being, first, a potential teacher for other learners and, second, an informant to the teacher concerning his own learning progress. In this latter role, the learner can offer the teacher and other learners a source for new directions in the learning-teaching process of the group. Essentially, a communicative methodology would allow both the teacher and the learner to be interdependent participants in a communicative process of learning and teaching.

THE CONTENT

Language teaching curricula have often been traditionally defined by their content. Such content has itself been derived from a target repertoire in terms of some selected inventories of items analysed prior to the commencement of the teaching-learning process and often acting as predeterminants of it. Similarly, sets of formal items taken from an analytic grammar of the language, or sets of 'functions' taken from some list of semantic categories, have been linked to themes and topics deemed in advance to be appropriate to the expectations of the particular learners.

Communicative curricula, on the other hand, do not look exclusively to a selected target repertoire as a specifier of curriculum content, for a number of reasons. First, the emphasis on the process of bringing certain basic abilities to bear on the dynamic conventions of communication precludes any specification of content in terms of a static inventory of language items—grammatical or 'functional'—to be learned in some prescribed way. Second, the central concern for the development and refinement of underlying competence as a basis for a selected target repertoire requires a distinction between that target and *any* content which could be used as a potential means towards it. Third, the importance of the curriculum as a means for the activation and refinement of the process competences of different learners, presupposes differentiation, ongoing change, and only short-term predictability in what may be appropriate content.

The communicative curriculum would place content within methodology and provide it with the role of servant to the learning-teaching process. Thus, content would not necessarily be prescribed by purposes but selected and organised *within* the communicative and differentiated process by learners and teachers as participants in that process. Therefore, the learner would use the content of the curriculum as the 'carrier' of his process competence and as the provider of opportunities for communicative experiences through which personal routes may be selected and explored as a means to the ultimate target competence.

From this concern with means rather than ends—with the process of learning-teaching rather than with the product—the communicative curriculum will adopt criteria for the selection and organisation of content which will be subject to, and defined by, communicative learning and teaching. The content of any curriculum can be selected and organised on the basis of some adopted criteria, and these criteria will influence five basic aspects of the content: its focus, its sequence, its subdivision (or breakdown), its continuity, and its direction (or routing). We will now consider the possible criteria for the selection and organisation of content within the communicative curriculum with reference to each of these five aspects in turn:

(a) Focus

From what has been proposed in this section so far, it follows that content within communicative methodology is likely to focus upon knowledge—both cognitive and affective—which is personally significant to the learner. Such knowledge would be placed in an interpersonal context which can motivate personal and joint negotiation through the provision of authentic and problem-posing texts. If content is to be sensitive to the process of learning and to the interpersonal concerns of the group, it needs to reflect and support the integration of language with other forms of human experience and behaviour.

(b) Sequence

If we accept that the communicative process requires that we deal with dynamic and creative conventions, we cannot assume that any step-by-step or cumulative sequence of content will necessarily be appropriate. In learning, the various and changing routes of the learners crucially affect any ordering of content, so that sequencing derives from *the state of the learners* rather than from the implicit 'logic' of the content itself. Just as any movement from 'simple' to 'complex' is a very misleading way of perceiving the relationship between any text and its meaning potential—a simple text may realise complex meaning, and vice-versa—so it may be wrong to assume that what may be 'simple' for any one learner is likely to be 'simple' for all the learners. Sequencing in communicative content is therefore likely to be a cyclic process where learners are continually developing related frameworks or aggregations of knowledge and ability use, rather than accumulating separable blocks of 'static' knowledge or a sequence of ordered skills. Learners would typically move from global to particular perspectives—and vice-versa—in their negotiation with the content. Thus, content becomes something which

learners move into and out from, and to which they return in a process of
finer analysis and refined synthesis. Curriculum designers cannot, therefore,
predict with any certainty the 'levels' of content on which learners will decide
to evolve their own sequencing in learning. All such designers can do is to
anticipate a range of content which will richly activate process competences
so that the ultimate target repertoire becomes accessible and its specific demands recognised by the learner.

(c) Subdivision

Traditionally content has been subdivided into serialised categories of structures or 'functions'. A communicative view of content precludes this frag-
mentation and argues for subdivision in terms of whole frameworks wherein
there is interaction between all the various components of the knowledge
system—ideational, interpersonal and textual—and all the abilities involved
in using such knowledge. Content would be subdivided or broken down in
terms of activities and tasks to be undertaken, wherein both knowledge and
abilities would be engaged in the learners' communication and metacommunication. The various activities and tasks would be related by sharing a holistic 'core' of knowledge and abilities. So, we would not be concerned with
'units' of content, but with 'units' of activity which generate communication
and metacommunication.

(d) Continuity

The need to provide continuity for the learner has, in the past, been based
upon content. Within a communicative methodology, continuity can be identified within at least four areas. First, continuity can reside in the activities
and the tasks within each activity; and from one activity to another and from
one task to another. An activity or task sets up its own requirements for its
progressive accomplishment, and it is the pursuit of these requirements
which can provide tangible continuity for the learner. Second, continuity potentially resides within communicative acts during the learning and teaching:
either at the 'macro' level in terms of the whole lesson and its 'micro' sequences of negotiation, or within the structure of discourse in terms of the
'macro' communicative act with its own coherent sequence of utterances.[2]
Third, continuity is provided through the ideational system which can also
be seen in terms of 'macro' and 'micro' levels. At the 'macro' level the learner
may have access to continuity of theme, while at the 'micro' level the learner
can have access to conceptual or notional continuity. Because ideational continuity is realised through a refinement of textual knowledge—the refinement
of a concept, for example, can imply a refinement of its linguistic expression,
and vice-versa—there is a parallel continuity of ideation and text. Fourth, and
finally, continuity can reside within a skills repertoire or a cycle of skill-use
during an activity. For example, there could be a progression from reading to

note-taking to speaking for the achievement of a particular activity. A communicative methodology would exploit each of these areas of continuity as clusters of potential continuities, rather than exploit any one alone. All can be inherent in a single activity. These kinds of continuity offer two important advantages. They can serve the full process competencies of learners—knowledge systems and abilities—and they can allow for differentiation. Learners need to be enabled to seek and achieve their own continuity and, therefore, the criteria for their own progress. In the process of accomplishing some immediate activity, learners will impose their own personal and interpersonal order and continuity upon that activity, the communication which the activity generates, the interpersonal, ideational and textual data which they act upon, and on the skills they need to use in the activity's achievement. As a result, the progressive refinement of the learner's own process competence can provide an overall *learning* continuity. Once the teacher can accept that each of these areas provides potential continuity for different learners, it ceases to be a problem if different learners pursue several routes or progress at different rates.

(e) Direction

Traditionally, learners have been expected to follow the direction implicit in some prescribed content. Typically an emphasis on content led the learner from the beginning, through the middle, to the end. From what has been indicated so far, a communicative methodology would not exploit content as some pre-determined route with specific entry and exit points. In a communicative methodology, content ceases to become some external control over learning-teaching procedures. Choosing directions becomes a part of the curriculum itself, and involves negotiation between learners and learners, learners and teachers, and learners and text. Who or what directs content becomes a justification for communication about the selection and organisation of content with methodology, and about the various routes to be adopted by the learners through any agreed content. Content can be predicted within methodology only to the extent that it serves the communicative learning process of the participants in the group. It might well be that the teacher, in negotiation with learners, will propose the adoption of aspects of the target repertoire as appropriate content. However, the teacher would recognise that the central objective of developing underlying communicative knowledge and abilities can be achieved through a range of alternative content, *not necessarily* including aspects of the target repertoire. Such 'carrier' content can be as diverse as the different routes learners may take towards a common target: perhaps content can be more various and more variable. Also, the teacher would remain free to build upon the contributions of learners—their initial competences and expectations—and exploit the inevitably different ways in which learners may attain the ultimate target. Further, the teacher would not regard any surface performance as synonymous with its underlying knowledge and abilities, and he will avoid transferring this possible confusion to the learners.

NOTES

[1]Some readers may feel that the main roles of facilitator and interdependent participant within a communicative methodology present teachers with unaccustomed challenges. However, if we more closely consider the problems for the teacher within more traditional methodologies (see for example: Rogers, 1969; Allwright, 1978), we can discover quite separate motivations for the roles suggested here.

[2]On lessons seen in terms of 'macro' and 'micro' levels see Sinclair and Coulthard (1975). On discourse as 'macro speech acts' and 'micro speech acts' see van Dijk (1977).

RELATED READING 4

THEORIES OF SECOND LANGUAGE ACQUISITION

Rod Ellis

INTRODUCTION

There has been no shortage of theorizing about second language acquisition (SLA). The research literature abounds in approaches, theories, models, laws, and principles. It is arguable that there has been a superfluity of theorizing. Schouten (1979, p. 4), for instance, claims:

> . . . in second language learning, too many models have been built and taken for granted too soon, and this has stifled relevant research.

He believes that theorizing should only follow extensive and rigorous empirical research. However, it might also be argued that theorizing should precede and, therefore, inform empirical study, guiding the specific hypotheses it seeks to examine. Irrespective of these methodological issues, SLA research has gone ahead and spawned a plethora of theories.

The main aim of this reading is to review a number of theories of SLA. The ones that have been selected for discussion have assumed a central place

Rod Ellis, ''Theories of Second Language Acquisition,'' from *Understanding Second Language Acquisition* (Oxford: Oxford University Press, 1986), pp. 248–276.

in SLA research. They reflect the variety of perspectives evident in SLA studies. They are:

1. The Acculturation Model (and closely associated with it, the Nativization Model)
2. Accommodation Theory
3. Discourse Theory
4. The Monitor Model[1]
5. The Variable Competence Model
6. The Universal Hypothesis
7. A Neurofunctional Theory

The discussion of each theory will take the form of an account of its central premises, followed by a critical evaluation.

THE ROLE OF THEORY IN SLA RESEARCH

What is the role of theory in SLA research? Hakuta (1981, p. 1) sees the main goal of SLA research as follows:

> The game of language acquisition research can be described as the search for an appropriate level of description for the learner's system of rules.

In other words, the main goal of a theory of SLA is *description*—the characterization of the nature of the linguistic categories which constitute the learner's interlanguage at any point in development. However, most other researchers have aimed at more than just description. They have tried to discover why the learner develops the particular linguistic categories that he does. As Rutherford (1982, p. 85) puts it:

> We wish to know *what* it is that is acquired, *how* it is acquired and *when* it is acquired. But were we to have the answers even to these questions, we would still want to know *why* . . .

In other words, theory building is concerned with *explanation* as well as with description.

But the term 'explanation' is ambiguous. Firstly, it can refer to the way in which the learner works on samples of the input data, converting them into intake and then using his knowledge to produce output. Explanation in this sense covers the acquisition sequence and order and the processes responsible for it. Secondly, the term 'explanation' can also refer to what motivates the learner to learn and what causes him to cease learning (i.e., fossilize). Schumann (1976) distinguishes these two types of explanation, which he refers to respectively as 'cognitive processes' responsible for *how* SLA takes place and 'initiating factors' responsible for *why* SLA takes place. Ellis (1984a) refers to the two types as 'assembly mechanisms' and 'power mechanisms'. The distinction is an important one where SLA theorizing is concerned, because, as will be shown, whereas some theories focus on the *how*, others focus on the *why*. The kind of explanation they offer, therefore, is of a different order. A comprehensive theory of SLA will need to explain both assembly and power mechanism.

How do researchers set about building an explanation of how and why SLA takes place? Long (1983a), drawing on the work of Reynolds (1971), distinguishes two approaches to theory building: the *theory-then-research* approach and the *research-then-theory* approach. These will be discussed briefly.

The theory-then-research approach involves five stages:

1. Develop an explicit theory.
2. Derive a testable prediction from the theory.
3. Conduct research to test the prediction.
4. Modify (or abandon) the theory if the prediction is disconfirmed.
5. Test a new prediction if the first prediction is confirmed.

The starting point of this approach is to invent a theory using hunches and relevant research. The theory constitutes what Popper (1976) calls 'dogmatic thinking'. It is important that the theory is presented in such a way that it is falsifiable. That is, the researcher must not be able to interpret any conceivable event as verification of the theory, or, as Popper puts it, it must exclude some 'immunizations'. The strength of the theory rests both in its ability to 'cover' what is already known about the phenomenon under investigation and also to predict what will be observed in future. The prediction is a test of the theory. The process of testing and amending the theory is a continuous one that, in Popper's view, never ends. Thus it is possible to talk about a comprehensive theory which accounts for all the available facts, but it is not possible to talk about a true theory, as any theory must remain open to modification.

The research-then-theory approach has four stages:

1. Select a phenomenon for investigation.
2. Measure its characteristics.
3. Collect data and look for systematic patterns.
4. Formalize significant patterns as rules describing natural events.

The starting point of this approach is not a theory but a 'research question'—an area of interest into which the researcher wants to enquire. This area is likely to have been decided on as a result of hunches or reading the relevant research, but the research question is not formulated in such a way as to provide a testable prediction. The research-then-theory approach need never lead to a comprehensive theory—it can produce a 'bits-and-pieces' view of SLA, a series of insights into what motivates behaviour.

The study of SLA has involved both approaches. The experimental studies of the effects of motivation and attitudes undertaken by Canadian researchers (e.g., Gardner & Lambert, 1972) are examples of a theory-then-research approach. In contrast, many longitudinal studies of individual L2 learners follow a research-then-theory approach. Their aim is not so much to build a comprehensive theory as to examine specific aspects of SLA in detail.

As Long points out, both approaches have their strengths and weaknesses. The theory-then-research approach provides an approximate answer and a basis for systematically testing aspects of the overall theory. But researchers are not always prepared to abandon a theory even in the face of substantial disconfirmatory evidence. The research-then-theory approach means that the researcher is less likely to be 'wrong' at any time and can provide valuable insights into selected aspects of the whole process being investigated. But the claims that derive from this approach are necessarily limited, and it is not always clear how one claim relates to another.

Long argues that the theory-then-research approach leads to more efficient research because:

> . . . the theory governing the research at any point in time tells the investigator what the relevant data are, which is the crucial experiment to run. (1983a, p. 22)

The study of SLA, however, needs both approaches. First, there is no agreed initial theory to motivate an experimental hypothesis-testing approach, and it is doubtful whether there will be in the near future. The insights provided by a research-then-theory approach provide a basis for theory building. Second, there is a recognized need to construct theories in order to provide a general explanation of SLA. The fact that different researchers have used different approaches may, as Long suggests, be a reflection of their different personalities, but it probably also reflects the recognition that the field of SLA requires different research perspectives.

The subsequent sections of this reading review a number of theories of SLA. They differ in what they seek to explain—the 'assembly mechanisms' that govern how SLA takes place or the 'power mechanisms' that explain why it takes place, or both. They also differ in how they have been arrived at. Some are the result of a theory-then-research approach, while others owe more to a research-then-theory approach. The reader who seeks a tidy and exhaustive account of SLA is likely to be disappointed. The theories offer 'complementary alternatives', as Selinker and Lamendella (1978b, p. 168) put it; 'each perspective has advantages others lack, while at the same time embodying disadvantages'.

SEVEN THEORIES OF SLA

1. The Acculturation Model

Acculturation is defined by [H. D.] Brown (1980, p. 129) as 'the process of becoming adapted to a new culture'. It is seen as an important aspect of SLA, because language is one of the most observable expressions of culture and because in second (as opposed to foreign) language settings the acquisition of a new language is seen as tied to the way in which the learner's community and the target language community view each other. One view of how acculturation affects SLA has already been described. The account that follows is based on the work of John Schumann (see Schumann, 1978a, 1978b, 1978c). In addition, an elaborated version of Schumann's model—the Nativization Model—is discussed, with reference to Andersen (1980, 1981, 1983).

The central premise of the Acculturation Model is:

> . . . second language acquisition is just one aspect of acculturation and the degree to which a learner acculturates to the target language group will control the degree to which he acquires the second language. (Schumann, 1978a, p. 34)

Acculturation, and hence SLA, is determined by the degree of *social* and *psychological distance* between the learner and the target language culture. Social distance is the result of a number of factors which affect the learner as a member of a social group in contact with the target language group. Psychological distance is the result of various affective factors which concern the learner as an individual. The social factors are primary. The psychological factors come into play in cases where the social distance is indeterminant (i.e. where social factors constitute neither a clearly positive nor a clearly negative influence on acculturation), although they can also modify the modal level of learning associated with a particular social situation.

Schumann (1978c) lists the various factors which determine social and psychological distance. The social variables govern whether the overall learning situation is 'good' or 'bad'. An example of a 'good' learning situation is when (1) the target language and L2 groups view each other as socially equal; (2) the target language and L2 groups are both desirous that the L2 group will assimilate; (3) both the target language and L2 groups expect the L2 group to share social facilities with the target language group (i.e. there is low enclosure); (4) the L2 group is small and not very cohesive; (5) the L2 group's culture is congruent with that of the target language group; (6) both groups have positive attitudes to each other; and (7) the L2 group envisages staying in the target language area for an extended period. An example of a 'bad' learning situation is when the conditions are opposite to the ones described above.[2] It is, of course, possible to have varying degrees of social distance.

The psychological factors are affective in nature. They include (1) language shock (i.e. the learner experiences doubt and possible confusion when using the L2); (2) culture shock (i.e. the learner experiences disorientation, stress, fear, etc. as a result of differences between his or her own culture and that of the target language community); (3) motivation; and (4) ego boundaries.

Social and psychological distance influence SLA by determining the

amount of contact with the target language that the learner experiences, and
also the degree to which the learner is open to that input which is available.
Thus in 'bad' learning situations the learner will receive very little L2 input.
Also, when the psychological distance is great, the learner will fail to convert
available input into intake.

Schumann also describes the kind of learning which takes place. He suggests that the early stages of SLA are characterized by the same processes
that are responsible for the formation of pidgin languages. When social and/
or psychological distances are great, the learner fails to progress beyond the
early stages, with the result that his language is pidginized. Schumann refers
to this account of SLA as the *pidginization hypothesis*. He documents in detail
the pidginization that characterizes one adult Spanish speaker's acquisition
of L2 English in the United States. The learner, Alberto, was subject to a high
degree of social distance and failed to progress very far in learning English.
His English was characterized by many of the forms observed in pidgins, e.g.
'no + V' negatives, uninverted interrogatives, the absence of possessive and
plural inflections, and a restricted verb morphology. Schumann suggests
'pidginization may characterize all early second language acquisition and
. . . under conditions of social and psychological distance it persists' (1978b, p.
110). When pidginization persists, the learner fossilizes. That is, he no longer
revises his interlanguage system in the direction of the target language. Thus
early fossilization and pidginization are identical processes.[3]

Thus continued pidginization is the result of social and psychological distance. The degree of acculturation leads to pidgin-like language in two ways.
First, as suggested above, it controls the level of input that the learner receives. Second, it reflects the function which the learner wishes to use the L2
for. Following [D.] Smith (1972), Schumann distinguishes three broad functions of language: (1) the communicative function, which concerns the trans-
mission of purely referential, denotative information; (2) the integrative function, which involves the use of language to mark the speaker as a member of
a particular social group; and (3) the expressive function, which consists of
the use of language to display linguistic virtuosity (e.g. in literary uses). Initially L2 learners will seek to use the L2 for the communicative function. Pidgins and interlanguages which fossilize in the early stages of development
remain restricted to the communicative function. Native speakers of the target language use it for both the communicative and integrative functions, as
will those L2 learners who do not fossilize early on, but many native speakers
and L2 learners will never aspire to master the expressive uses of language.

The Nativization Model

Andersen builds on Schumann's Acculturation Model, in particular by providing a cognitive dimension which Schumann does not consider. For Schumann, SLA can be explained simply in terms of input and the general function the learner wants to use the L2 for. He is not concerned with the learner's

internal processing mechanisms. Andersen, to a much greater extent, is concerned with learning processes.

Andersen sees SLA as the result of two general forces, which he labels *nativization* and *denativization*. Nativization consists of assimilation; the learner makes the input conform to his own internalized view of what constitutes the L2 system. In terms of the typology of learner strategies, the learner simplifies the learning task by building hypotheses based on the knowledge he already possesses (e.g. knowledge of his first language; knowledge of the world). In this sense, then, he attends to an 'internal norm'. Nativization is apparent in pidginization and the early stages of both first and second language acquisition. Denativization involves accommodation (in the Piagetian sense); the learner adjusts his internalized system to make it fit the input. The learner makes use of inferencing strategies which enable him to remodel his interlanguage system in accordance with the 'external norm' (i.e. the linguistic features represented in the input language). Denativization is apparent in depidginization (i.e. the elaboration of a pidgin language which occurs through the gradual incorporation of forms from an external language source) and also in later first and second language acquisition. Figure 1 summarizes Andersen's Nativization Model.

Evaluation

The Acculturation and Nativist models focus on the power mechanisms of SLA. They provide explanations of why L2 learners, unlike first language learners, often fail to achieve a native-like competence. L2 learners may be cut off from the necessary input as a result of social distance, or they may fail to attend to it as a result of psychological distance. These models also indicate that SLA involves processes of a very general kind, which are also found in the formation and elaboration of pidgin languages. The notions of 'internal' and 'external norms' are elegant devices for explaining why early and late interlanguage systems are so very different. Characterizing SLA as the grad-

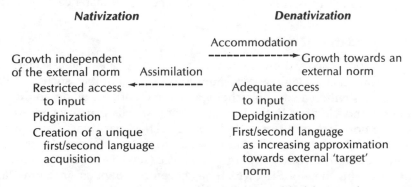

Figure 1. Andersen's Nativization Model (slightly simplified from Andersen, 1983, p. 11)

ual transition of attention from an internal to an external norm explains the
developmental sequence which has been observed in SLA, and the switch
that learners make from reliance on simplifying to reliance on inferencing
strategies.

Neither model sheds light on how L2 knowledge is internalized and used.
In other words, there is no specification of the learner's assembly mechanisms. This is quite evident in the Acculturation model. It is also true of the
Nativization model. Although this model does consider internal factors (in
the form of the assimilation/accommodation distinction), there is no discussion of how these operate. The relationship between primary linguistic data
and internal processing is an intricate one, requiring a detailed account of
how learner strategies operate on input and produce output. Thus, while
accepting that in the final analysis SLA is dependent on input and on a pre-
paredness of the learner to convert input into intake, a comprehensive theory
of SLA will also need to consider *how* input becomes intake and *how* this is
integrated into the existing interlanguage system. In particular it will need to
consider whether intake is controlled by the way the input is shaped in interaction involving the learner and other speakers or whether it is controlled by
the structure of the internal processing mechanisms themselves—the differential contribution of environment and 'black box'. Andersen's 'internal' and
'external norms' suggest that the internal mechanisms play a crucial part,
but this is not elaborated upon. And neither Andersen nor Schumann pays
attention to the potentially facilitating effects of input/interaction, as described by Hatch and Long. In short, what is missing from these models is
an account of the role of the interaction between situation and learner.

The Acculturation and Nativization Models address naturalistic SLA,
where the L2 learner has contact with the target language community. It is
not clear whether the models are also applicable to classroom SLA (i.e. foreign language instruction), where no such contact is possible. Presumably the
factors responsible for social distance are not relevant in foreign language
learning, although those responsible for psychological distance may be.[4]

2. Accommodation Theory

Accommodation Theory derives from the research of Giles and associates into
the intergroup uses of language in multilingual communities such as Britain.
Giles operates within a socio-psychological framework, drawing on the work
of Lambert and Gardner in the Canadian context. His primary concern is to
investigate how intergroup uses of language reflect basic social and psychological attitudes in inter-ethnic communication. As an offshoot of this, he has
also considered SLA from an intergroup stance (see Giles & Byrne, 1982) and
it is the resulting view of SLA which has become known as Accommodation
Theory.

The Accommodation Theory shares certain premises with the Acculturation Model, but it also differs from it in a number of significant ways. Like

Schumann, Giles is concerned to account for successful language acquisition. Both seek the answer in the relationships that hold between the learner's social group (termed the 'ingroup') and the target language community (termed the 'outgroup'). However, whereas Schumann explains these relationships in terms of variables that create *actual* social distance, Giles does so in terms of *perceived* social distance.[5] Giles argues that it is how the ingroup defines itself in relationship to the outgroup that is important for SLA. Also, where Schumann appears to treat social and psychological distance as absolute phenomena that determine the level of interaction between the learner and native speakers, Giles sees intergroup relationships as subject to constant negotiation during the course of each interaction. Thus, whereas for Schumann social and psychological distance are static (or at least change only slowly over time), for Giles intergroup relationships are dynamic and fluctuate in accordance with the shifting views of identity held by each group *vis-à-vis* the other. As will be discussed later, this enables Accommodation Theory to take account of the variability inherent in language-learner language and, also, the native speaker's input.

Giles agrees with Gardner (1979) that motivation is the primary determinant of L2 proficiency. He considers the level of motivation to be a reflex of how individual learners define themselves in ethnic terms. This, in turn, is governed by a number of key variables:

1. Identification of the individual learner with his ethnic ingroup:
    the extent to which the learner sees himself as a member of a specific ingroup, separate from the outgroup.
2. Inter-ethnic comparison:
    whether the learner makes favourable or unfavourable comparisons between his own ingroup and the outgroup. This will be influenced by the learner's awareness of 'cognitive alternatives' regarding the status of his own group's position, for instance when he perceives the intergroup situation as unfair.
3. Perception of ethno-linguistic vitality:
    whether the learner sees his ingroup as holding a low or high status and as sharing or excluded from institutional power.
4. Perception of ingroup boundaries:
    whether the learner sees his ingroup as culturally and linguistically separate from the outgroup (= hard boundaries) or as culturally and linguistically related (= soft boundaries).
5. Identification with other ingroup social categories:
    whether the learner identifies with few or several other ingroup social categories (e.g. occupational, religious, gender) and as a consequence whether he holds adequate or inadequate status within his ingroup.

Column A in Table 1 shows when the individual learner is likely to be highly motivated to learn the L2 and hence acquire a high level of proficiency. Conversely, column B shows when he is likely to be unmotivated and so achieve only a low level of proficiency. Where the motivation is high as a result of favourable socio-psychological attitudes (as described in column A in Table 1), the learner will not only benefit from formal instruction in the L2, but is also likely to avail himself of the opportunities for informal acquisition (in Seliger's (1977) terms, high input generators in the classroom are likely to also obtain a high level of exposure outside). In contrast, when motivation is low as a consequence of unfavourable socio-psychological attitudes (as described in column B of Table 1), whether the learner succeeds in formal language contexts will depend instead on intelligence and aptitude, because he is less likely to take advantage of informal acquisition contexts.

In addition to determining the overall level of proficiency achieved in SLA, Accommodation Theory also accounts for the learner's variable linguistic output. Giles, Bourhis, and Taylor (1977) write:

> . . . people are continually modifying their speech with others so as to reduce or accentuate the linguistic (and hence) social differences between them depending on their perceptions of the interactive situation.

Giles (1979) distinguishes two types of change which occur in the L2 speaker's use of 'ethnic speech markers' (i.e. linguistic features which mark the ingroup membership of the speaker).[6] *Upward convergence* involves the attenuation of ingroup speech markers. It occurs when the learner is positively motivated towards the outgroup community (i.e. when his socio-psychological set is favourable). *Downward divergence* involves the accentuation of ethnic speech markers. It occurs when the learner is not positively motivated towards the outgroup (i.e. when his socio-psychological set is unfavourable). In language *use* the occurrence of upward convergence or downward diver-

TABLE 1. DETERMINANTS OF SUCCESSFUL AND UNSUCCESSFUL LEARNING ACCORDING TO ACCOMMODATION THEORY

Key variables	A	B
	high motivation, high level of proficiency	*low motivation, low level of proficiency*
1. Identification with ingroup	weak identification	strong identification
2. Inter-ethnic comparison	makes favourable or no comparison, i.e. ingroup not seen as inferior	makes negative comparison, i.e. ingroup seen as inferior
3. Perception of ethno-linguistic vitality	low perception	high perception
4. Perception of ingroup boundaries	soft and open	hard and closed
5. Identification with other social categories	strong identification—satisfactory ingroup status	weak identification—inadequate group status

gence can fluctuate as a result of the L2 speaker's ongoing assessment of himself *vis-à-vis* his own group and the outgroup community. It follows, therefore, that the learner possesses a stylistic repertoire from which he selects in accordance with his shifting socio-psychological set, and that in any one situation the learner may employ different linguistic forms according to the extent to which he chooses to mark his speech as that of the ingroup. In language *acquisition*, progress takes place when the overall predisposition of the learner is towards upward convergence, although this need not be evident in every instance of use. Conversely, fossilization occurs when the overall predisposition of the learner is towards downward divergence.

Evaluation

Accommodation Theory, like the Acculturation Model, does not explain assembly mechanisms. It does not account for the developmental sequence. It is another 'black box' model in this respect. The strength of Accommodation Theory is that it encompasses language acquisition and language use within a single framework. It also relates the acquisition of a new dialect or accent to the acquisition of a L2, as both are seen as a reflection of the learner's perception of himself with regard to his own social group and the target language/dialect group.

   Accommodation Theory provides an explanation of language-learner language variability. Variable language use is the result of conflicting socio-psychological attitudes in different situations. Variability of use is related to acquisition, in the sense that the same set of factors is responsible for both. Tarone accounts for variability in terms of varying degrees of attention to form, but she does not address what motivates this. Attention to form can be seen as a consequence of the kind of factors that Giles considers. That is, the learner's perception of himself *vis-à-vis* the target-language community in face-to-face interaction governs when he attends to form. Upward convergence will be characterized by attention to form and to the use of the careful style. Downward divergence will be characterized by an absence of attention to form and a reliance on the vernacular style, through which the learner displays his ingroup membership. Thus diverging or converging may represent aspects of style-shifting involving the vernacular–careful style continuum. However, it is doubtful whether Accommodation Theory can be applied to foreign language learning, when intergroup relationships are not an obvious issue. Foreign language learners also style-shift. This suggests that although ethnic identity is an important aspect of variability in SLA, it does not account for total variability.

3. Discourse Theory

It follows from a theory of language use, in which communication is treated as the matrix of linguistic knowledge (as proposed for instance in Hymes's description of communicative competence), that language development should be considered in terms of how the learner discovers the meaning potential of language by participating in communication. This is how Halliday (1975) views first language acquisition. In a study of how his own child acquired language, Halliday shows that the development of the formal linguistic devices for realizing basic language function grows out of the interpersonal uses to which language is put. Because the structure of language is itself a reflection of the functions it serves, it can be learnt through learning to communicate. As [L.] Cherry (1979, p. 122) puts it:

> Through communicating with other people, children accomplish actions in the world and develop the rules of language structure and use.

It is because the L2 learner is similarly motivated to 'accomplish actions' (at least in informal SLA) that a parallel can be drawn between first and second language acquisition. In SLA this view of how development takes place has become known as the Discourse Theory.

Only the main principles of Discourse Theory, proposed by Hatch (1978b, 1978c), are considered here:

1. SLA follows a 'natural' route in syntactical development.
2. Native speakers adjust their speech in order to negotiate meaning with non-native speakers.
3. The conversational strategies used to negotiate meaning, and the resulting adjusted input, influence the rate and route of SLA in a number of ways:
   a. the learner learns the grammar of the L2 in the same order as the frequency order of the various features in the input;
   b. the learner acquires commonly occurring formulas and then later analyses these into their component parts;
   c. the learner is helped to construct sentences vertically; vertical structures are the precursors of horizontal structures.
4. Thus, the 'natural' route is the result of learning how to hold conversations.

Evaluation

Whereas Schumann and Giles are interested in explaining the rate of SLA and the level of proficiency achieved, Hatch is interested in explaining *how* SLA takes place. As Hatch says:

> The basic question that second language acquisition research addresses is: how can we describe the *process* of second language acquisition. (1980, p. 177—my [Ellis's] italics)

Hatch tries to provide an answer to this question by qualitative analyses of face-to-face interactions involving L2 learners. The route of development is explained in terms of the properties of these interactions. The strength of

Hatch's approach lies in the detailed insights it provides into how the process of constructing discourse contributes to the process of building an interlanguage.

It is arguable, however, that notwithstanding these insights, Hatch has not been able to demonstrate conclusively that negotiation of input is the necessary and sufficient condition of SLA. Hatch herself notes:

> We have not been able (nor have we tried) to show how, or if, making messages simpler or more transparent promotes language learning. (1980, p. 181)

Hatch is only too aware of the huge leap that is made from 'low-inference descriptions' to 'high-inference explanations'. The relationship between negotiated input and SLA is, therefore, likely but not substantiated. SLA research still needs to carry out the kind of empirical studies which have taken place in first language acquisition research and which demonstrate that where rate of development is concerned, at least some discourse features are facilitative (e.g. Cross, 1978; Ellis & Wells, 1980). Moreover, the Discourse Theory needs to accommodate the fact that, as Larsen-Freeman (1983a) has observed, successful SLA can take place even when there is no negotiated input (e.g. in self-study).

The Discourse Theory, like the two preceding theories, does not address the nature of the learner strategies responsible for SLA. When Hatch talks of *processes*, she means external processes—those which can be observed in face-to-face interaction—not internal processes, those that can only be inferred by observing how learners perform. Hatch does not look at the cognitive processes that control how the learner (and native speaker) construct discourse, or how data made available through discourse are sifted and internalized. There is no specification of the relationship between external and internal processing. In fairness, though, it should be noted that Hatch does not intend to dismiss the cognitive side of SLA. Hatch writes:

> While social interaction may give the learner the 'best' data to work with, the brain in turn must work out a fitting and relevant model of that input. (1983, p. 186)

The Discourse Theory, however, is not concerned with what this model consists of.

4. The Monitor Model

Krashen's Monitor Model has enjoyed considerable prominence in SLA research. In so far as it is probably the most comprehensive of existing theories, this is justified. However, as I shall attempt to show later, the theory is seriously flawed in a number of respects, in particular in its treatment of language-learner variability.

The Monitor Model consists of five central hypotheses. In addition, it makes reference to a number of other factors which influence SLA and which relate to the central hypotheses. Each hypothesis is briefly summarized below. Krashen's views on the different causative variables of SLA are also considered. A full account of the Monitor Model is available in Krashen (1981b, 1982), and in Krashen and Terrell (1983).

The Five Hypotheses

1. The Acquisition Learning Hypothesis

The 'acquisition–learning' distinction lies at the heart of Krashen's theory. It is applicable to the process of internalizing new L2 knowledge, to storing this knowledge, and also to using it in actual performance. 'Acquisition' occurs subconsciously as a result of participating in natural communication where the focus is on meaning. 'Learning' occurs as a result of conscious study of the formal properties of the language. In storage, 'acquired' knowledge is located in the left hemisphere of the brain (in most users) in the language areas; it is available for automatic processing. 'Learnt' knowledge is metalinguistic in nature. It is also stored in the left hemisphere, but not necessarily in the language areas; it is available only for controlled processing. Thus, 'acquired' and 'learnt' knowledge are stored separately. In performance, 'acquired' knowledge serves as the major source of initiating both the comprehension and production of utterances. 'Learnt' knowledge is available for use only by the Monitor (see Hypothesis 3 below).

2. The Natural Order Hypothesis

The natural order hypothesis draws on the SLA research literature that indicates that learners may follow a more or less invariant order in the acquisition of formal grammatical features. The hypothesis affirms that grammatical structures are 'acquired' in a predictable order. Thus when the learner is engaged in natural communication tasks, he will manifest the standard order. But when he is engaged in tasks that require or permit the use of metalinguistic knowledge, a different order will emerge.

3. The Monitor Hypothesis

The Monitor is the device that learners use to edit their language performance. It utilizes 'learnt' knowledge by acting upon and modifying utterances generated from 'acquired' knowledge. This can occur either before the utterance is uttered or after (see Figure 2). In either case its use is optional. Krashen argues that Monitoring has an extremely limited function in language performance, even where adults are concerned. He gives three conditions for its use: (1) there must be sufficient time; (2) the focus must be on form and not meaning; and (3) the user must know the rule. Krashen recognizes that editing can also take place using 'acquired' competence. He refers to this as edit-

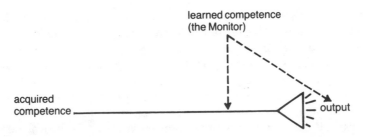

Figure 2. A Model of Adult Second Language Performance (Krashen & Terrell, 1983, p. 30)

ing by 'feel'. However, this aspect of L2 performance is not developed. Figure 2, for instance, does not show how editing by 'feel' takes place.

4. The Input Hypothesis
This states that 'acquisition' takes place as a result of the learner having understood input that is a little beyond the current level of his competence (i.e. the i + 1 level). Input that is comprehensible to the learner will automatically be at the right level.

5. The Affective Filter Hypothesis
This deals with how affective factors relate to SLA, and covers the ground of the Acculturation Model. Krashen incorporates the notion of the Affective Filter as proposed by Dulay and Burt (1977). The filter controls how much input the learner comes into contact with, and how much input is converted into intake. It is 'affective' because the factors which determine its strength have to do with the learner's motivation, self-confidence, or anxiety state. Learners with high motivation and self-confidence and with low anxiety have low filters and so obtain and let in plenty of input. Learners with low motivation, little self-confidence, and high anxiety have high filters and so receive little input and allow even less in. The Affective Filter influences the rate of development, but it does not affect the route.

Causative Variables Taken into Account in the Monitor Model
Krashen also discusses a number of other factors, each of which figures conspicuously in the SLA research literature.

    1. Aptitude
       Krashen argues that aptitude only relates to 'learning'. That is, the learner's aptitude predicts how well he will perform on grammar-type

tests that provide the right conditions for the operation of the Monitor. In contrast, attitude is related to 'acquisition' (see Hypothesis 5 above).

2. Role of the first language

Krashen rejects the view that the first language interferes with SLA. Rather, he sees the use of the first language as a performance strategy. The learner falls back on his first language when he lacks a rule in the L2. He initiates an utterance using his first language (instead of 'acquired' L2 knowledge) and then substitutes L2 lexical items, also making small repairs to the resulting string by means of the Monitor.

3. Routines and patterns

Krashen rejects the view that formulaic speech (consisting of routines and patterns) contributes to 'acquisition'. In his opinion, formulas play a performance role only by helping the learner to 'outperform his competence'. They are not broken down, and their separate parts are not, therefore, incorporated into the learner's creative rule system. Rather 'acquisition' catches up with the routines and patterns; that is, the structural knowledge contained in the formulas is developed separately.

4. Individual differences

Krashen claims that 'acquisition' follows a natural route (Hypothesis 2). Thus there is no individual variation in the acquisition process itself. However, there is variation in the rate and the extent of acquisition as a result of the amount of comprehensible input received, and the strength of the Affective Filter. There is also variation in performance, brought about by the extent of the learner's reliance on 'learnt' knowledge. Krashen indicates three types of Monitor Users: (1) over-users, (2) under-users, and (3) optimal users (i.e. those who apply conscious knowledge when it is appropriate).

5. Age

Age influences SLA in a number of ways. It affects the amount of comprehensible input that is obtained; younger learners may get more than older learners. Age also affects 'learning'; older learners are better suited to study language form and also to use 'learnt' knowledge in monitoring. Finally, age influences the affective state of the learner; after puberty the Affective Filter is likely to increase in strength.

Evaluation

Perhaps as a result of its prominence in SLA research, the Monitor Model has also attracted a lot of criticism. I shall select three central issues for detailed consideration. These are the 'acquisition—learning' distinction, the Monitor, and Krashen's treatment of variability. A fourth issue—Krashen's conceptualization of the role of input—has already been examined and will, therefore, not be treated here.

THE 'ACQUISITION—LEARNING' DISTINCTION. The 'acquisition—learning' distinction has been called 'theological', in that it has been formulated in order to confirm a specific goal, namely that successful SLA is the result of 'acquisition' ([J.] James, 1980). McLaughlin (1978) argues that the Monitor Model is unreliable, because the 'acquisition—learning' distinction is defined in terms of 'subconscious' and 'conscious' processes, which are not open to inspection. The first criticism, then, is a methodological one. The 'acquisition—learning' hypothesis is not acceptable, because it cannot be tested in empirical investigation.

A further objection concerns Krashen's claims that 'acquisition' and 'learning' are entirely separate, and that 'acquired' knowledge cannot turn into 'learnt' knowledge. Krashen refers to this as *the non-interface position*. McLaughlin (1978), Rivers (1980), Stevick (1980), Sharwood-Smith (1981), and Gregg (1984) have all challenged this position on the basis that when 'learnt' knowledge is automatized through practice it becomes 'acquired' i.e. available for use in spontaneous conversation.

Irrespective of whether the 'acquisition—learning' distinction is valid or not, it can also be criticized on the grounds that Krashen does not really explicate the cognitive processes that are responsible either for 'acquisition' or 'learning'. As Larsen-Freeman (1983b) observes, Krashen does not explain what the learner does with input. If the 'acquisition—learning' distinction is to have any power, it is surely necessary to specify in what way the processes responsible for each knowledge type are different from each other. This Krashen does not do. Thus, despite its comprehensiveness, the Monitor Model is still a 'black box' theory.

MONITORING. There are several difficulties with Krashen's account of Monitoring. One of these is again methodological. The only evidence for Monitoring lies in the language user's own account of trying to apply explicit rules (e.g. Cohen & Robbins, 1976). But both McLaughlin (1978) and Rivers (1980) point to the difficulty of distinguishing introspectively 'rule' application (as in Monitoring) and 'feel' (the implicit use of 'acquired' knowledge to judge or modify an utterance). Editing by 'feel' (or 'monitoring' with a small 'm') subsumes Monitoring (with a big 'M'). Both can be seen as aspects of what Morrison and Low (1983) refer to as the 'critical faculty'. This enables us to become critically aware of what we have created and hence allows us to control it. We are able to attend to the form of our utterances without using conscious rules, and without being able to make explicit how modifications in the initial output have been effected. This happens all the time in writing when we seek to conform to the conventions of the written medium, and it also happens in speech.

Morrison and Low offer a number of other criticisms of Monitoring. They point out that Monitoring does not account for the reception of utterances (i.e. as explained by Krashen, it refers only to production). They also note that Monitoring is limited to syntax, but in fact learners and users have the ability to edit their pronunciation, lexis, and, perhaps most important of all, their discourse. Krashen does not give any consideration to Monitoring as a collaborative activity involving both the learner and his interlocutor. To this list, I would also draw attention to the fact that Krashen tends to conflate Monitoring and 'learning', although the former refers to performance and the latter to rule internalization. As commented on above, there is no detailed discussion of how 'learning' takes place.

VARIABILITY. The Monitor Model is a 'dual competence' theory of SLA. That is, it proposes that the learner's knowledge of the L2, which is reflected in variable performance, is best characterized in terms of two separate competences, which Krashen labels 'acquisition' and 'learning'. The alternative position is to build a variable competence model (see next section), in which the learner's variable performance is seen as a reflection of a stylistic continuum. Which model—the Monitor Model or a variable competence model—best fits the known facts about SLA?

The available evidence indicates that learners produce utterances which are formally different even when it is evident that they are focused on meaning. Consider two utterances from Ellis (1984b) produced by one classroom learner within seconds of each other, each performing the same communicative function:

> No look my card.   (instruction to another pupil during a word
> Don't look at my card.   bingo game)

Data such as these, which are common in SLA research literature (see the case studies in Hatch, 1978a, for instance), demonstrate that even what Krashen calls 'acquired' knowledge is not homogeneous. But once claims about the homogeneity or 'acquired' knowledge are seen to be ill-founded, it makes little sense to maintain a dual competence explanation. The kinds of performance that result from focusing on meaning and on form are best treated as aspects of a single but variable competence which contains alternative rules for realizing the same meanings, in much the same way as does the native speaker's competence.

In summary, despite the comprehensiveness of the Monitor Model, it poses serious theoretical problems regarding the validity of the 'acquisition—learning' distinction, the operation of Monitoring, and the explanation of variability in language-learner language. Also the input hypothesis does not account for the fact that acquisition can take place without two-way negotiation of meaning, nor does it recognize that output also plays an important role.

5. The Variable Competence Model

Here I shall summarize the Variable Competence theory proposed by Ellis (1984a). This draws on and extends the work of Tarone (1982, 1983), Widdowson (1979b, 1984), and Bialystok (1982).

The Model is based on two distinctions—one of which refers to the process of language use, and the other to the product. The theory also proposes to account for SLA within a framework of language use. In other words, it claims that the way a language is learnt is a reflection of the way it is used.

The *product* of language use comprises a continuum of discourse types ranged from entirely unplanned to entirely planned. To summarize briefly, unplanned discourse is discourse that lacks forethought and preparation. It is associated with spontaneous communication, e.g. everyday conversation or brainstorming in writing. Planned discourse is discourse that is thought out prior to expression. It requires conscious thought and the opportunity to work out content and expression. Examples are a prepared lecture or careful writing.

The *process* of language use is to be understood in terms of the distinction between linguistic knowledge (or *rules*) and the ability to make use of this knowledge (*procedures*). Widdowson (1984) refers to a knowledge of rules as *competence* and to a knowledge of the procedures involved in using rules to construct discourse as *capacity*. Widdowson points out that the narrow concept of linguistic competence has been widened to include appropriate use as well as correct use (i.e. communicative competence). But he argues that even this broader view of competence does not account for the language user's ability 'to create meanings by exploiting the potential inherent in the language for continual modification . . . ' (Widdowson, 1984, p. 8). It is for this reason that he adds the term *capacity*. The language user possesses procedures for realizing the meaning potential of rules in context. In other words, the language user makes his knowledge of linguistic rules work by exploiting them in relationship to both the situational and linguistic context. He actualizes his abstract knowledge of sentences to create utterances in discourse.

It follows from this view of the process of language use that the product (i.e. the different types of discourse) is the result of either or both of the following:

1. a variable competence, i.e. the user possesses a heterogeneous rule system;
2. variable application of procedures for actualizing knowledge in discourse.

The Variable Competence Model of SLA claims that both (1) and (2) occur. Furthermore, it claims that they are related.

The variability of the learner's rule system is described with reference

·to Bialystok's (1982) dual distinction between automatic/non-automatic and analytic/unanalytic. The first distinction concerns the relative access that the learner has to L2 knowledge. Knowledge that can be retrieved easily and quickly is automatic. Knowledge that takes time and effort to retrieve is non-automatic. The second distinction concerns the extent to which the learner possesses a 'propositional mental representation which makes clear the structure of the knowledge and its relationship to other aspects of knowledge' (op. cit., 183). Bialystok points out that unanalysed knowledge is the general form in which we know most things, in that we are usually not aware of the way in which our knowledge is structured. Both the automatic/non-automatic and the analysed/unanalysed distinctions represent continua rather than dichotomies. There are degrees of automatic and analysed knowledge.

Procedures for actualizing knowledge are of two types, which Ellis (1984a) refers to as primary and secondary processes.[7] Each set of processes has an external and internal representation, referred to as discourse and cognitive processes respectively. Primary processes are responsible for engaging in unplanned discourse. They draw on knowledge that is relatively unanalysed and automatic. Secondary processes come into play in planned discourse and draw on knowledge towards the analysed end of the continuum. An example of a primary process is *semantic simplification* (i.e. the omission of elements from a proposition in production). An example of a secondary process is *monitoring* (i.e. the editing of language performance). As an example of what is meant by discourse and cognitive processes, semantic simplification can be accounted for as follows:

Discourse process:

> Simplify the semantic structure of a message by omitting meaning elements that are communicatively redundant or that can be realized by a non-verbal device (e.g. mime).

Cognitive process:

> a. Construct an underlying conceptual structure of a message.
> b. Compare this structure with the frame of reference shared with an interlocutor.
> c. Eliminate redundant elements and elements for which no lexical item is available.

Primary and secondary processes account for how L2 learners actualize their linguistic knowledge in discourse. They account for the variability of language-learner language by positing that both different types of knowledge and different procedures are involved in the construction of different discourse types. They also account for acquisition. To explain how, it is necessary to return to what Widdowson has to say about rules and procedures.

Widdowson argues that through using procedures, not only does the language user utilize his existing linguistic knowledge but he also, potentially at least, creates new linguistic rules. As Widdowson (1979b, p. 62) puts it:

> We draw upon our knowledge of rules to *make sense*. We do not simply measure discourse up against our knowledge of pre-existing rules, we create discourse and commonly bring new rules into existence by so doing. All competence is transitional in this sense.

In other words, language acquisition is the result of our capacity to make sense. New rules are created when we endeavour to use existing knowledge in relation to the linguistic and situational context in order to create shared frames of reference. A theory of language use is the matrix of a theory of language acquisition.

Ellis (1984a) goes one step further and suggests that SLA follows the sequence that it does because the processes that the learner calls on to participate in discourse are themselves developmental. That is, their prominence in SLA coincides with different stages of development. Thus, for instance, early SLA is characterized by the heavy use of semantic simplification, because this is a procedure that requires little L2 knowledge. Later procedures, such as those used to reduce reliance on shared knowledge and non-verbal devices, by making explicit the relationship between one proposition and another and between each proposition and its situational context (see Widdowson (1984, pp. 67ff)), are characteristic of later SLA. Also knowledge that to begin with is available only for use via secondary processes (because it exists only in analysed form) can eventually be accessed by means of primary processes and so used in unplanned as well as planned discourse.

To summarize, the Variable Competence Model proposes:

1. There is a single knowledge store containing variable interlanguage rules according to how automatic and how analysed the rules are.
2. The learner possesses a capacity for language use which consists of primary and secondary discourse and cognitive processes.
3. L2 performance is variable as a result of whether primary processes employing unanalysed L2 rules are utilized in unplanned discourse, or secondary processes employing analysed L2 rules are utilized in planned discourse.
4. Development occurs as a result of
   a. acquisition of new L2 rules through participation in various types of discourse (i.e. new rules originate in the application of procedural knowledge);

   b. activation of L2 rules which initially exist in either a non-automatic unanalysed form or in an analysed form so they can be used in unplanned
discourse.

These proposals are shown in Figure 3.

Evaluation

The Variable Competence Model of SLA attempts to account for (1) the variability of language-learner language, and (2) the external and internal processes responsible for SLA. It incorporates within the same framework a theory of language use and a theory of SLA. As it stands at the moment, the
Model is in need of development in two directions. First it needs to provide
a more detailed analysis of the primary and secondary processes responsible
for use and acquisition. Second, it needs to incorporate the role of input into
the overall framework. Learners do not construct discourse in isolation (at
least not in face-to-face interaction), so how input is negotiated must be considered. SLA is the result of the exchange of linguistic information which
occurs in the process of discourse construction involving both the learner and
an interlocutor.

6. The Universal Hypothesis

The Universal Hypothesis states that there are linguistic universals which determine the course of SLA as follows:

   1. Linguistic universals impose constraints on the form that interlanguages can take.

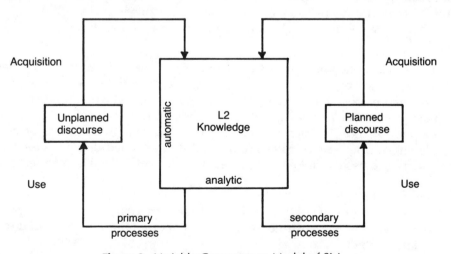

Figure 3. Variable Competence Model of SLA

2. Learners find it easier to acquire patterns that conform to linguistic universals than those that do not. The linguistic markedness of L2 rules explains the developmental route.
3. Where the L1 manifests linguistic universals, it is likely to assist interlanguage development through transfer.

Linguistic universals have been investigated by the in-depth study of a single language. Those working in this tradition argue that there is a Universal Grammar that constrains the kind of hypotheses that the learner can form and that is innate. An alternative approach to investigating linguistic universals is to study a large number of languages from different language families in order to discover typological universals.[8] A number of possible explanations for universals are entertained by those working in this tradition, including pragmatic explanations.

In both L1 and L2 acquisition the effect of linguistic universals has been investigated primarily in terms of markedness theory. This states that some rules are unmarked or weakly marked and others marked or more strongly marked. Various criteria have been proposed for determining the markedness of a rule. Chomsky proposes that an unmarked rule is one that requires no or minimal 'triggering' from the environment. A typological universal or a strong universal tendency can also be considered as unmarked. There is some evidence to suggest that language acquisition proceeds by mastering the easier unmarked properties before the more difficult marked ones. In SLA there is also some evidence to suggest that when the L2 rule is marked, the learner will turn to his L1, particularly if this has an equivalent unmarked rule.

A few evaluative comments are below.

Evaluation

The Universal Hypothesis provides an interesting account of how the linguistic properties of the target language and the learner's first language may influence the course of development. It constitutes an attempt to explain SLA in terms of an independent language faculty, rather than in more general cognitive terms. One advantage of this is that it brings SLA studies into line with current linguistic research that follows the Chomskyan tradition. It also avoids the quagmire of explanations based on learner strategies.

The value of the Universal Hypothesis for SLA theory is twofold: (1) it focuses attention on the nature of the target language itself, lending support to Wode's (1980, pp. 136–137) claim that 'the linguistic devices used in a given language are the major variable(s) determining . . . linguistic sequences'; and (2) it provides a subtle and persuasive reconsideration of transfer as an important factor in SLA.

One of the major problems of the Universal Hypothesis lies in the difficulty in defining the markedness construct. Various criteria have been used to explicate it—core vs peripheral grammar, complexity and explicitness.

Moreover, it is not clear whether markedness is to be seen as just a linguistic construct or whether it has psycholinguistic validity.

Even if linguistic markedness is a major determinant of SLA (and this is not yet proven, as it is possible that many of the facts explained in terms of markedness theory might also be explained by other factors, such as the frequency of occurrence of different structures in the input), it is unlikely that it will be able to explain the complexity of SLA by itself. In addition, the Universal Hypothesis operates on the assumption that linguistic knowledge is homogeneous, and, therefore, ignores variability.

7. A Neurofunctional Theory

Whereas all the previous models discussed have attempted to explain SLA in linguistic or *psycholinguistic* terms, the theory considered in this section draws on *neurolinguistic* research. It constitutes, therefore, a different type of explanation. Lamendella (1979, pp. 5–6) defines the scope of a neurofunctional approach as follows:

> A neurofunctional perspective on language attempts to characterize the neurolinguistic information processing systems responsible for the development and use of language.

The account of a neurofunctional theory of SLA that follows draws primarily on the work of Lamendella (1977, 1979; Selinker & Lamendella, 1978b).

The basic premise of a neurofunctional view of SLA is that there is a connection between language function and the neural anatomy. It is important, however, to recognize that, as Hatch (1983, p. 213) puts it, 'there is no single "black box" for language in the brain'. It is not possible to identify precisely which areas of the brain are associated with language functioning. Therefore it is better to speak of 'the relative contribution of some areas more than others under certain conditions' (Seliger, 1982, p. 309). The adult's brain never entirely loses the plasticity of the new-born baby's brain, with the result that in cases of damage to specific areas of neural tissue (as in aphasia), the functions associated with those areas need not be completely lost, but transferred to other areas.

Neurofunctional accounts of SLA have considered the contribution of two areas of the brain: (1) the right (as opposed to the left) hemisphere, and (2) the areas of the left hemisphere (in particular those known as Wernicke's and Broca's areas), which clinical studies have shown to be closely associated with the comprehension and production of language. Neurofunctional accounts have also tended to focus on specific aspects of SLA: (1) age differences, (2) formulaic speech, (3) fossilization, and (4) pattern practice in classroom SLA. The relationship between the maturation of neural mechanisms and SLA has already been considered and so will not be dealt with again here. The other issues are considered briefly below in a discussion of the two areas of the brain that research has focused on.

Right Hemisphere Functioning

Right hemisphere functioning is generally associated with holistic processing, as opposed to serial or analytic processing, which occurs in the left hemisphere. Not surprisingly, therefore, it has been suggested (e.g. by Obler, 1981; Krashen, 1981b) that the right hemisphere is responsible for the storing and processing of formulaic speech. The routines and patterns which comprise formulaic speech are unanalysed wholes and as such belong to the 'gestalt' perception of the right hemisphere. It has also been suggested that right hemisphere involvement in L2 processing will be more evident in the early, non-proficient stages than in later, more advanced stages of SLA. This hypothesis is compatible with the link between the right hemisphere and formulaic speech, as the early stages of SLA are more likely to be characterized by heavy use of formulaic speech. However, Genesee (1982), reviewing this hypothesis, found conflicting evidence. Out of the thirteen studies he examined, three provided positive support, six found comparable patterns of left hemisphere involvement, and four were opposed to the stage hypothesis. Genesee concluded that the stage hypothesis has received insufficient support. He found greater support for another hypothesis concerning right hemisphere involvement, namely that it is associated to a greater extent with informal than formal language acquisition. This hypothesis is also compatible with the right hemisphere connection with formulaic speech, which is generally considered to be more prominent in settings where natural language use is common. It seems, therefore, that there is considerable evidence to associate the acquisition and use of formulaic speech with the right hemisphere.

The right hemisphere may also be involved in pattern practice in classroom SLA. Seliger (1982) suggests that the right hemisphere may act as an initial staging mechanism for handling patterns which can then be re-examined later in left hemisphere functioning. Pattern practice and minimal pair drills may utilize right hemisphere abilities in the adult learner and so contribute to what Seliger calls 'primitive hypotheses'. If subsequent analysis by the left hemisphere does not take place, the learner will not be able to utilize the language forms that have been drilled in the construction of spontaneous, creative speech. This offers an interesting neurolinguistic explanation of why formal language practice does not appear to facilitate natural language use immediately.

Left Hemisphere Functioning

Where the left hemisphere is concerned, there is less clarity regarding the location of specific language functions. In general the left hemisphere is associated with creative language use, including syntactic and semantic processing and the motor operations involved in speaking and writing. However, the extent to which these different functions can be localized is not clear (see Hatch, 1983, for a detailed review of this issue). Walsh and Diller (1981) distinguish two broad types of functioning: (1) lower order functioning and (2) higher order functioning. The former, associated with Wernicke's and Broca's areas, involves basic grammatical processing, together with the motor operations. The latter, associated with a different area of the cerebral cortex, involves semantic processing and verbal cognition. Walsh and Diller suggest that lower-order processing is a function of early maturing, while higher-order processing depends on late developing neural circuitry. Thus whereas younger learners rely primarily on lower-order processing, older learners make use of higher-order processing. There have also been suggestions that different levels of language processing (e.g. pronunciation vs. syntax) are linked to different neural mechanisms. The fact that different aspects of language fossilize at different times (e.g. learners with native-like syntax but non-native pronunciation are not uncommon) is evidence of this. Seliger (1978) develops an interesting argument based on neurolinguistic evidence to support a differential fossilization hypothesis. In general, though, claims about localized functions need to be treated circumspectly.

These various observations do not amount to a theory of SLA. However, Lamendella has attempted to formulate a neurofunctional theory of SLA. This is described below.

Lamendella's Neurofunctional Theory
Lamendella distinguishes two basic types of language acquisition: (1) Primary Language Acquisition and (2) Secondary Language Acquisition. (1) is found in the child's acquisition of one or more languages from 2 to 5 years. (2) is subdivided into (a) foreign language learning (i.e. the formal classroom learning of a L2), and (b) second language acquisition (i.e. the natural acquisition of a L2 after the age of five).

Linked to these two types of language acquisition are different neurofunctional systems, each of which consists of a hierarchy of functions. Each system has a different overall role in information processing. Lamendella pinpoints two systems as particularly important for language functioning:

1. The communication hierarchy: this has responsibility for language and other forms of interpersonal communication.
2. The cognitive hierarchy: this controls a variety of cognitive information processing activities that are also part of language use.

Primary language acquisition and also second language acquisition (i.e. (2b)) are marked by the use of the communication hierarchy, whereas foreign language acquisition, i.e. (2a), is marked by the use of the cognitive hierarchy. Pattern pratice drills are likely to involve the cognitive hierarchy and hence material learnt in this way is not available in language behaviour that draws on the communicative hierarchy. As Lamendella puts it:

> . . . the executive functions of the communication hierarchy do not seem to have the capacity to call up automated subroutines whose construction was directed by the cognitive hierarchy. (1979, p. 17)

Thus the theory posits a different neurolinguistic base for the kind of acquisition and language use typically found in natural SLA and tutored SLA. The distinction between the communicative and cognitive hierarchies seems to parallel the psycholinguistic distinction between 'acquisition' and 'learning' in the Monitor Model.

Each neurofunctional system is composed of different levels, ranged from higher to lower order, and each associated with different levels of neural organization (which Lamendella does not specify). The different levels can be interconnected, but they can also be disassociated. Thus, for instance, it is possible to engage what Lamendella calls 'copying circuits' in order to repeat what someone has said, without engaging other circuits that are responsible for language comprehension or formulation (e.g. a typist can type out a letter without bothering to understand its content). Furthermore, L2 forms acquired by means of higher-level systems can be stored as automatic sub-routines at lower levels of the communication hierarchy. In language performance, lower-level sub-routines can be accessed without calling upon higher levels within the same hierarchy.

Lamendella sums up the task facing the language learner:

> When first confronted with the need to acquire new information structures . . . a learner must identify the functional hierarchy best suited to this learning, then establish the appropriate level and subsystems within the hierarchy with which to begin the learning process. (1979, p. 15)

In other words, Lamendella claims that SLA can be explained neurofunctionally with reference to (1) which neurofunctional system is used—the communication or the cognitive—and (2) which level within the chosen neurofunctional system is engaged.

Evaluation

Neurofunctional explanations of SLA are based on the premise that it is possible to trace the neurolinguistic correlates of specific language functions. However, there is still considerable uncertainty regarding the identification of specific neurofunctions and their neurolinguistic correlates. The evidence from clinical studies (see Genesee, 1982) is conflicting. Also it is not clear to what extent studies of language *processing* based on tests where linguistic stimuli are presented separately to the left and right ear (i.e. dichotic listening tests) or studies of aphasia, which together serve as the major sources of information about neurofunctioning, provide reliable insights into the neurolinguistic bases of language *acquisition*.

Lamendella's neurofunctional theory offers an interesting account of a number of facts about SLA (e.g. the inutility of material learnt through pattern practice in spontaneous communication). But there are many facts which it does not explain (or even seek to). In particular it is not clear how it can account for the natural sequence of development. Also the distinction between foreign and second language learning is a simplification. It is not so much the type of setting which is important, as the type of interaction which occurs in these settings. Thus natural communication in a L2 is quite possible in a foreign language classroom.

Neurolinguistic and neurofunctional explanations are perhaps best treated as affording additional understanding about SLA, rather than an explanation of it. However, in the long run it will be useful if psycholinguistic constructs used to explain SLA can be matched up with neurofunctional mechanisms. . . .

A FRAMEWORK FOR INVESTIGATING SLA

A number of components of SLA need to be considered. These are (1) situational factors, (2) the linguistic input, (3) learner differences, (4) learner processes, and (5) linguistic output. Figure 4 shows the interrelationship between

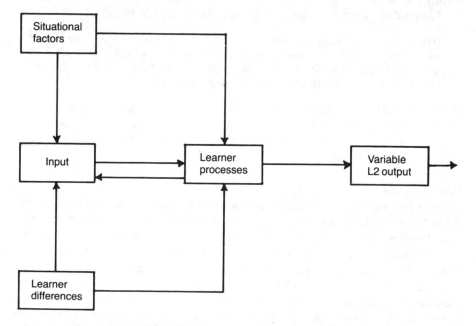

Figure 4. A Framework for Examining the Components of SLA

these components. Situational factors influence input (e.g. input in a classroom setting is likely to differ from that in a natural setting) and also the use of learner processes (e.g. communication strategies). Learner differences on such variables as motivation and personality help to determine the quantity and quality of the input and also affect the operation of learner strategies (e.g. the use of metalingual strategies). Input comprises (1) the inherent properties of the target language system, and (2) the formally and interactionally adjusted features found in foreigner and teacher talk. Input constitutes the data upon which the learner strategies work, but also the input is itself in part determined by the learner's use of communication strategies. Thus the relationship between input and learner processes is an interactive one. The learner's strategies (composed of learning, production, and communication strategies) produce a variable L2 output. This in turn is part of the input. Thus the framework is cyclical. . . .

NOTES

[1]Krashen's Monitor Model and Dulay and Burt's Creative Construction Theory are closely related, sharing many premises. The former is considered in this reading, as a recognition of the considerable interest it has aroused in SLA research.

[2]More than one type of 'bad' learning situation is possible, as many of the variables permit three-way alternatives. For instance, a 'bad' situation arises when the target language group sees itself as either dominant *or* subordinate.

[3]Schumann's (1978b) study of Alberto lasted ten months. This is perhaps too short a period to conclude that fossilization has taken place. Ellis (1984a) observed little syntactical development in three classroom learners over a similar period, but another twelve months showed evidence of considerable development.

[4]To the best of my knowledge, neither Schumann nor Andersen has discussed the application of their theories to classroom SLA. The psychological factors which Schumann considers are likely to be relevant to the classroom, as Gardner and Lambert's (1972) work on motivation and attitude has shown.

[5]H. D. Brown (1980) has in fact criticized Schumann's theory on the grounds that there is no objective means of measuring actual social distance. He points out that it is how the learner views his own culture in relation to the culture of the target language community that affects SLA.

[6]Giles also identifies a third type of speech marker—*upward divergence*—which occurs when an outgroup speaker accentuates speech markers that distinguish him from the ingroup speaker. In so doing the outgroup speaker may deviate from the standard forms of his language. Thus the L2 learner may find the prestige dialect 'an ever-moving target' (Giles & Byrne, 1982, p. 22).

[7]The terms 'primary' and 'secondary processes' are chosen to reflect the primacy of unplanned discourse. It is not intended to suggest that 'primary processes' are more important than 'secondary processes', only that they are responsible for the style associated with spontaneous face-to-face communication.

[8]In order to carry out a cross-linguistic comparison it is, of course, necessary to work on hypothetical assumptions about what the universal categories will be.

RELATED READING 5

PROVIDING INPUT FOR ACQUISITION

Stephen Krashen

THE POTENTIAL OF THE SECOND
LANGUAGE CLASSROOM

. . . The classroom is of benefit when it is the major source of comprehensible
input. When acquirers have rich sources of input outside the class, and when
they are proficient enough to take advantage of it (i.e. understand at least
some of it), the classroom does not make an important contribution. . . . If,
however, we fill our second language classrooms with input that is optimal
for acquisition, it is quite possible that we can actually do better than the
informal environment, at least up to the intermediate level. The informal environment is not always willing to supply comprehensible input to the older
second language student. As Hatch and her colleagues have pointed out,
input to the adult is more complicated grammatically, contains a wider range
of vocabulary, deals with more complex topics, and is generally harder to
understand. This is simply a reflection of the fact that the adult world is more
complex than the world of the child, and our expectations for adult comprehension are much higher.

In the case of the adult beginner, the classroom can do much better than
the informal environment. In the second language classroom, we have the
potential of supplying a full 40–50 minutes per day of comprehensible input,
input that will encourage language acquisition. The true beginner in the informal environment, especially if he or she is not adept at skills of conversational
management and negotiation of meaning (see Scarcella & Higa, 1982), may
require days or even weeks before he or she can ''pick out'' that much comprehensible input from the barrage of language heard. The beginning student
will simply not understand most of the language around him. It will be noise,
unusable for acquisition.

The value of second language classes, then, lies not only in the grammar
instruction, but in the simpler ''teacher talk'', the comprehensible input. It
can be an efficient place to achieve at least the intermediate levels rapidly, as
long as the focus of the class is on providing input for acquisition.

LIMITATIONS OF THE CLASSROOM

Despite my enthusiasm for the second language classroom, there are several
ways in which the outside world clearly excels (or some ''modification'' of

Stephen Krashen, ''Providing Input for Acquisition,'' from *Principles and Practice in Second Language Acquisition* (Oxford: Pergamon, 1982), pp. 58–73.

the outside world), especially for the intermediate level second language student. First, it is very clear that the outside world can supply *more* input. Living in the country where the language is spoken can result in an all-day second language lesson! As we mentioned earlier, however, for the informal environment to be of any use, the input language has to be comprehensible. The informal environment will therefore be of more and more use as the acquirer progresses and can understand more and more.

Second, as many scholars have pointed out, the range of discourse that the student can be exposed to in a second language classroom is quite limited, no matter how "natural" we make it. There is simply no way the classroom can match the variety of the outside world, although we can certainly expand beyond our current limitations.

The classroom will probably never be able to completely overcome its limitations, nor does it have to. Its goal is not to substitute for the outside world, but to bring students to the point where they can begin to use the outside world for further acquisition, to where they can begin to understand the language used on the outside. It does this in two ways: by supplying input so that students progress in language acquisition, so that they understand "real" language to at least some extent, and by making the student conversationally competent, that is, by giving the student tools to manage conversations despite a less than perfect competence in the second language. We return to both of these important points in the discussion that follows.

THE ROLE OF OUTPUT

A second point that needs to be dealt with before describing the characteristics of optimal input for acquisition is the role of output, most commonly, the role of speech, in language acquisition.[1]

The Input Hypothesis makes a claim that may seem quite remarkable to some people—we acquire spoken fluency *not* by practicing talking but by understanding input, by listening and reading. It is, in fact, theoretically possible to acquire language without ever talking. This has been demonstrated for first language acquisition by Lenneberg (1962), who described the case of a boy with congenital dysarthria, a disorder of the peripheral speech organs, who was never able to speak. When Lenneberg tested the boy, he found that the child was able to understand spoken English perfectly. In other words, he had acquired "competence" without ever producing. The child was tested at age eight, and there is no way to tell directly whether his lack of output had slowed down his language acquisition. It is quite possible that if he had been able to speak, he would have acquired language somewhat faster, due to the *indirect* contribution speaking can make to acquisition.

Output has a contribution to make to language acquisition, but it is not a direct one: Simply, the more you talk, the more people will talk to you! Actual speaking on the part of the language acquirer will thus affect the *quantity* of input people direct at you.

It will also affect the *quality* of the input directed at the acquirer. Conversational partners often try to help you understand by modifying their speech ("foreigner talk"). They judge how much to modify by seeing whether you understand what is said, and also *by listening to you talk.* A second language speaker who makes lots of mistakes, has a poor accent, and is hesitant, will most likely receive, in general, more modified input than a speaker who appears competent and fluent.

Engaging in conversation is probably much more effective than "eavesdropping" for language acquisition. In conversation, the second language acquirer has some degree of control of the topic, can signal to the partner that there is a comprehension problem, etc. In other words, he can manage and regulate the input, and make it more comprehensible. There is no such control in eavesdropping! But in order to participate in conversation, there must be at least some talk, some output, from each partner. Hence, the indirect contribution of speech.

1. "Conversation" and Language Acquisition

Some scholars have suggested that "participation in conversation" is responsible for language acquisition. In the light of the above discussion, we can see that this is true, in a sense. "Conversation", however, is not in itself the causative variable in second language acquisition. It is one way, and a very good way, to obtain input. It is theoretically quite possible to acquire without participating in conversation, however.[2]

Figure 1 illustrates the indirect, but often considerable, contribution output can make to language acquisition.

2. Output and Learning

Output can play a fairly direct role in helping language *learning,* although even here it is not necessary. Output aids learning because it provides a domain for error correction. When a second language user speaks or writes, he

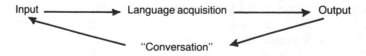

Figure 1. How Output Contributes to Language Acquisition Indirectly

Comprehensible *input* is responsible for progress in language acquisition.
***Output* is possible as a result of acquired competence.**
When performers *speak*, they encourage *input* (people speak to them). This is *conversation*.

or she may make an error. When this error is corrected, this supposedly helps the learner change his or her conscious mental representation of the rule or alter the environment of rule application.

We may thus compare an "output approach" to the input approach promoted here. Could we teach language primarily by encouraging production, with little or no input, and correcting all errors? Such a technique, in addition to being maddening, relies entirely on the students' ability to learn grammar.

This is not to say that error correction is totally useless and that learning is of no value. Learning has a role to play, and error correction may be of use in certain situations.

CHARACTERISTICS OF OPTIMAL INPUT FOR ACQUISITION

I will attempt in this section to present a set of requirements that should be met by any activity or set of materials aimed at subconscious language acquisition. The (testable) prediction that this set of characteristics makes is that an activity that fits the characteristics fully will encourage acquisition at the fastest possible rate. An activity that fits none of them could result in zero acquisition, or very little acquisition. (The latter, "very little", is more likely. The "language acquisition device" may be so powerful, even in the adult, that some minimal acquisition may occur as a result of *any* exposure to language.) . . .

We discuss each characteristic separately, showing what predictions each characteristic makes with respect to different aspects of method, materials, and informal input.

1. Optimal Input Is Comprehensible

This is clearly the most important input characteristic. It amounts to the claim that when the acquirer does not understand the message, there will be no acquisition. In other words, incomprehensible input, or "noise", will not help.

Positing *comprehensibility* as a fundamental and necessary (but not sufficient) requirement makes several predictions that appear to be correct. It explains why it is practically impossible for someone to acquire a second or foreign language merely by listening to the radio, unless the acquirer speaks a very closely related language. A monolingual English speaker, for example, hearing Polish on the radio, would acquire nothing because the input would be only "noise".[3]

This requirement also explains the apparent failure of educational TV programs to teach foreign languages. The input is simply not comprehensible. My own children watched programs such as Ville Allegre faithfully for years, and acquired about as much as I did: They could count from one to ten in Spanish and recognize a few words such as *casa* and *mesa*! The comprehensibility requirement predicts that TV would, in general, be somewhat more successful than radio as a language teacher, but that even TV would be inadequate in beginning stages. Ervin-Tripp (1973) has noted that hearing children of deaf parents do not acquire language from TV or radio, an observation consistent with this requirement.[4]

This characteristic also explains why children sometimes fail to pick up family languages. My own case is, I think, quite typical. My parents spoke Yiddish around the house for years, occasionally to each other (to tell secrets), and constantly to my grandparents. Nevertheless, my sister and I failed to acquire Yiddish, with the exception of a few phrases and routines. On the other hand, in many families children do grow up speaking the family language as well as the language of the community. What appears to be crucial is whether the family language is directed at the child, in other words, whether an attempt is made to make the language *comprehensible*. What we heard via eavesdropping was not comprehensible. It dealt with topics that were not easily identified and that were also often beyond our range of experience. Language directed at us in Yiddish would have been simplified, and more relevant to us, and hence more comprehensible.

Another prediction that the comprehensibility requirement makes is that "just talking", or "free conversation", is not language teaching. In other words, simply being a native speaker of a language does not in and of itself qualify one as a teacher of that language. Conscious and extensive knowledge of grammar does not make one a language teacher either. Rather, the defining characteristic of a good teacher is someone who can make input comprehensible to a non-native speaker, regardless of his or her level of competence in the target language. This leads naturally to another topic, how teachers make input comprehensible.

(a) How to Aid Comprehension

If we are correct in positing comprehensibility as a crucial requirement for optimal input for acquisition, the question of how to aid comprehension is a very central one for second language pedagogy. Indeed, the comprehension requirement suggests that *perhaps the main function of the second language teacher is to help make input comprehensible*, to do for the adult what the "outside world" cannot or will not do.

There are basically two ways in which the teacher can aid comprehension, linguistic and non-linguistic. Studies have shown that there are many things speakers do linguistically to make their speech more comprehensible to less competent speakers. Hatch (1979) has summarized the linguistic aspects of simplified input which appear to promote comprehension. Among these characteristics are:

1. slower rate and clearer articulation, which helps acquirers to identify word boundaries more easily, and allows more processing time;
2. more use of high frequency vocabulary, less slang, fewer idioms;
3. syntatic simplification, shorter sentences.

Such characteristics and others appear to be more or less common to different types of simple codes, such as caretaker speech, foreigner-talk, and teacher-talk (see also Krashen, 1980), and clearly help make input language more comprehensible. There is considerable empirical evidence that these codes are significantly "simpler" than native speaker—native speaker language, and there is evidence of some correlation between the linguistic level of the acquirer and the complexity of the input language: more advanced acquirers tend to get more complex input.

Does this mean that teachers should consciously try to simplify their speech when they talk to students? Should they think about slowing down, using more common vocabulary, using shorter sentences, less complex syntax with less embedding, etc.? Consciously referring to these "rules" might be helpful on occasion, but it appears to be the case that we make these adjustments automatically when we focus on trying to make ourselves understood. . . . If we focus on comprehension and communication, we will meet the syntatic requirements for optimal input.

While we free teachers of the responsibility to consciously control the grammar of their output speech, other responsibilities become more important. One is to make sure that the input is indeed comprehensible. I have nothing startling to add to the literature on comprehension checking, other than to underscore and emphasize its importance. Comprehension checking can range from simply asking "Do you understand?" occasionally, to monitoring comprehension via students' verbal and non-verbal responses.

Another main task of the teacher is to provide non-linguistic means of encouraging comprehension. In my view, providing extra-linguistic support in the form of realia and pictures for beginning classes is not a frill, but a very important part of the tools the teacher has to encourage language acquisition. The use of objects and pictures in early second language instruction corresponds to the caretaker's use of the "here and now" in encouraging first language acquisition, in that they all help the acquirer understand messages containing structures that are "a little beyond" them.

Good teachers also take advantage of the student's knowledge of the world in helping comprehension by discussing topics that are familiar to the student. Certainly, discussing or reading about a topic that is totally unknown will make the message harder to understand. There is a danger, however, in making the input too "familiar". If the message is completely known, it will be of no interest, and the student will probably not attend. We want the student to focus on the message, and there must be some message, something that the student really wants to hear or read about. This requirement is perhaps the hardest one to meet, and we shall have more to say about it below, in our discussion of characteristic II.[5]

As pointed out just a moment ago, comprehension is a *necessary* condition for language acquisition, but it is not *sufficient*. It is quite possible to understand input language, and yet not acquire. This can happen in several different ways: First, it is quite possible that the input simply does not contain $i + 1$ [see Chapter 3], that it does not include structures that are "a bit beyond" the student. Second, in many cases we do not utilize syntax in understanding—we can often get the message with a combination of vocabulary, or lexical information, plus extra-linguistic information. Finally, the "affective filter" may be "up", which can result in the acquirer understanding input, even input with $i + 1$, but not utilizing it for further acquisition.

2. Optimal Input Is Interesting and/or Relevant

Optimal input focusses the acquirer on the message and not on form. To go a step further, the best input is so interesting and relevant that the acquirer may even "forget" that the message is encoded in a foreign language.

Creating materials and providing input that meet this characteristic may appear to be an easy and obvious task, but my view is that, in reality, this requirement is not easy to meet, nor has the profession considered it obvious. It is very *difficult* to present and discuss topics of interest to a class of people whose goals, interests, and backgrounds differ from the teacher's and from each other's. I also claim that relevance and interest have not been widely perceived as requirements for input, since so many materials fail to meet this requirement!

It is fairly easy to think up examples of input that, while comprehensible, are universally perceived to be uninteresting and irrelevant. Among the most obvious examples are pattern drill, and most dialogue type exercises. Experimental evidence suggests that students pay little or no attention to meaning after the first few repetitions in pattern drill (Lee, McCune, & Patton, 1970), and the same result is most likely true for dialogues that are memorized by rote. Grammatical exercises also fail as input for acquisition on similar grounds. Granted, the goals of these exercises are not "acquisition", and we will have occasion to examine whether these input-types fill other needs in the second language program. Nevertheless, they fail this requirement dismally.

Somewhat less obvious is the failure of "meaningful drill" to qualify as optimal input for acquisition. "Meaningful drill" is distinguished from "mechanical drill", in that the former requires that real meaning be involved (Paulston, 1972). Since meaningful drill is designed to provide practice on particular grammatical structures, however, it is very difficult to also build in the exchange of truly relevant or interesting information, as in:

What time does he get up in the morning?

What time do they get up in the morning?

At best, such information is of only mild interest to members of a language class. I believe that it is an impossible task for teachers to embed truly interesting or relevant information into the form of a meaningful drill on a daily basis!

Some other fairly widespread input types that fall very short of the mark of true relevance are the reading assignments that most foreign langauge students work through in introductory courses. Generally, these selections bear very little resemblance to the kind of reading the students would do in their first language on their own time. . . .

3. Optimal Input Is Not Grammatically Sequenced

In acquisition-oriented materials, we should not be consciously concerned about including $i + 1$ in the input. The Input Hypothesis claims that when input is comprehensible, when meaning is successfully negotiated, $i + 1$ will be present automatically, in most cases.[6]

This requirement could be stated in a weaker form. It could be rephrased as follows: there is no *need* to deliberately include $i + 1$, since it will occur naturally. The strong form may be called for instead: it may be better not to even attempt to include $i + 1$! The arguments against a deliberate attempt to grammatically sequence will be expanded on here.

1. If we sequence, and each lesson, or group of lessons, focusses on one structure, this assumes that everyone in the class has the same $i + 1$, that everyone is at the same developmental stage in the second langauge. Because there are individual differences in the rate of acquisition (due to the strength of the affective filter and the amount of comprehensible input obtained), and differences among students as to out of class contact with the language, it is extremely unlikely that all the students in any class are at the same stage. Unsequenced but natural input, it is hypothesized, will contain a rich variety of structure—if it is comprehensible, there will be $i + 1$ for everyone as long as there is *enough* input (we return to the *quantity* question below).

2. When we attempt to present a "finely-tuned" sequence, we generally present each structure or rule once. (There is the "review" lesson and there are attempts at recycling, but review does not usually work through the entire sequence of activities—its goal is generally to "remind" and provide some additional practice for a rule that is supposedly already "internalized".[7] What happens to the student who misses the rule the first time around? Traditional review, meant as a reminder, will often not help. In traditional foreign language learning, as done in the United States, the student may even have to wait until next year, when the rule is presented again! Unsequenced communicative input contains built-in review. We don't have to worry if we miss the progressive tense today, it will be part of the input again . . . and again!

Comprehensible input thus guarantees us natural review and recycling, as-suming, as mentioned above, that there is enough of it.

Some readers may feel that I am setting up and attacking a straw man. It can be argued that some grammatically-based courses, despite a lockstep structural orientation, do provide input at $i + 1$ as well. While there may be a "structure of the day", not every utterance contains the target structure. For example, if the lesson's focus is the progressive tense marker, other tenses will be used as well in both classroom input and in the readings.

This may appear to be the case, but there is, nevertheless, a real problem with this approach. With a grammatical focus, communication will *always* suf-fer, there will always be less genuinely interesting input. The teacher's mind, and the materials writer's mind, is focussed on "contextualizing" a particular structure, and not on communicating ideas.

As my colleague Steven Sternfeld has pointed out to me, what is pro-posed here is fundamentally different from "contextualization". Contextual-ization involves inventing a *realistic* context for the presentation of a gram-matical rule or vocabulary item. The goal in the mind of the teacher is the learning or acquisition of the rule or word. What is proposed here is that the goal, in the mind of both the teacher and the students, is the idea, the message.

This objection can be summarized as follows:

3. The very orientation of the grammatically-based syllabus reduces the quality of comprehensible input and distorts the communicative focus. Teach-ers will be concerned with *how* they are speaking, reading selections will be aimed at including x number of examples of structure y along with a certain vocabulary sample, a sure guarantee of boring and wooden language.

4. Still another problem is that the grammatical sequence attempts to guess the order of acquisition. Several years ago, I suggested (Krashen, Mad-den, & Bailey, 1975) that an application of the Natural Order Hypothesis was the construction of "natural syllabi" following the natural order. My position has changed. As Fathman (1979) has pointed out, the practical implication of the Natural Order Hypothesis may lie in what it has taught us about the underlying process of language acquisition.

Comprehensible input, it is claimed, will automatically follow a nat-ural order insofar as $i + 1$ will be provided (along with many other structures).

4. Optimal Input Must Be in Sufficient Quantity

It is difficult to say just how much comprehensible/low filter input is neces-sary to achieve a given level of proficiency in second langauge acquisition, due to a lack of data. We know enough now, however, to be able to state with some confidence that the profession has seriously underestimated the amount of comprehensible input necessary to achieve even moderate, or "intermediate" levels of proficiency in second language acquisition.

Theoretical arguments for quantity derive from the immediately preceding discussion. I hypothesized that natural communicative input could supply $i + 1$ for all students if two conditions were met:

1. The input was not artificially constrained (limited range of discourse types)
2. It was supplied in sufficient quantity.

Clearly, five minutes of talk, or a single paragraph of reading, has little chance of including a given student's $i + 1$. Rather than take a more careful aim at that student's needs, rather than "overindividualizing" instruction, it is far easier, I am suggesting, to increase the amount of comprehensible input. Again, if there is enough, $i + 1$ will be provided, and will be provided over and over!

As mentioned above, we do not have enough data to state, with confidence, how much input is necessary to reach a given stage. The literature does provide us with enough to state some initial hypotheses, however. Below, we briefly examine what the literature implies about reaching the initial "readiness to speak" stage, and more advanced levels.

(a) Quantity Requirements for Initial Readiness to Speak

How much input is needed to end the "silent period"? How much input is necessary so that second language acquirers can produce utterances using acquired competence?

Asher's work on Total Physical Response teaching, a method that requires students to obey commands given in the second language, often with a "total physical response" (e.g. standing up), gives us some idea as to how much input is necessary for initial speaking readiness. The chief virtue of Total Physical Response may be its ability to supply concentrated comprehensible input. Asher has noted in several papers that TPR students are generally ready to start production in the target language after about ten hours of Total Physical Response input.[8]

Informal language acquisition research presents what at first may seem to be a different picture. The "silent period" seen in informal child second language acquisition may last as long as six months! During this time, the child may produce very little in the second language, other than routines and a few patterns. The greater length of the "natural" silent period, as compared to Asher's observation that ten hours may suffice may be due to the fact that a great deal of the input that the child in the natural environment receives may be incomprehensible. As stated earlier in this reading, the main advantage of "formal instruction" may be its potential for providing comprehensible input in early stages, bringing the acquirer to the point where he or she can begin to take advantage of the natural environment. The long silent period in informal child second language acquisition may be further evidence that the informal environment is inefficient in early stages.[9]

(b) Quantity Requirements
for Higher Levels of Proficiency

We know even less about the amount of low filter/comprehensible input necessary for progress to higher levels for competence. We can get some idea from the United States Foreign Service Institute chart, an estimate of the amount of class time necessary to achieve a FSI 2+ rating in different foreign languages (2+ is defined as "halfway between minimal professional proficiency and working professional proficiency", Diller, 1978, p. 100) for adult English speakers. According to the Foreign Service Institute estimates (reproduced in Diller, 1978), European languages such as German, French, and Italian require approximately 720 hours of classtime for the "average" student to attain the 2+ level, while more "exotic" languages (such as Arabic, Korean, and Chinese) require 1950 hours of classtime.[10]

These figures may, however, represent an upper bound. They are based on "classroom hours", which, if traditional methods are employed, may not entail optimal input. In other words, we can do better!

"How much input?" remains an empirical question, one that can probably be adequately answered by research. To be more precise, we would like to know: "How much low filter/comprehensible input is necessary for students to acquire enough competence in the second language, so that they can use the informal environment to continue improving?" Despite our current paucity of data, what seems clear to me now is that we are not using enough of the available instruction time for supplying comprehensible input, and that we will be able to stimulate more rapid (and more comfortable) second language acquisition if we put greater focus on input.

NOTES

[1]Speech production can come from any of three different sources. First, we can use our acquired competence as illustrated in the Monitor model. According to the input hypothesis, this sort of production takes some time to develop. Another way is via memorized patterns and routines (see Krashen & Scarcella, 1978). A third way is by extensive use of first language structures. The latter two methods of speech production are ways of "performing without competence" (borrowing R. Clark's terminology). A second language performer can "learn to speak" very quickly using these methods, and they are explicitly encouraged by some techniques. They are severely limited modes, however. (Krashen & Scarcella, 1978; Krashen, 1981b)

[2]This raises the interesting question of whether participation in conversation is even *practically* necessary for truly successful second language acquisition. It probably is. In addition to being an effective means of obtaining comprehensible input, conversation offers some other real advantages that will become clearer as we proceed. Scarcella (forthcoming) points out that there are many aspects of "communicative competence" that are probably not acquirable by observa-

tion and input alone. Also, Scarcella points out that real conversation entails "a high degree of personal involvement", what Stevick (1976a) terms "depth" and a lowered affective filter.

[3]In a review of the science fiction literature, Hatch (1976) points out several examples in which authors assume that it is possible to acquire human languages by listening to radio broadcasts. Even these authors seem to understand, however, that acquiring language by listening to incomprehensible input is an ability possessed only by certain aliens with different, and apparently superior "language acquisition devices".

[4]There are anecdotal cases of people who have picked up second languages via television. Larsen-Freeman (1979), for example, cited a case of a German speaker who acquired Dutch via TV. This is not at all strange, as much input in Dutch would be comprehensible to a speaker of such a closely related language. Note that I am not claiming that it is *impossible* to acquire language from TV. I am only saying that comprehensible input is necessary for acquisition and that television provides little comprehensible input for a beginner. Intermediate level students may profit quite a bit from television and even radio.

[5]Another way teachers help students understand messages containing structures that are "beyond" them is by emphasizing vocabulary. Both Evelyn Hatch and I have stated the argument for increased vocabulary work in recent years (Hatch, 1978b, Krashen, 1981b), and our argumentation is, I think, similar. While knowledge of vocabulary may not be sufficient for understanding all messages, there is little doubt that an increased vocabulary helps the acquirer understand more of what is heard or read (see e.g. Ulijn & Kempen, 1976; Macha, 1979, on the role of vocabulary in reading comprehension). Thus, more vocabulary should mean more comprehension of input, and more acquisition of grammar. This "new view" is quite different from earlier positions. Language teachers had been told to restrict introduction of new vocabulary in order to focus on syntax. Now we are saying that vocabulary learning will actually contribute to the acquisition of syntax.

The practical implications of this position are not clear to me, however. Should we teach vocabulary in isolation in an effort to boost the amount of input that is comprehensible? Unfortunately, there is little research that speaks directly to the question of how vocabulary is best acquired, and, most important, retained. There is some agreement among teachers that vocabulary should be taught in context, rather than by rote memorization of lists (see Celce-Murcia & Rosenzweig, 1979, for several techniques), but it may even be the case that vocabulary should not be directly taught at all! It may be the case that if we supply enough comprehensible input, vocabulary acquisition will in fact take care of itself.

Let me restate this suggestion in the form of an informal experiment: Given ten minutes of study time (waiting for a bus, etc.), which activity would be more useful for the language acquirer interested in long-term retention of vocabulary?

(1) Rote learning of a list, using flash cards or some equivalent technique.
(2) Reviewing a story that has "new words" carefully included (Contextualization).
(3) Reading for pleasure, trying only to understand the message and looking up new words only when they seem to be essential to the meaning or when the acquirer is curious as to their meaning.

Method (3) relies on comprehensible input to supply new vocabulary in enough frequency, and to help the acquirer determine the meaning. In method (3) there is no conscious focus on vocabulary, only on meaning. The prediction (hope?) is that really important words will reoccur naturally and their meanings will be made increasingly obvious by the context. It does not exclude the possibility that the acquirer may be helped by occasional glances at the dictionary or occasional definitions by a teacher.

[6]There are exceptions, examples of comprehensible input in which $i + 1$ may not be present. These include situations in which the discourse is limited, as in many classrooms, where the possibilities for discourse variation are limited, and in many instrumental uses of language in which familiarity with a few routines and patterns may suffice for successful communication (e.g. dealing with gas station attendants, clerks, etc.).

[7]"Internalization", in my interpretation, seems to mean the acquisition of a rule that was first learned, where learning is assumed to have *caused* the subsequent acquisition. According to the theory of second language acquisition presented in Chapter II [of *Principles and Practice in Second*

Language Acquisition], this does not occur. I have discussed this in several technical papers (Krashen, 1977).

[8]Varvel (1979) describes a silent period in formal instruction (Silent Way methodology) that lasted considerably longer, indicating that there may be a fair amount of individual variation in the duration of the silent period for adults in language classes:

> "There was a woman from Taiwan who after several weeks was still conspicuously silent in class. She never talked, and when called upon would only answer in a whisper, saying only what was required. It was clear, however, that she was one of the most attentive students in the class, had a clear understanding of what was being done, and seemingly enjoyed the class. She also had a positive attitude towards what and how she was learning. At no time was she coerced into active participation.
>
> Then one day in the ninth week of school she sat in the front row and actively participated throughout the whole hour. From that point on, she continued to participate actively in a more limited way and at times helped others and was helped by others . . ," (p. 491)

While there may have been other reasons for this student's silence, this example suggests that the silent period should be respected, and that some students develop speaking readiness later than others.

[9]Given the same amount of comprehensible input, the child's silent period in second language acquisition may turn out to be longer than the average adult silent period for other reasons. What I am suggesting here is that the silent period in child second language acquisition would not be as long if more of the input the child hears is comprehensible.

[10]Note that if we assume that an acquirer in the natural environment receives about two hours per day of comprehensible input, 720 hours translates into about one year "abroad". This assumes that classtime = comprehensible input, which may not be true with the traditional methods the FSI chart is based on. It is, however, in accord with the informally accepted idea that a year abroad will result in a fair degree of fluency in the case of European languages.

RELATED READING 6

INTERACTION BETWEEN LEARNING AND DEVELOPMENT

Lev S. Vygotsky

The problems encountered in the psychological analysis of teaching cannot be correctly resolved or even formulated without addressing the relation between learning and development in school-age children. Yet it is the most unclear of all the basic issues on which the application of child development theories to educational processes depends. Needless to say, the lack of theoretical clarity does not mean that the issue is removed altogether from current research efforts into learning; not one study can avoid this central theoretical issue. But the relation between learning and development remains methodologically unclear because concrete research studies have embodied theoretically vague, critically unevaluated, and sometimes internally contradictory

From L. S. Vygotsky, *Mind in Society: Development of Higher Psychological Processes*, edited by M. Cole, S. Scribner, V. John-Steiner, and E. Souberman. (Cambridge, MA.: Harvard University Press, 1978), pp. 79–91.

postulates, premises, and peculiar solutions to the problem of this fundamental relationship; and these, of course, result in a variety of errors.

Essentially, all current conceptions of the relation between development and learning in children can be reduced to three major theoretical positions.

The first centers on the assumption that processes of child development are independent of learning. Learning is considered a purely external process that is not actively involved in development. It merely utilizes the achievements of development rather than providing an impetus for modifying its course.

In experimental investigations of the development of thinking in school children, it has been assumed that processes such as deduction and understanding, evolution of notions about the world, interpretation of physical causality, and mastery of logical forms of thought and abstract logic all occur by themselves, without any influence from school learning. An example of such a theory is Piaget's extremely complex and interesting theoretical principles, which also shape the experimental methodology he employs. The questions Piaget [1955] uses in the course of his "clinical conversations" with children clearly illustrate his approach. When a five-year-old is asked "why doesn't the sun fall?" it is assumed that the child has neither a ready answer for such a question nor the general capabilities for generating one. The point of asking questions that are so far beyond the reach of the child's intellectual skills is to eliminate the influence of previous experience and knowledge. The experimenter seeks to obtain the tendencies of children's thinking in "pure" form, entirely independent of learning.

Similarly, the classics of psychological literature, such as the works by Binet and others, assume that development is always a prerequisite for learning and that if a child's mental functions (intellectual operations) have not matured to the extent that he is capable of learning a particular subject, then no instruction will prove useful. They especially feared premature instruction, the teaching of a subject before the child was ready for it. All effort was concentrated on finding the lower threshold of learning ability, the age at which a particular kind of learning first becomes possible.

Because this approach is based on the premise that learning trails behind development, that development always outruns learning, it precludes the notion that learning may play a role in the course of the development or maturation of those functions activated in the course of learning. Development or maturation is viewed as a precondition of learning but never the result of it. To summarize this position: Learning forms a superstructure over development, leaving the latter essentially unaltered.

The second major theoretical position is that learning *is* development. This identity is the essence of a group of theories that are quite diverse in origin.

One such theory is based on the concept of reflex, an essentially old notion that has been extensively revived recently. Whether reading, writing, or arithmetic is being considered, development is viewed as the mastery of conditioned reflexes; that is, the process of learning is completely and inseparably blended with the process of development. This notion was elaborated by James, who reduced the learning process to habit formation and identified the learning process with development.

Reflex theories have at least one thing in common with theories such as Piaget's: in both, development is conceived of as the elaboration and substitution of innate responses. As [W.] James expressed it, "Education, in short, cannot be better described than by calling it the organization of acquired habits of conduct and tendencies to behavior" [1958, pp. 36–37]. Development itself is reduced primarily to the accumulation of all possible responses. Any acquired response is considered either a more complex form of or a substitute for the innate response.

But despite the similarity between the first and second theoretical positions, there is a major difference in their assumptions about the temporal relationship between learning and developmental processes. Theorists who hold the first view assert that developmental cycles precede learning cycles; maturation precedes learning and instruction must lag behind mental growth. For the second group of theorists, both processes occur simultaneously; learning and development coincide at all points in the same way that two identical geometrical figures coincide when superimposed.

The third theoretical position on the relation between learning and development attempts to overcome the extremes of the other two by simply combining them. A clear example of this approach is Koffka's theory [1924], in which development is based on two inherently different but related processes, each of which influences the other. On the one hand is maturation, which depends directly on the development of the nervous system; on the other hand is learning, which itself is also a developmental process.

Three aspects of this theory are new. First, as we already noted, is the combination of two seemingly opposite viewpoints, each of which has been encountered separately in the history of science. The very fact that these two viewpoints can be combined into one theory indicates that they are not opposing and mutually exclusive but have something essential in common. Also new is the idea that the two processes that make up development are mutually dependent and interactive. Of course, the nature of the interaction is left virtually unexplored in Koffka's work, which is limited solely to very general remarks regarding the relation between these two processes. It is clear that for Koffka the process of maturation prepares and makes possible a specific process of learning. The learning process then stimulates and pushes forward the maturation process. The third and most important new aspect of this theory is the expanded role it ascribes to learning in child development. This emphasis leads us directly to an old pedagogical problem, that of formal discipline and the problem of transfer.

Pedagogical movements that have emphasized formal discipline and urged the teaching of classical languages, ancient civilizations, and mathematics have assumed that regardless of the irrelevance of these particular subjects for daily living, they were of the greatest value for the pupil's mental development. A variety of studies have called into question the soundness of this idea. It has been shown that learning in one area has very little influence on overall development. For example, reflex theorists Woodworth and Thorndike found that adults who, after special exercises, had achieved considerable success in determining the length of short lines, had made virtually no progress in their ability to determine the length of long lines. These same adults were successfully trained to estimate the size of a given two-dimensional figure, but this training did not make them successful in estimating the size of a series of other two-dimensional figures of various sizes and shapes.

According to Thorndike [1914], theoreticians in psychology and education believe that every particular response acquisition directly enhances overall ability in equal measure: Teachers believed and acted on the basis of the theory that the mind is a complex of abilities—powers of observation, attention, memory, thinking, and so forth—and that any improvement in any specific ability results in a general improvement in all abilities. According to this theory, if the student increased the attention he paid to Latin grammar, he would increase his abilities to focus attention on any task. The words "accuracy," "quick-wittedness," "ability to reason," "memory," "power of observation," "attention," "concentration," and so forth are said to denote actual fundamental capabilities that vary in accordance with the material with which they operate; these basic abilities are substantially modified by studying particular subjects, and they retain these modifications when they turn to other areas. Therefore, if someone learns to do any single thing well, he will also be able to do other entirely unrelated things well as a result of some secret connection. It is assumed that mental capabilities function independently of the material with which they operate, and that the development of one ability entails the development of others.

Thorndike himself opposed this point of view. Through a variety of studies he showed that particular forms of activity, such as spelling, are dependent on the mastery of specific skills and material necessary for the performance of that particular task. The development of one particular capability seldom means the development of others. Thorndike argued that specialization of abilities is even greater than superficial observation may indicate. For example, if, out of a hundred individuals we choose ten who display the ability to detect spelling errors or to measure lengths, it is unlikely that these ten will display better abilities regarding, for example, the estimation of the weight of objects. In the same way, speed and accuracy in adding numbers are entirely unrelated to speed and accuracy in being able to think up antonyms.

This research shows that the mind is not a complex network of *general* capabilities such as observation, attention, memory, judgment, and so forth, but a set of specific capabilities, each of which is, to some extent, independent of the others and is developed independently. Learning is more than the acquisition of the ability to think; it is the acquisition of many specialized abilities for thinking about a variety of things. Learning does not alter our overall ability to focus attention but rather develops various abilities to focus attention on a variety of things. According to this view, special training affects overall development only when its elements, material, and processes are similar across specific domains; habit governs us. This leads to the conclusion that because each activity depends on the material with which it operates, the development of consciousness is the development of a set of particular, independent capabilities or of a set of particular habits. Improvement of one function of consciousness or one aspect of its activity can affect the development of another only to the extent that there are elements common to both functions or activities.

Developmental theorists such as Koffka and the Gestalt School—who hold to the third theoretical position outlined earlier—oppose Thorndike's point of view. They assert that the influence of learning is never specific. From their study of structural principles, they argue that the learning process can never be reduced simply to the formation of skills but embodies an intellectual order that makes it possible to transfer general principles discovered in solving one task to a variety of other tasks. From this point of view, the child, while learning a particular operation, acquires the ability to create structures of a certain type, regardless of the diverse materials with which she is working and regardless of the particular elements involved. Thus, Koffka does not conceive of learning as limited to a process of habit and skill acquisition. The relationship he posits between learning and development is not that of an identity but a more complex relationship. According to Thorndike, learning and development coincide at all points, but for Koffka, development is always a larger set than learning. Schematically, the relationship between the two processes could be depicted by two concentric circles, the smaller symbolizing the learning process and the larger the developmental process evoked by learning.

Once a child has learned to perform an operation, he thus assimilates some structural principle whose sphere of application is other than just the operations of the type on whose basis the principle was assimilated. Consequently, in making one step in learning, a child makes two steps in development, that is, learning and development do not coincide. This concept is the essential aspect of the third group of theories we have discussed.

ZONE OF PROXIMAL DEVELOPMENT:
A NEW APPROACH

Although we reject all three theoretical positions discussed above, analyzing them leads us to a more adequate view of the relation between learning and development. The question to be framed in arriving at a solution to this problem is complex. It consists of two separate issues: first, the general relation between learning and development; and second, the specific features of this relationship when children reach school age.

That children's learning begins long before they attend school is the starting point of this discussion. Any learning a child encounters in school always has a previous history. For example, children begin to study arithmetic in school, but long beforehand they have had some experience with quantity— they have had to deal with operations of division, addition, subtraction, and determination of size. Consequently, children have their own preschool arithmetic, which only myopic psychologists could ignore.

It goes without saying that learning as it occurs in the preschool years differs markedly from school learning, which is concerned with the assimilation of the fundamentals of scientific knowledge. But even when, in the period of her first questions, a child assimilates the names of objects in her environment, she is learning. Indeed, can it be doubted that children learn speech from adults; or that, through asking questions and giving answers, children acquire a variety of information; or that, through imitating adults and through being instructed about how to act, children develop an entire repository of skills? Learning and development are interrelated from the child's very first day of life.

Koffka, attempting to clarify the laws of child learning and their relation to mental development, concentrates his attention on the simplest learning processes, those that occur in the preschool years. His error is that, while seeing a similarity between preschool and school learning, he fails to discern the difference—he does not see the specifically new elements that school learning introduces. He and others assume that the difference between preschool and school learning consists of nonsystematic learning in one case and systematic learning in the other. But "systematicness" is not the only issue; there is also the fact that school learning introduces something fundamentally new into the child's development. In order to elaborate the dimensions of school learning, we will describe a new and exceptionally important concept without which the issue cannot be resolved: the zone of proximal development.

A well known and empirically established fact is that learning should be matched in some manner with the child's developmental level. For example, it has been established that the teaching of reading, writing, and arithmetic should be initiated at a specific age level. Only recently, however, has attention been directed to the fact that we cannot limit ourselves merely to determining developmental levels if we wish to discover the actual relations of the developmental process to learning capabilities. We must determine at least two developmental levels.

The first level can be called the *actual developmental level*, that is, the level of development of a child's mental functions that has been established as a result of certain already *completed* developmental cycles. When we determine a child's mental age by using tests, we are almost always dealing with the actual developmental level. In studies of children's mental development it is generally assumed that only those things that children can do on their own are indicative of mental abilities. We give children a battery of tests or a variety of tasks of varying degrees of difficulty, and we judge the extent of their mental development on the basis of how they solve them and at what level of difficulty. On the other hand, if we offer leading questions or show how the problem is to be solved and the child then solves it, or if the teacher initiates the solution and the child completes it or solves it in collaboration with other children—in short, if the child barely misses an independent solution of the problem—the solution is not regarded as indicative of his mental development. This "truth" was familiar and reinforced by common sense. Over a decade even the profoundest thinkers never questioned the assumption; they never entertained the notion that what children can do with the assistance of others might be in some sense even more indicative of their mental development than what they can do alone.

Let us take a simple example. Suppose I investigate two children upon entrance into school, both of whom are ten years old chronologically and eight years old in terms of mental development. Can I say that they are the same age mentally? Of course. What does this mean? It means that they can independently deal with tasks up to the degree of difficulty that has been standardized for the eight-year-old level. If I stop at this point, people would imagine that the subsequent course of mental development and of school learning for these children will be the same, because it depends on their intellect. Of course, there may be other factors, for example, if one child was sick for half a year while the other was never absent from school; but generally speaking, the fate of these children should be the same. Now imagine that I do not terminate my study at this point, but only begin it. These children seem to be capable of handling problems up to an eight-year-old's level, but not beyond that. Suppose that I show them various ways of dealing with the problem. Different experimenters might employ different modes of demonstration in different cases: some might run through an entire demonstration and ask the children to repeat it, others might initiate the solution and ask the child to finish it, or offer leading questions. In short, in some way or another I propose that the children solve the problem with my assistance. Under these circumstances it turns out that the first child can deal with problems up to a twelve-year-old's level, the second up to a nine-year-old's. Now, are these children mentally the same?

When it was first shown that the capability of children with equal levels of mental development to learn under a teacher's guidance varied to a high degree, it became apparent that those children were not mentally the same age and that the subsequent course of their learning would obviously be different. This difference between twelve and eight, or between nine and eight, is what we call *the zone of proximal development. It is the distance between the*

*actual developmental level as determined by independent problem solving and the level
of potential development as determined through problem solving under adult guidance
or in collaboration with more capable peers.*

If we naively ask what the actual developmental level is, or, to put it more
simply, what more independent problem solving reveals, the most common
answer would be that a child's actual developmental level defines functions
that have already matured, that is, the end products of development. If a
child can do such-and-such independently, it means that the functions for
such-and-such have matured in her. What, then, is defined by the zone of
proximal development, as determined through problems that children cannot
solve independently but only with assistance? The zone of proximal development defines those functions that have not yet matured but are in the process
of maturation, functions that will mature tomorrow but are currently in an
embryonic state. These functions could be termed the "buds" or "flowers"
of development rather than the "fruits" of development. The actual developmental level characterizes mental development retrospectively, while the
zone of proximal development characterizes mental development prospec-
tively.

The zone of proximal development furnishes psychologists and educators
with a tool through which the internal course of development can be understood. By using this method we can take account of not only the cycles and
maturation processes that have already been completed but also those processes that are currently in a state of formation, that are just beginning to mature and develop. Thus, the zone of proximal development permits us to
delineate the child's immediate future and his dynamic developmental state,
allowing not only for what already has been achieved developmentally but
also for what is in the course of maturing. The two children in our example
displayed the same mental age from the viewpoint of developmental cycles
already completed, but the developmental dynamics of the two were entirely
different. The state of a child's mental development can be determined only
by clarifying its two levels: the actual developmental level and the zone of
proximal development.

I will discuss one study of preschool children to demonstrate that what
is in the zone of proximal development today will be the actual developmental level tomorrow—that is, what a child can do with assistance today she
will be able to do by herself tomorrow.

The American researcher Dorothea McCarthy [1930] showed that among
children between the ages of three and five there are two groups of functions:
those the children already possess, and those they can perform under guidance, in groups, and in collaboration with one another but which they have
not mastered independently. McCarthy's study demonstrated that this second group of functions is at the actual developmental level of five-to-seven-
year-olds. What her subjects could do only under guidance, in collaboration,
and in groups at the age of three-to-five years they could do independently

when they reached the age of five-to-seven years. Thus, if we were to determine only mental age—that is, only functions that have matured—we would have but a summary of completed development, while if we determine the maturing functions, we can predict what will happen to these children between five and seven, provided the same developmental conditions are maintained. The zone of proximal development can become a powerful concept in developmental research, one that can markedly enhance the effectiveness and utility of the application of diagnostics of mental development to educational problems.

A full understanding of the concept of the zone of proximal development must result in reevaluation of the role of imitation in learning. An unshakable tenet of classical psychology is that only the independent activity of children, not their imitative activity, indicates their level of mental development. This view is expressed in all current testing systems. In evaluating mental development, consideration is given to only those solutions to test problems which the child reaches without the assistance of others, without demonstrations, and without leading questions. Imitation and learning are thought of as purely mechanical processes. But recently psychologists have shown that a person can imitate only that which is within her developmental level. For example, if a child is having difficulty with a problem in arithmetic and the teacher solves it on the blackboard, the child may grasp the solution in an instant. But if the teacher were to solve a problem in higher mathematics, the child would not be able to understand the solution no matter how many times she imitated it.

Animal psychologists, and in particular Köhler [1925], have dealt with this question of imitation quite well. Köhler's experiments sought to determine whether primates are capable of graphic thought. The principal question was whether primates solved problems independently or whether they merely imitated solutions they had seen performed earlier, for example, watching other animals or humans use sticks and other tools and then imitating them. Köhler's special experiments, designed to determine what primates could imitate, reveal that primates can use imitation to solve only those problems that are of the same degree of difficulty as those they can solve alone. However, Köhler failed to take account of an important fact, namely, that primates cannot be taught (in the human sense of the word) through imitation, nor can their intellect be developed, because they have no zone of proximal development. A primate can learn a great deal through training by using its mechanical and mental skills, but it cannot be made more intelligent, that is, it cannot be taught to solve a variety of more advanced problems independently. For this reason animals are incapable of learning in the human sense of the term; *human learning presupposes a specific social nature and a process by which children grow into the intellectual life of those around them.*

Children can imitate a variety of actions that go well beyond the limits of their own capabilities. Using imitation, children are capable of doing much more in collective activity or under the guidance of adults. This fact, which seems to be of little significance in itself, is of fundamental importance in that it demands a radical alteration of the entire doctrine concerning the relation between learning and development in children. One direct consequence is a change in conclusions that may be drawn from diagnostic tests of development.

Formerly, it was believed that by using tests, we determine the mental development level with which education should reckon and whose limits it should not exceed. This procedure oriented learning toward yesterday's development, toward developmental stages already completed. The error of this view was discovered earlier in practice than in theory. It is demonstrated most clearly in the teaching of mentally retarded children. Studies have established that mentally retarded children are not very capable of abstract thinking. From this the pedagogy of the special school drew the seemingly correct conclusion that all teaching of such children should be based on the use of concrete, look-and-do methods. And yet a considerable amount of experience with this method resulted in profound disillusionment. It turned out that a teaching system based solely on concreteness—one that eliminated from teaching everything associated with abstract thinking—not only failed to help retarded children overcome their innate handicaps but also reinforced their handicaps by accustoming children exclusively to concrete thinking and thus suppressing the rudiments of any abstract thought that such children still have. Precisely because retarded children, when left to themselves, will never achieve well-elaborated forms of abstract thought, the school should make every effort to push them in that direction and to develop in them what is intrinsically lacking in their own development. In the current practices of special schools for retarded children, we can observe a beneficial shift away from this concept of concreteness, one that restores look-and-do methods to their proper role. Concreteness is now seen as necessary and unavoidable only as a stepping stone for developing abstract thinking—as a means, not as an end in itself.

Similarly, in normal children, learning which is oriented toward developmental levels that have already been reached is ineffective from the viewpoint of a child's overall development. It does not aim for a new stage of the developmental process but rather lags behind this process. Thus, the notion of a zone of proximal development enables us to propound a new formula, namely that the only "good learning" is that which is in advance of development.

The acquisition of language can provide a paradigm for the entire problem of the relation between learning and development. Language arises initially as a means of communication between the child and the people in his environment. Only subsequently, upon conversion to internal speech, does it come to organize the child's thought, that is, become an internal mental function. Piaget and others have shown that reasoning occurs in a children's group as an argument intended to prove one's own point of view before it occurs as an internal activity whose distinctive feature is that the child begins to perceive and check the basis of his thoughts. Such observations prompted Piaget [1955] to conclude that communication produces the need for checking and confirming thoughts, a process that is characteristic of adult thought. In the same way that internal speech and reflective thought arise from the interactions between the child and persons in her environment, these interactions provide the source of development of a child's voluntary behavior. Piaget has shown that cooperation provides the basis for the development of a child's moral judgment. Earlier research established that a child first becomes able to subordinate her behavior to rules in group play and only later does voluntary self-regulation of behavior arise as an internal function.

These individual examples illustrate a general developmental law for the higher mental functions that we feel can be applied in its entirety to children's learning processes. We propose that an essential feature of learning is that it creates the zone of proximal development; that is, learning awakens a variety of internal developmental processes that are able to operate only when the child is interacting with people in his environment and in cooperation with his peers. Once these processes are internalized, they become part of the child's independent developmental achievement.

From this point of view, learning is not development; however, properly organized learning results in mental development and sets in motion a variety of developmental processes that would be impossible apart from learning. Thus, learning is a necessary and universal aspect of the process of developing culturally organized, specifically human, psychological functions.

To summarize, the most essential feature of our hypothesis is the notion that developmental processes do not coincide with learning processes. Rather, the developmental process lags behind the learning process; this sequence then results in zones of proximal development. Our analysis alters the traditional view that at the moment a child assimilates the meaning of a word, or masters an operation such as addition or written language, her developmental processes are basically completed. In fact, they have only just begun at that moment. The major consequence of analyzing the educational process in this manner is to show that the initial mastery of, for example, the four arithmetic operations provides the basis for the subsequent development of a variety of highly complex internal processes in children's thinking.

Our hypothesis establishes the unity but not the identity of learning processes and internal developmental processes. It presupposes that the one is converted into the other. Therefore, it becomes an important concern of psychological research to show how external knowledge and abilities in children become internalized.

Any investigation explores some sphere of reality. An aim of the psychological analysis of development is to describe the internal relations of the intellectual processes awakened by school learning. In this respect, such analysis will be directed inward and is analogous to the use of x-rays. If successful, it should reveal to the teacher how developmental processes stimulated by the course of school learning are carried through inside the head of each individual child. The revelation of this internal, subterranean developmental network of school subjects is a task of primary importance for psychological and educational analysis.

A second essential feature of our hypothesis is the notion that, although learning is directly related to the course of child development, the two are never accomplished in equal measure or in parallel. Development in children never follows school learning the way a shadow follows the object that casts it. In actuality, there are highly complex dynamic relations between developmental and learning processes that cannot be encompassed by an unchanging hypothetical formulation.

Each school subject has its own specific relation to the course of child development, a relation that varies as the child goes from one stage to another. This leads us directly to a reexamination of the problem of formal discipline, that is, to the significance of each particular subject from the viewpoint of overall mental development. Clearly, the problem cannot be solved by using any one formula; extensive and highly diverse concrete research based on the concept of the zone of proximal development is necessary to resolve the issue.

RELATED READING 7

PERSONALITY FACTORS

H. Douglas Brown

If we were to devise theories of second language acquisition or teaching methods which were based only on cognitive considerations, we would be omitting the most fundamental side of human behavior. Over two decades ago Ernest Hilgard, well known for his study of human learning and cognition, noted that "purely cognitive theories of learning will be rejected unless a role is assigned to affectivity" (1963, p. 267). In recent years there has been an increasing awareness of the necessity in second language research and teaching to examine human personality in order to find solutions to perplexing problems.

From H. D. Brown, *Principles of Language Learning and Teaching*, 2d ed. (Englewood Cliffs, NJ: Prentice-Hall, Inc., 1987), pp. 99–110, 114–119.

The affective domain is impossible to describe within definable limits. An overwhelming set of variables is implied in considering the emotional side of human behavior in the second language learning process. One difficulty in striving for affective explanations for language success is presented by the task of subdividing and categorizing the factors of the affective domain. We are often guilty of using rather sweeping terms as if they were carefully defined. For example, it is easy enough to say that "culture conflict" accounts for most language learning problems, or that "motivation" is the key to success in a foreign language; but it is quite another matter to define such terms with precision. Psychologists also experience a difficulty in defining terms. Abstract concepts such as empathy, aggression, extroversion, and other common terms are difficult to define operationally. Standardized psychological tests often form an empirical definition of such concepts, but constant revisions are evidence of an ongoing struggle for validity. Nevertheless, the elusive nature of affective and cognitive concepts need not deter us from seeking answers to questions. Careful, systematic study of the role of personality in second language acquisition has already led to a greater understanding of the language learning process and to improved language teaching methods.

THE AFFECTIVE DOMAIN

What is the affective domain? How is it to be delimited and understood? *Affect* refers to emotion or feeling. The affective domain is the emotional side of human behavior, and it may be juxtaposed to the cognitive side. The development of affective states or feelings involves a variety of personality factors, feelings both about ourselves and about others with whom we come into contact.

Benjamin Bloom and his colleagues (Krathwohl, Bloom, & Masia, 1964) provided a useful extended definition of the affective domain, outlining five levels of affectivity.

1. At the first fundamental level, the development of affectivity begins with *receiving*. Persons must be aware of the environment surrounding them, be conscious of situations, phenomena, people, objects; be willing to receive, willing to tolerate a stimulus, not avoid it, and give a stimulus their controlled or selected attention.
2. Next, persons must go beyond receiving to *responding*, committing themselves in at least some small measure to a phenomenon or a person. Such responding in one dimension may be in acquiescence, but in another, higher, dimension the person is willing to respond voluntarily without coercion, and then to receive satisfaction from that response.
3. The third level of affectivity involves *valuing*, placing worth on a thing, a behavior, or a person. Valuing takes on the characteristics of beliefs

or attitudes as values are internalized. Individuals do not merely accept a value to the point of being willing to be identified with it, but commit themselves to the value to pursue it, seek it out, and to want it, finally to the point of conviction.

4. The fourth level of the affective domain is the *organization* of values into a system of beliefs, determining interrelationships among them, and establishing a hierarchy of values within the system.

5. Finally, individuals become characterized by and understand themselves in terms of their *value system*. Individuals act consistently in accordance with the values they have internalized and integrate beliefs, ideas, and attitudes into a total philosophy or world view. It is at this level that problem solving, for example, is approached on the basis of a total, self-consistent system.

Bloom's taxonomy was devised for educational purposes, but it has been widely used for a general understanding of the affective domain in human behavior. The fundamental notions of receiving, responding, and valuing are universal. In second language acquisition the learner needs to be receptive both to those with whom he or she is communicating and to the language itself, responsive to persons and to the context of communication, and to place a certain value on the communicative act of interpersonal exchange.

Lest you feel at this point that the affective domain as described by Bloom is just a bit too far removed from the essence of language, it is appropriate to recall that language is inextricably bound up in virtually every aspect of human behavior. Language is so pervasive a phenomenon in our humanity that it cannot be separated from the larger whole—from the whole persons that live and breathe and think and feel. Kenneth Pike (1967, p. 26) said that

> language is behavior, that is, a phase of human activity which must not be treated in essence as structurally divorced from the structure of nonverbal human activity. The activity of man constitutes a structural whole in such a way that it cannot be subdivided into neat "parts" or "levels" or "compartments" with language in a behavioral compartment insulated in character, content, and organization from other behavior.

Understanding how human beings feel and respond and believe and value is an exceedingly important aspect of a theory of second language acquisition.

We turn now to a consideration of specific personality factors in human behavior and how they relate to second language acquisition.

SELF-ESTEEM

Self-esteem is probably the most pervasive aspect of any human behavior. It could easily be claimed that no successful cognitive or affective activity can be carried out without some degree of self-esteem, self-confidence, knowl-

edge of yourself, and belief in your own capabilities for that activity. Malinowski (1923) noted that all human beings have a need for *phatic communion*—
defining oneself and finding acceptance in expressing that self in relation to
valued others. Personality development universally involves the growth of a
person's concept of self, acceptance of self, and reflection of self as seen in
the interaction between self and others.

The following is a well-accepted definition of *self-esteem* (Coopersmith,
1967, pp. 4–5):

> By self-esteem, we refer to the evaluation which the individual makes and
> customarily maintains with regard to himself; it expresses an attitude of ap-
> proval or disapproval, and indicates the extent to which an individual
> believes himself to be capable, significant, successful and worthy. In short,
> self-esteem is a personal judgement of worthiness that is expressed in the
> attitudes that the individual holds towards himself. It is a subjective experi-
> ence which the individual conveys to others by verbal reports and other overt
> expressive behavior.

People derive their sense of self-esteem from the accumulation of experiences
with themselves and with others and from assessments of the external world
around them. General, or *global*, self-esteem is thought to be relatively stable
in a mature adult, and is resistant to change except by active and extended
therapy. But since no personality or cognitive trait is predictably stable for all
situations and at all times, self-esteem has been categorized into three levels,
only the first of which is global self-esteem. *Situational* or *specific* self-esteem
is a second level of self-esteem, referring to one's appraisals of oneself in
certain life situations, such as social interaction, work, education, home, or
on certain relatively discretely defined traits—intelligence, communicative
ability, athletic ability, or personality traits like gregariousness, empathy, and
flexibility. The degree of specific self-esteem a person has may vary depending upon the situation or the trait in question. The third level, *task* self-
esteem, relates to particular tasks within specific situations. For example,
within the educational domain task self-esteem might refer to particular
subject-matter areas. In an athletic context, skill in a particular sport—or even
a facet of a sport such as net play in tennis or pitching in baseball—would be
evaluated on the level of task self-esteem. Specific self-esteem might refer to
second language acquisition in general, and task self-esteem might appropriately refer to one's self-evaluation of a particular aspect of the process: speaking, writing, a particular class in a second language, or even a special kind of
classroom exercise.

Adelaide Heyde (1979) studied the effects of the three levels of self-
esteem on performance of an oral production task by American college students learning French as a foreign language. She found that all three levels
of self-esteem correlated positively with performance on the oral production
measure, with the highest correlation occurring between task self-esteem and

performance on oral production measures. Brodkey and Shore (1976) and Gardner and Lambert (1972) both included measures of self-esteem in their studies of success in language learning. While no conclusive statistical evidence emerged from these studies, the results of both revealed that self-esteem appears to be an important variable in second language acquisition, particularly in view of cross-cultural factors of second language learning.

What we do not know at this time is the answer to the classic chicken-or-egg question: does high self-esteem cause language success or does language success cause high self-esteem? Clearly, both are interacting factors. It is difficult to say whether teachers should try to ''improve'' global self-esteem or simply improve a learner's proficiency and let self-esteem take care of itself. Heyde (1979) found that certain sections of a beginning college French course had better oral production and self-esteem scores than other sections after only 8 weeks of instruction. This finding suggests that teachers really can have a positive and influential effect on both the linguistic performance and the emotional well-being of the student. Perhaps those ''good'' teachers succeeded because they gave optimal attention to linguistic goals and to the personhood of their students.

INHIBITION

Closely related to and in some cases subsumed under the notion of self-esteem is the concept of inhibition. All human beings, in their understanding of themselves, build sets of defenses to protect the ego. The newborn baby has no concept of its own self; gradually it learns to identify a self that is distinct from others. Then in childhood, the growing degrees of awareness, responding, and valuing begin to create a system of affective traits which individuals identify with themselves. In adolescence, the physical, emotional, and cognitive changes of the preteenager and teenager bring on mounting defensive inhibitions to protect a fragile ego, to ward off ideas, experiences, and feelings that threaten to dismantle the organization of values and beliefs on which appraisals of self-esteem have been founded. The process of building defenses continues on into adulthood. Some persons—those with higher self-esteem and ego strength—are more able to withstand threats to their existence and thus their defenses are lower. Those with weaker self-esteem maintain walls of inhibition to protect what is self-perceived to be a weak or fragile ego, or a lack of self-confidence in a situation or task.

The human ego encompasses what Guiora has called the *language ego* to refer to the very personal, egoistic nature of second language acquisition. Meaningful language acquisition involves some degree of identity conflict as language learners take on a new identity with their newly acquired competence. An adaptive language ego enables learners to lower the inhibitions that may impede success. Guiora, Beit-Hallami, Brannon, Dull, and Scovel (1972) produced one of the few studies on inhibition in relation to second language learning. Claiming that the notion of ego boundaries is relevant to language learning, Guiora designed an experiment using small quantities of alcohol to induce temporary states of less than normal inhibition in an experimental group of subjects. The performance on a pronunciation test in Thai of subjects given the alcohol was significantly better than the performance of a control group. Guiora concluded that a direct relationship existed between inhibition (a component of language ego) and pronunciation ability in a second language. But there were some serious problems in his conclusion. Alcohol may lower inhibitions, but alcohol also tends to affect muscular tension, and while "mind" and "body" in this instance may not be clearly separable, the physical effect of the alcohol may have been a more important factor than the mental effect in accounting for the superior pronunciation performance of the subjects given alcohol. Furthermore, pronunciation may be a rather poor indicator of overall language competence. Nevertheless, Guiora provided an important hypothesis which has tremendous intuitive—if not experimental—support.

In another experiment (Guiora, Acton, Erard, & Strickland, 1980), Guiora and his associates studied the effect of Valium on pronunciation of a second language. Inspired by a study (Schumann, Holroyd, Campbell, & Ward, 1978) that showed that hypnotized subjects performed well on pronunciation tests, Guiora and colleagues hypothesized that various amounts of a chemical relaxant would have a similar effect on subjects' pronunciation performance. Unfortunately, the results were nonsignificant, but interestingly enough the tester made a significant difference. In other words, the person doing the testing made a bigger difference on scores than did the dosage of Valium. I wonder if this result says something about the importance of teachers!

Some have facetiously suggested that the moral to Guiora's experiments is that we should provide cocktails—or prescribe tranquilizers—for foreign language classes! While students might take delight in such a proposal, the experiments have highlighted a most interesting possibility: that the inhibitions, the defenses, which we place between ourselves and others can prevent us from communicating in a foreign language. Since Guiora's experiments were conducted, a number of giant steps have been taken in foreign language teaching methodology to create methods that reduce these defenses. Language teaching methods in the last quarter of this century have been characterized by the creation of contexts for meaningful classroom communication such that the interpersonal ego barriers are lowered to pave the way for free, unfettered communication.

Anyone who has learned a foreign language is acutely aware that second language learning actually necessitates the making of mistakes. We test out hypotheses about language by trial and many errors; children learning their first language and adults learning a second can really only make progress by learning from making mistakes. If we never ventured to speak a sentence until we were absolutely certain of its total correctness, we would likely never communicate productively at all. But mistakes can be viewed as threats to one's ego. They pose both internal and external threats. Internally, one's critical self and one's performing self can be in conflict: the learner performs something "wrong" and becomes critical of his or her own mistake. Externally, the learner perceives others exercising their critical selves, even judging his very person when he or she blunders in a second language. Earl Stevick (1976b) spoke of language learning as involving a number of forms of *alienation*, alienation between the critical me and the performing me, between my native culture and my target culture, between me and my teacher, and between me and my fellow students. This alienation arises from the defenses that we build around ourselves. These defenses do not facilitate learning; rather they inhibit learning, and their removal therefore can promote language learning, which involves self-exposure to a degree manifested in few other endeavors.

RISK-TAKING

One of the prominent characteristics of good language learners, according to Rubin (1975), was a willingness to "guess." Impulsivity was also described as a style which could have positive effects on language success. And we have just seen that inhibitions, or building defenses around our egos, can be a detriment. These factors suggest that risk-taking is an important characteristic of successful learning of a second language. Learners have to be able to "gamble" a bit, to be willing to try out hunches about the language and take the risk of being wrong.

Beebe (1983, p. 40) says risk-taking is important in both classroom and natural settings:

> In the classroom, these ramifications might include a bad grade in the course, a fail on the exam, a reproach from the teacher, a smirk from a classmate, punishment or embarrassment imposed by oneself. Outside the classroom, individuals learning a second language face other negative consequences if they make mistakes. They fear looking ridiculous; they fear the frustration coming from a listener's blank look, showing that they have failed to communicate; they fear the danger of not being able to take care of themselves; they fear the alienation of not being able to communicate and thereby get close to other human beings. Perhaps worst of all, they fear a loss of identity.

On a continuum ranging from high to low risk-taking, we may be tempted to assume that high risk-taking will yield positive results in second language learning; however, such is not usually the case. Beebe (1983, p. 41) cited a study which claimed that "persons with a high motivation to achieve are . . . moderate, not high, risk-takers. These individuals like to be in control and like to depend on skill. They do not take wild, frivolous risks or enter into no-win situations." Successful second language learners appear to fit the same paradigm. A learner might be too bold in blurting out meaningless verbal garbage which no one can quite understand, while success lies in an optimum point where calculated guesses are ventured. As Rubin (1975) noted, the good language learner makes willing and *accurate* guesses.

Risk-taking variation seems to be a factor in a number of issues in second language acquisition and pedagogy. The silent student in the classroom is one who is unwilling to appear foolish when mistakes are made. Self-esteem seems to be closely connected to a risk-taking factor: when those foolish mistakes are made, a person with high global self-esteem is not daunted by the possible consequences of being laughed at. Beebe (1983) notes that fossilization, or the relatively permanent incorporation of certain patterns of error, may be due to a lack of willingness to take risks. It is "safe" to stay within patterns that accomplish the desired function even though there may be some errors in those patterns. The implications for teaching are important. In a few uncommon cases, overly high risk-takers, as they dominate the classroom with wild gambles, may need to be "tamed" a bit by the teacher. But most of the time our problem as a teacher will be to encourage students to guess somewhat more willingly than the usual student is prone to do, and to value them as persons for those risks that they take.

ANXIETY

Intricately intertwined with self-esteem and inhibition and risk-taking, the construct of anxiety, as it has been studied in the psychological domain, plays an important affective role in second language acquisition. Anxiety is almost impossible to define in a simple sentence. It is associated with feelings of uneasiness, self-doubt, apprehension, or worry. Scovel (1978, p. 134) defined anxiety "as a state of apprehension, a vague fear. . . ." We all know what anxiety is and we all have experienced feelings of anxiousness. How does this construct relate to second language learning? Any complex task we undertake can have elements of anxiety in it, aspects in which we doubt our own abilities and wonder if we will indeed succeed. Second language learning is no exception to a long list of complex tasks that are susceptible to our human anxieties.

The research on anxiety suggests that, like self-esteem, anxiety can be experienced at various levels. At the deepest, or global, level, *trait* anxiety is a more permanent predisposition to be anxious. Some people are predictably and generally anxious about many things. At a more momentary, or situational level, *state* anxiety is experienced in relation to some particular event or act. As we learned in the case of self-esteem, then, it is important in a classroom for a teacher to try to determine whether a student's anxiety stems from a more global trait or whether it comes from a particular situation at the moment.

A somewhat more relevant aspect of the research on anxiety lies in the distinction between *debilitative* and *facilitative* anxiety (Alpert & Haber, 1960, cited by Scovel, 1978). We may be inclined to view anxiety as a negative factor, something to be avoided at all costs. For example, we are all familiar with the feeling of "test anxiety" before a big examination (see Madsen, 1982, for a study of test anxiety in ESL tests). But the notion of facilitative anxiety is that some concern—some apprehension—over a task to be accomplished is a positive factor. Otherwise, a learner might be inclined to be "wishy-washy," lacking that facilitative tension that keeps one poised, alert, and just slightly unbalanced to the point that one cannot relax entirely. The feeling of nervousness before giving a public speech is, in experienced speakers, often a sign of facilitative anxiety, a symptom of just enough tension to get the job done.

In [K.] Bailey's (1983) study of competitiveness and anxiety in second language learning, facilitative anxiety was one of the keys to success, and closely related to competitiveness. Rogers' humanistic theory of learning promotes low anxiety among learners and a nondefensive posture where learners do not feel they are in competition with one another. Bailey found in her self-analysis, however, that while competitiveness sometimes hindered her progress (for example, the pressure to outdo her peers sometimes caused her to retreat even to the point of skipping class), at other times it motivated her to study harder (as in the case of carrying out an intensive review of material in order to feel more at ease in oral work in the classroom). She explained the positive effects of competitiveness by means of the construct of facilitative anxiety.

So the next time your language students are "anxious," you do well to ask yourself if that anxiety is truly debilitative. It could well be that a little nervous tension in the process is a good thing. Once again, we find that a construct has an optimal point along its continuum: Both too much and too little anxiety may hinder the process of successful second language learning.

EMPATHY

The human being is a social animal, and the chief mechanism for maintaining the bonds of society is language. Some highly sophisticated methods of language teaching have failed to accomplish the goal of communicativity in the learner by overlooking the social nature of language. While we tend to recognize the importance of the social aspect of language, we also tend to oversimplify that aspect by not recognizing the complexity of the relation between language and society, or by considering socially oriented problems in language learning as a simple matter of "acculturation." Acculturation is no simple process. The social *transactions* which the second language learner is called upon to make constitute complex endeavors.

Transaction is the process of reaching out beyond the self to others. The tools of language help to accomplish these feats. A variety of transactional variables comes to bear on second language learning: imitation, modeling, identification, empathy, extroversion, aggression, styles of communication, and others. Two of these variables, chosen for their relevance to a global understanding of second language acquisition, will be treated here: empathy and extroversion.

Empathy, like so many personality variables, defies adequate definition. In common terminology, empathy is the process of "putting yourself into someone else's shoes," of reaching beyond the self and understanding and feeling what another person is understanding or feeling. It is probably the major factor in the harmonious coexistence of individuals in society. Language is one of the primary means of empathizing, but nonverbal communication facilitates the process of empathizing and must not be overlooked.

In more sophisticated terms, empathy is usually described as the projection of one's own personality into the personality of another in order to understand him or her better. Empathy is not synonymous with *sympathy*. Empathy implies more possibility of detachment; sympathy connotes an agreement or harmony between individuals. Guiora, Brannon, and Dull (1972, p. 142) defined empathy as "a process of comprehending in which a temporary fusion of self-object boundaries permits an immediate emotional apprehension of the affective experience of another." The affective side of that definition could apply to the cognitive as well. Psychologists have found it difficult to define empathy. Hogan (1969, p. 309), one of the leading researchers in empathy, at one point defined empathy as "a relatively discrete social phenomenon recognizable in the experience of laymen and psychologists alike." The circularity of this definition is reminiscent of the zoologist's definition of a *dog* as a four-legged animal recognizable as a dog by other dogs! Despite the difficulty of defining the concept, there is general consensus on what empathy is. Psychologists generally agree with Guiora's definition above, and add that there are two necessary aspects to the development and exercising of empathy: first, an awareness and knowledge of one's own feelings, and second, identification with another person (Hogan, 1969). In other words, you cannot fully empathize—or know someone else—until you adequately know yourself.

Communication requires a sophisticated degree of empathy. In order to communicate effectively you need to be able to understand the other person's effective and cognitive states; communication breaks down when false presuppositions or assumptions are made about the other person's state. From the very mechanical, syntactic level of language to the most abstract, meaningful level, we assume certain structures of knowledge and certain emotional states in any communicative act. In order to make those assumptions correctly we need to transcend our own ego boundaries, or using Guiora's term, to "permeate" our ego boundaries so that we can send and receive messages clearly.

Oral communication is a case in which, cognitively at least, it is easier to achieve empathic communication since there is immediate feedback from the hearer. A misunderstood word, phrase, or idea can be questioned by the hearer, and then rephrased by the speaker until a clear message is interpreted. Written communication requires a special kind of empathy—a "cognitive" empathy in which the writer, without the benefit of immediate feedback from the reader, must communicate ideas by means of a very clear empathic intuition and judgment of the reader's state of mind and structure of knowledge.

So in a second language learning situation the problem of empathy becomes acute. Not only must learner-speakers correctly identify cognitive and affective sets in the hearer, but they must do so in a language in which they are insecure. Then, learner-hearers, attempting to comprehend a second language, often discover that their own states of thought are misinterpreted by a native speaker, and the result is that linguistic, cognitive, and affective information easily passes "in one ear and out the other."

Guiora, in the two studies with his colleagues (mentioned earlier), found that a modified version of the Micro-Momentary Expression (MME) test, a test claiming to measure degrees of empathy, successfully predicted authenticity of pronunciation of a foreign language. Naiman, Fröhlich, and Stern (1978) included an empathy measure (Hogan's Empathy Scale—see Hogan, 1969) in their battery of tests used to try to discover characteristics of the "good language learner," but found no significant correlation between empathy and language success as measured by an imitation test and a listening test. However, their finding was not unexpected since they found field independence to be positively correlated with language success; the presumed antithesis of field independence—field dependence—has been shown to correlate highly with empathy (Witkin, Oltman, Raskin, & Karp, 1971). But a great deal of the problem of the study of most personality variables lies in the accuracy of the tests used to measure traits. Serious methodological problems surround such measurement; the MME and Hogan's Empathy Scale are cases in point. It has been shown that such tests accurately identify personality *extremes* (schizophrenic, paranoid, or psychotic behavior, for example) but fail to differentiate among the vast "normal" population.

If indeed a high degree of empathy is predictive of success in language learning, it would be invaluable to discover how one could capitalize on that possibility in language teaching. It is one thing to claim to be able to predict success and quite another matter to cause success by fostering empathy in the language classroom. One would need to determine if empathy is something one can "learn" in the adult years, especially cross-culturally. If so, then it would not be unreasonable to incorporate empathy in language teaching methods. What kinds of drills and exercises could be devised which require a person to predict or guess another person's response? How worthwhile would it be to attempt to organize foreign language classes which operate on a high-empathy basis, as in Community Language Learning, in which principles of T-group therapy are used to aid the language learning process? These and other questions give rise to some creative issues in language teaching methodology.

Probably the most interesting implication of the study of empathy is the need to define empathy cross-culturally—to understand how different cultures express empathy. Most of the empathy tests devised in the United States are culture-bound to Western North American middle-class society.

EXTROVERSION

Extroversion, and its counterpart, introversion, are also potentially important factors in the acquisition of a second language. The terms are often misunderstood because of a tendency to stereotype extroversion. We are prone to think of an extroverted person as a gregarious, "life of the party" person. Introverted people, conversely, are thought of as quiet and reserved, with tendencies toward reclusiveness. Western society values the stereotypical extrovert. Nowhere is this more evident than in the classroom where teachers admire the talkative, outgoing student who participates freely in class discussions. On the other hand, introverts are sometimes thought of as not being as bright as extroverts.

Such a view of extroversion is misleading. Extroversion is the extent to which a person has a deep-seated need to receive ego enhancement, self-esteem, and a sense of wholeness *from other people* as opposed to receiving that affirmation within oneself. Extroverts actually need other people in order to feel "good." However, extroverts are not necessarily loudmouthed and talkative. They may be relatively shy, but still need the affirmation of others. Introversion, on the other hand, is the extent to which a person derives a sense of wholeness and fulfillment apart from a reflection of this self from other people. Contrary to our stereotypes, introverts can have an inner strength of character that extroverts do not have.

Unfortunately, these stereotypes have influenced teachers' perceptions of students. Ausubel (1968, p. 413) noted that introversion and extroversion are a "grossly misleading index of social adjustment," and other educators have warned against prejudging students on the basis of perceived extroversion. In language classes, where oral participation is highly valued, it is easy to view active participants with favor, and to assume that their visibility in the classroom is due to an extroversion factor (which may not be so). Culturally, American society differs considerably from a number of other societies where it is improper to speak out extensively in the classroom. Teachers need to consider cultural norms in their assessment of a student's presumed "passivity" in the classroom.

Extroversion is commonly thought to be related to empathy, but such may not be the case. The extroverted person may actually behave in an extroverted manner in order to protect his or her own ego, with extroverted behavior being symptomatic of defensive barriers and high ego boundaries. At the same time the introverted, quieter, more reserved person may show high empathy—an intuitive understanding and apprehension of others—and simply be more reserved in the outward and overt expression of empathy.

It is not clear then, that extroversion or introversion helps or hinders the process of second language acquisition. The Toronto study (Naiman, Fröhlich, & Stern, 1978) found no significant effect for extroversion in characterizing the good language learner. Busch (1982), in the most comprehensive study to date on extroversion, explored the relationship of introversion and extroversion to English proficiency in adult Japanese learners of English in Japan. She hypothesized that extroverted students (as measured by a standard personality inventory) would be more proficient than introverts. Her hypothesis was not supported. In fact, introverts were significantly *better* than extroverts in their pronunciation (one of four factors which were measured in an oral interview)! This latter result tends to blow apart our stereotype of the extroverted language learner who is presumably a frequent and willing participant in class activities. Busch's study, however, is just one study, and it was done in one culture with one group of learners. Much more research is needed before we can draw conclusions.

Even in the light of an appropriate definition of extroversion, it is nevertheless conceivable that extroversion may be a factor in the development of general oral communicative competence, which requires face to face interaction, but not in listening, reading, and writing. It is also readily apparent that cross-cultural norms of nonverbal and verbal interaction vary widely, and what in one culture (say, the United States) may appear as introversion is in another culture (say, Japan), respect and politeness. Nevertheless, on a practical level, the facilitating or interfering effects of certain methods which invoke extroversion need to be carefully considered. How effective are methods that incorporate drama, pantomime, humor, role plays, and overt personality exposure? A teacher needs to beware of trying to "create" in a student more so-called extroversion than is really necessary. We need to be sensitive to cultural norms, to a student's willingness to speak out in class, and to optimal points between extreme extroversion and introversion that may vary from student to student.

MOTIVATION

Motivation is probably the most often used catch-all term for explaining the success or failure of virtually any complex task. It is easy to figure that success in a task is due simply to the fact that someone is "motivated." It is easy in second language learning to claim that a learner will be successful with the proper motivation. Such claims are of course not erroneous, for countless studies and experiments in human learning have shown that motivation is a key to learning. But these claims gloss over a detailed understanding of exactly what motivation is and what the subcomponents of motivation are. What does it mean to say that someone is motivated? How do you create, foster, and maintain motivation?

Motivation is commonly thought of as an inner drive, impulse, emotion, or desire that moves one to a particular action. More specifically, human beings universally have needs or drives that are more or less innate, yet their intensity is environmentally conditioned. Six desires or needs of human organisms are commonly identified (see Ausubel, 1968, pp. 368–379) which undergird the construct of motivation: (1) the need for *exploration*, for seeing "the other side of the mountain," for probing the unknown; (2) the need for *manipulation*, for operating—to use Skinner's term—on the environment and causing change; (3) the need for *activity*, for movement and exercise, both physical and mental; (4) the need for *stimulation*, the need to be stimulated by the environment, by other people, or by ideas, thoughts, and feelings; (5) the need for *knowledge*, the need to process and internalize the results of exploration, manipulation, activity, and stimulation, to resolve contradictions, to quest for solutions to problems and for self-consistent systems of knowledge; (6) finally, the need for *ego enhancement*, for the self to be known and to be accepted and approved of by others.

There are other possible factors that could be listed in accounting for motivation. Maslow (1970) listed hierarchical human needs, from fundamental physical necessities (air, water, food) to higher needs of security, identity, and self-esteem, the fulfillment of which leads to *self-actualization*. Other psychologists have noted further basic needs: achievement, autonomy, affiliation, order, change, endurance, aggression, and other needs. The six needs listed above appear to capture the essence of most general categories of needs, and are especially relevant to second language acquisition.

Examples abound to illustrate the sixfold concept of motivation. Consider children who are "motivated" to learn to read. They are motivated because certain needs are important to them, perhaps all six of the needs mentioned above, particularly exploration, stimulation, and knowledge. Children who are not motivated to read see no way in which reading meets the needs they have. The adult who learns to ski and learns to do so well no doubt is motivated by a need for exploration and stimulation and activity and maybe even ego enhancement. The foreign langauge learner who is either intrinsically or extrinsically meeting needs in learning the language will be positively motivated to learn.

Motivation, then, is an inner drive or stimulus which can, like self-esteem, be global, situational, or task-oriented. Learning a foreign language clearly requires some of all three levels of motivation. For example, a learner may possess high "global" motivation but low "task" motivation to perform well on, say, the written mode of the language. It is easy to see how virtually any aspect of second language learning can be related to motivation. Nelson and Jakobovits (1970), in a lengthy report on motivation in foreign language learning, cited just about every possible factor as relevant to the role of motivation in second language learning. A number of instructional, individual, and sociocultural factors were considered which could enhance or deter motivation. Among learner factors, for example, were included intelligence, aptitude, perseverance, learning strategies, interference, and self-evaluation! It is not difficult to see how all of those factors could contribute either positively or negatively to motivation. But it is fruitless merely to list a host of variables which can be subsumed under motivation without examining the relationship of each variable to the basic needs underlying motivation. Why, for example, do learners persevere in their task? Or how can the less intelligent person appeal to his or her inner needs and enhance motivation? How can a teacher provide extrinsic motivation where intrinsic motivation is lacking? Answers to these questions necessitate probing the fundamental nature of human psychology, but such probing will ultimately lead to a deeper and richer understanding of both motivation and the second language learning process in general.

Motivation, seen as the fulfillment of needs, is closely connected to behavioristic reinforcement theory. Inasmuch as certain needs are being satisfactorily met in a person, reinforcement occurs. If learning to speak a foreign language enhances one's ego, for example, the ego enhancement is in itself an internal reinforcer of the desired behavior.

INSTRUMENTAL AND INTEGRATIVE MOTIVATION

One of the best-known studies of motivation in second language learning was carried out by Robert Gardner and Wallace Lambert (1972). Over a period of 12 years they extensively studied foreign language learners in Canada, several parts of the United States, and the Philippines in an effort to determine how attitudinal and motivational factors affect language learning success.

Motivation was examined as a factor of a number of different kinds of attitudes. Two different clusters of attitudes divided two basic types of motivation: instrumental and integrative motivation. *Instrumental* motivation refers to motivation to acquire a language as means for attaining instrumental goals: furthering a career, reading technical materials, translation, and so forth. An *integrative* motive is employed when learners wish to integrate themselves within the culture of the second language group, to identify themselves with and become a part of that society. Many of Lambert's studies (see Lambert, 1972) and one study by Spolsky (1969) found that integrative motivation generally accompanied higher scores on proficiency tests in a foreign language. The conclusion from these studies was that integrative motivation may indeed be an important requirement for successful language learning. And some teachers and researchers have even gone so far as to claim that integrative motivation is absolutely essential for successful second language learning.

Soon evidence began to accumulate which challenged such a claim. Yasmeen Lukmani (1972) demonstrated that among Marathi-speaking Indian students learning English in India, those with higher *instrumental* motivation scored higher in tests of English proficiency. Braj Kachru (1977) noted that Indian English is but one example of a variety of English*es*, which, especially in Third World countries where English has become an international language, can be acquired very successfully for instrumental reasons alone.

The more recent findings are not necessarily contradictory to Lambert's. They point out once again that there is no single means of learning a second language: some learners in some contexts are more successful in learning a language if they are integratively oriented, and others in different contexts benefit from an instrumental orientation. The findings also suggest that the two types of motivation are not necessarily mutually exclusive. Second language learning is rarely motivated by attitudes that are exclusively instrumental or exclusively integrative. Most situations involve a mixture of each type of motivation. Arabic speakers learning English in the United States for academic purposes may be relatively balanced in their desire to learn English both for academic (instrumental) purposes and to understand and become somewhat integrated with the culture and people of the United States. Macnamara (1973, p. 64) noted that the dichotomy is not as important as searching "for the really important part of motivation in the act of communication itself, in the student's effort to make his own meaning clear."

The instrumental/integrative construct does, however, help to put some of the recent interest in affective variables into some perspective. It is easy to conclude that second language learning is an emotional activity involving countless affective variables, or to assert that learning a second language involves taking on a new identity. But the findings of studies like those of Lukmani and Kachru warn us that while perhaps some contexts of foreign language learning involve an identity crisis, there are a good many legitimate language learning contexts in which that identity crisis may be minimized, or at least seen as less of a personal affective crisis and more of a cognitive crisis. Do children in French-speaking Africa, who must learn French in order to succeed in educational settings, and who are quite instrumentally motivated to do so, meet with an identity crisis? Must they take on a "French" identity? It is possible that they do not, just as children learning English in India tend to learn *Indian* English as an integral part of their own culture. In some cases, then, the foreign language does not carry with it the heavy cultural loading that some have assumed to be characteristic of all language learning contexts.

In an expansion of the construct of integrative motivation, [C. R.] Graham (1984) claims that integrative motivation has been too broadly defined in previous research. He makes a distinction between integrative and *assimilative* motivation. Integrative motivation is the desire on the part of a language learner to learn the second language in order to communicate with, or find out about, members of the second language culture, and does not necessarily imply direct contact with the second language group. Assimilative motivation is the drive to become an indistinguishable member of a speech community, and it usually requires prolonged contact with the second language culture. Assimilative motivation is characteristic of persons who, perhaps at a very young age, learn a second language and second culture in order to identify almost exclusively with that second culture. Seen in this light, integrative motivation takes on less of a pervading affective character and becomes more of a simple contrast to instrumental motivation. One can be integratively oriented without desiring to "lose oneself" in the target culture.

Yet another dimension of the integrative/instrumental dichotomy is brought to light by looking at *intrinsic* and *extrinsic* differences in motivation. These differences are a factor of the source of motivation. Does the motivation generally stem from within oneself or from other people? Kathleen Bailey (1986) illustrated this dichotomy with the following table:

	Intrinsic	Extrinsic
Integrative	L2 learner wishes to integrate with the L2 culture (e.g., for immigration or marriage)	Someone else wishes the L2 learner to know the L2 for integrative reasons (e.g., Japanese parents send kids to Japanese-language school)
Instrumental	L2 learner wishes to achieve goals utilizing L2 (e.g., for a career)	External power wants L2 learner to learn L2 (e.g., corporation sends Japanese businessman to U.S. for language training)

Teachers, therefore, may need to discern the source of a student's motivation in order to meet particular, possibly specialized, needs.

IN THE CLASSROOM:
COMMUNITY LANGUAGE LEARNING

The age of audiolingualism, with its emphasis on surface forms and on the rote practice of scientifically produced patterns, began to wane when the Chomskyan revolution in linguistics turned linguists and language teachers toward the "deep structure" of language and when psychologists began to recognize the fundamentally affective and interpersonal nature of all learning. The decade of the 1970s was a chaotic but exceedingly fruitful era during which second language research not only came into its own, but also began to inspire innovative methods for language teaching. As we increasingly recognized the importance of the affective domain, some of these innovative methods took on a distinctly affective nature. Community Language Learning became the classic example of an affectively based method.

In his "Counseling-Learning" model of education Charles Curran (1972) was inspired by Carl Rogers' view of education in which learners in a classroom are regarded as a "group" rather than a "class"—a group in need of certain therapy and counseling. The social dynamics of such a group are of primary importance. In order for any learning to take place, as has already been noted in Carl Rogers' model, what is first needed is for the members to interact in an interpersonal relationship in which students and teacher join together to facilitate learning in a context of valuing and prizing each individual in the group. In such a surrounding each person lowers the defenses that prevent open interpersonal communication. The anxiety caused by the educational context is lessened by means of the supportive community. The teacher's presence is not perceived as a threat, nor is it the teacher's purpose to impose limits and boundaries, but rather, as a true counselor, to center his or her attention on the clients (the students) and their needs. "Defensive" learning is made unnecessary by the empathic relationship between teacher and students. Curran's Counseling-Learning model of eduation thus capitalizes on the primacy of the needs of the learners—clients—who have gathered together in the educational community to be counseled.

Curran's Counseling-Learning model of education has been extended to language learning contexts in the form of Community Language Learning (CLL). While particular adaptations of CLL are numerous, the basic methodology is explicit. The group of clients (learners), having first established in their native language an interpersonal relationship and trust, are seated in a circle with the counselor (teacher) on the outside of the circle. The clients may be complete beginners in the foreign language. When one of the clients wishes to say something to the group or to an individual, he says it in his native language (say, English) and the counselor translates the utterance back to the learner in the second language (say, Japanese). The learner then repeats that Japanese sentence as accurately as she can. Another client responds, in English; the utterance is translated by the counselor; the client repeats it;

and the conversation continues. If possible the conversation is taped for later listening, and at the end of each session the learners inductively attempt together to glean information about the new language. If desirable, the counselor may take a more directive role and provide some explanation of certain linguistic rules or items.

The first stage of intense struggle and confusion may continue for many sessions, but always with the support of the counselor and of the fellow clients. Gradually the learner becomes able to speak a word or phrase directly in the foreign language, without translation. This is the first sign of the learner's moving away from complete dependence upon the counselor. As the learners gain more and more familiarity with the foreign language, more and more direct communication can take place with the counselor providing less and less direct translation and information, until after many sessions, perhaps many months or years later, the learner achieves fluency in the spoken language. The learner has at that point become independent. CLL reflects not only the principles of Carl Rogers' view of education but also basic principles of the dynamics of counseling, in which the counselor, through careful attention to the client's needs, aids the client in moving from dependence and helplessness to independence and self-assurance.

There are advantages and disadvantages to a method like CLL. The affective advantages are evident. CLL is an attempt to put Carl Rogers' philosophy into action and to overcome some of the threatening affective factors in second language learning. The threat of the all-knowing teacher, of making blunders in the foreign language in front of classmates, of competing against peers—all threats which can lead to a feeling of alienation and inadequacy—are presumably removed. The counselor allows the learner to determine the type of conversation and to analyze the foreign language inductively. It is interesting to note that the teacher can also become a client at times: in situations with which explanation or translation seems to be impossible, it is often the client-learner who steps in and becomes a counselor to aid the teacher. The student-centered nature of the method can provide extrinsic motivation and capitalize on intrinsic motivation.

But there are some practical and theoretical problems with CLL. The counselor-teacher can become *too* nondirective. The student often needs direction, especially in the first stage, in which there is such seemingly endless struggle within the foreign language. Supportive but assertive direction from the counselor could strengthen the method. Another problem with CLL is its reliance upon an inductive strategy of learning. Deductive learning is both a viable and efficient strategy of learning. Adults particularly can benefit from deduction as well as induction. While some intense inductive struggle is a necessary component of second language learning, the initial grueling days and weeks of floundering in ignorance in CLL could be alleviated by more directed, deductive, learning ''by being told.'' Perhaps only in the second or third stage, when the learner has moved to more independence, is an inductive strategy really successful. Finally, the success of CLL depends largely on the translation expertise of the counselor. Translation is an intricate and complex process that is often "easier said than done"; if subtle aspects of language are mistranslated, there could be a less than effective understanding of the target language.

Despite its weaknesses CLL is a potentially useful method for the foreign language classroom as long as teachers are willing to adapt it to their own curricular constraints. That adaptation requires a relaxing of certain aspects of the method. For example, you might avoid the initial, complete dependence stage by using CLL in an intermediate language class. Or you might provide more directiveness than CLL advocates. As is the case with virtually any method, if you have solid theoretical foundations—a broad, cautiously enlightened, eclectic view—you can derive valuable insights from diverse points of view and apply them creatively to your own situation.

RELATED READING 8

DISCRETE POINT, INTEGRATIVE, OR PRAGMATIC TESTS

John Oller, Jr.

DISCRETE POINT VERSUS INTEGRATIVE TESTING

In recent years, a body of literature on language testing has developed which distinguishes two major categories of tests. John Carroll (1961) was the person credited with first proposing the distinction between *discrete point* and *integrative* language tests. Although the types are not always different for practical purposes, the theoretical bases of the two approaches contrast markedly and the predictions concerning the effects and relative validity of different testing procedures also differ in fundamental ways, depending on which of the two approaches one selects. The contrast between these two philosophies, of course, is not limited to language testing *per se*, but can be seen throughout the whole spectrum of educational endeavor.

Traditionally, a *discrete point* test is one that attempts to focus attention on one point of grammar at a time. Each test item is aimed at one and only one element of a particular component of a grammar (or perhaps we should say hypothesized grammar), such as phonology, syntax, or vocabulary. Moreover, a discrete point test purports to assess only one skill at a time (e.g.,

From John Oller, Jr., *Language Tests at School* (London: Longman Group Ltd., 1979), pp. 36–50.

listening, or speaking, or reading, or writing) and only one aspect of a skill (e.g., productive versus receptive or oral versus visual). Within each skill, aspect, and component, discrete items supposedly focus on precisely one and only one phoneme, morpheme, lexical item, grammatical rule, or whatever the appropriate element may be (Lado, 1961). For instance, a phonological discrete item might require an examinee to distinguish between minimal pairs, e.g., *pill* versus *peel,* auditorily presented. An example of a morphological item might be one which requires the selection of an appropriate suffix such as *-ness* or *-ity* to form a noun from an adjective like *secure,* or *sure.* An example of a syntactic item might be a fill-in-the-blank type where the examinee must supply the suffix *-s* as in *He walk— to town each morning now that he lives in the city.*

The concept of an *integrative* test was born in contrast with the definition of a discrete point test. If discrete items take language skill apart, integrative tests put it back together. Whereas discrete items attempt to test knowledge of language one bit at a time, integrative tests attempt to assess a learner's capacity to use many bits all at the same time, and possibly while exercising several presumed components of a grammatical system, and perhaps more than one of the traditionally recognized skills or aspects of skills.

However, to base a definition of integrative language testing on what would appear to be its logical antithesis and in fact its competing predecessor is to assume a fairly limiting point of view. It is possible to look to other sources for a theoretical basis and rationale for so-called integrative tests.

A DEFINITION OF PRAGMATIC TESTS

The term *pragmatic test* has sometimes been used interchangeably with the term *integrative test* in order to call attention to the possibility of relating integrative language testing procedures to a theory of pragmatics, or pragmatic expectancy grammar. Whereas integrative testing has been somewhat loosely defined in terms of what discrete point testing is not, it is possible to be somewhat more precise in saying what a pragmatic test is: it is any procedure or task that causes the learner to process sequences of elements in a language that conform to the normal contextual constraints of that language, and which requires the learner to relate sequences of linguistic elements via pragmatic mappings to extralinguistic context.

Integrative tests are often pragmatic in this sense, and pragmatic tests are always integrative. There is no ordinary discourse situation in which a learner might be asked to listen to and distinguish between isolated minimal pairs of phonological contrasts. There is no normal language use context in which one's attention would be focussed on the syntactic rules involved in placing appropriate suffixes on verb stems or in moving the agent of an active declarative sentence from the front of the sentence to the end in order to form a passive (e.g., *The dog bit John* in the active form becoming *John was bitten by the dog* in the passive). Thus, *discrete point tests cannot be pragmatic, and conversely, pragmatic tests cannot be discrete point tests.* Therefore, pragmatic tests must be integrative.

But integrative language tasks can be conceived which do not meet one or both of the naturalness criteria which we have imposed in our definition of pragmatic tests. If a test merely requires an examinee to use more than one of the four traditionally recognized skills and/or one or more of the traditionally recognized components of grammar, it must be considered integrative. But to qualify as a pragmatic test, more is required.

In order for a test user to say something meaningful (valid) about the efficiency of a learner's developing grammatical system, the pragmatic naturalness criteria require that the test invoke and challenge that developing grammatical system. This requires processing sequences of elements in the target language (even if it is the learner's first and only language) subject to temporal contextual constraints. In addition, the tasks must be such that for examinees to do them, linguistic sequences must be related to extralinguistic contexts in meaningful ways.

Examples of tasks that do not qualify as pragmatic tests include all discrete points tests, the rote recital of sequences of material without attention to meaning; the manipulation of sequences of verbal elements, possibly in complex ways, but in ways that do not require awareness of meaning. In brief, if the task does not require attention to meaning in temporally constrained sequences of linguistic elements, it cannot be construed as a pragmatic language test. Moreover, the constraints must be of the type that are found in normal uses of the language, not merely in some classroom setting that may have been contrived according to some theory of how languages should be taught. Ultimately, the question of whether or not a task is pragmatic is an empirical one. It cannot be decided by theory based preferences, or opinion polls.

DICTATION AND CLOZE PROCEDURE AS EXAMPLES OF PRAGMATIC TESTS

The traditional dictation, rooted in the distant past of language teaching, is an interesting example of a pragmatic language testing procedure. If the sequences of words or phrases to be dictated are selected from normal prose, or dialogue, or some other natural form of discourse (or perhaps if the sequences are carefully contrived to mirror normal discourse, as in well-written fiction) and if the material is presented orally in sequences that are long enough to challenge the short-term memory of the learners, a simple traditional dictation meets the naturalness requirements for pragmatic language tests. First, such a task requires the processing of temporally constrained sequences of material in the language and second, the task of dividing up the stream of speech and writing down what is heard requires understanding the meaning of the material—i.e., relating the linguistic context (which in a sense is given) to the extralinguistic context (which must be inferred). . . .

Another example of a pragmatic language testing procedure is the cloze technique. The best known variety of this technique is the sort of test that is constructed by deleting every fifth, sixth, or seventh word from a passage of prose. Typically each deleted word is replaced by a blank of standard length, and the task set the examinee is to fill in the blanks by restoring the missing words. Other varieties of the procedure involve deleting specific vocabulary items, parts of speech, affixes, or particular types of grammatical markers.

The word *cloze* was invented by Wilson Taylor (1953) to call attention to the fact that when an examinee fills in the gaps in a passage of prose, he is doing something similar to what Gestalt psychologists call 'closure', a process related to the perception of incomplete geometric figures, for example. Taylor considered words deleted from prose to present a special kind of closure problem. From what is known of the grammatical knowledge the examinee brings to bear in solving such a closure problem, we can appreciate the fact that the problem is a very special sort of closure.

Like dictation, cloze tests meet both of the naturalness criteria for pragmatic language tests. In order to give correct responses (whether the standard of correctness is the exact word that originally appeared at a particular point, or any other word that fully fits the context of the passage), the learner must operate _____ the basis of, both immediate and long-range _____ constraints. Whereas some of the blanks in a cloze test (say of the standard variety deleting every *n*th word) can be filled by attending only to a few words on either side of the blank, as in the first blank in the preceding sentence, other blanks in a typical cloze passage require attention to longer stretches of linguistic context. They often require inferences about extralinguistic context, as in the case of the second blank in the preceding sentence.

The word *on* seems to be required in the first blank by the words *operate* and *the basis of*, without any additional information. However, unless long range constraints are taken into account, the second blank offers many possibilities. If the examinee attended only to such constraints as are afforded by the words from *operate* onward, it could be filled by such words as *missile*, *legal*, or *leadership*. The intended word was *contextual*. Other alternatives which might have occurred to the reader, and which are in the general semantic target area might include *temporal*, *verbal*, *extralinguistic*, *grammatical*, *pragmatic*, *linguistic*, *psycholinguistic*, *sociolinguistic*, *psychological*, *semantic*, and so on.

In taking a cloze test, the examinee must utilize information that is inferred about the facts, events, ideas, relationships, states of affairs, social settings and the like that are pragmatically mapped by the linguistic sequences contained in the passage. Examples of cases where extralinguistic context and the linguistic context of the passage are interrelated are obvious in so-called deictic words such as *here* and *now, then* and *there, this* and *that*, pronouns that refer to persons or things, tense indicators, aspect markers on verbs, adverbs of time and place, determiners and demonstratives in general, and a host of others.

For a simple example, consider the sentence, *A horse was fast when he was tied to a hitching post, and the same animal was also fast when he won a horse-race.* If such a sentence were part of a larger context, say on the difficulties of the English language, and if we deleted the first *a*, the blank could scarcely be filled with the definite article *the* because no horse has been mentioned up to that point. On the other hand, if we deleted the *the* before the words *same animal*, the indefinite article could not be used because of the fact that the horse referred to by the phrase *A horse* at the beginning of the sentence is the same horse referred to by the phrase *the same animal*. This is an example of a pragmatic constraint. Consider the oddity of saying, *The horse was fast when he was tied to a hitching post, and a same animal was also fast when he won a horse-race.*

Even though the pragmatic mapping constraints involved in normal discourse are only partially understood by the theoreticians, and though they cannot be precisely characterized in terms of grammatical systems (at least not yet), the fact that they exist is well-known, and the fact that they can be tested by such pragmatic procedures and the cloze technique has been demonstrated.

All sorts of deletions of so-called content words (e.g., nouns, adjectives, verbs, and adverbs), and especially grammatical connectors such as subordinating conjunctions, negatives, and a great many others carry with them constraints that may range backward or forward across several sentences or more. Such linguistic elements may entail restrictions that influence items that are widely separated in the passage. This places a strain on short-term memory which presses the learner's pragmatic expectancy grammar into operation. The accuracy with which the learner is able to supply correct responses can therefore be taken as an index of the efficiency of the learner's developing grammatical system.

OTHER EXAMPLES OF PRAGMATIC TESTS

Pragmatic testing procedures are potentially innumerable. The techniques discussed so far, dictation, cloze, and variations of them, by no means exhaust the possibilities. Probably they do not even begin to indicate the range of reasonable possibilities to be explored. There is always a danger that minor empirical advances in educational research in particular, may lead to excessive dependence on procedures that are associated with the progress. However, in spite of the fact that some of the pragmatic procedures thus far investigated do appear to work substantially better than their discrete point predecessors, there is little doubt that pragmatic tests can also be refined and expanded. It is important that the procedures which now exist and which have been studied should not limit our vision concerning other possibilities. Rather, they should serve as guideposts for subsequent refinement and development of still more effective and more informative testing procedures.

Therefore, the point of this section is not to provide a comprehensive list of possible pragmatic testing procedures, but rather to illustrate some of the possible types of procedures that meet the naturalness criteria concerning the temporal constraints on language in use, and the pragmatic mapping of linguistic contexts onto extralinguistic ones.

COMBINED CLOZE AND DICTATION. The examinee reads material from which certain portions have been deleted and simultaneously (or subsequently) hears the same material without deletions either live or on tape. The examinee's task is to fill in the missing portions the same as in the usual cloze procedure, but he has the added support of the auditory signal to help him fill in the missing portions. Many variations on this procedure are possible. Single words, or even parts of words, or sequences of words, or even whole sentences or longer segments may be deleted. The less material one deletes, presumably, the more the task resembles the standard cloze procedure, and the more one deletes, the more the task looks like a standard dictation.

ORAL CLOZE PROCEDURE. Instead of presenting a cloze passage in a written format, it is possible to use a carefully prepared tape recording of the material with numbers read in for the blanks, or with pauses where blanks occur. Or, it is possible merely to read the material up to the blank, give the examinee the opportunity to guess the missing word, record the response, and at that point either tell the examinee the right answer (i.e., the missing word), or simply go on without any feedback as to the correctness of the examinee's response. Another procedure is to arrange the deletions so that they always come at the end of a clause or sentence. Any of these oral cloze techniques have the advantage of being usable with non-literate populations.

DICTATION WITH INTERFERING NOISE. Several varieties of this procedure have been used, and for a wide range of purposes. The best known examples are the versions of the Spolsky-Gradman noise tests used with non-native speakers of English. The procedure simply involves superimposing white noise (a wide spectrum of random noise sounding roughly like radio static or a shhhhshing sound at a constant level) onto taped verbal material. If the linguistic context under the noise is fully meaningful and subject to the normal extralinguistic constraints, this procedure qualifies as a pragmatic testing technique. Variations include noise throughout the material versus noise over certain portions only. It is argued, in any event, that the noise constitutes a situation somewhat parallel to many of the everyday contexts where language is used in less than ideal acoustic conditions, e.g., trying to have a conversation in someone's livingroom when the television and air conditioner are producing a high level of competing noise, or trying to talk to or hear someone else in the crowded lobby of a hotel, or trying to hear a message over a public address system in a busy air terminal, etc.

PARAPHRASE RECOGNITION. In one version, examinees are asked to read a sentence and then to select from four or five alternatives the best paraphrase for the given sentence. The task may be made somewhat more difficult by having examinees read a paragraph or longer passage and then select from several alternatives the one which best represents the central meaning or idea of the given passage. This task is somewhat similar to telling what a conversation was about, to what the main ideas of a speech were, and the like. Typically, such tests are interpreted as being tests of reading comprehension. However, they are pragmatic language tests inasmuch as they meet the naturalness criteria related to meaning and temporal constraints.

A paraphrase recognition task may be either in a written format or an oral format or some combination of them. An example of an oral format comes from the *Test of English as a Foreign Language* produced by Educational Testing Service, Princeton, New Jersey. Examinees hear a sentence like, *John dropped the letter in the mailbox.* Then they must choose between (a) *John sent the letter;* (b) *John opened the letter;* (c) *John lost the letter;* (d) *John destroyed the letter.*[1] Of course, considerably more complicated items are possible. The discrete point theorist might object that since the first stimulus is presented auditorily and since the choices are then presented in a written format, it becomes problematic to say what the test is a test of—whether listening comprehension, or reading comprehension, or both.

QUESTION ANSWERING. In one section of the *TOEFL*, examinees are required to select the best answer from a set of written alternatives to an auditorily presented question (either on record or tape). For instance, the examinee might hear, *When did Tom come here?* In the test booklet he reads, (a) *By taxi;* (b) *Yes, he did;* (c) *To study history;* and (d) *Last night.* He must mark on his answer sheet the letter corresponding to the best answer to the given question.

A slightly different question answering task appears in a different section of the test. The examinee hears a dialogue such as:

MAN'S VOICE: Hello Mary. This is Mr. Smith at the office. Is Bill feeling any better today?

WOMAN'S VOICE: Oh, yes, Mr. Smith. He's feeling much better now. But the doctor says he'll have to stay in bed until Monday.

THIRD VOICE: Where is Bill now?

Possible answers from which the examinee must choose include: (a) *At the office*; (b) *On his way to work*; (c) *Home in bed*; and (d) *Away on vacation*.

Perhaps the preceding example, and other multiple choice examples may seem somewhat contrived. For this and other reasons good items of the preceding type are quite difficult to prepare. Other formats which allow the examinee to supply answers to questions concerning less contrived contexts may be more suitable for classroom applications. For instance, sections of a television or radio broadcast in the target language may be taped. Questions formed in relation to those passages could be used as part of an interview technique aimed at testing oral skills.

A colorful, interesting, and potentially pragmatic testing technique is the *Bilingual Syntax Measure* (Burt, Dulay, & Hernandez-Chavez, 1975). It is based on questions concerning colorful cartoon style pictures like the one shown in Figure 1.

The test is intended for children between the ages of four and nine, from kindergarten through second grade. Although the authors of the test have devised a scoring procedure that is essentially aimed at assessing control of

Figure 1. A cartoon drawing illustrating the style of the *Bilingual Syntax Measure*.

less than twenty so-called functors (morphological and syntactic markers like the plural endings on nouns, or tense markers on verbs), the procedure itself is highly pragmatic. First, questions are asked in relation to specific extralinguistic contexts in ways that require the processing of sequences of elements in English, or Spanish, or possibly some other language. Second, those meaningful sequences of linguistic elements in the form of questions must be related to the given extralinguistic contexts in meaningful ways.

For instance, in relation to a picture such as the one shown in Figure 1, the child might be asked something like, *How come he's so skinny*? The questioner indicates the guy pushing the wheelbarrow. The situation is natural enough and seems likely to motivate a child to want to respond.

ORAL INTERVIEW. In addition to asking specific questions about pictured or real situations, oral tests may take a variety of other forms. In effect, every opportunity a learner is given to talk in an educational setting can be considered a kind of oral language test. The score on such a test may be only the subjective impression that it makes on the teacher (or another evaluator), or it may be based on some more detailed plan of counting errors. Surprisingly perhaps, the so-called objective procedures are not necessarily more reliable. In fact, they may be less reliable in some cases. Certain aspects of language performances may simply lend themselves more to subjective judgement than they do to quantification by formula. For instance, Richards (1970) has shown that naive native speakers are fairly reliable judges of word frequencies. Also, it has been known for a long time that subjective rankings of passages of prose are sometimes more reliable than rankings (for relative difficulty) based on readability formulas (Klare, 1974).

An institutional technique that has been fairly well standardized by the Foreign Service Institute uses a training procedure for judges who are taught to conduct interviews and to judge performance on the basis of carefully thought-out rating scales.

COMPOSITION OR ESSAY WRITING. Most free writing tasks necessarily qualify as pragmatic tests. Because it is frequently difficult to judge examinees relative to one another when they may have attempted to say entirely different sorts of things, and because it is also difficult to say what constitutes an error in writing, various modified writing tasks have been used. For example, there is the so-called dehydrated sentence, or dehydrated essay. The examinee is given a telegraphic message and is asked to expand it. An instance of the dehydrated sentence is *child/ride/bicycle/off embankment/last month*. A dehydrated narrative might continue, *was taken to hospital/lingered near death/family reunited/back to school/two weeks in hospital*.

Writing tasks may range from the extreme case of allowing examinees to select their own topic and to develop it, to maximally controlled tasks like filling in blanks in a pre-selected (or even contrived) passage prepared by the teacher or examiner. The blanks might require open-ended responses on the order of whole paragraphs, or sentences, or phrases, or words. In the last case, we have arrived back at a rather obvious form of cloze procedure.

Another version of a fairly controlled writing task involves either listening to or reading a passage and then trying to reproduce it from recall. If the original material is auditorily presented, the task becomes a special variety of dictation.

NARRATION. One of the techniques sometimes used successfully to elicit relatively spontaneous speech samples is to ask subjects to talk about a frightening experience or an accident where they were almost 'shaded out of the picture' (Paul Anisman, personal communication). With very young children, story re-telling, which is a special version of narration, has been used. It is important that such tasks seem natural to the child, however, in order to get a realistic attempt from the examinee. For instance, it is important that the person to whom the child is expected to re-tell the story is not the same person who has just told the story in the first place (he obviously knows it). It should rather be someone who has not (as far as the child is aware) heard the story before—or at least not the child's version.

TRANSLATION. Although translation, like other pragmatic procedures, has not been favored by the testing experts in recent years, it still remains in at least some of its varieties as a viable pragmatic procedure. It deserves more research. It would appear from the study by Swain, Dumas, and Naiman (1974) that if it is used in ways that approximate its normal application in real life contexts, it can provide valuable information about language proficiency. If the sequences of verbal material are long enough to challenge the short-term memory of the examinees, it would appear that the technique is a special kind of pragmatic paraphrase task. . . .

NOTES

[1]This example and subsequent ones from the TOEFL are based on mimeographed hand-outs prepared by the staff at Educational Testing Service to describe the new format of the TOEFL in relation to the format used from 1961–1975.

LANGUAGE PROFICIENCY, BILINGUALISM AND ACADEMIC ACHIEVEMENT

Jim Cummins

EVOLUTION OF A THEORETICAL FRAMEWORK FOR CONCEPTUALIZING LANGUAGE PROFICIENCY

Skutnabb-Kangas & Toukomaa (1976) initially drew attention to the distinction between "surface fluency" in a language and academically-related aspects of language proficiency. They noted that Finnish immigrant students who were either born in Sweden or who immigrated at a relatively young (i.e. pre-school) age appeared to converse in peer-appropriate ways in everyday face-to-face situations (in both L1 and L2), despite literacy skills that were very much below age-appropriate levels in both languages. Following Skutnabb-Kangas and Toukomaa (1976), a distinction was introduced between "surface fluency" and "conceptual-linguistic knowledge" (Cummins, 1979b) and was later (Cummins, 1979a, 1980) formalized in terms of basic interpersonal communicative skills (BICS) and cognitive/academic language proficiency (CALP). The former was defined in terms of "the manifestation of language proficiency in everyday communicative contexts" whereas CALP was conceptualized in terms of the manipulation of language in decontextualized academic situations.

This distinction was applied to a broad range of theoretical and educational situations: for example, it was used to dispute Oller's (1979) theoretical claim that one global dimension could account for all individual differences in "language proficiency" as well as to emphasize the consequences of extrapolating from L2 BICS to L2 CALP in psychological assessment and bilingual education situations.

The distinction between BICS and CALP was expressed in terms of the "iceberg" metaphor adapted from Roger Shuy (1978, 1981). Shuy used the iceberg metaphor to highlight the distinction between the "visible", quantifiable, formal aspects of language (e.g. pronunciation, basic vocabulary, grammar) and the less visible and less easily measured aspects dealing with semantic and functional meaning ("pragmatic" aspects of proficiency in Oller's (1979) terms). He pointed out that most language teaching (whether L1 or L2) attempted to develop functional or communicative proficiency by fo-

From Jim Cummins, *Bilingualism and Special Education: Issues in Assessment and Pedagogy* (San Diego, CA: College-Hill, 1984), pp. 136–151.

cusing on the surface forms despite the fact that the direction of language acquisition was from deeper communicative functions of language to the surface forms.

Shuy's (1978, 1981) analysis can be seen as elaborating some of the linguistic realizations of the BICS/CALP distinction. Chamot (1981) and Skinner (1981) have suggested that the cognitive aspects can be elaborated in terms of Bloom's taxonomy of educational objectives (Bloom & Krathwohl, 1977). Specifically, the surface level would involve Knowledge (remembering something previously encountered or learned), Comprehension (grasp of basic meaning, without necessarily relating it to other material), Application (use of abstractions in particular and concrete situations), while the deeper levels of cognitive/academic processing would involve Analysis (breaking down a whole into its parts so that the organization of elements is clear), Synthesis (putting elements into a coherent whole) and Evaluation (judging the adequacy of ideas or material for a given purpose.

The conceptualization of language proficiency to which these notions gave rise is depicted in Figure 1. Clearly what is suggested here is not a precise model of proficiency but rather a series of parallel distinctions that are generally consistent with research evidence and appear to have important heuristic value. The major points embodied in the BICS/CALP distinction are that some heretofore neglected aspects of language proficiency are considerably more relevant for students' cognitive and academic progress than are the surface manifestations of proficiency frequently focused on by educators, and that educators' failure to appreciate these differences can have particularly unfortunate consequences for minority students.

However, any dichotomy inevitably oversimplifies the reality and it became clear that the terms "BICS" and "CALP" had the potential to be misinterpreted (see e.g. Edelsky, Hudelson, Flores, Barkin, Altweger, & Jilbert, 1983; Rivera, 1984). Consequently, the theoretical framework was elaborated in terms of the contextual and cognitive dimensions underlying language per-

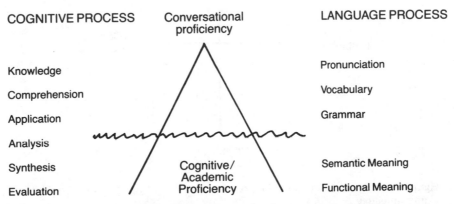

Figure 1. Surface and Deeper Levels of Language Proficiency

formance while still maintaining the essential aspects of the BICS/CALP distinction.

The framework in Figure 2 proposes that "language proficiency" can be conceptualized along two continuums. First is a continuum relating to the range of contextual support available for expressing or receiving meaning. The extremes of this continuum are described in terms of "context-embedded" versus "context-reduced" communication. They are distinguished by the fact that in context-embedded communication the participants can actively negotiate meaning (e.g. by providing feedback that the message has not been understood) and the language is supported by a wide range of meaningful paralinguistic and situational cues; context-reduced communication, on the other hand relies primarily (or at the extreme of the continuum, exclusively) on linguistic cues to meaning and thus successful interpretation of the message depends heavily on knowledge of the language itself. In general, context-embedded communication is more typical of the everyday world outside the classroom, whereas many of the linguistic demands of the classroom (e.g. manipulating text) reflect communicative activities which are closer to the context-reduced end of the continuum.

The upper parts of the vertical continuum consist of communicative tasks and activities in which the linguistic tools have become largely automatized (mastered) and thus require little active cognitive involvement for appropriate performance. At the lower end of the continuum are tasks and activities in which the communicative tools have not become automatized and thus require active cognitive involvement. Persuading another individual that your

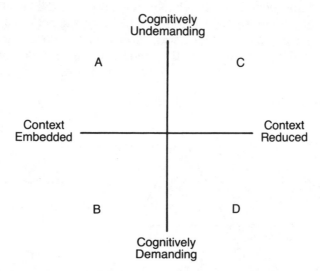

Figure 2. Range of Contextual Support and Degree of Cognitive involvement in Communicative Activities

point of view is correct and writing an essay are examples of quadrant B and D skills respectively.

The framework is compatible with several other theoretical distinctions elaborated to elucidate aspects of the relationships between language proficiency and academic development; for example, Bruner's (1975) distinction between communicative and analytic competence, Olson's (1977) distinction between utterance and text, Donaldson's (1978) embedded and disembedded thought and language and Bereiter and Scardamelia's (1981) distinction between conversation and composition (see Cummins, 1981, 1983b). The current framework owes most to Donaldson's distinction and thus it is briefly considered here.

Embedded and Disembedded Thought and Language

Donaldson (1978) distinguishes between embedded and disembedded cognitive processes from a developmental perspective and is especially concerned with the implications for children's adjustment to formal schooling. She points out that young children's early thought processes and use of language develop within a "flow of meaningful context" in which the logic of words is subjugated to perception of the speaker's intentions and salient features of the situation. Thus, children's (and adults') normal productive speech is embedded within a context of fairly immediate goals, intentions, and familiar patterns of events. However, thinking and language that move beyond the bounds of meaningful interpersonal context make entirely different demands on the individual, in that it is necessary to focus on the linguistic forms themselves for meaning rather than on intentions.

Donaldson offers a re-interpretation of Piaget's theory of cognitive development from this perspective and reviews a large body of research which supports the distinction between embedded and disembedded thought and language. Her description of pre-school children's comprehension and production of language in embedded contexts is especially relevant to current practices in assessment of language proficiency in bilingual programmes. She points out that

> the ease with which pre-school children often seem to understand what is said to them is misleading if we take it as an indication of skill with language *per se*. Certainly they commonly understand us, but surely it is not our words alone that they are understanding—for they may be shown to be relying heavily on cues of other kinds (1978, p. 72).

She goes on to argue that children's facility in producing langauge that is meaningful and appropriate in interpersonal contexts can also give a misleading impression of overall language proficiency:

> When you produce language, you are in control, you need only talk about what you choose to talk about. . . . The child is never required, when he is himself producing language, to go counter to his own preferred reading of

the situation—to the way in which he himself spontaneously sees it. But this is no longer necessarily true when he becomes the listener. And it is frequently not true when he is the listener in the formal situation of a psychological experiment or indeed when he becomes a learner at school (1978, pp. 73–74).

The relevance of this observation to the tendency of psychologists and teachers to overestimate the extent to which ESL students have overcome difficulties with English is obvious.

Donaldson provides compelling evidence that children are able to manifest much higher levels of cognitive performance when the task is presented in an embedded context, or one that makes "human sense". She goes on to argue that the unnecessary "disembedding" of early instruction in reading and other academic tasks from students' out-of-school experiences contributes significantly to educational difficulties.

Application of the Theoretical Framework

How does the framework elaborated in Figure 2 clarify the conceptual confusions that have been considered above? The framework has been applied to a variety of issues which will be only briefly noted here.

First, the context-embedded/context-reduced distinction suggests reasons why ESL students acquire peer-appropriate L2 conversational proficiency sooner than peer-appropriate academic proficiency, specifically the fact that there are considerably more cues to meaning in face-to-face context-embedded situations than in typical context-reduced academic tasks. The implications for psychological assessment and exit from bilingual programmes have already been noted.

A *second* application of the framework relates to language pedagogy. A major aim of schooling is to develop students' ability to manipulate and interpret cognitively-demanding context-reduced text. The more initial reading and writing instruction can be embedded in a meaningful communicative context (i.e. related to the child's previous experience), the more successful it is likely to be. The same principle holds for L2 instruction. The more context-embedded the initial L2 input, the more comprehensible it is likely to be, and paradoxically, the more successful in ultimately developing L2 skills in context-reduced situations. A central reason why minority students have often failed to develop high levels of L2 academic skills is because their initial instruction has emphasized context-reduced communication insofar as instruction has been through English and unrelated to their prior out-of-school experience.

A *third* application concerns the nature of the academic difficulties experienced by most children characterized as "learning disabled" or "language disordered". These students' language and academic problems are usually confined to context-reduced cognitively-demanding situations (see e.g. Cummins & Das, 1977; Das & Cummins, 1982). For example, children with "language learning disabilities" (Stark & Wallach, 1980) have extreme difficulty acquiring French in typical French-as-a-second language classes where the language is taught as a subject, yet acquire fluency in French in context-embedded French immersion programmes (Bruck, 1984). This suggests that it may be especially important for these children to experience instruction that is embedded in a meaningful context.

The framework is also relevant to theories of communicative competence (see e.g. Oller, 1983a), in that it provides a means for carrying out a task analysis of proficiency measures and predicting relationships among them. For example, it is immediately apparent why the issue of the relationship between "oral" language and reading is so confused. Measures of "oral" language can be located in any one of the four quadrants and consequently they often have very low correlations with each other (compare, for example, the WISC-R vocabulary subtest with a measure of conversational fluency).

In conclusion, the framework proposed above has the advantage of allowing the academic difficulties of both minority students and students characterized as "learning disabled" to be conceptualized in terms of more general relationships between language proficiency and academic achievement. The context-embedded/context-reduced and cognitively-undemanding/cognitively-demanding continuums are clearly not the only dimensions that would require consideration in a theoretical framework designed to incorporate all aspects of language proficiency or communicative competence. However, it is suggested that these dimensions are directly relevant to the relationships between language proficiency and educational achievement and that they facilitate the interpretation of research data on the linguistic and academic progress of minority students. In the next section, the cross-lingual dimensions of language proficiency are considered.

CONCEPTUALIZING BILINGUAL PROFICIENCY

On the basis of the fact that in bilingual programme evaluations little relationship has been found between amount of instructional time through the majority language and academic achievement in that language, it has been suggested that first and second language academic skills are interdependent, i.e. manifestations of a common underlying proficiency. The interdependence principle has been stated formally as follows (Cummins, 1981, p. 29):

> To the extent that instruction in Lx is effective in promoting proficiency in Lx, transfer of this proficiency to Ly will occur provided there is adequate exposure to Ly (either in school or environment) and adequate motivation to learn Ly.

In concrete terms what this principle means is that in a Spanish-English bilingual programme, Spanish instruction that develops first language reading skills for Spanish-speaking students is not just developing Spanish skills, it is also developing a deeper conceptual and linguistic proficiency that is strongly related to the development of English literacy and general academic skills. In other words, although the surface aspects (e.g. pronunciation, fluency) of, for example, Spanish and English or Chinese and English are clearly separate, there is an underlying cognitive/academic proficiency which is common across languages. This "common underlying proficiency" makes possible the transfer of cognitive/academic or literacy-related skills across languages. Transfer is much more likely to occur from minority to majority language because of the greater exposure to literacy in the majority language and the strong social pressure to learn it.

Continuing with the "iceberg" metaphor, bilingual proficiency is represented in Figure 3 as a "dual-iceberg" in which common cross-lingual proficiencies underlie the obviously different surface manifestations of each language. The interdependence or common underlying proficiency principle implies that experience with *either* language can promote development of the proficiency underlying both languages, given adequate motivation and exposure to both either in school or in the wider environment.

What are some of the literacy-related skills involved in the common underlying proficiency? Conceptual knowledge is perhaps the most obvious example. An immigrant child who arrives in North America at, for example, age 15, understanding the concept of "honesty" in his or her L1 only has to acquire a new *label* in L2 for an already-existing concept. A child, on the other hand, who does not understand the meaning of this term in his or her L1 has a very different, and more difficult, task to acquire the *concept* in L2. By the same token, subject matter knowledge, higher-order thinking skills, reading strategies, writing composition skills etc. developed through the medium of L1 transfer or become available to L2 given sufficient exposure and motivation.

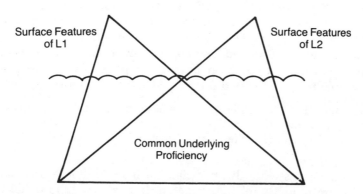

Figure 3. The "Dual Iceberg" Representation of Bilingual Proficiency

Common experience also indicates the existence of some form of common underlying proficiency. For example, as John Macnamara (1970) has pointed out, if L1 and L2 proficiencies were separate (i.e. if there were *not* a common underlying proficiency) this would leave the bilingual in a curious predicament in that "he would have great difficulty in 'communicating' with himself. Whenever he switched languages he would have difficulty in explaining in L2 what he had heard or said in L1" (1970, pp. 25–26).[1]

Comprehensive reviews of the extremely large amount of data supporting the common underlying proficiency principle have been carried out. The supporting evidence is derived from (1) results of bilingual education programmes (see Baker & de Kanter, 1981; Cummins, 1983a), (2) studies relating both age on arrival and L1 literacy development to immigrant students' L2 acquisition (see Cummins, 1983b), (3) studies relating bilingual language use in the home to academic achievement, (4) studies of the relationships of L1 and L2 cognitive/academic proficiency (Cummins, 1979a), and (5) experimental studies of bilingual information processing (Katsaiti, 1983).

Three bilingual education programme evaluations that are of particular interest are reviewed in the next section in order to illustrate the process of L1–L2 transfer and the potency of the interdependence principle to predict the academic outcomes of bilingual programmes. The first example carries important implications with respect to the appropriacy of bilingual programmes for students of low academic ability while the latter two point to the potential academic benefits of strong L1 promotion for minority students who are academically at risk.

ILLUSTRATIVE BILINGUAL PROGRAMME EVALUATIONS

Malherbe's Afrikaans–English Bilingual Education Study

In 1938 E. G. Malherbe conducted a survey of almost 19,000 South African students from Afrikaans and English backgrounds in different types of school programmes. The results were published in 1946 in his book entitled *The Bilingual School*. The aim of the study was to compare the effects of having children from each language background in bilingual as compared to monolingual schools. In the bilingual schools children generally received their instruction in the early grades through L1 and thereafter through both languages. Both intelligence level and home language were kept constant in comparisons of the effects of these two types of school. At the time of the survey, 32% of students spoke only English at home, 25% only Afrikaans and 43% were from homes that were bilingual in varying degrees. Fifty-one percent of students received English-only instruction, 28% only Afrikaans, and 21% were in bilingual schools receiving instruction through both English and Afrikaans.

Some of the major findings of the study were as follows (see Malherbe, 1946, 1969, 1978):

1. South African students gained considerably in their L2 when it was used as a medium of instruction and not merely taught as a school subject.

2. The proficiency of students in their L1 was not adversely affected either by having the two languages represented in the same school or by using the L2 as a medium of instruction. In other words, as in French immersion programmes, instructional time through the medium of L2 did not entail any loss in L1 academic skills.

3. Again as in French immersion programmes, an initial lag in mastery of subjects taught through L2 was experienced by children from monolingual home backgrounds: however, this lag became progressively less and tended to disappear by the end of elementary school (grade 6).

4. In order to test the hypothesis that bilingual instruction might be appropriate for bright students but be too "challenging" for those who are less bright, Malherbe compared the performance of children at different IQ levels in bilingual and monolingual schools. It is worth quoting Malherbe (1969) in some detail on this point in view of the assumption of some teachers and special educators that bilingual instruction will add to the difficulties of students who are academically at risk:

   > Not only the bright children but also the children with below normal intelligence do better school work all round in the bilingual school than in the unilingual school. What is most significant is that the greatest gain for the bilingual school was registered in the second language by the lower intelligence groups. Not only do they more than hold their own in the first language [in comparison to equivalent IQ children in monolingual schools], but in their second language their gain was nearly twice as big as that registered by the higher intelligence groups (1969, p. 48)

   In other words, low ability children are especially disadvantaged when taught the second language in a traditional (context-reduced) programme; however, they appear to fare well in acquiring L2 in a bilingual programme where the L2 is used as a meaningful medium of communication. This result parallels the findings of French immersion programmes.

In short, Malherbe's massive and well-controlled study illustrates the transfer of academic skills across languages and also suggests that bilingual programmes are appropriate for students with potential learning difficulties.

The San Diego Spanish–English Language "Immersion" Programme

This demonstration project, implemented in 1975 in the San Diego City Schools, involved approximately 60% Spanish L1 and 40% English L1 students. Instruction was predominantly in Spanish from pre-school through grade 3 after which half the time was spent through the medium of each language. Twenty minutes of English instruction was included at the pre-school level, 30 minutes at grades K-1, and 60 minutes at grades 2–3. Originally implemented in just one school, the project has now spread to several others. The original project was located in a lower-middle class area and, although participation was (and is) voluntary, the Spanish-background students appear typical of most limited-English proficient students in regular bilingual programmes.

The project evaluation shows that although students lag somewhat behind grade norms in both Spanish and English reading skills until near the end of elementary school, by grade 6 they were performing above grade norms in both languages. Math achievement also tended to be above grade norms. The evaluation results for both groups of students are summarized as follows:

> Native-English-speaking project students—because they do not receive instruction in English reading as early as do students in the district's regular elementary level program—begin to develop English reading skills somewhat later than regular-program students. However, project students make rapid and sustained progress in English reading once it is introduced and, as has been noted, ultimately meet or exceed English language norms for their grade levels. Also, though native-Spanish-speaking project students are not exposed to English reading and writing as early as they would be in the regular English-only instructional program, they eventually acquire English language skills which are above the norm for students in regular, English-only instructional programs and, in addition, develop their native-language skills (San Diego City Schools, 1982, p. 183).

Although clearly these demonstration project results must be treated with caution, confidence in their potential generalizability is increased by the fact that they are entirely predictable from the interdependence hypothesis and consistent with data from similar programmes involving minority francophones in the Canadian context (Carey & Cummins, 1983; Hébert et al., 1976). The results strongly support the feasibility of bilingual programmes designed to promote additive bilingualism among minority children who are academically at risk. This conclusion is also supported by the findings of the Carpinteria evaluation examined in the next section.

The Carpinteria Spanish-Language Pre-school Program

The proposal to implement an intensive Spanish-only pre-school programme in the Carpinteria School District near Santa Barbara, California, derived from district findings showing that a large majority of the Spanish-speaking students entering kindergarten each year lacked adequate skills to succeed in the kindergarten programme. On the *School Readiness Inventory*, a district-wide screening measure administered to all incoming kindergarten students, Spanish-speaking students tended to average about eight points lower than English-speaking students despite the fact that the test was administered in students' dominant language (approximately 14.5 compared to 23.0, averaged over four years from 1979 to 1982). A score of 20 or better was viewed by the district as predicting a successful kindergarten year for the child. Prior to the implementation of the experimental programme, the Spanish-background children attended a bilingual pre-school programme (operated either by Head Start or the Community Day Care Center) in which both English and Spanish were used concurrently, but with strong emphasis on the development of English skills. According to the district kindergarten teachers, children who had attended these programmes often mixed English and Spanish into a ''Spanglish''.

The major goal of the experimental Spanish-only pre-school programme was to bring Spanish-dominant children entering kindergarten up to a level of readiness for school similar to that attained by English-speaking children in the community. The project also sought to make parents of the programme participants aware of their role as the child's ''first teacher'' and to encourage them to provide specific types of experiences for their children in the home.

The pre-school programme itself involved the integration of language with a large variety of concrete and literacy-related experiences. As summarized in the evaluation report:

> The development of language skills in Spanish was foremost in the planning and attention given to every facet of the pre-school day. Language was used constantly for conversing, learning new ideas, concepts and vocabulary, thinking creatively, and problem-solving to give the children the opportunity to develop their language skills in Spanish to as high a degree as possible within the structure of the pre-school day (Carpinteria Unified School District, 1982, p. 25).

Participation in the programme was on a voluntary basis and students were screened only for age and Spanish-language dominance. Family characteristics of students in the experimental programme were typical of other Spanish-speaking families in the community. More than 90% were of low socio-economic status, and the majority worked in agriculture and had an average educational level of about sixth grade.

The programme proved to be highly successful in developing students' readiness skills as evidenced by the average score of 21.6 obtained by the

1982/83 incoming kindergarten students who had been in the programme compared to the score of 23.2 obtained by English-speaking students. A score of 14.6 was obtained by Spanish-speaking students who experienced the regular bilingual pre-school programme.

Of special interest is the performance of the experimental programme students on the English and Spanish versions of the Bilingual Syntax Measure (BSM) (Hernandez-Chavez, Burt, & Dulay, 1976), a test of oral syntactic development. Despite the fact that they experienced an exclusively Spanish pre-school programme, they outperformed the other Spanish-speaking students in both English and Spanish. Eighty-one percent of the 1982 programme students scored at the fluent speaker level (i.e. 5 on a five-point scale) on the Spanish version compared to only 53% of the other Spanish-speaking students; in English, 76% of the programme students scored 3 or higher compared to 35% of the other Spanish-speaking students. It appears likely that the highly effective language promotion that was going on in the experimental pre-school allowed children to acquire more of the English to which they were exposed in the environment.

The major relevance of these findings for special educators derives from their demonstration that educational programmes *can* succeed in preventing the academic failure experienced by many minority students. Among the students who did not experience the experimental pre-school programme, the typical pattern of low levels of academic readiness and limited proficiency in both languages was observed. These are the students who are likely to be referred for psychological assessment early in their school careers. By contrast, students who experienced a pre-school programme in which meaningful use of language was integrated into every aspect of daily activities developed high levels of conceptual and linguistic skills in both languages. The reinforcement of children's cultural identity in the programme and the involvement of parents are also likely to have positively influenced outcomes.

The findings clearly suggest that for minority students who are academically at risk, strong promotion of first language conceptual skills may be more effective than either a half-hearted bilingual approach or a monolingual English "immersion" approach.

CONCLUSION

In this reading, research findings on how long it takes minority language students to acquire "English proficiency" were reviewed and interpreted within a theoretical framework concerned with the nature of language proficiency and its cross-lingual dimensions. The fact that immigrant students require, on the average, 5–7 years to approach grade norms in L2 academic skills, yet show peer-appropriate L2 conversational skills within about two years of arrival, suggests that conversational and academic aspects of language proficiency need to be distinguished. It is apparent that, as a result of failure to take account of these two dimensions of language proficiency, many of the psychological assessments underestimated children's academic potential by assessing students whose academic functioning still reflected insufficient time to attain age appropriate levels of English proficiency.

Some of the reasons why minority children acquire L2 conversational skills more rapidly than age-appropriate L2 academic skills are apparent from the dimensions hypothesized to underlie the relationships between language proficiency and academic development. Considerably less knowledge of the L2 itself is required to function appropriately in conversational settings than in academic settings as a result of the greater contextual support available for communicating and receiving meaning.

A large amount of data suggests that L1 and L2 context-reduced cognitively-demanding proficiencies are interdependent or manifestations of a common underlying proficiency. This theoretical principle accounts for the fact that instruction through the medium of a minority language does not result in lower levels of academic performance in the majority language.

Thus, there is little justification for the frequent scepticism expressed by educators about the value of bilingual or heritage language programmes, especially for students with potential language or learning difficulties. As the Carpinteria and South African findings suggest, it is this type of student who appears to need and to benefit most from the promotion of L1 literacy skills and the development of an additive form of bilingualism.

These same findings also suggest how ill-advised it is for educators to encourage parents of bilingual children with learning difficulties to switch to English in the home. This is not only unnecessary in view of the common underlying proficiency principle but it will often have damaging emotional and cognitive effects as a result of the lower quality and quantity of interaction that parents are likely to provide in their weaker language.

Finally, it is clear on the basis of the data supporting the common underlying proficiency principle that policy in regard to the education of minority students is not as bereft of research evidence as most educators and policymakers appear to believe. Although the causes of minority students' underachievement are not yet fully understood, we do have a partial theoretical basis for policy in that we can predict with confidence the academic outcomes of bilingual programmes implemented in a variety of societal contexts; specifically, we can predict that students instructed through a minority language for all or a part of the school day will perform in majority language academic skills as well as or better than equivalent students instructed entirely through the majority language. For minority students academically at risk there is evidence that strong promotion of L1 proficiency represents an effective way of developing a conceptual and academic foundation for acquiring English literacy.

NOTES

[1]Research data (Cummins, Swain, Nakajima, Handscombe, Green, & Tran, 1984) suggest that some aspects of context-embedded language skills are also interdependent across languages. Specifically it was found that Japanese immigrant students in Canada manifested similar interactional styles in both Japanese and English and that these styles in L1 and L2 were related to personality variables. On the basis of these results, Cummins *et al.* suggest a distinction between "attribute-based" and "input-based" aspects of language proficiency: the former are cross-lingual in nature and reflect stable attributes of the individual (e.g. cognitive skills, personality) while the latter are largely a function of quality and quantity of exposure to the language in the environment.

References

Adams, M., & Collins, A. (1979). A schema-theoretic view of reading. In R. Freedle (Ed.), *New directions in discourse processing*. Norwood, NJ: Ablex.

Adams, S. (1982). Scripts and the recognition of unfamiliar vocabulary: Enhancing second language reading skills. *Modern Language Journal, 66*(2), 155–159.

Allen, J., & VanBuren, P. (1971). *Chomsky: Selected readings*. London: Oxford University.

Allwright, R. (1978). Abdication and responsibility in teaching. Paper presented at the Berne Colloquium on Applied Linguistics.

Allwright, R. (1979). Language learning through communication practice. In Brumfit & Johnson, pp. 167–182.

Alpert, R., & Haber, R. (1960). Anxiety in academic achievement situations. *Journal of Abnormal and Social Psychology, 61*, 207–215.

Andersen, R. (1980). The role of creolization in Schumann's Pidginization Hypothesis for second language acquisition. In R. Scarcella and S. Krashen (Eds.), *Research in second language acquisition*. Rowley, MA: Newbury House.

Andersen, R. (1981). *New dimensions in second language acquisition research*. Rowley, MA: Newbury House.

Andersen, R. (1983). Introduction: A language acquisition interpretation of pidginization and creolization. In R. Andersen (Ed.), *Pidginization and creolization as language acquisition*. Rowley, MA: Newbury House.

Anthony, E. (1963). Approach, method and technique. *English Language Teaching, 17*, 63–67.

Armstrong, B., Johnson, D. W., & Balow, B. (1981). Effects of cooperative versus individualistic learning experiences on interpersonal attraction between learning-disabled and normal-progress elementary school students. *Contemporary Educational Psychology, 6*, 102–109.

Arthur, B., Weiner, R., Culver, M., Young, J., & Thomas, D. (1980). The register of impersonal discourse to foreigners: Verbal adjustments to foreign accent. In D.

Larsen-Freeman (Ed.), *Discourse analysis in second language research* (pp. 111–124). Rowley, MA: Newbury House.

Asher, J. (1972). Children's first language as a model for second language learning. *Modern Language Journal, 56,* 133–139.

Asher, J. (1982). *Learning another language through actions: The complete teachers' guidebook.* Los Gatos, CA: Sky Oaks.

Asher, J. (1983). Motivating children and adults to acquire a second language. In Oller & Richard-Amato, pp. 329–336. Also in *SPEAQ Journal* (1979), *3,* 87–99.

Asher, J., Kusudo, J., & de la Torre, R. (1974). Learning a second language through commands: The second field test. *Modern Language Journal, 58,* 24–32.

Austin, J. (1962). *How to do things with words.* Oxford: Clarendon.

Ausubel, D. (1968). *Educational psychology: A cognitive view.* New York: Holt, Rinehart, & Winston.

Bailey, K. (1983). Competitiveness and anxiety in adult second language learning: Looking at and through the diary studies. In Seliger & Long, pp. 67–103.

Bailey, K. (1986, Spring). Class lecture, Monterey Institute of International Studies.

Bailey, N., Madden, C., & Krashen, S. (1974). Is there a "natural sequence" in adult second language learning? *Language Learning, 21,* 235–243.

Baker, K., & de Kanter, A. (1981). *Effectiveness of bilingual education: A review of the literature.* Washington, DC: Office of Planning and Budget, U.S. Department of Education.

Banks, J. (1981). *Multiethnic education: Theory and practice.* Boston: Allyn & Bacon.

Bassano, S., & Christison, M. (1983). *Drawing out.* Hayward, CA: Alemany.

Becker, J. (1973). A model for the encoding of experiential information. In R. Schank and K. Colby (Eds.), *Computer models of thought and language.* San Francisco: Freeman.

Beebe, L. (1983). Risk-taking and the language learner. In Seliger and Long, pp. 39–66.

Bereiter, C., & Scardamelia, M. (1981). From conversation to composition: The role of instruction in a developmental process. In R. Glaser (Ed.), *Advances in instructional psychology* (Vol. 2). Hillsdale, NJ: Erlbaum.

The best from Sunburst. Pleasantville, NY: Sunburst Communications.

Beyond language: Social and cultural factors in schooling language minority students. (1986). Office of Bilingual Bicultural Education, California State Department of Education, Sacramento. Los Angeles: Evaluation, Dissemination and Assessment Center, California State University.

Bialystok, E. (1982). On the relationship between knowing and using forms. *Applied Linguistics, 3,* 181–206.

Bialystok, E., and Fröhlich, M. (1977). Aspects of second language learning in classroom settings. *Working Papers on Bilingualism, 13,* 2–26.

Bialystok, E., & Fröhlich, M. (1978). Variables of classroom achievement in second-language learning. *Modern Language Association Journal, 62,* 327–336.

Bloom, B., & Krathwohl, D. (1977). *Taxonomy of educational objectives: Handbook I: Cognitive domain.* New York: Longman.

Bonne, R. (1973). (Pam Adams, Illus.). *There was an old lady who swallowed a fly.* Purton Wilts, England: Child's Play (International).

Breen, M., & Candlin, C. (1979). Essentials of a communicative curriculum. *Applied Linguistics, 1*(2), 90–112.

Brinton, D., & Neuman, R. (1982). *Getting along (book 2)* (p. 33). Englewood Cliffs, NJ: Prentice-Hall.

Brodkey, D., & Shore, H. (1976). Student personality and success in an English language program. *Language Learning, 26,* 153–159.

Brown, H. D. (1980). *Principles of language learning and teaching.* Englewood Cliffs, NJ: Prentice-Hall.

Brown, H. D., Yorio, C., & Crymes, R. (Eds.). (1977). *On TESOL '77.* Washington, DC: Teaching English to Speakers of Other Languages.

Brown, R. (1973). *A first language: The early stages.* Cambridge, MA: Harvard University.

Brown, R. (1977). Introduction. In C. Snow and C. Ferguson (Eds.), *Talking to children* (pp. 1–30). Cambridge: Cambridge University.

Brown, R., Cazden, C., & Bellugi, U. (1973). The child's grammar from I to III. In C. Ferguson and D. Slobin (Eds.), *Studies of child language development* (pp. 295–333). New York: Holt, Rinehart, & Winston.

Brown, S. (1979). Life situations: Incorporating community resources into the adult ESL curriculum. *CATESOL Occasional Papers,* No. 5, pp. 48–65.

Brown, S., & Dubin, F. (1975). Adapting human relations training techniques for ESL classes. In Burt & Dulay, pp. 204–209.

Bruck, M. (1984). The feasibility of an additive bilingual program for language-impaired children. In M. Paradis & Y. Lebrun (Eds.), *Early bilingualism and child development.* Amsterdam: Swets and Zeitlinger.

Brumfit, C. J., & Johnson, K. (Eds.). (1979). *The communicative approach to language teaching.* Oxford: Oxford University.

Bruner, J. (1975). Language as an instrument of thought. In A. Davies (Ed.), *Problems of language and learning.* London: Heinemann.

Bruner, J. (1978a). From communication to language: A psychological perspective. In I. Markova (Ed.), *The social context of language* (pp. 17–48). New York: Wiley.

Bruner, J. (1978b). The role of dialogue in language acquisition. In A. Sinclair, R. Javella, & W. Levelt (Eds.), *The child's conception of language* (pp. 241–256). New York: Springer-Verlag.

Burt, M., & Dulay, H. (Eds.). (1975). *New directions in second language learning, teaching, and bilingual education.* Washington, DC: Teaching English to Speakers of Other Languages.

Burt, M., & Dulay, H. (1983). Optimal language learning environments. In Oller and Richard-Amato, pp. 38–48. Also in J. E. Alatis, H. Altman, and P. Alatis (Eds.), (1981), *The second language classroom* (pp. 177–192). New York: Oxford University.

Burt, M., Dulay, H., & Finocchiaro, M. (Eds.). (1977). *Viewpoints on ESL* (pp. 172–184). New York: Regents.

Burt, M., Dulay, H., & Hernandez-Chavez, E. (1975). *Bilingual syntax measure: Technical handbook.* New York: Harcourt Brace Jovanovich.

Busch, D. (1982). Introversion-extraversion and the EFL proficiency of Japanese students. *Language Learning, 32,* 109–132.

Byrd, D., & Clemente-Cabetas, I. (1980). *React interact: Situations for communication.* New York: Regents.

Byrne, D. (1967). *Progressive picture compositions.* New York: Longman.

Canale, M., & Barker, G. (1986). How creative language teachers are using microcomputers. *TESOL Newsletter 20*(1), Supplement (3), 1–3.

Carey, S., & Cummins, J. (1983). Achievement, behavioral correlates and teachers' perceptions of Francophone and Anglophone immersion students. *Alberta Journal of Educational Research, 29,* 159–167.

Carpinteria Unified School District. (1982). Title VII evaluation report 1981–82. Unpublished report.

Carrell, P. (1983). Some issues in studying the role of schemata, or background knowledge, in second language comprehension. *Reading in a Foreign Language, 1*(2), 81–92.

Carroll, J. (1960). Wanted: A research basis for educational policy on foreign language teaching. *Harvard Educational Review, 30,* 128–140.

Carroll, J. (1961). Fundamental considerations in testing for English proficiency of foreign students. In *Testing the English proficiency of foreign students* (pp. 31–40). Washington, DC: Center for Applied Linguistics.

Carroll, J. (1963). The prediction of success in intensive foreign language training. In R. Glazer (Ed.), *Training, research, and education.* Pittsburgh: University of Pittsburgh.

Carroll, J. (1967). Foreign language proficiency levels attained by language majors near graduation from college. *Foreign Language Annals, 1*(2), 131–151.

Cathcart, R. (1972). *Report on a group of Anglo children after one year of immersion in Spanish.* Unpublished master's thesis, UCLA.

Cazden, C. (1972). *Child language and education.* New York: Holt, Rinehart & Winston.

Celce-Murcia, M., and Rosenzweig, F. (1979). Teaching vocabulary in the ESL classroom. In M. Celce-Murcia and L. McIntosh (Eds.), *Teaching English as a second or foreign language* (pp. 241–257). Rowley, MA: Newbury House.

Chamot, A. (1981). Applications of second language acquisition research to the bilingual classroom. *Focus,* 8.

Chastain, K. (1975). Affective and ability factors in second language learning. *Language Learning, 25,* 153–161.

Chaudron, C. (1985). A method for examining the input/intake distinction. In Gass and Madden, pp. 285–302.

Cherry, C. (1957). *On human communication.* Cambridge, MA: M.I.T.

Cherry, L. (1979). A sociolinguistic approach to language development and its implications for education. In O. Garnica and M. King (Eds.), *Language, children, and society.* Oxford: Pergamon.

Chomsky, N. (1959). Review of B.F. Skinner, ''Verbal Behavior.'' *Language, 35,* 26–58.

Chomsky, N. (1971). *Problems of knowledge and freedom.* New York: Pantheon.

Chomsky, N. (1975). *Reflections on language.* New York: Pantheon.

Chomsky, N. (1980). *Rules and representations.* New York: Columbia University.

Christison, M. (1982). *English through poetry.* Hayward, CA: Alemany.

Christison, M., & Bassano, S. (1981). *Look who's talking.* San Francisco: Alemany.

Clark, H., & Clark, E. (1977). *Psychology and language.* New York: Harcourt Brace Jovanovich.

Cohen, A. (1974). The Culver City Spanish immersion program: The first two years. *Modern Language Journal, 58,* 95–103.

Cohen, A., & Robbins, M. (1976). Toward assessing interlanguage performance: The relationship between selected errors, learners' characteristics and learners' explanations. *Language Learning, 26,* 45–66.

Condon, C. (1983). Treasure hunts for English practice. In Oller and Richard-Amato, pp. 309–312. Also in *English Language Teaching* (1979), 34(1), 53–55.

Coopersmith, S. (1967). *The antecedents of self-esteem.* San Francisco: W. H. Freeman.

Corder, S. P. (1978). Language-learner language. In Richards, pp. 94–116.

Cross, T. (1978). Mothers' speech and its association with rate of linguistic development in young children. In N. Waterson and C. Snow (Eds.). *The development of communication.* New York: Wiley.

Crymes, R. 1979. Current trends in ESL instruction. Paper presented at the Indiana TESOL Convention, October. In J. Haskell (Ed.) *Selected Articles* From the TESOL Newsletter (1966-1983): Washington, D.C.: TESOL.

Cummins, J. (1976). The influence of bilingualism on cognitive growth: A synthesis of research findings and explanatory hypotheses. *Working Papers on Bilingualism, 9,* 1–43.

Cummins, J. (1979a). Cognitive/academic language proficiency, linguistic interdependence, the optimum age question and some other matters. *Working Papers on Bilingualism, 19,* 121–129.

Cummins, J. (1979b). Linguistic interdependence and the educational development of bilingual children. *Review of Educational Research, 49*(2), 222–251.

Cummins, J. (1980). The entry and exit fallacy in bilingual education. *NABE Journal, 4,* 25–60.

Cummins, J. (1981). The role of primary language development in promoting educational success for language minority students. In *Schooling and language minority students: A theoretical framework* (pp. 3–49). Office of Bilingual Bicultural Education, California State Department of Education, Sacramento. Los Angeles: Evaluation, Dissemination and Assessment Center, California State University.

Cummins, J. (1983a). *Heritage language education: A literature review.* Toronto: Ministry of Education, Ontario.

Cummins, J. (1983b). Language proficiency and academic achievement. In J. Oller, Jr. (Ed.), *Issues in language testing research.* Rowley, MA: Newbury House.

Cummins, J. (1984). *Bilingualism and special education: Issues in assessment and pedagogy.* San Diego: College-Hill.

Cummins, J., and Das, J. (1977). Cognitive processing and reading difficulties: A framework for research. *Alberta Journal of Educational Research, 23,* 245–256

Cummins, J., Swain, M., Nakajima, K., Handscombe, J., Green, D., & Tran, C. (1984). Linguistic interdependence among Japanese and Vietnamese immigrant students. In C. Rivera (Ed.), *Communicative competence approaches to language proficiency assessment: Research and application.* Clevedon, England: Multilingual matters.

Curran, C. (1972). *Counseling-learning: A whole-person model for education.* New York: Grune and Stratton.

d'Anglejan, A. (1978). Language learning in and out of classrooms. In Richards, pp. 218–278.

Das, J., & Cummins, J. (1982). Language processing and reading disability. In K. Gadow and I. Bialer (Eds.), *Advances in learning and behavioral disabilities: A research annual.* Greenwich, CT: JAI

Day, R. (1984). Student participation in the ESL classroom or some imperfections in practice. *Language Learning, 34*(3), 69–102.

DeVilliers, P., & DeVilliers, J. (1973). A cross-sectional study of the acquisition of grammatical morphemes in child speech. *Journal of Psycholinguistic Research, 2,* 267–278.

de Saussuré, F. (1959). *Course in general linguistics.* New York: Philosophical Library.

Diller, K. (1978). *The language teaching controversy.* Rowley, MA: Newbury House.

DiPietro, R. (1983). Scenarios, discourse, and real-life roles. In Oller and Richard-Amato, pp. 226–238.

Dixon, C., & Nessel, D. (1983). *Language experience approach to reading (and writing).* Hayward, CA: Alemany.

DLM teaching resources comprehensive catalog. Allen, TX: DLM Teaching Resources.

Donaldson, M. (1978). *Children's minds.* Glasgow: Collins.

Dulay, H., & Burt, M. (1974). Natural sequences in child second language acquisition. *Language Learning, 25*(1), 37–53.

Dulay, H., & Burt, M. (1977). Remarks on creativity in language acquisition. In Burt, Dulay, & Finocchiaro, pp. 95–126.

Edelsky, C., Hudelson, S., Flores, B., Barkin, F., Altweger, B., & Jilbert, K. (1983). Semilingualism and language deficit. *Applied Linguistics, 4,* 1–22.

Ellis, R. (1984a). *Classroom second language development.* Oxford: Pergamon.

Ellis, R. (1984b). Sources of variability in interlanguage. Paper presented at the Interlanguage Seminar in Honor of Pit Corder, Edinburgh.

Ellis, R. (1984c). Formulaic speech in early classroom second language development. In J. Handscombe, R. Orem, & B. Taylor (Eds.), *On TESOL '83: The question of control.* Washington, DC: Teachers of English to Speakers of Other Languages.

Ellis, R. (1985). Teacher-pupil interaction in second language development. In Gass & Madden, pp. 69–85.

Ellis, R. (1986). *Understanding second language acquisition.* Oxford: Oxford University.

Ellis, R., and Wells, G. (1980). Enabling factors in adult–child discourse. *First Language, 1,* 46–82.

Enright, D. S., & McCloskey, M. L. (1985). Yes, talking! Organizing the classroom to promote second language acquisition. *TESOL Quarterly, 19*(3), 431–453.

Ervin-Tripp, S. (1973). Some strategies for the first and second years. In A. Dil (Ed.), *Language acquisition and communicative choice* (pp. 204–238). Stanford, CA: Stanford University.

Ervin-Tripp, S. (1974). Is second language learning like the first? *TESOL Quarterly, 8,* 111–127.

Evans, J., & Moore, J. (1979). *Art moves the basics along: Animal units.* Carmel, CA: Evan-Moor, 80.

Evans, J., & Moore, J. (1982). *Art moves the basics along: Units about children.* Carmel, CA: Evan-Moor, 57.

Farnette, C., Forte, I., & Loss, B. (1977). *I've got me and I'm glad.* ABC Unified School District, Cerritos, California. Nashville, TN: Incentive Publications.

Fathman, A. (1979). The value of morpheme order studies for second language learning. *Working Papers on Bilingualism, 18,* 179–199.

Feenstra, H. J. (1967). Aptitude, attitude, and motivation in second language acquisition. Unpublished doctoral dissertation, Univesity of Western Ontario, London, Ont.

Ferguson, C. (1975). Toward a characterization of English foreigner talk. *Anthropological Linguistics, 17*(1), 1–14.

Findley, C. (1986). Interactive videodisc: A powerful new technology in language learning. *TESOL Newsletter, 20*(1), Supplement (3), 10–11.

Flack, M. (1977). *The story about Ping.* New York: Penguin.

Ford, C., & Silverman, A. (1981). *American cultural encounters.* San Francisco: Alemany.

Francois, L. (1983). *English in action.* Southgate, CA: Linda Francois.

Freed, B. (1978). Foreigner talk: A study of speech adjustments made by native speakers of English in conversation with non-native speakers. Unpublished doctoral dissertation, University of Pennsylvania, Philadelphia.

Freire, P. (1970). *Pedagogy of the oppressed.* New York: Seabury.

Freud, S. (1920). *A general introduction to psychoanalysis.* New York: Liveright.

Fries, C. (1945). *Teaching and learning English as a foreign language.* Ann Arbor: University of Michigan.

Gaies, S. (1977). The nature of linguistic input in formal second language learning: Linguistic and communicative strategies in ESL teachers' classroom language. In Brown, Yorio, & Crymes, pp. 204–212.

Galyean, B. (1976). *Language from within: A handbook of teaching strategies for personal growth and self-reflection in the language classes.* Long Beach, CA: Ken Zel.

Galyean, B. (1982). A confluent design for language teaching. In R. Blair (Ed.), *Innovative approaches to language teaching* (pp. 176–188). Rowley, MA: Newbury House.

Gardner, R. (1973). Attitudes and motivation: Their role in second language acquisition. In J. Oller, Jr., & J. Richards (Eds.), *Focus on the learner: Pragmatic perspectives for the language teacher* (pp. 235–245). Rowley, MA: Newbury House.

Gardner, R. (1979). Social psychological aspects of second language acquisition. In H. Giles and R. St. Clair (Eds.), *Language and social psychology.* Oxford: Basil Blackwell.

Gardner, R., Lalonde, R., & Moorcroft, R. (1985). The role of attitudes and motivation in second language learning: Correlational and experimental considerations. *Language Learning, 35*(2), 207–227.

Gardner, R., & Lambert, W. (1959). Motivational variables in second-language acquisition. *Canadian Journal of Psychology, 13,* 266–272.

Gardner, R., & Lambert, W. (1972). *Attitudes and motivation in second-language learning.* Rowley, MA: Newbury House.

Gardner, R., Smythe, P., Clement, R., & Gliksman, L. (1976). Second-language learning: a social-psychological perspective. *Canadian Modern Language Review, 32,* 198–213.

Gary, J. (1975). Delayed oral practice in initial stages of second language learning. In Burt & Dulay, pp. 89–95.

Gass, S., & Madden, C. (Eds.) (1985). *Input in second language acquisition.* Rowley, MA: Newbury House.

Gass, S., & Varonis, E. (1985). Task variation and nonnative/nonnative negotiation of meaning. In Gass & Madden, pp. 149–161.

Genesee, F. (1982). Experimental neuropsychological research on second language processing. *TESOL Quarterly, 16,* 315–324.

Gessler: The foreign language experts. New York: Gessler Educational Software.

Giles, H. (1979). Ethnicity markers in speech. In K. Scherer & H. Giles (Eds.), *Social markers in speech.* Cambridge: Cambridge University.

Giles, H., Bourhis, R., and Taylor, D. (1977). Toward a theory of language in ethnic group relations. In H. Giles (Ed.), *Language ethnicity and intergroup relations.* New York: Academic.

Giles, H., & Byrne, J. (1982). An intergroup approach to second language acquisition. *Journal of Multilingual and Multicultural Development, 3,* 17–40.

Gliedman, J. (1983). Interview (with Noam Chomsky). *Omni, 6*(2), 113–118.

Goodman, J., & Tenney, C. (1979). Teaching the total language with readers theater. *CATESOL Occasional Papers,* No. 5, pp. 84–89.

Goodman, K. (1982). Acquiring literacy is natural: Who skilled Cock Robin? In F. Gollasch (Ed.), *Language and literacy: Selected writings of Kenneth S. Goodman, Volume II.* Boston: Routledge and Kegan Paul.

Graham, C. (1978). *Jazz chants.* New York: Oxford University.

Graham, C. (1978). *Jazz chants for children.* New York: Oxford University.

Graham, C. (1986). *Small talk.* New York: Oxford University.

Graham, C. R. (1984). Beyond integrative motivation: The development and influence of assimilative motivation. Paper presented at the TESOL Convention, Houston, Texas, March.

Green, K. (1983). Values clarification theory in ESL and bilingual education. In Oller & Richard-Amato, pp. 179–189. Also in *TESOL Quarterly* (1975), 9(2), 155–164.

Gregg, K. (1984). Krashen's monitor and Occam's razor. *Applied Linguistics* 5(2), 79–100.

Grice, H. P. (1975). Logic and conversation. In P. Cole and J. L. Morgan (Eds.), *Syntax and semantics: Speech acts 3* (pp. 365–372). New York: Seminar Press.

Grunfeld, F. (Ed.). (1975). *Games of the world.* Versailles, KY: Rand McNally.

Guiora, A., Acton, W., Erard, R., & Strickland, F. (1980). The effects of benzodiazepine (Valium) on permeability of ego boundaries. *Language Learning, 30,* 351–363.

Guiora, A., Beit-Hallami, B., Brannon, R., Dull, C., & Scovel, T. (1972). The effects of experimentally induced changes in ego states on pronunciation ability in second language: An exploratory study. *Comprehensive Psychiatry, 13,* 421–428.

Guiora, A., Brannon, R., & Dull, C. (1972). Empathy and second language learning. *Language Learning, 22,* 111–130.

Hakuta, K. (1981). Some common goals for second and first language acquisition research. In R. Andersen (Ed.), *Pidginization and creolization as language acquisition.* Rowley, MA: Newbury House.

Halliday, M.A.K. (1975). *Learning how to mean.* London: Edward Arnold.

Halliday, M.A.K. (1979). Towards a sociological semantics. In Brumfit & Johnson, pp. 27–46.

Hatch, E. (1976). Language in outer space. Paper presented at the UCLA-USC Second Language Acquisition Forum, Fall.

Hatch, E. (Ed.) (1978a). *Second language acquisition: A book of readings.* Rowley, MA: Newbury House.

Hatch, E. (Ed.) (1978b). Discourse analysis and second language acquisition. In Hatch, *Second language acquisition,* pp. 401–474.

Hatch, E. (1978c). Discourse analysis, speech acts and second language acquisition. In W. Ritchie (Ed.), *Second language acquisition research.* New York: Academic.

Hatch, E. (1979). Apply with caution. *Studies in Second Language Acquisition, 2,* 123–143.

Hatch, E. (1980). Second language acquisition—avoiding the question. In S. Felix (Ed.), *Second language development.* Tübingen: Gunther Narr.

Hatch, E. (1983). *Psycholinguistics: A second language perspective.* Rowley, MA: Newbury House.

Hatch, E., Shapira, R., & Gough, J. (1978). "Foreigner-talk" discourse. *ITL Review of Applied Linguistics, 39–40,* 39–60.

Hébert, R., et al. (1976). *Rendement academique et langue d'enseignement chez les élèves Franco-Manitobains.* Saint-Boniface, Manitoba: Centre de recherches du Collège Universitaire de Saint-Boniface.

Henzl, V. (1973). Linguistic register of foreigner language instruction. *Language Learning*, 2, 203–222.

Hernandez-Chavez, E., Burt, M., & Dulay, H. (1976). *The bilingual syntax measure*. New York: Psychological Corporation.

Heyde, A. (1977). The relationship between self-esteem and the oral production of a second language. In H. D. Brown, C. Yorio, and R. Crymes, pp. 226–240.

Heyde, A. (1979). The relationship between self-esteem and the oral production of a second language. Unpublished doctoral dissertation, Univeristy of Michigan, Ann Arbor.

Hilgard, E. (1963). Motivation in learning theory. In S. Koch (Ed.), *Psychology: A study of science 5*. New York: McGraw-Hill.

Hogan, R. (1969). Development of an empathy scale. *Journal of Consulting and Clinical Psychology*, 33, 307–316.

Hook, J. N. (1963). *Writing creatively*. Boston: Heath.

Hooker, D., & Gallagher, R. (1984). *I am gifted, creative, and talented*. New York: Educational Design. EDI 331.

Howes, D., & Osgood, C. (1961). On the combination of associative probabilities in linguistic contexts. In Saporta & Bastian, pp. 214–227.

Hunter, M., & Russell, D. (1977). How can I plan more effective lessons? *Instructor*, 87, 74–75.

Hymes, D. (1970). On communicative competence. In J. Gumperz & D. Hymes (Eds.), *Directions in sociolinguistics* (pp. 35–71). New York: Holt, Rinehart, & Winston.

The immersion phenomenon. (1984). *Language and Society* (12).

Jain, M. (1969). Error analysis of an Indian English corpus. Unpublished manuscript, University of Edinburgh.

James, J. (1980). Learner variation: The monitor model and language learning. *Interlanguage Studies Bulletin*, 2, 99–111.

James, W. (1958). *Talks to teachers*. New York: Norton.

Jamieson, J., & Chapelle, C. (1984). Prospects in computer assisted language lessons. *CATESOL Occasional Papers*, No. 10, pp. 17–34.

Jespersen, O. (1904). *How to teach a foreign language*. London: Allen and Unwin.

Johnson, C. (1979). Choosing materials that do the job. In J. Phillips (Ed.), *Building on experience—Building for success*. Skokie, IL: National Textbook.

Johnson, K. (1979). Communicative approaches and communicative processes. In Brumfit & Johnson, pp. 192–205.

John-Steiner, V. (1985). The road to competence in an alien land: A Vygotskian perspective on bilingualism. In J. Wertsch (Ed.), *Culture, communication, and cognition: Vygotsky in perspective*. Cambridge: Cambridge University.

John-Steiner, V., & Souberman, E. (1978). Afterword. In Vygotsky, pp. 121–140.

Jones, L., & von Baeyer, C. (1983). *Functions of American English: Communication activities for the classroom* (p. 17). New York: Cambridge University.

Kachru, B. (1977). The Englishes and old models. *English Language Forum*, July.

Kagan, S. (1981). Cooperative learning and sociocultural factors in schooling. In *Beyond language: Social and cultural factors in schooling language minority students* (pp. 231–298). Los Angeles: Evaluation, Dissemination and Assessment Center, California State University, Los Angeles.

Kagan, S. (1985). *Cooperative learning: Resources for teachers*. Riverside, CA: Spencer Kagan (University of California).

Kalivoda, T., Morain, G., & Elkins, R. (1971). The audio-motor unit: A listening comprehension strategy that works. *Foreign Language Annals, 4*, 392–400. Also in Oller & Richard-Amato, pp. 337–347.

Katsaiti, L. (1983). Interlingual transfer of a cognitive skill in bilinguals. Unpublished master's thesis, University of Toronto.

Kind, U. (1980). *Tune in to English: Learning English through familiar melodies*. New York: Regents.

Klare, G. (1974). Assessing readability. *Reading Research Quarterly, 10*, 62–102.

Kleifgen, J. (1985). Skilled variation in a kindergarten teacher's use of foreigner talk. In Gass & Madden, pp. 59–68.

Koestler, A. (1964). *The act of creation*. New York: Macmillan.

Koffka, K. (1924). *The growth of the mind*. London: Routledge and Kegan Paul.

Köhler, W. (1925). *The mentality of apes*. New York: Harcourt Brace.

Krashen, S. (1973). Lateralization, language learning, and the critical period: Some new evidence. *Language Learning, 23*, 63–74.

Krashen, S. (1977). Some issues relating to the Monitor Model. In H. D. Brown, C. Yorio, & R. Crymes, pp. 144–158.

Krashen, S. (1980). The theoretical and practical relevance of simple codes in second language acquisition. In Scarcella and Krashen, pp. 7–18.

Krashen, S. (1981a). The fundamental pedagogical principle in second language teaching. *Studia Linguistica, 61*.

Krashen, S. (1981b). *Second language acquisition and second language learning*. Oxford: Pergamon.

Krashen, S. (1982). *Principles and practice in second language acquisition*. Oxford: Pergamon.

Krashen, S. (1984). Immersion: Why it works and what it has taught us. *Language and Society*, (12), 61–64.

Krashen, S. (1985). *The input hypothesis: Issues and implications*. New York: Longman.

Krashen, S., Madden, C., & Bailey, N. (1975). Theoretical aspects of grammatical sequencing. In M. Burt & H. Dulay (Eds.), *Second language learning, teaching, and bilingual education* (pp. 44–54). Washington, DC: TESOL.

Krashen, S. & Pon, P. (1975). An error analysis of an advanced ESL learner. *Working Papers on Bilingualism, 7*, 125–129.

Krashen, S., & Scarcella, R. (1978). On routines and patterns in language acquisition and performance. *Language Learning, 28*, 283–300.

Krashen, S., & Terrell, T. (1983). *The natural approach: Language acquisition in the classroom*. Oxford: Pergamon.

Krathwohl, D., Bloom, B., & Masia, B. (1964). *Taxonomy of educational objectives*, Handbook H: Affective Domain. New York: David McKay.

Lado, R. (1961). *Language testing*. New York: McGraw-Hill.

Lado, R. (1977). *Lado English series*. New York: Regents.

LaForge, P. (1971). Community language learning: A pilot study. *Language Learning, 20*, 103–108.

Lambert, W. (1972). *Language, psychology, and culture: Essays by Wallace E. Lambert*. Stanford, CA: Stanford University.

Lambert, W. (1974). Culture and language as factors in learning and education. Paper presented at the Annual TESOL Convention, Denver.

Lambert, W., & Tucker, G. (1972). *Bilingual education of children: The St. Lambert experiment*. Rowley, MA: Newbury House.

Lamendella, J. (1977). General principles of neurofunctional organization and their manifestations in primary and non-primary acquisition. *Language Learning, 27,* 155–196.

Lamendella, J. (1979). The neurofunctional basis of pattern practice. *TESOL Quarterly, 13,* 5–20.

Lapkin, S., & Swain, M. (1984). Research update. *Language and Society,* (12), 48–54.

Larsen, D., & Smalley, W. (1972). *Becoming bilingual: A guide to language learning.* New Canaan, CT: Practical Anthropology.

Larsen-Freeman, D. (1978). An explanation for the morpheme accuracy order of learners of English as a second language. In Hatch, *Second Language Acquisition: A Book of Readings,* pp. 371–382.

Larsen-Freeman, D. (1979). The importance of input in second language acquisition. Paper presented at the Linguistic Society of America, Los Angeles, December.

Larsen-Freeman, D. (1983a). The importance of input in second language acquisition. In R. Andersen (Ed.), *Pidginization and creolization as language acquisition.* Rowley, MA: Newbury House.

Larsen-Freeman, D. (1983b). Second language acquisition: Getting the whole picture. In K. Bailey, M. Long, & S. Peck (Eds.), *Second language acquisition research.* Rowley, MA: Newbury House.

Lashley, K. (1961). The problem of serial order in behavior. In Saporta & Bastian, pp. 176–197.

Lawson, J. (1971). Should foreign language be eliminated from the curriculum? *Foreign Language Annals, 4,* 427. Also in J. W. Dodge (Ed.), *The case for foreign language study.* New York: Northeast Conference on the Teaching of Foreign Languages.

Lee, H. (1960). *To kill a mockingbird.* Philadelphia: J. B. Lippincott.

Lee, R., McCune, L., & Patton, L. (1970). Physiological responses to different modes of feedback in pronunciation testing. *TESOL Quarterly, 4,* 117–122.

Lenneberg, E. (1962). Understanding language without ability to speak: A case report. *Journal of Abnormal and Social Psychology, 65,* 419–425.

Lenneberg, E. (1967). *Biological foundations of language.* New York: Wiley.

Lewis, S. (1985). *One-minute favorite fairy tales.* Garden City, NY: Doubleday.

Long, M. (1981). Input, interaction, and second language acquisition. In H. Winitz (Ed.), *Native language and foreign language acquisition: Annals of the New York Academy of Sciences, 379,* 259–278.

Long, M. (1983a). Input and second language acquisition theory. Paper presented at the Tenth University of Michigan Conference on Applied Linguistics.

Long, M. (1983b). Linguistic and conversational adjustments to non-native speakers. *Studies in Second Language Acquisition,* (5.2), 177–193.

Long, M. (1983c). Native speaker/non-native speaker conversation in the second language classroom. In M. Clarke & J. Handscombe (Eds.), *On TESOL '82: Pacific perspectives on language learning and teaching.* Washington, DC: Teachers of English to Speakers of Other Languages.

Long, M. (1984). Process and product in ESL program evaluation. *TESOL Quarterly, 18*(3), 409–426.

Long, M., Adams, L., McLean, M., & Castanos, F. (1976). Doing things with words—verbal interaction in lockstep and small group classroom situations. In J. Fanselow & R. Crymes (Eds.), *On TESOL '76* (pp. 137–153). Washington, DC: Teachers of English to Speakers of Other Languages.

Long, M., & Porter, P. (1984). Group work, interlanguage talk and classroom second language acquisition. Paper presented at TESOL 1984, Houston.

Lorton, M. B. (1976). *Mathematics their way.* Menlo Park, CA: Addison-Wesley.

Lozanov, G. (1978). *Suggestology and outlines of suggestopedy.* New York: Gordon and Breach.

Lukmani, Y. (1972). Motivation to learn and language proficiency. *Language Learning, 22,* 261–273.

Macha, D. (1979). Reading comprehension of non-native students in English composition at the freshman level. *TESOL Quarterly, 13,* 425–427.

Macnamara, J. (1970). Bilingualism and thought. In J. Alatis (Ed.), *Georgetown round table on languages and linguistics.* Washington, DC: Georgetown University.

Macnamara, J. (1973). The cognitive strategies of language learning. In Oller and Richards, pp. 57–65.

Macnamara, J. (1983). Nurseries, streets, and classrooms: Some comparisons and deductions. In Oller & Richard-Amato, pp. 259–266. Also in *Modern Language Journal, 57*(5–6) (1981), 250–254.

Madden, C., & Swales, J. (1986). A description of the activities of the English Language Institute: The University of Michigan. Unpublished document.

Madsen, H. (1982). Determining the debilitative impact of test anxiety. *Language Learning, 32,* 133–143.

Making choices campaign. (1986). In *Canadian Parents for French, 24,* 8.

Maley, A., & Duff, A. (1983). *Drama techniques in language learning: A resource book of communication activities for language teachers.* Cambridge: Cambridge University.

Malherbe, E. (1946). *The bilingual school.* Johannesburg: Bilingual School Association.

Malherbe, E. (1969). Introductory remarks. In L. G. Kelly (Ed.), *UX (Description and measurement of bilingualism).* Toronto: Canadian National Commission for UNESCO and University of Toronto.

Malherbe, E. (1978). Bilingual education in the Republic of South Africa. In B. Spolsky & R. Cooper (Eds.), *Case studies in bilingual education.* Rowley, MA: Newbury House.

Malinowski, B. (1923). The problem of meaning in primitive languages. In C. Ogden & I. A. Richards (Eds.), *The meaning of meaning.* London: Kegan Paul.

Marino, E., Martini, M., Raley, C., & Terrell, T. (1984). *A rainbow collection: A natural approach to teaching English as a Second Language.* Norwalk, CA: Santillana.

Markstein, L., & Grunbaum, D. (1981). *What's the story?* New York: Longman.

Martino, L., & Johnson, D. W. (1979). Cooperative and individualistic experiences among disabled and normal children. *Journal of Social Psychology, 107,* 177–183.

Maslow, A. (1970). *Motivation and personality* (2nd ed.). New York: Harper & Row.

McCallum, G. (1980). *101 word games.* Oxford: Oxford University.

McCarthy, D. (1930). *The language development of the pre-school child.* Minneapolis: University of Minnesota.

McLaughlin, B. (1978). The Monitor Model: Some methodological considerations. *Language Learning, 28,* 309–332.

McLaughlin, B., Rossman, T., & McLeod, B. (1984). Second language learning: An information-processing perspective. *Language Learning, 33*(2), 135–158.

Mchan, H. (1979). *Learning lessons.* Cambridge, MA: Harvard University.

Michener, D., & Muschlitz, B. (1979). *Teacher's gold mine.* Nashville: Incentive Publications.

Minsky, M. (1975). A framework for representing knowledge. In P. Winston (Ed.), *The psychology of computer vision* (pp. 211–277). New York: McGraw-Hill.

Morley, J., Robinett, B. W., Selinker, L., & Woods, D. (1984). ESL theory and the Fries legacy. *JALT Journal, 6*(2), 171–207.

Morrison, D. M., & Low, G. (1983). Monitoring and the second language learner. In J. Richards & R. Schmidt (Eds.), *Language and communication*. London: Longman.

Moskowitz, G. (1978). *Caring and sharing in the foreign language class: A source book on humanistic techniques*. Rowley, MA: Newbury House.

Moskowitz, G. (1981). Effects of humanistic techniques on attitude, cohesiveness, and self-concept on foreign language students. *Modern Language Journal, 65,* 149–157.

Murray, D. (1982). *Learning by teaching: Selected articles on writing and teaching*. Upper Montclair, NJ: Boynton Cook.

Naiman, N., Fröhlich, M., & Stern, H. H. (1978). *The good language learner.* Toronto: Ontario Institute for Studies in Education.

Nelson, G., & Winters, T. (1980). *ESL operations: Techniques for learning while doing.* Rowley, MA: Newbury House.

Nelson, R., & Jakobovits, L. (1970). Motivation in foreign language learning. In J. Tursi (Ed.), *Foreign languages and the ''new'' student, reports of the working committees.* New York: Northeast Conference on the Teaching of Foreign Languages.

Newmark, L. (1979). How not to interfere with language learning. In Brumfit & Johnson, pp. 160–166. Also in Oller & Richard-Amato, pp. 49–58.

Obler, L. (1981). Right hemisphere participation in second language acquisition. In K. Diller (Ed.), *Universals in language learning aptitude.* Rowley, MA: Newbury House.

Oller, J., Jr. (1974). Expectancy for successive elements: Key ingredient to language use. *Foreign Language Annals, 7,* 448–452.

Oller, J., Jr. (1975). Cloze, discourse and approximations to English. In Burt & Dulay, pp. 345–356.

Oller, J., Jr. (1979). *Language tests at school.* London: Longman.

Oller, J., Jr. (1981). Research on the measurements of affective variables: Some remaining questions. In Andersen, pp. 14–27.

Oller, J., Jr. (1983a). *Issues in language testing research.* Rowley, MA: Newbury House.

Oller, J., Jr. (1983b). Some working ideas for language teaching. In Oller & Richard-Amato, pp. 3–19.

Oller, J., Jr. (1983c). Story writing principles and ESL teaching. *TESOL Quarterly, 17*(1), 39–53.

Oller, J., Jr., Baca, L., & Vigil, A. (1977). Attitudes and attained proficiency in ESL: A sociolinguistic study of Mexican-Americans in the southwest. *TESOL Quarterly, 11,* 173–183.

Oller, J., Jr., Hudson, A., & Liu, P. (1977). Attitudes and attained proficiency in ESL: A sociolinguistic study of native speakers of Chinese in the United States. *Language Learning, 27*(1), 1–27.

Oller, J., Jr., & Obrecht, D. (1969). The psycholinguistic principle of informational sequence: An experiment in second language learning. *International Review of Applied Linguistics in Language Teaching, 7*(2), 117–123.

Oller, J., Jr., & Perkins, K. (Eds.). (1978). *Language in education: Testing and tests.* Rowley, MA: Newbury House.

Oller, J., Jr., & Richard-Amato, P. (Eds.). (1983). *Methods that work.* Rowley, MA: Newbury House.

Oller, J., Jr., and Richards, J. (Eds.). (1973). *Focus on the learner: Pragmatic perspectives for the language teacher.* Rowley, MA: Newbury House.

Olson, D. (1977). From utterance to text: The bias of language in speech and writing. *Harvard Educational Review, 47,* 257–281.

Osman, A., & McConochie, J. (1979). *If you feel like singing*. White Plains, NY: Longman.

Palmer, H. (1971). *Songbook: Learning basic skills through music I*. Freeport, NJ: Educational Activities.

Palmer, H., & Palmer, D. (1925). *English through actions* (reprinted ed., 1959). London: Longman Green.

Papert, S. (1980). *Mindstorms: Children, computers, and powerful ideas*. New York: Basic Books.

Parkhurst, C. (1984). Using C.A.L.L. to teach composition. In P. Larson, E. Judd, & D. Messerschmitt (Eds.), *On TESOL '84: A brave new world for TESOL* (pp. 255–260). Washington, DC: Teachers of English to Speakers of Other Languages.

Paulston, C. (1972). Structural pattern drills: A classification. *Foreign Language Annals, 4*, 187–193.

Penfield, W., & Roberts, L. (1959). *Speech and brain-mechanisms*. Princeton: Princeton University.

Piaget, J. (1955). *The language and thought of the child*. New York: Meridian Books.

Piaget, J. (1979). *The development of thought*. New York: Viking.

Pica, T., & Doughty, C. (1985). Input and interaction in the communicative language classroom: A comparison of teacher-fronted and group activities. In Gass & Madden, pp. 115–132.

Pike, K. (1967). *Language in relation to a unified theory of the structure of human behavior*. The Hague: Mouton.

Plann, S. (1977). Acquiring a second language in an immersion classroom. In H. D. Brown, C. Yorio, & R. Crymes, pp. 213–225.

Pollock, C. (1982). *Communicate what you mean* (p. 7). Englewood Cliffs, NJ: Prentice-Hall.

Popper, K. (1976). *Unended quest*. London: Fontana Collins.

Porter P. 1986. How learners talk to each other: input and interaction in task-centered discussions. In. R. Day (Ed.), *Talking to learn: Conversation in Second Language Acquisition*. Rowley, Massachusetts: Newbury House, pp. 200–222.

Porter, R. (1977). A cross-sectional study of morpheme acquisition in first language learners. *Language Learning, 27*, 47–62.

Postovsky, V. (1974). Effects of delay in oral practice at the beginning of second language learning. *Modern Language Journal, 58*, 5–6.

Postovsky, V. (1977). Why not start speaking later? In Burt, Dulay, & Finocchiaro, pp. 17–26.

The Random House book of poetry for children. (1983). New York: Random House.

Raths, L., Merrill, H., & Simon, S. (1966). *Values and teaching*. Columbus, OH: Charles E. Merrill.

Reynolds, P. (1971). *A primer in theory construction*. Indianapolis: Bobbs-Merrill.

Richard, P., & Lucero, R. (1980). Foreigner talk strategies in the ESL classroom. Course paper written for C. Cazden at the University of New Mexico, TESOL Institute.

Richard-Amato, P. (1983). ESL in Colorado's Jefferson County Schools. In Oller & Richard-Amato, pp. 393–397.

Richard-Amato, P. (1987). Teacher talk in the classroom: Native and foreigner. Paper presented at the 21st Annual Convention of TESOL, April 21–25, Miami Beach, FL.

Richards, J. (1970). A psycholinguistic measure of vocabulary selection. *IRAL, 8*, 87–102.

Richards, J. (1975). The context for error analysis. In Burt & Dulay, pp. 70–79.

Richards, J. (1978). *Understanding second and foreign language learning.* Rowley, MA: Newbury House.

Richards, J. (1980). Conversation. *TESOL Quarterly, 14*(4), 413–431.

Richards, J., & Rodgers, T. (1986). *Approaches and methods in language teaching: A description and analysis.* New York: Cambridge.

Rivera, C. (1984). *Language proficiency and academic achievement.* Clevedon, England: Multilingual Matters.

Rivers, W. (1980). Foreign language acquisition: Where the real problems lie. *Applied Linguistics, 1*(1), 48–59.

Rodgers, T. (1978). Strategies for individualized language learning and teaching. In Richards, *Understanding second and foreign language learning,* pp. 251–273.

Rogers, C. (1969). *Freedom to learn.* Columbus, OH: Merrill.

Romijn, E., & Seely, C. (1980). *Live action English for foreign students (LAEFFS).* San Francisco: Alemany.

Rubin, J. (1975). What the "good language learner" can teach us. *TESOL Quarterly, 9,* 41–51.

Rumelhart, D. E. (1980). Schemata: The building blocks of cognition. In R. Spiro, B. Bruce, & W. Brewer (Eds.), *Theoretical issues in reading comprehension.* Hillsdale, NJ: Lawrence Erlbaum.

Rutherford, W. (1982). Markedness in second language acquisition. *Language Learning, 32,* 85–107.

San Diego City Schools. (1982). *An exemplary approach to bilingual education: A comprehensive handbook for implementing an elementary-level Spanish-English language immersion program.* San Diego: San Diego City Schools.

Saporta, S. (Ed.), & Bastian, J. (1961). *Psycholinguistics: A book of readings.* New York: Holt, Rinehart & Winston.

Savignon, S. (1983). *Communicative competence: Theory and classroom practice: Texts and contexts in second language learning.* Reading, MA: Addison-Wesley.

Saville-Troike, M. (1976). *Foundations for teaching ESL.* Englewood Cliffs, NJ: Prentice-Hall.

Scarcella, R. (1983). Sociodrama for social interaction. In Oller & Richard-Amato, pp. 239–245. Also in *TESOL Quarterly, 12*(1) (1978), 41–46.

Scarcella, R. Developing conversational competence in a second language. Forthcoming.

Scarcella, R., & Higa, C. (1982). Input and age differences in second language acquisition. In S. Krashen, R. Scarcella, & M. Long (Eds.), *Child-adult differences in second language acquisition* (pp. 175–201). Rowley, MA: Newbury House.

Scarcella, R., & Krashen, S. (Eds.). (1980). *Research in second language acquisition.* Rowley, MA: Newbury House.

Schallert, D. (1976). Improving memory for prose: The relationship between depth of processing and context. *Journal of Verbal Learning and Verbal Behavior, 15,* 621–632.

Schank, R., & Abelson, R. (1977). *Scripts, plans, goals, and understanding.* Hillsdale, NJ: Lawrence Erlbaum.

Schmidt, R. (1984). The strengths and limitations of acquisition: A case study of an untutored language learner. *Language Learning and Communication, 3*(1), 1–16.

Schouten, M. (1979). The missing data in second language learning research. *Interlanguage Studies Bulletin, 4,* 3–14.

Schumann, J. (1976). Second language acquisition research: Getting a more global look at the learner. In H. D. Brown (Ed.), *Papers in second language acquisition. Language Learning Special Issue, 4.*

Schumann, J. (1978a). The acculturation model for second-language acquisition. In R. Gingras (Ed.), *Second language acquisition and foreign language teaching* (pp. 27–50). Arlington, VA: Center for Applied Linguistics.

Schumann, J. (1978b). *The pidginization process: A model for second language learning.* Rowley, MA: Newbury House.

Schumann, J. (1978c). Second language acquisition: The pidginization hypothesis. In Hatch, *Second language acquisition: A book of readings,* pp. 256–276.

Schumann, J. (1979). Lecture presented at the First TESOL Institute, University of California, Los Angeles.

Schumann, J. (1980). Affective factors and the problem of age in second language acquisition. In K. Croft (Ed.), *Readings in ESL* (pp. 222–247). Cambridge, MA: Winthrop.

Schumann, J., Holroyd, J., Campbell, R., & Ward, F. (1978). Improvement of foreign language pronunciation under hypnosis: A preliminary study. *Language Learning, 28,* 143–148.

Scovel, T. (1978). The effect of affect on foreign language learning: A review of the anxiety research. *Language Learning, 28,* 129–142.

Scovel, T. (1981). The effects of neurological age on nonprimary language acquisition. In Andersen, pp. 58–61.

Segal, B. (1984). *Teaching English as a second language: Shortcuts to success.* Paso Robles, CA: Bureau of Education and Research.

Seliger, H. (1975). Inductive method and deductive method in language teaching: A re-examination. *IRAL, 13,* 1–8.

Seliger, H. (1977). Does practice make perfect? A study of interaction patterns and L2 competence. *Language Learning, 27*(2), 263–278.

Seliger, H. (1978). Implications of a multiple critical periods hypothesis for second language learning. In W. Ritchie (Ed.), *Second language acquisition research.* New York: Academic.

Seliger, H. (1982). On the possible role of the right hemisphere in second language acquisition. *TESOL Quarterly, 16,* 307–314.

Seliger, H., & Long, M. (1983). *Classroom oriented research in second language acquisition.* Rowley, MA: Newbury House.

Selinker, L. (1972). Interlanguage. *International Review of Applied Linguistics, 10,* 209–230.

Selinker, L., & Lamendella, J. (1978a). Fossilization in interlanguage. In C. Blatchford & J. Schachter (Eds.), *On TESOL '78: EFL policies, programs, practices.* Washington, DC: Teachers of English to Speakers of Other Languages.

Selinker, L., & Lamendella, J. (1978b). Two perspectives on fossilization in interlanguage learning. *Interlanguage Studies Bulletin, 3,* 143–191.

Selinker, L., Swain, M., & Dumas, G. (1975). The interlanguage hypothesis extended to children. *Language Learning, 25,* 139–152.

Shaftel, F., and Shaftel, G. (1967). *Role-playing for social values.* Englewood Cliffs, NJ: Prentice-Hall.

Sharwood-Smith, M. (1981). Consciousness-raising and the second language learner. *Applied Linguistics, 2,* 159–169.

Shuy, R. (1978). Problems in assessing language ability in bilingual education programs. In H. Lafontaine, H. Persky, & L. Golubchick (Eds.), *Bilingual education.* Wayne, NJ: Avery Publishing Group.

Shuy, R. (1981). Conditions affecting language learning and maintenance among Hispanics in the United States. *NABE Journal, 6,* 1–18.

Silverstein, S. (1981). *A light in the attic.* New York: Harper & Row.

Simon, S., Howe, L., & Kirschenbaum, H. (1972). *Values clarification.* New York: Hart.

Sinclair, J., and Coulthard, M. (1975). *Towards an analysis of discourse.* London: Oxford University.

Skinner, D. (1981). Bi-modal learning and teaching: Concepts and methods. Unpublished manuscript. Hispanic Training Institute.

Skutnabb-Kangas, T., & Toukomaa, P. (1976). *Teaching migrant children's mother tongue and learning the language of the host country in the context of the socio-cultural situation of the migrant family.* Helsinki: The Finnish National Commission for UNESCO.

Slavin, R. (1983). When does cooperative learning increase student achievement? *Psychological Bulletin, 94*(3), 429–445.

Slobin, D. (1971). *Psycholinguistics.* Glenview, IL: Scott Foresman.

Slobin, D. (1973). Cognitive prerequisites for the development of grammar. In C. Ferguson & D. Slobin (Eds.), *Studies of child language development.* New York: Holt, Rinehart & Winston.

Slobodkina, E. (1984). *Caps for sale.* New York: Blue Ribbon Books.

Smith, D. (1972). Some implications for the social status of pidgin languages. In D. Smith & R. Shuy (Eds.), *Sociolinguistics in cross-cultural analysis.* Washington, DC: Georgetown University.

Smith, E. B., Goodman, K., & Meredith, R. (1970). *Language and thinking in school.* New York: Holt, Rinehart & Winston.

Smith, F. (1978). *Understanding reading,* 2d ed. New York: Holt, Rinehart & Winston.

Smith, P. (1981). *Second language teaching: A communicative strategy.* Boston: Heinle and Heinle.

Spolsky, B. (1969). Attitudinal aspects of second language learning. *Language Learning, 19,* 271–283.

Srole, L. (1956). Social integration and certain corollaries: An exploration study. *American Sociological Review, 21,* 709–716.

Stafford, C., & Covitt, G. (1978). Monitor use in adult language production. *Review of Applied Linguistics, 39–40,* 103–125.

Stanford, G. (1977). *Developing effective classroom groups.* New York: Hart.

Stark, I., & Wallach, G. (1980). The path to a concept of language learning disabilities. *Topics in Languages Disorders, 1,* 1–14.

Stauble, A. (1980). Acculturation and second language acquisition. In Scarcella & Krashen, pp. 43–50.

Steinbeck, J. (1947). *The pearl.* New York: Viking.

Stern, S. (1983). Why drama works: A psycholinguistic perspective. In Oller & Richard-Amato, pp. 207–225. Also in *Language Learning 30*(1) (1980), 77–100.

Stevick, E. (1976a). *Memory, meaning, and method.* Rowley, MA: Newbury House.

Stevick, E. (1976b). Teaching English as an alien language. In J. Fanselow & R. Crymes, *On TESOL '76* (pp. 225–228). Washington, DC: Teaching English to Speakers of Other Languages.

Stevick, E. (1980). *Teaching languages: A way and ways.* Rowley, MA: Newbury House.

Stevick, E. (1982). *Teaching and learning languages.* Cambridge, MA: Cambridge University.

Strevens, P. (1978). The nature of language teaching. In Richards, pp. 179–203.

Sutherland, K. (1979). *Accuracy vs. fluency in the second language classroom. CATESOL occasional papers,* California Association of Teachers of English to Speakers of Other Languages, No. 5, pp. 25–29.

Sutherland, K. (1981). *English alfa* (teachers ed.) (p. 11). Boston: Houghton Mifflin.

Swaffer, J., & Woodruff, M. (1978). Language for comprehension: Focus on reading. *Modern Language Journal, 62,* 27–32.

Swain, M. (1975). Writing skills of grade 3 French immersion pupils. *Working Papers on Bilingualism,* 7: 1–38.

Swain, M. (1985). Communicative competence: Some roles of comprehensible input and comprehensible output in its development. In Gass & Madden, pp. 235–253.

Swain, M., Dumas, G., & Naiman, N. (1974). Alternatives to spontaneous speech: Elicited translation and imitation as indicators of second language competence. *Working Papers on Bilingualism: Special Issue on Language Acquisition Studies, 3:* 68–79.

Swain, M., Lapkin, S., & Barik, H. (1976). The cloze test as a measure of second language proficiency for young children. *Working Papers on Bilingualism, 11:* 32–43.

Tarone, E. (1981). Some thoughts on the notion of communication strategy. *TESOL Quarterly, 15(3),* 285–295.

Tarone, E. (1982). Systematicity and attention interlanguage. *Language Learning, 32,* 69–82.

Tarone, E. (1983). On the variability of interlanguage systems. *Applied Linguistics, 4(2),* 143–163.

Taylor, B. (1980). Adult language learning strategies and their pedagogical implications. In K. Croft (Ed.), *Readings in English as a second language* (pp. 144–152). Cambridge, MA: Winthrop.

Taylor, B. (1983). Teaching ESL: Incorporating a communicative, student-centered component. *TESOL Quarterly, 17(1),* 69–87.

Taylor, W. (1953). Cloze procedure: A new tool for measuring readability. *Journalism Quarterly, 30,* 415–433.

Terrell, T. (1983). The natural approach to language teaching: An update. In Oller & Richard-Amato, pp. 267–283. Also in *Modern Language Journal, 66(2)* (1982), 121–132.

Terrell, T. (1987). Presentation in a colloquium entitled ''Achieving Grammatical Accuracy: Advice for ESL/EFL Students'' at the 21st Annual Convention, April 21–25, Miami Beach, FL.

Thonis, E. 1984. Reading instruction for language minority students. In *Schooling and language minority students: a theoretical framework.* Office of Bilingual Education, California State Department of Education, Sacramento, California. Los Angeles: Evaluation, Dissemination and Assessment Center, California State University, Los Angeles, pp. 147–181.

Thorndike, E.L. (1914). *The psychology of learning.* New York: Teachers College.

Tucker, G., & d'Anglejan, A. (1971). Language learning process. In *The Britannica Review of Foreign Language Education* (3) (pp. 163–182). Chicago: Encyclopedia Britannica.

Tucker, G., & d'Anglejan, A. (1972). An approach to bilingual education: The St. Lambert Experiment. In M. Swain (Ed.), *Bilingual schooling: Some experiences in Can-*

ada and the United States (pp. 15–21). Toronto: The Ontario Institute for Studies in Ontario.

Ulijn, J., & Kempen, G. (1976). The role of the first language in second language reading comprehension—Some experimental evidence. *Proceedings of the Fourth International Congress of Applied Linguistics* (pp. 495–507). Stuttgart: Hochschul Verlag.

Van Allen, R., & Allen, C. (1967). *Language experience activities.* Boston: Houghton Mifflin.

van Dijk, T. (1977). *Text and context: Explorations in the semantics and pragmatics of discourse.* London: Longman.

Varvel, T. (1979). The silent way: Panacea or pipedream? *TESOL Quarterly, 13,* 483–494.

Voge, W. (1981). Testing the validity of Krashen's input hypothesis. Paper presented at the International Congress of Applied Linguistics, Lund, Sweden.

Vygotsky, L. (1962). *Thought and language.* Cambridge, MA: M.I.T.

Vygotsky, L. (1978). *Mind in society.* Cambridge, MA: Harvard University.

Wagner-Gough, J., & Hatch, E. (1975). The importance of input data in second language acquisition studies. *Language Learning, 25,* 297–308.

Wallerstein, N. (1983). *Language and culture in conflict: Problem posing in the ESL classroom.* Reading, MA: Addison-Wesley.

Walsh, T., & Diller, K. (1981). Neurolinguistic considerations on the optimum age for second language learning. In K. Diller (Ed.), *Universals in language learning aptitude.* Rowley, MA: Newbury House.

Wells, G. (1981). *Learning through interaction: The study of language development.* Cambridge: Cambridge University.

Wesche, M., & Ready, D. (1985). Foreigner talk in the university classroom. In Gass & Madden, pp. 89–114.

Whitecloud, T. (1938). Blue winds dancing. *Scribner's Magazine,* February. Also in *Variations: A contemporary literature program: In touch* (pp. 148–152). New York: Harcourt Brace Jovanovich, 1975.

Widdowson, H. (1978). *Teaching language as communication.* Oxford: Oxford University.

Widdowson, H. (1979a). *Explorations in applied linguistics.* Oxford: Oxford University.

Widdowson, H. (1979b). Rules and procedures in discourse analysis. In T. Myers (Ed.), *The development of conversation and discourse.* Edinburgh: Edinburgh University.

Widdowson, H. (1984). *Learning purpose and language use.* Oxford: Oxford University.

Wilkins, D. A. (1976). *Notional syllabuses.* London: Oxford University.

Wilkins, D. A. (1979a). Grammatical, situational, and notional syllabuses. In Brumfit & Johnson, pp. 82–90.

Wilkins, D. A. (1979b). Notional syllabuses and the concept of a minimum adequate grammar. In Brumfit & Johnson, pp. 91–98.

Winn-Bell Olsen, J. (1977). *Communication starters and other activities for the ESL classroom.* Hayward, CA: Alemany.

Winn-Bell Olsen, J. (1984). *Look again pictures.* Hayward, CA: Alemany.

Witkin, H., Oltman, P., Raskin, E., & Karp, S. (1971). *Embedded figures test manual.* Palo Alto, CA: Consulting Psychologists.

Wode, H. (1978). Developmental sequences in naturalistic L2 acquisition. In Hatch, *Second language acquisition: A book of readings,* pp. 101–117.

Wode, H. (1980). Operating principles and "universals" in L1, L2 and FLT. In D. Nehls (Ed.), *Studies in language acquisition.* Heidelberg: Julius Groos.

Wong-Fillmore, L. (1976). The second time around: Cognitive and social strategies in second language acquisition. Unpublished doctoral dissertation, Stanford University, Stanford, CA.

Wong-Fillmore, L. (1985). When does teacher talk work as input? In Gass & Madden, pp. 17–50.

Wright, A., Betteridge, D., & Buckby, M. (1984). *Games for language learning*. Cambridge: Cambridge University.

Yorio, C. (1980). The teacher's attitude toward the students' output in the second language classroom. *CATESOL Occasional Papers*. California Association of Teachers of English to Speakers of Other Languages, No. 6, pp. 1–8.

Zanger, V. (1985). *Face to face: The cross-cultural workbook*. Rowley, MA: Newbury House.

Index